MILLER'S
Collectables
PRICE GUIDE

MILLER'S COLLECTABLES PRICE GUIDE 1995/96

Compiled, edited and designed by
Miller's Publications
The Cellars, High Street
Tenterden, Kent TN30 6BN
Telephone: 01580 766411

Consultants: Judith & Martin Miller

General Editor: Madeleine Marsh
Editorial & Production Co-ordinator: Sue Boyd
Editorial Assistants: Sue Montgomery, Marion Rickman, Jo Wood
Production Assistants: Gillian Charles, Karen Taylor
Design: Jody Taylor, Kari Reeves, Matthew Leppard, Darren Manser
Photographic Co-ordinator and Advertising Executive: Elizabeth Smith
Display Advertisements: Liz Warwick, Melinda Williams
Index compiled by: DD Editorial Services, Beccles, Suffolk
Additional photography: Ian Booth, Robin Saker

First published in Great Britain in 1995
by Miller's
an imprint of Reed Consumer Books Limited
Michelin House, 81 Fulham Road
London SW3 6RB
and Auckland, Melbourne, Singapore and Toronto

© 1995 Reed International Books Limited

Bromide output: Perfect Image, Hurst Green, E. Sussex
Illustrations: G. H. Graphics, St. Leonard's-on-Sea, E. Sussex
Colour origination: Scantrans, Singapore
Printed and bound in England by William Clowes Ltd,
Beccles and London

Miller's is a trademark of
Reed International Books Ltd

MILLER'S
Collectables
PRICE GUIDE

Consultants
Judith and Martin Miller

General Editor
Madeleine Marsh

1995-96
(Volume VII)

6

KEY TO ILLUSTRATIONS

Each illustration and descriptive caption is accompanied by a letter code. By referring to the following list of Auctioneers (denoted by *) and Dealers (•), the source of any item may be immediately determined. Inclusion in this edition in no way constitutes or implies a contract or binding offer on the part of any of our contributors to supply or sell the goods illustrated, or similar articles, at the prices stated. Advertisers in this year's directory are denoted by (†).

If you require a valuation for an item, it is advisable to check whether the dealer or specialist will carry out this service and if there is a charge. Please mention Miller's when making an enquiry. Having found a specialist who will carry out your valuation it is best to send a photograph and description of the item to the specialist together with a stamped addressed envelope for the reply. A valuation by telephone is not possible.

Most dealers are only too happy to help you with your enquiry, however, they are very busy people and consideration of the above points would be welcomed.

AA • Ambeline Antiques, By George Antique Centre, St. Albans, Herts. Tel: 01727 53032 & 0181 445 8025

AAM • Anything American (Chris Pearce), 33-35 Duddenhill Lane, London NW10. Tel: 0181 451 0320

AAV * Academy Auctioneers & Valuers, Northcote House, Northcote Avenue, Ealing, London W5 Tel: 0181 579 7466

ACA •† Acorn Antiques, Sheep Street, Stow-on-the-Wold. Tel: 01451 831519

ACC •† Albert's, 113 London Rd., Twickenham, Middlesex. Tel: 0181 891 3067

AH * Andrew Hartley, Victoria Hall, Little Lane, Ilkley, W. Yorks. Tel: 01943 816363

AHL • Adrian Hornsey Ltd, Three Bridge Mill, Twyford, Bucks. Tel: 01296 738373

AI • Antiques & Interiors, Romney Bay House, Coast Road, Littlestone, New Romney, Kent, TN28 8QY. Tel: 01797 364747

AJ •† A. J. Partners, Stand J28, Gray's In The Mews, Davies Mews, London W1. Tel: 0171 629 1649

AL •† Ann Lingard, Ropewalk Antiques, Ropewalk, Rye, East Sussex. Tel: 01797 223486

ALI •† Alien Enterprises, The Antiques Shop, 30 Henley Street, Stratford-upon-Avon. Tel: 01789 292485

AMH • Amherst Antiques, 23 London Road, Riverhead, Kent. Tel: 01732 455047.

AND • Joan & Bob Anderson, Hatch End Antiques Centre, 294 Uxbridge Rd, Hatch End, Middx. Tel: 0181 561 4517

AnE • The Antiques Emporium, The Old Chapel, Long Street, Tetbury, Gloucestershire. Tel: 01666 505281

APES •† APES Rocking Horses, Ty Gwyn, Llannefydd, Denbigh, Clwyd LL16 5HB. Tel: 0174 579 365

APO • Apollo Antiques Ltd, The Saltisford, Birmingham Road, Warwick. Tel: 01926 494746

ARE • Arenski, 185 Westbourne Grove, London W11 2SB. Tel: 0171 727 8599

ASA • AS Antiques & Decorative Arts, 26 Broad Street, Pendleton, Salford 6, Manchester, M6 5BY. Tel: 0161 737 5938

ASB •† Andrew Spencer Bottomley, The Coach House, 173A Huddersfield Road, Thongsbridge, Holmfirth, Huddersfield, Yorks. Tel: 01484 685234

B * Boardman, Station Road Corner, Haverhill, Suffolk. Tel: 01440 730414

BAf •† Books Afloat, 66 Park Street, Weymouth, Dorset, DT4 7DE. Tel: 01305 779774

BAL •† A.H. Baldwin & Sons Ltd, Numismalists, 11 Adelphi Terrace, London WC2N 6BJ. Tel: 0171 930 6879

BAT • Bartlett Street Antique Centre, Bartlett Street, Bath, Avon. Tel: 01225 466689

Bea * Bearnes, Rainbow, Avenue Rd, Torquay, Devon. Tel: 01803 296277

BeG •† Bears Galore, 8 The Fairings, Tenterden, Kent TN30 6QX. Tel: 01580 765233

BER • Douglas Berryman, Bartlett St Antiques Centre, Bath, Avon. Tel: 01225 446841

BFB • Books For Cooks, 4 Blenheim Crescent, London W11 1NN. Tel: 0171 221 1992/88102

BHA • Beaubush House Antiques, 95 High St. Sandgate, Folkestone, Kent, CT20 3BY. Tel: 01303 249099/251121

BHE •† British Heritage Telephones, 11 Rhodes Drive, Unsworth, Bury, Lancs. Tel: 0161 767 9259

BKK •† Bona Arts Decorative, 19 Princesmead, Farnborough, Hants. Tel: 01252 372188/544130

Bon * Bonhams, Montpelier Galleries, Montpelier Street, London SW7 1HH. Tel: 0171 584 9161

BRD • Birdham Antiques, The Old Bird & Ham, Main Rd, Birdham, Chichester, West Sussex PO2 7HS. Tel: 01243 51141

BT ‡ BT Museum, The Story of Telecommunications, 14 Queen Victoria Street, London EC4. Tel: 0171 248 7444

BTA •† Brian Taylor Antiques, 24 Molesworth Road, Plymouth. Tel: 01752 569061

Bur • Burlington Gallery, 10 Burlington Gardens, London W1X 1LG. Tel: 0171 734 9228/9984

CA •† Crafers Antiques, The Hill, Wickham Market, Suffolk. Tel: 01728 747347

CAB •† Candlestick & Bakelite, PO Box 308, Orpington, Kent. Tel: 0181 467 3743

CAG * Canterbury Auction Galleries, 40 Station Road West, Canterbury, Kent. Tel: 01227 763337

CAI • Cain Antiques, Littleton House, Littleton, Nr. Somerton, Somerset. Tel: 01458 272341

CBa • Catherine Barlow, 14 Windsor Rd. Selston, Nottingham NG16 6JJ. Tel: 01773 860933

CBS • The Canterbury Bookshop, 37 Northgate, Canterbury, Kent CT1 1BL. Tel: 01227 464 773

CCC •† The Crested China Co., The Station House, Driffield, E. Yorks, YO25 7PY. Tel: 01377 257042

CD • The China Doll, 31 Walcot Street, Bath, Avon. Tel: 01225 465849

CEMB• Christine Bishop's Kitchenware, Westway, Portobello Road Market, London W11. Tel: 0171 221 4688

CK •† Claire Kinloch, Bulmer House, The Green, Sedlescombe, East Sussex. Tel: 01424 870364

CMF •† Childhood Memories, The Farnham Antique Centre, 27 South Street, Farnham, Surrey. Tel: 01252 724475

COB •† Cobwebs, 78 Northam Road, Southampton. Tel: 01703 227458

COL •† Collectables, PO Box 130, Chatham, Kent. Tel: 01634 828767

COp Co-Operative Chemists, 35 High Street, Tenterden, Kent TN30 6BJ. Tel: 01580 763313

CPA • Country Pine Antiques, The Barn, Upper Bush Farm, Upper Bush, Kent. Tel: 01634 717982

CRA • Cranks Antiques, Powerscourt Townhouse Centre, Dublin 2.

CRO •† Coronets & Crowns (Robert Taylor), Unit J12, Grays in the Mews, 1-7 Davies Mews, London W1Y 1AR. Tel: 0171 493 3448

CS •† Christopher Sykes Antiques, The Old Parsonage, Woburn, Bucks. Tel: 01525 290259

CSA •† Church Street Antiques, 15 Church Street, Godalming, Surrey. Tel: 01483 860894

CSK *† Christie's (South Kensington) Ltd, 85 Old Brompton Road, London SW7 3LD. Tel: 0171 581 7611

CtC Clinton Cards PLC, 8 High Street, Tenterden, Kent TN30 6AP. Tel: 010580 762090

DAL •† Dalkeith Auctions, Dalkeith Hall, Dalkeith Steps, (Rear of) 81 Old Christchurch Road, Bournemouth. Tel: 01202 292905

DAN • Andrew Dando, 4 Wood Street, Queen Square, Bath, Avon. Tel: 01225 422702

DAV • Davies Antiques, 44a Kensington Church St., London W8. Tel: 0171 937 9216

DEL • Ann Delores, Bartlett Street Antiques Centre, Bath, Avon. Tel: 01225 466689

DLF • David Linley Furniture Ltd., 60, Pimlico Road, London SW1 W8LP. Tel: 0171 730 7300

DMa • David March, Abbots Leigh, Bristol. Tel: 01275 372422

DN * Dreweatt Neate, Donnington Priory, Donnington, Newbury, Berks. Tel: 01635 31234

DON • Donay Antiques, 35 Camden Passage, London N1 8EA. Tel: 0171 359 1880

DP • David Payne, Bartlett Street Antiques Market, 9 Bartlett Street, Bath, Avon. Tel: 01225 466689

DUN • Richard Dunton, 920 Christchurch Road, Boscombe, Bournemouth, Dorset. Tel: 01202 425963

EaJ •† Eaton and Jones, 120 High Street, Tenterden, Kent, TN30 6HT. Tel: 01580 763357

EP * Evans & Partridge, Agriculture House, High Street, Stockbridge, Hants. Tel: 01264 810702

FMN •† Forget Me Knot Antiques (Heather Sharp), By George Antique Centre, 23 George Street, St. Albans, Herts. Tel: 01727 53032 & 01923 261172

G&CC•† Goss and Crested China Ltd, 62 Murray Road, Horndean, Hants. Tel: 01705 597440

GHA •† Garden House Antiques, 116-118 High Street, Tenterden, Kent. Tel: 01580 763664

GHa • Graham Hale, Bartlett Street Antiques Centre, Bath, Avon. Tel: 01225 446322

GKR • GKR Bonds Ltd., P.O. Box 1, Kelvedon, Essex. Tel: 01376 71711

GRF • Grange Farm Ltd., Grange Farm, Tongham, Surrey. Tel: 01258 2993/2804

GRG • Gordon Reece Gallery, Finkle Street, Knaresborough, N. Yorks. Tel: 01423 866219

GWe • Graham Webb, 59A Ship Street, Brighton, Sussex, BN1 1AE. Tel: 01273 321803

HAC •† Halifax Antiques Centre, Queens Road, Halifax, W. Yorks. Tel: 01422 366657

HaH * Hayman & Hayman, Antiquarius M15/L3, 135/7, Kings Road, London SW3 4PW. Tel 0171 351 6568

HAL •† John & Simon Haley, 89 Northgate, Halifax, W. Yorks. Tel: 01422 822148

HAY • Hayloft Woodwork, Box Dept, 3 Bond St, Chiswick, London W4. Tel: 0181 747 3510

HB •† Harrington Bros, The Chelsea Antique Market, 253 King's Road, London SW3 Tel: 0171 352 5689/1720.

HCH * Hobbs & Chambers, Market Place, Cirencester. Tel: 01285 654736

HEG •† Stuart Heggie, 58 Northgate, Canterbury, Kent. Tel: 01227 470422

HEW •† Muir Hewett, Halifax Antiques Centre, Queen's Road Mills, Queen's Road/Gibbet St., Halifax, W. Yorks. Tel: 01422 347377

HEY • Heyford Antiques, 7 Church Street, Nether Heyford, Northampton. Tel: 01327 340749

HOL • Holmfirth Antiques, (Ken Priestley) Halifax Antiques Centre, Queen's Road, Halifax. Tel: 01422 366657

HOLL * Holloways, 49 Parsons St. Banbury, Oxon. Tel: 01295 253197

HSS * Henry Spencer & Sons, 20 The Square, Retford, Notts. Tel: 01777 708633.

HW Harriet Wortley, The Rockery, The Moor, Hawkhurst, Kent.

IW • Islwyn Watkins, 1 High Street, 29 Market Street, Knighton, Powys. Tel: 01547 520145

JAC • John & Anne Clegg, 12 Old Street, Ludlow, Shropshire. Tel: 01584 873176

JCr • John Croft Antiques, 3 George Street, Bath, BA1 2EH. Tel: 01225 466211

JDC • J & D Collectables, Canterbury, Kent. Tel: 01227 452873

JMC • J & M Collectables. Tel: 01580 891657

JMG •† c/o Timeless Tackle, 1 Blackwood Crescent, Edinburgh EH9 1QZ. Tel: 0131 6671407

JO •† Jacqueline Oosthuizen, The Georgian Village & 23 Cale Street, Chelsea, London, SW3. Tel: 0171 352 6071

JP • Janice Paull, Beehive House, 125 Warwick Road, Kenilworth, Warwicks, CV18 1HV. Tel: 01926 55253

JPr • Joanna Proops Antiques & Textiles, No. 3, Saville Row, Bath, Avon BA1 2QP. Tel: 01225 310795

JTA • J.T. Antiques, 16 Christchurch House, Christchurch Rd, London SW2. Tel: 0181 671 2354

JUN •† Junktion, The Limes, Fen Road, Stickford, Boston, Lincs. Tel: 01205 480087

KAC • Kensington Antique Centre, 58-60 Kensington Church Street, London W8. Tel: 0171 376 0425

KES •† Keystones, Stafford. Tel: 01785 56648

LB •† The Lace Basket, 116 High Street, Tenterden, Kent. Tel: 01580 763664

LBL • Laurance Black Ltd., Antiques of Scotland, 45 Cumberland Street, Edinburgh. Tel: 0131 557 4545

LF * Lambert & Foster, 77 Commercial Road, Paddock Wood, Kent. Tel: 01892 832325

LIO • Lion's Den, 11 St. Mary's Crescent, Leamington Spa, Warks, CV31 1JL. Tel: 01926 339498.

LL • Linen & Lace, (Jo Watson & Maggie Adams), The Great Western Antique Centre, Bartlett Street, Bath. Tel: 01225 310388

MA • Danny Ma, 5/10 Bartlett Street Antiques Centre, Bartlett St., Bath, Avon. Tel: 01225 316889

MAP • Marine Art Posters, 42 Ravenspur Road, Bilton, Hull. Tel: 01482 874700 & 815115

MAS • Maskerade (Lynn Waller), Unit 15, The Antique Centre, 58 Kensington Church Street, London W8. Tel: 0171 937 8974

MAW * Thos Mawer & Son, The Lincoln Saleroom, 63 Monks Road, Lincoln. Tel: 01522 524984

MBg •† Martyn Bagley. Tel: 01825 760067

MCh •† Michael Chapman. Tel: 01789 773897

MCR • Mary Cruz Antiques, 15 Broad Street, Bath, BA1 5LJ. Tel: 01225 334174

MDI • Martin Dodge Interiors, 15/16 Broad Street, Bath, Avon, BA1 5LJ. Tel: 01225 462202

MJW • Mark J. West, Cobb Antiques Ltd, 39a High Street, Wimbledon Village, London SW19. Tel: 0181 946 2811

MLa •† Marion Langham, J30/31, Grays Mews, Davies St., London W1. Tel: 0171 629 2511

MofC • Millers of Chelsea Antiques Ltd, Netherbrook House, 86 Christchurch Rd, Ringwood, Hants. Tel: 01425 472062

MRT • Mark Rees Tools. Tel: 01225 837031

MSh • Manfred Schotten, The Crypt Antiques, 109 High Street, Burford, Oxon. Tel: 0199382 2302

MUR •† Murray Cards (International) Ltd, 51 Watford Way, Hendon Central, London NW4. Tel: 0181 202 5688

NAS •† Nashers Music Store, 72 Walcot Street, Bath, Avon. Tel: 01225 332298

NCA •† New Century Antiques, 69 Kensington Church Street, London W8. Tel: 0171 376 2810

NEW •† New Ashgate Gallery, Waggon Yard, Farnham, Surrey, GU9 7PS. Tel: 01252 713208

NM • Nick Marchant, Bartlett Street Antiques Centre, Bartlett Street, Bath, Avon. Tel: 01225 310457

NOS • Nostalgia Comics, 14-16 Smallbrook Queensway, City Centre, Birmingham. Tel: 0121 643 0143

OCA • The Old Cinema, 160 Chiswick High Road, London W4. Tel: 0181 995 4166

OCS •† The Old Curiosity Shop, 30 Henley Street, Stratford Upon Avon. Tel: 01789 292485

ONS * Onslow's Auctions Ltd., Metrostore, Townmead Road, London SW6 2RZ. Tel: 0171 793 0240

OO •† Pieter Oosthuizen, De Verzamelaar, Georgian Village, Camden Passage, London N1. Tel: 0171 359 3322/376 3852

ORA • Ora Gordon, J27 Grays in the Mews, 1-7 Davies Mews, London WIY 1AR. Tel: 0171 499 1319

ORG • Oriental Rug Gallery, 42 Verulam Road, St. Albans, Herts. Tel: 01727 841046

OTA •† On The Air, 42 Bridge Street Row, Chester. Tel: 01244 348468

OTW • Otterswick Antiques, 6 Lady Lawson Street, Edinburgh, EH3 9DS. Tel: 0131 228 3690

P * Phillips, Blenstock House, 101 New Bond Street, London W1. Tel: 0171 629 6602

PAR •† Park House Antiques, Park Street, Stow-on-the-Wold, Nr Cheltenham, Glos.

PBr • Pamela Brooks, Leicester. Tel: 01533 302625

PC Private Collection

PCh * Peter Cheney, Western Road Auction Rooms, Western Road, Littlehampton, Sussex. Tel: 01903 722264 & 713428

PHay• Peggy Hayden, Lincoln. Tel: 01507 343261

PIA •† The Pianola Shop, 134 Islingword Road, Brighton, East Sussex, BN2 2SH. Tel: 01273 608999

PMB •† Pooks Motor Bookshop, Fowke Street, Rothley, Leics. Tel: 0116 2376222

POW •† Sylvia Powell Decorative Arts, 28 The Mall, Camden Passage, London N1. Tel: 0171 354 2977/0181 458 4543.

PSA • Pantiles Spa Antiques, 6 Union House, Eridge Road, Tunbridge Wells, Kent. Tel: 01892 541377

PSC • Peter and Sonia Cashman, Bartlett Street Antique Centre, Barlett Street, Bath, Avon. Tel: 01225 310451

PUR • The Purple Shop, Antiquarius, 135 Kings Road, Chelsea, London SW3. Tel: 0171 352 1127

RA • Roberts Antiques. Tel: Cleveleys 01253 827794

RAM • Ram Chandra, Grays Portobello, 138 Portobello Road, London W8. Tel: 0181 740 0655

RAN • L. Randall, J16 Grays in the Mews, 1-7 Davies Mews, London WIY 1AR.

RAS Royal Academy Shop, The Royal Academy of Arts, Piccadilly, London W1 Tel: 0171 439 7438

RBA •† Roger Bradbury Antiques, Church Street, Coltishall, Norfolk. Tel: 01603 737444

RdeR • Rogers de Rin, 76 Hospital Road, Paradise Walk, London SW3. Tel: 0171 352 9007

RE • Ron's Emporium, 98 Church Lane, Sholden, Deal, Kent. Tel: 01304 374784.

RMV • Radio Memories & Vintage Wireless, 203 Tankerton Road, Whitstable, Kent. Tel: 01227 262491

RR • Jonathan Hill, 2-4 Brook Street, Bampton, Devon. Tel: 01398 331532

RUM •† Rumours Decorative Arts, 10 The Mall, Upper Street, Camden Passage, Islington, London N1. Tel: 01582 873561

RWB • Roy W. Bunn Antiques, 34-36 Church Street, Barnoldswick, Colne, Lancs. Tel: 01282 813703

S * Sotheby's, 34-35 New Bond Street, London W1A 2AA. Tel: 0171 493 8080

S(S) * Sotheby's Sussex, Summers Place, Billingshurst, W. Sussex, RH14 9AD. Tel: 01403 783933

SAM • Samarkand Galleries, 2 Brewery Yard, Sheep Street, Stow-on-the-Wold, Glos. Tel: 01451 832322

SBa • Simon Barlow, 14 Windsor Road, Selston, Nottingham NG16 6JJ. Tel: 01773 860933

SCR •† The Scripophily Shop, Britannia House, Grosvenor Square, London W1. Tel: 0171 495 0580

SHA • Shambles, 22 North Street, Ashburton, Devon. Tel: 01364 653848

SIG • Sigma Antiques, Water Skellgate, Ripon, North Yorks. Tel: 01765 603163

Som • Somervale Antiques, 6 Radstock Road, Midsomer Norton, Bath, Avon. Tel: 01761 41268

SP •† Sue Pearson, 13 Prince Albert Street, Brighton, East Sussex. Tel: 01273 329247

SRA *† Sheffield Railwayana Auctions, 43 Little Norton Lane, Sheffield, Yorks. Tel: 0114 274 5085 & 0860 921519

STA • Michelina & George Stacpoole, Main St., Adare, Co. Limerick, Ireland. Tel: 010 353 61396409

STK • Stockbridge Antiques, 8 Deanhaugh Street, Edinburgh. Tel: 0131 332 1366

SUL • Sullivan Antiques (Chantal O'Sullivan), 43-44 Francis Street, Dublin 8. Tel: 00353 1 541143

SWB •† Sweetbriar Gallery, Robin Hood Lane, Helsby, Cheshire WA6 9NH. Tel: 01928 723851

SWO * Sworders, G. E. Sworder & Sons, 15 Northgate End, Bishops Stortford, Herts. Tel: 01279 651388

TAR • Lorraine Tarrant Antiques, 7-11 Market Place, Ringwood, Hampshire. Tel: 01425 461123

TEM • Teddy's Emporium, 50 Northgate, Canterbury, Kent. Tel: 01227 769987

TER • Terrace Antiques, 10 & 12 South Ealing Road, London W5. Tel: 0181 567 5194/567 1223

TMN • The Magpie's Nest, 14 Palace Street, Canterbury, Kent, CT1 2DZ. Tel: 01227 764883

TOM •† Shirley Tomlinson, Halifax Antiques Centre, Queens Road, Halifax, W. Yorks. Tel: 01422 366657

TP •† Tom Power, The Collector, 9 Church Street, London NW8 8DT. Tel: 0171 706 4586

TRU • The Trumpet, West End, Minchinhampton, Glos. Tel: 01453 883027

TTM • The Talking Machine, 30 Watford Way, London NW4. Tel: 0181 202 3473

TVM •† Teresa Vanneck-Murray, Vanneck House, 22 Richmond Hill, Richmond Upon Thames, Surrey TW10 6QX. Tel: 0181 940 2035

VB •† Variety Box, 16 Chapel Place, Tunbridge Wells, Kent, TN1 1YQ Tel: 01892 531868

VMA * Vectis Model Auctions, Ward House, 12 York Avenue, East Cowes, Isle of Wight. Tel: 01983 292272

VS *† T. Vennett-Smith, 11 Nottingham Road, Gotham, Nottingham, NG11 OHE Tel: 0115 98330541

W * Walter's, No. 1 Mint Lane, Lincoln. Tel: 01522 525454

WA • Windmill Antiques, 4 Montpellier Mews, Harrogate, Yorks. Tel: 01423 530502 & 01845 401330

WAB •† Warboys Antiques, Old Church School, High Street, Warboys, Cambridge. Tel: 01487 823686

WAG • The Weald Antiques Gallery, 106 High Street, Tenterden, Kent. Tel: 01580 762939

WAL *† Wallis & Wallis, West Street Auction Galleries, Lewes, E. Sussex, BN7 2NJ. Tel: 01273 480208

WEL • Wells Reclamation & Co., The Old Cider Farm, Coxley, Nr Wells, Somerset Tel: 01749 77087/77484

WIL * Peter Wilson, Victoria Gallery, Market Street, Nantwich, Cheshire. Tel: 01270 623878

WHB * William H. Brown, Olivers Rooms, Burkitt's Lane, Sudbury, Suffolk. Tel: 01787 880305

WP •† West Promotions, PO Box 257, Sutton, Surrey, SM3 9WW. Tel: 0181 641 3224

WTA • Witney and Airault, Prinny's Gallery, 3 Meeting House Lane, The Lanes, Brighton, BN1 1HB. Tel: 01273 204554

WW * Woolley & Wallis, The Castle Auction Mart, Castle Street, Salisbury, Wilts. Tel: 01722 321711

YY • Yesteryear, 24D, Magdalen Street, Norwich, Norfolk. Tel: 01603 622908

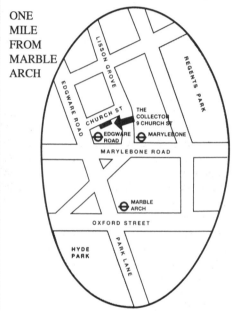

CONTENTS

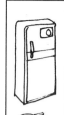

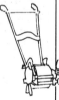

INTRODUCTION

The great joy of the collectables market is that it is ever-expanding. Items in this year's *Miller's Collectables Price Guide* range from Greek and Roman antiquities, to modern-day toys. In today's culture, it takes very little time for an object to acquire the status of a collectable. Take phonecards for example (see page 314). The first phonecard was not introduced until 1975, and in just 20 years, phonecard collecting, or 'fusilately', is popular all over the world and the rarest cards can fetch hundreds or even thousands of pounds at auction.

Last year we held a competition asking readers for their suggestions for 'Collectables of the Future'. The winning entry came from Pauline Gill of West Yorkshire who proposed McDonald's Happy Meal toys which, as every parent knows, are already avidly sought after by children. In compiling this year's *Miller's Collectables Price Guide* we found an adult enthusiast who already specialised in McDonald's material and discovered that in the USA there were established McDonald's collectors' societies. It can only be a matter of time before a similar club is started up in the UK.

Several of the collectables in this book started life as promotional 'freebies', for example cigarette cards (see Ephemera page 166) and Butlin's souvenirs, to which we devote a special section this year. Equally, many objects now commanding distinctly adult prices were originally intended for children. The toy and doll market continues to perform healthily with dealers noting an increasing interest in 1950s material.

A similar movement can be observed in other fields. This year we interviewed the famous ceramic designer, Susie Cooper, a remarkable woman now in her mid-90s. Her 1920s and '30s ceramics are extremely collectable and command high prices.

This has prompted collectors to become interested in her 1950s designs, until recently very undervalued, but which Miss Cooper herself considers some of her most significant work.

As the millenium draws to a close, attention will be turned back to the 1950s and period collectables will undoubtedly increase in value. This year we have included a selection of '50s dresses, and next year we would like to feature a specific section of 1950s collectables. If you specialise in this area, either as a dealer or private collector, we would like to hear from you.

Each year the *Miller's Collectables Price Guide* features different subjects – new entries this year include ammunition, contemporary crafts and British historical medals. Our ceramics coverage includes several new categories and features on increasingly popular areas such as SylvaC and Wade.

Then there is 'the lucky find', 'the great discovery', the *raison d'être* for many collectors. One of this year's surprises includes a very rare 1933 GECophone, which had spent a considerable portion of its life forgotten and collecting dust in a warehouse. When a dealer spotted the telephone it was not long before the importance of his find became apparent. (See page 399).

Although collecting antiques can be regarded as an expensive business, you do not need to be a millionaire to be a collector. We have included for the first time a section on collectables for under five pounds. In 'Collectables of the Future' we have picked a few items that might prove to be an investment in years to come. If you can spot what next year's hottest collectable might be, let us know, and the best answer will win a free copy of *Miller's Collectables Price Guide* until the year 2000!

As ever, happy hunting!

ACKNOWLEDGEMENTS

The publishers would like to acknowledge the great assistance given by our consultants.

BOOKS: **Adrian Harrington,** Harrington Bros., The Chelsea Antiques Market, 253 King's Road, London SW3 5EL

ART DECO CERAMICS: **Beverley,** 30 Church Street, Marylebone, London NW8 8EP. **Susie Cooper,** Isle of Man

DENBY POTTERY SARREGUEMINES: **Keystones, Graham & Alva Key,** Tel: 01785 56648 **Marty** 0181 876 1427

TROIKA POTTERY: **Harry Lyon,** New Century Antiques, 69 Kensington Church Street, W8 4BG

VUNG TAU: **Andrew Dando,** 4 Wood Street, Queen Square, Bath BA1 2JQ

WADE: **Catherine Barlow,** 14 Windsor Road, Selston, Nottingham NG16 6JJ

DOLLS AND TOYS: **Maureen Anne Stanford,** Childhood Memories, Farnham Antique Centre, 27 South Street, Farnham GU9 7QN

EPHEMERA: **Trevor Vennett-Smith,** 11 Nottingham Road, Gotham, Nottingham, NG11 OHE

CIGARETTE CARDS: **John Wooster,** Albert's Cigarette Cards, 113 London Road Twickenham, TW1 1EE

FANS: **The Fan Museum,** 22 Crooms Hill, Greenwich, London SE10 8ER

McDONALD'S: **Stuart Barlow,** 14 Windsor Road, Selston, Nottingham NG16 6JJ

MEDALS: **Timothy Millett,** A.H. Baldwin & Sons Ltd., 11 Adelphi Terrace, London WC2N 6BJ

PAPERWEIGHTS: **Marion Langham,** J30/31 Grays Mews, Davies Street, London W1Y 1AR

PHONECARDS: **Graham Lister,** Lister Art Books, P.O. Box 31, Southport, Lancs, PR9 8BF

RADIOS: **Steve Harris,** On the Air, 42 Bridge Street Row, Chester CH1 1NN

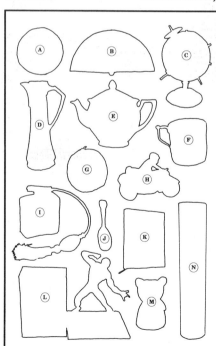

A. A John Deacon 'Crowns' paperweight, c1993, 2½in (6cm) high. **£55–65** *SWB*

B. A Victorian hand painted fan. **£40–50** *VB*

C. A 'sputnick' barometer, 1960s, 8in (20cm) high. **£50–85** *CRA*

D. A Shelley lustre jug, 1920s, 12in (30.5cm) high. **£200–225** *AJ*

E. A Crown Devon teapot, part of a six-piece set, 1930s. **£200–250 the set** *HEW*

F. A Derby coffee can, c1810, 2½in (6cm) high. **£60–90** *LIO*

G. A leather football, c1930, 6in (15cm) diam. **£20–30** *MSh*

H. A toy tinplate motorcycle and sidecar, made in China, c1950, with original box. **£50–75** *LIO*

I. An Art Deco scent bottle, 5in (12.5cm) high. **£200–250** *HEW*

J. A silver caddy spoon, 1878. **£150–200** *PC*

K. *Stories of William Tell*, by H.E. Marshall, c1930. **£3–5** *OCS*

L. A Marvel Universe Model Kit of Spider-Man, by Horizon, 12in (30.5cm) high. **£30–45** *ALI*

M. A Crown Devon 'Sooty' money box, 5½in (14cm) high. **£60–75** *HEW*

N. A taper box, complete with tapers, 1920s, 11½in (29cm) high. **£25–40** *OCA*

ADVERTISING & PACKAGING

Nostalgia is a major spur for many collectors and few objects inspire sweeter memories than the tins and wrappers of products from the past and our own childhood. It is only within the last 30 years that advertising and packaging material has become collectable.

A leading pioneer in this field is Robert Opie, founder of the Museum of Advertising and Packaging in Gloucester. The collection began in 1963, when the teenage Opie purchased a packet of Munchies from a railway station vending machine and suddenly realised that if he threw its paper away, a little piece of history would disappear forever. 'It was like a blinding flash of light,' he enthuses, 'and since that day I have saved the wrapper off every product I have ever used.'

Opie's museum now houses the largest collection of its kind in the world, ranging from Victorian packaging, through wartime material ('Nasti Toilet Rolls – Use Hess Paper for Mess Paper') to the present day. It is a treasure trove for anyone interested in this field.

A Canadian Pacific Railway Company calendar, showing the fleet, 1911, 28 by 20in (71 by 51cm).
£40–50 *JUN*

A French cheese label, 1960s, 8in (20cm) diam.
£6–7 *COB*

A clock advertising Stones Best Bitter, 1970s, 8in (20cm) high.
£10–12 *HAC*

A Cadbury's advertising mug, brown glazed, c1970, 3½in (9cm) square.
£4–5 *HAC*

A white ceramic Bovril mug, c1900, 3½in (9cm) high.
£8–10 *AL*

A papier mâché Hovis advertising figure, 1930s, 35in (89cm) high.
£125–150 *JUN*

A Café Bénédictine goblet, green with gold lettering, red mark, 6in (15cm) high, and a D.O.M. Café mug, 20thC, 2½in (7cm) high.
50p–£1 each *HAC*

A Homepride cruet set, in original box, c1975.
£10–15 *PC*

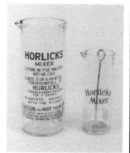

A Whitbread crate with four beer bottles, c1930, 13½in (34.5cm) high.
£15–20 *JUN*

Two glass Horlicks mixers, 1940s, tallest 8in (20cm) high.
£5-8 each *AL*

A Spratts enamel dog bowl, c1925, 10in (25cm) diam.
£25–35 *JUN*

A selection of 43 thin coloured card illustrated advertising cut-outs, Victorian to 1930s.
£250–300 *DAL*

Signs

A shop sign in the form of a carved wooden head of a bullock, with painted decoration and long horns, 19thC, 38in (96.5cm) wide.
£1,700–2,200 *B*

A shop sign, inscribed 'To Eveline Xmas 1889, Mother and Father' on reverse.
£75–100 *CK*

A Hignett's Smoking Mixture enamel sign, 1910, 20in (51cm) square.
£150–175 *JUN*

An Afrikander Tobaccos enamel sign, c1925, 30 by 20in (76 by 50.5cm).
£250–300 *PMB*

A Duckham's Adcoids enamel sign, with thermometer, 1930, 45in (114cm) high.
£175–200 *JUN*

An Our Boys Tea tin sign, c1920, 29in (74cm) wide.
£25–30 *JUN*

A Player's Please enamel sign, c1935, 58in(147cm) high.
£200–250 *PMB*

A Wills's Flag Cigarettes enamel sign, c1930, 36in (92cm) high.
£150–180 *PMB*

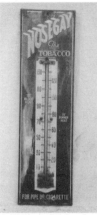

A Nosegay Tobacco enamel sign, with thermometer, 1930, 24½in (62cm) high.
£55–65 *JUN*

A Bird's Custard enamel sign, 1920s, 30 by 24in (76 by 61cm).
£500–600 *PMB*

A Dunlop Accessories, enamel sign, 1930, 13 by 11½in (33 by 29cm).
£65–75 *JUN*

An enamel sign showing Lloyd George, with Churchill in the background, c1918.
£400–500 *PMB*

A Burma Sauce enamel sign, 1920s, 30 by 20in (76 by 50.5cm).
£400–450 *PMB*

A Huntley & Palmers enamel sign, 1930s, 18in (46cm) square.
£300–350 *PMB*

A John Bull enamel sign, c1918, 28in (71cm) high.
£400–450 *PMB*

A Fordson Tractors enamel sign, c1955, 36in (92cm) high.
£100–120 *PMB*

A Zebra Grate Polish enamel sign, 1930s, 36in (92cm) high.
£100–120 *PMB*

A Campbell Brand and Palm
Brand Footwear enamel sign,
1910, 26in (66cm) long.
£70–80 *JUN*

A Punch enamel sign, c1925,
48in (122cm) long.
£200–220 *PMB*

A Waterman's Fountain Pen
enamel sign, c1920, 30 by 20in
(76 by 50.5cm).
£200–250 *PMB*

An Alfa Nr. 56 Margarine
convex enamel sign, 1920s,
24in (61cm) high.
£300–350 *PMB*

An Oceanic Foot-Wear
enamel sign, c1900, 13 by 19in
(33 by 48cm).
£425–450 *PMB*

An enamel warning sign,
1920s, 16in (41cm) long.
£40–50 *JUN*

A Redfern Rubber Heels & Soles
enamel sign, c1935, 48in
(122cm) long.
£100–135 *JUN*

Tins

The great age of the British tin was between the 1870s and 1930s. Many were designed for the Christmas market or to celebrate specific events. Shaped tins often command the highest prices. Commemorative and decorative pictorial tins can also be very collectable, as can examples with interesting period copy. In this field of mass production, condition is all-important. Tins should not be too battered, dented or rusted. Check the hinges and the condition of the paintwork.

A Huntley & Palmers printed biscuit tin, c1865, 8½in (21cm) long.
£45–50 *JUN*

A Huntley & Palmers paper covered biscuit tin, c1890, 4½ by 9½in (11 by 24cm).
£25–30 *JUN*

A Huntley & Palmers tin in the form of a snakeskin bag, 1908, 8in (20cm) long.
£70–75 *JUN*

A Huntley & Palmers biscuit tin, 1910, 9¼ by 9½in (23.5 by 24cm).
£20–30 *JUN*

A Hitchens of Leeds pictorial tin, c1932, 4in (10cm) square.
£8–10 *JUN*

Museum of Advertising & Packaging
The Albert Warehouse
Gloucester Docks
Gloucester GL1 2EH
Tel: 0452 302309

A Weston's display biscuit tin, with glass lid, c1930, 8½in (21cm) square.
£25–30 *AL*

A Lipton's British Empire Exhibition souvenir tea caddy, c1925, 5½in (14cm) high.
£18–25 *NM*

A Needler's Toffee tin, c1935, 6½ by 4¼in (16 by 11cm).
£10–15 *JUN*

A reproduction brass Queen Mary tin, c1953, 5in (12.5cm).
£20–25 *DUN*

These tins were originally a gift made by Queen Mary to soldiers during WWI. They were filled with cigarettes and chocolate.

AERONAUTICA

Air Force museums can be of considerable assistance when it comes to researching aeronautical memorabilia. Probably the most important museum in this field is the Royal Air Force Museum, Britain's national museum of aviation, covering the story of flight and the history of the RAF. Consultations with staff members are available by appointment or by post and the museum library is open to the public by appointment. When investigating an object, always make sure that you have taken down its full details - for example, wooden aeroplane propellers, now very collectable, can possibly be identified, as long as you have the correct serial number.

A collection of aircraft brochures, 1947.
£5–10 each *COB*

Models

A propeller, c1916.
£125–250 *WAB*

A WWII sheepskin flying jacket.
£250–280 *JUN*

A Japanese model of a Spitfire, c1950, 10in (25.5cm).
£40–45 *PC*

A carved wooden Spitfire, c1918, 17in (43cm) wingspan.
£75–100 *PC*

A model of a Bristol/Westland Belvedere HC1, Serial XG463, No. 66 Sqn. RAF, 20thC, 8½in (21cm).
£180–220 *CSK*

A model of a Short S17 Kent G-ABFC, Imperial Airways livery, 20thC, 19in (48cm).
£1,500–2,000 *CSK*

A model of a Handley Page 0/400, Serial 9672, 20thC, 16½in (42cm).
£450–500 *CSK*

A model of a Handley Page Heyford I, Serial K3495, No. 99 Sqn. RAF, 12½in (32cm).
£720–820 *CSK*

A model of a Supermarine Scapa, Serial K4196, No. 202 Flying Boat Sqn. RAF, 12½in (32cm).
£280–330 *CSK*

A model of a Avro Shackleton MR3, Serial XF711, No. 201 Sqn. RAF, 20thC, 20in (51cm).
£360–420 *CSK*

A model of an Armstrong Whitworth Argosy, I G-EBLF 'City of Glasgow', Imperial Airways livery, 15in (38cm).
£400–450 *CSK*

A model of an Armstrong Whitworth Argosy, I G-EBLF 'City of Glasgow', Imperial Airways livery, 20thC, 15in (38cm).
£400–450 *CSK*

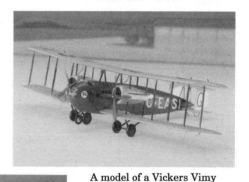

A model of a Vickers Vimy Commercial G-EASI, 'City of London', S. Instone & Co. Ltd. livery, 11½in (29cm).
£850–950 *CSK*

A model of British Aerospace B.Ae 146-100 G-BKMN, Dan-Air London livery, 20thC, 14½in (37cm).
£610–700 *CSK*

A model of a Handley Page Victor K2, Serial XM715, No. 55 Sqn. RAF, 20in (50cm).
£2,300–3,000 *CSK*

Royal Air Force Museum
Grahame Park Way
Hendon
London NW9 5LL
Tel: 081 205 2266

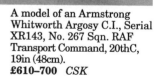

A model of an Armstrong Whitworth Argosy C.I., Serial XR143, No. 267 Sqn. RAF Transport Command, 20thC, 19in (48cm).
£610–700 *CSK*

A model of a Bristol Brabazon I G-AGPW, 20thC, 38½in (97cm), with box.
£3,500–4,000 *CSK*

A model of an Avro York G-AGOE 'Medway', BOAC livery, 17in (43cm).
£610–700 *CSK*

AMUSEMENT, VENDING & SLOT MACHINES

A poulet automatique, for dispensing tin eggs with chocolates or sweets inside, French, c1897.
£3,500–4,000 *DON*

An Imperial Electric Co., shocker, c1901.
£1,000–1,500 *DON*

A penny-in-the-slot platform weighing machine, manufactured by Watling, Chicago, c1920, 75in (190.5cm) high.
£800–875 *JUN*

A Bradwin penny-in-the-slot machine, c1930.
£250–300 *JUN*

An Allwin de Luxe penny-in-the-slot machine, c1920, 24in (61cm) high.
£350–400 *JUN*

A dice game slot machine, c1935, 14in (35.5cm) long.
£100–120 *JUN*

A Challenger penny-in-the-slot machine, pre-WWII.
£250–300 *JUN*

A punch 'Try Your Strength' machine, by Caille Brothers Co., USA, c1904.
£5,000–6,000 *DON*

A Craven 'A' cigarette vending machine, 1930s, 30in (76cm) high.
£125–150 *JUN*

A wooden cigarette vending machine, 1940s, 33in (84cm) high.
£40–45 *JUN*

ANTIQUITIES
Classical & Medieval

One of the more remarkable things about small antiquities is not only how old they are, but how cheap they can be. At the top of the range prices can run into millions, but at the other end of the scale you can buy a Roman coin for under five pounds, or an ancient Mesopotamian oil lamp for £20–30. Objects become available from the sale of old collections and from new excavations where once museums and major collectors have taken their pick of the finest items, but there is plenty left for the more modest purchaser.

Collectables include ceramics, glass, votive offerings, weaponry etc. Ancient jewellery can be stunningly beautiful and perfectly wearable – what more romantic present could there be than a ring which perhaps once adorned the finger of a Roman senator? Antiquities can be obtained from auctions, specialist dealers and also coin dealers who are a well known source for supplies.

A Sung Dynasty green glazed vase, c1200, 5in (12.5cm) high.
£90–100 *OCS*

A Ming Dynasty terracotta green glazed horse and rider, with detachable head, c1550, 15in (38cm) high.
£650–700 *OCS*

A pottery votive chicken, left in a tomb as an offering, original paint, circa 1st Century B.C.
£40–50 *OCS*

A Roman glass vase, with loop handle, all-over iridescence, 6in (15cm) high.
£150–175 *OCS*

A Tibetan repoussé copper head, circa 14th Century, 2in (5cm) high.
£200–250 *RAM*

A Chinese Bronze Age spearhead, circa 1st Century B.C.
£60–75 *OCS*

An Iron Age Cypriot bowl, with two loop handles, restored, 900–600 B.C., 8in (20cm) diam.
£40–50 *OCS*

A Tang Dynasty glazed pottery bowl, in the form of a bulbous chicken, circa 10th Century A.D.
£140–150 *OCS*

A pewter spoon, found in the River Thames, 16thC, 7in (17.5cm) long.
£60–75 *OCS*

A Roman multi-coloured glass bracelet, found near Sidon, 300–400 A.D.
£50–55 *OCS*

AUTOMOBILIA
General

A motoring helmet, and a pair of Triplex C2 goggles, 1920s.
£25–45 *WAB*

Two Shell oil measures, c1940.
£25–30 each *JUN*

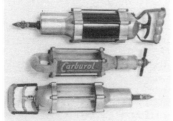

A Chemico Lightcar repair outfit tin, 9½in (24cm) long.
£20–25 *JUN*

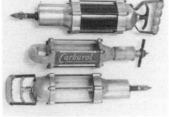

A selection of one-shot oil lubricators, 19in (48cm) long.
£30–40 each *JUN*

A Schrader Gauge garage display cabinet, early 20thC, 27in (68.5cm) high.
£225–250 *JUN*

A leather motoring coat, 1920s.
£100–120 *JUN*

A petrol can with Shell Motor Oil tin insert, 1930s.
£150–175 *JUN*

A crate of empty Essolube oil bottles, c1940, 16½in (42cm) high.
£45–50 *JUN*

A Redex oil and fuel additive gun, 20thC.
£20–25 *JUN*

A smoker's companion for a Morris, inscribed, early 20thC.
£80-85 *JUN*

A set of graduated oil cans, 1930s.
£35–40 *JUN*

A BP Motor Spirit two gallon petrol can, 1930s–40s.
£25–30 *JUN*

Two bus maps, 1923 and 1924.
£6–7 each *COB*

A Bell Punch London Transport bus ticket machine and rack, c1930.
£75–80 *CAB*

A British Grand Prix programme for Brands Hatch, 20th July 1974.
50p–£2 *PC*

A Paraffin glass pump globe, 20thC, 19in (48cm) high.
£50–60 *JUN*

A Duckham's Quest magazine showing James and Susie Hunt on the cover, 1973.
£3–5 *PC*

An Indylantic programme for Brands Hatch, 3rd October 1976.
50p–£2 *PC*

Mascots

A nickel plated brass Targa Florio cupid mascot, by Sasportas, marked on base, 20thC, 4in (10cm) high, mounted on a radiator cap.
£700–800 *S*

A Diana the Huntress mascot, attributed to H. Moreau by Susse Frères, c1920, 4½in (11.5cm) high, mounted on a radiator cap.
£450–550 *S*

FURTHER READING
Miller's Collectors Cars Price Guide,
Reed Consumer Books Ltd.

A Parisien policeman mascot, by M. Le Verrier, signed, with factory marks, c1920, 6in (15cm) high, mounted on a radiator cap.
£700–800 *S*

A chrome plated Pegasus mascot, registered design 1922, 5in (13cm) high, mounted on a display base.
£300–400 *S*

A cast aluminium 'V' for Victory Winston Churchill mascot, 1940s, 5in (12.5cm) high, mounted on a winged radiator cap.
£200–300 *S*

During WWII these mascots were sold to boost war funds, and were supposedly made from shot down enemy aircraft.

A chrome plated mascot of three wise monkeys, c1930, 3in (8cm) wide, mounted on a radiator cap.
£250–350 *S*

A nickel plated pewter baker's boy mascot, attributed to Louis Kley, c1909, 7in (17.5cm) high, mounted on a radiator cap.
£100–175 *S*

A lovebirds mascot, by H. Payen, signed, c1920, 4in (10cm) high, mounted on a radiator cap above a marble base.
£550–650 *S*

A mal de chien mascot, by M. Baise, signed, with R. Patrilleau, Fondeur, Paris founders marks, c1925, 3in (8cm) high, mounted on a radiator cap.
£850–1,000 *S*

A solid nickel Maltese cross mascot, by Cutajar Works, 1920s, 4½in (11.5cm) high, mounted on a wooden base.
£120–200 *S*

A nickel plated girl mascot, by H. Fugère, signed, c1920, 5in (12cm) high, on a display base.
£330–400 *S*

A nickel plated frog mascot, by Bofil, signed, with MMA pre-1914 founders mark, 3in (8cm) high, mounted on radiator cap.
£950–1,200 *S*

An Adler nickel plated brass eagle mascot, mounted with a calorimeter, c1925, 3½in (9cm) high, on original radiator cap.
£300–400 *S*

A bronze mascot of a scared boy running away from a frog on his arm, German, c1910, 5½in (14cm) high, mounted on a radiator cap.
£480–520 *S*

Range Rover & Land Rover

A Range Rover special edition brochure, produced with *Vogue* magazine models, 1980s.
£3–5 *PC*

A Range Rover brochure, 1974/75.
£3–5 *PC*

A Land Rover brochure, early 1970s.
£3–5 *PC*

An original Range Rover press release, in bound form, with black and white photographs, June 1970.
£50–60 *PC*

A Range Rover press release, with photographs, June 1970.
£3–5 *PC*

A Range Rover owner's manual, with colour and trim charts, 1980s.
£3-5 *PC*

A Land Rover parts and equipment calendar, 1987.
£3–5 *PC*

BAROMETERS

A barograph, by Negretti & Zambra, early 20thC, 17in (43cm) wide.
£60–65 *JUN*

A barometer, with silvered dial, signed J. Hicks, 8, 9 & 10 Hatton Garden, London, in a lancet satinwood veneered case decorated with ebonised wood, early 20thC, 11in (28cm) high.
£150-250 *WIL*

A George III mahogany veneered signpost barometer, with crossbanding and gadroon moulded pediment, the silvered dial in a glazed ogee pediment case, with vernier scale, inscribed Whitehurst, Derby 1772.
£5,500–7,000 *WW*

BICYCLES & CYCLING MEMORABILIA

As cycling grows increasingly popular, interest in bicycle history and collectables expands. Bicycles were first produced in the early 19thC. The first official bicycle race took place in the Parc de Saint Cloud, Paris, in 1868, won by Englishman James Moore, who was also the victor of the first road race (Paris–Rouen), held the following year. 1903 saw the inception of the Tour de France, which remains the world's most famous cycling event. Early machines and memorabilia are rare and command strong prices, and even contemporary material, for example modern Tour de France memorabilia, is well worth keeping.

A lady's bicycle, by Taylor, Christchurch, pre-WWII.
£45–55 *JUN*

An Ordinary penny farthing bicycle, restored, 19thC, 48in (122cm) high.
£1,500–1,750 *JUN*

A lady's bicycle, by New Hudson, frame number C26659, with lever brakes, leather Mansfield & Co. 'Onward' saddle, and Lucas bell, 20thC.
£100–150 *S*

A Victorian child's tricycle, with solid tyres, c1880.
£450–550 *MCh*

A Victorian child's 'safety cycle', with solid tyres, c1890.
£400–600 *MCh*

A Dursley Pedersen bicycle, with 3 speeds, c1902.
£1,200–1,500 *JUN*

An embossed metal and wooden sign, c1920.
£70–85 *COB*

A penny farthing bicycle, by Petty & Sharpe, with pneumatic tyres, 19thC, 54in (137cm) high.
£2,000–2,500 *MCh*

Two Victorian penny farthing rumble bells, on leather handlebar straps.
£100–140 each *MCh*

BOOKS

Rarity and condition are the important features of collectable books and the presence of a dust jacket is crucial. A recent auction included two 1930 first editions of Evelyn Waugh's comic masterpiece *Vile Bodies*. The novel with its original wrapper made £1,100, the one without £130, a considerable difference! First editions by leading 20thC novelists are becoming increasingly collectable.

Illustrated books have grown enormously in popularity and this year's Guide includes a special feature on children's books. Like any other area of the collectables market, books are affected by fashion. The fascination with cooking during the 1980s, and the adulation of popular chefs, has stimulated interest in old and antique cookery books to which we devote an extensive section this year.

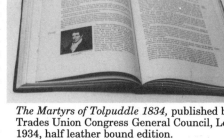

The Martyrs of Tolpuddle 1834, published by The Trades Union Congress General Council, London 1934, half leather bound edition.
£30–40 *BAf*

This book was published to commemorate the centenary of the struggle of the Tolpuddle Martyrs.

Sir Henry Chauncy, KT, *The Historical Antiquities of Hertfordshire,* 2 volume set, 1826 edition, full calf prize binding.
£250–300 *BAf*

W. A. Baillie-Graham, *Sport in the Alps,* printed by Adam and Charles Black, London, 1896.
£50–70 *BAf*

The Star Reciter, comedy and tragedy selected and arranged by J. A. Ferguson, published by John Heywood, c1880.
£7–9 *OCS*

Goldsmith's Poetical Works, published by V. & C. Brown & Co., c1880.
£8–10 *OCS*

The Complete Works of Oliver Goldsmith, published by George Routledge & Sons, leather bound presentation copy, c1870.
£35–45 *OCS*

The Poetical Works of Mrs. Hemans, with photographs, published by Frederick Warne & Co., c1889.
£10–15 *OCS*

Thomas Ingoldsby, *The Ingoldsby Legends,* c1911.
£8–10 *OCS*

Frederic Hervey and others, *Novel History of Great Britain,* 5 volumes, published London 1779, rebound, quarter leather with original title plates.
£400–500 *BAf*

Alexander William Kinglake, *The Invasion of the Crimea, Its Origin, and An Account of its Progress down to the Death of Lord Raglan,* 8 volumes, second edition, published by William Blackwood & Sons, Edinburgh and London, 1863–87, full calf decorated bindings.
£350–400 *BAf*

R. Talbot Kelly, *Burma,* published by A. & C. Black Ltd., London, second revised edition, with colour illustrations, 1933.
£12–18 *BAf*

Llewelyn Powys, *Dorset Essays,* first edition, 1935.
£25–30 *BAf*

R. L. G. Irving, *The Romance of Mountaineering,* reprinted 1946, first edition, 1935.
£10–15 *BAf*

A. E. Shepherd, *Links with the Past,* illustrated by E. Coffin, leather bound, c1917.
£6–10 *OCS*

Whitbread's *Reduced Ordnance Map of London,* c1883.
£20–25 *COB*

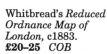

Logan Marshall, *Our National Calamity of Fire, Flood and Tornado,* including photographs and sketches, published in USA, c1913.
£10–15 *BAf*

Reverend C. A. Johns, *Flowers of the Field,* leather bound presentation copy for the Society for Promoting Christian Knowledge, c1899.
£40–45 *OCS*

Richard South, *The Moths of the British Isles,* published by Frederick Warne & Co., c1908.
£4–6 *OCS*

Jane's Fighting Ships, 1954–55, published by Sampson Low, Marston & Co. Ltd., London, W1, 1957.
£55–65 *BAf*

Lloyd's Register of British and Foreign Shipping, from 1st July 1854 to 3rd June 1855, original binding.
£80–100 *BAf*

The Steamship, an illustrated journal of progress in Marine Engineering, Steamship Building and Steam Navigation, edited by H. Holt-Butterfill, Volume I, 1883.
£60–70 *BAf*

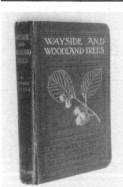

Edward Step, *Wayside and Woodland Trees,* published by Frederick Warne & Co., c1907.
£4–6 *OCS*

Frank Finn, *Eggs & Nests of British Birds,* published by Hutchinson & Co., c1910.
£4–6 *OCS*

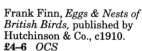

The New Book of Gardening, edited by Walter Brett, illustrated in colour and black and white, published by George Newnes Ltd., 3 volumes, leather spines and corners, c1930.
£25–30 *OCS*

Children's Books

Children's books do not necessarily mean juvenile prices. In recent months Beatrix Potter mania has been dominating the salerooms with bidders snapping up early books, letters and watercolours for decidedly adult prices, including an auction record of £55,000 for an inscribed first edition of Peter Rabbit. At the other end of the scale there is still a wide selection of children's books available for under £10. Canny collectors are already laying down contemporary children's books for the future, waiting for them to mature in value. A first edition of Maurice Sendak's *Where the Wild Things Are* could be worth over £100 and certain children's books by modern day illustrators and authors will undoubtedly become the adult collectables of the future.

Beatrix Potter, *The Tale of Peter Rabbit,* first commercial edition published in London and New York by Edmund Evans for Frederick Warne, November-December 1902.
£2,500–3,000   CSK

Harry Golding, *The Goblin Scouts,* The Little Wonder Books, published by Ward-Lock & Co., early 20thC, 5½ by 4in (13.5 by 10cm).
£20–25   CBS

Aunt Mavor's Everlasting Toy Books, *History of our Pets,* a cloth book, published by Routledge, Warne & Routledge, c1890, 9½ by 7in (24 by 17.5cm).
£15–20   HB

Dean's Movable Books, *The History of How Ned Nimble Built His Cottage,* 10 by 7in (25 by 17.5cm).
£250–300   CBS

My Playtime Album of Beautiful Transfer Pictures, published by Raphael Tuck, c1940, 8½ by 7in (21 by 17.5cm).
£6–8   COL

The Pets, a cloth book, published by Frederick Warne & Co., c1890, 9½ by 7½in (23.5 by 18.5cm).
£15–20   HB

Movable ABC, published by Dean, containing eight leaves with hand coloured engravings, the movable parts operated by a single lever at the bottom of the page, restored, covers very worn, early 20thC, 11 by 8in (28 by 20cm).
£600–700   CBS

Harriet Beecher Stowe, *Uncle Tom's Cabin,* published by Ward-Lock & Co., c1940.
£3–5   OCS

Fred E. Weatherly, *The Merry Musicians,* illustrated by A.M. Lockyer, 3½ by 5in early 20thC, (8.5 by 12.5cm). **£20–25** *CBS*

A Juvenile Child's Library, four volumes, one missing, 19thC, 3½ by 3in (8.5 by 7.5cm). **£200–275** *CBS*

Edgar Rice Burroughs, *Tarzan and the City of Gold,* first edition, c1936, 7½ by 5in (19 by 12.5cm). **£80–100** *CBS*

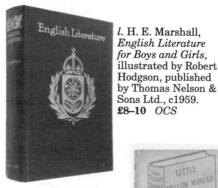

l. H. E. Marshall, *English Literature for Boys and Girls,* illustrated by Robert Hodgson, published by Thomas Nelson & Sons Ltd., c1959. **£8–10** *OCS*

Roald Dahl, *Charlie and the Chocolate Factory,* illustrated by Joseph Schindelman, 1960s, 9½ by 6¼in (24 by 15.5cm). **£40–50** *CBS*

r. M. C. Bell, *Little Yellow Wang-Lo,* The Dumpy Books for Children, first edition, 1903, 5 by 3in (12.5 by 7.5cm). **£40–45** *CBS*

A. A. Milne, *The King's Breakfast,* first edition, with music and illustrations, published by Methuen & Co. Ltd., c1928, 10 by 7in (25 by 17.5cm). **£15–20** *HB*

Laurence Whistler, *!Oho!,* drawings by Rex Whistler, first edition, 1946, published by John Lane, The Bodley Head, London. **£15–25** *BAf*

Annuals

Playbox Annual, 1911. **£5–20** *PC*

Playbox *was published from 1909 to 1956.*

Girl Annual, No. 8, 1959, 10 by 8½in (25.5 by 21.5cm). **£4–5** *CBS*

Chatterbox, first edition, c1894,
9 by 7in (23 by 17.5cm).
£50–60 *PC*

Chatterbox, 1898 edition,
published by Wells Gardner,
Darton & Co., London,
10 by 7½in (25.5 by 19cm)
£50–60 *PC*

The Rainbow Annual, 1927.
£5–20 *PC*

Rainbow Annual *was
published between 1924
and 1957.*

Rupert Annual, 1962.
£7–10 *BAf*

Peter Pan, Walt Disney, 1953,
published by Brockhampton
Press, 3 by 6in (7.5 by 15cm).
£7–8 *CBS*

© *Walt Disney Productions.*

The Rainbow Annual, 1950,
11 by 8in (28 by 20cm).
£5–6 *CBS*

Rupert Annual, 1975.
£4–6 *BAf*

Mickey Mouse Annual, c1939,
9 by 6½in (23 by 16.5cm).
£60–75 *CBS*

© *Walt Disney Productions.*

*More Adventures of Rupert, the
Daily Express Annual,* 1953,
good condition.
£15–20 *BAf*

*Mickey Mouse and the Bat
Bandit,* Walt Disney, published
by Whitman Publishing Co.,
Wisconsin, 1935, 4½ by
4in (11.5 by 10cm).
£30–35 *CBS*

© *Walt Disney Productions.*

Cookery Books

J. Worlidge, *Vinetum Britannicum or a Treatise of Cider,* published by Thomas Dring, 1691.
£250–350 *HB*

Cold Dishes for Hot Weather, published by Ysaguirre and La March, New York, c1896, 7 by 4½in (17.5 by 11.5cm).
£20–30 *HB*

Elizabeth Raffald, *The Experienced English Housekeeper,* written purely from practice, dedicated to the Hon. Lady Elizabeth Warburton, published by All the Booksellers and R. & W. Dean, Manchester, 1807.
£50–70 *HB*

William Terrington, *Cooling Cups and Dainty Drinks,* first edition, 1869, published by George Routledge & Son, London and New York.
£25–35 *HB*

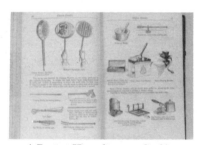

A Boston Housekeeper, *Cook's Own Book,* containing 2,500 recipes, published by James Miller, New York, c1880, 8 by 5in (20 by 12.5cm).
£40–50 *HB*

Cassell's Dictionary of Cookery, containing 9,000 recipes, c1880, 9½ by 6½in (24 by 16.5cm).
£25–35 *HB*

Mrs. S. T. Rorer, *Mrs Rorer's Cook Book,* published by Arnold and Company, Philadelphia, c1898.
£20–30 *HB*

Mrs Beeton, *The Book of Household Management, The Gas Cookery Section,* c1920, 8 by 5½in (20 by 14cm).
£30–50 *HB*

K. Burrill and Annie M. Booth, *The Amateur Cook,* dedicated to Ellen Terry, illustrations by Mabel Lucie Attwell, c1910.
£60–70 *HB*

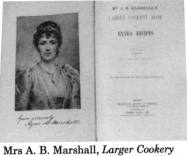

Mrs A. B. Marshall, *Larger Cookery Book of Extra Recipes*, dedicated by permission of HRH Princess Christian, published by Robert Hayes Ltd., early 20thC, 10 by 7½in (25.5 by 19cm). **£50-75** *HB*

Ambrose Heath, *Small Meat Dishes,* published by Faber & Faber, 1940s, 7½ by 5in (18.5 by 12.5cm). **£4–5** *BFB*

Mrs. C. S. Peel, OBE, *My Own Cookery Book,* c1939, 7½ by 5in (18.5 by 12.5cm). **£2–3** *BFB*

r. *Favourite Recipes,* paperback, published by *The Daily Telegraph,* c1945, 7 by 5in (17.5 by 12.5cm). **£5–6** *PC*

Ethelind Fearon, *Savoury Supper Dishes,* c1957, 6½ by 4in (16.5 by 10cm). **£1–2** *BFB*

Frances Parkinson Keyes, *Cook Book,* published by Muller, c1956, 8 by 5½in (20 by 14cm). **£8–10** *BFB*

Elizabeth David, *Mediterranean Food,* illustrated by John Minton, published by The Cookery Book Club, c1958. **£10–15** *BFB*

Jean Bothwell, *Onions Without Tears,* published by The World Work Ltd., Surrey, c1951.
£8–10 *BFB*

Cooking Price-Wise, with Vincent Price, published by Corgi, c1971, 7 by 4½in (18 by 11.5cm).
£2–3 *BFB*

Elizabeth David, *Mediterranean Food,* illustrated by John Minton, published by Penguin, c1958, 7 by 4½in (17.5 by 12cm).
£10–12 *PC*

Lady Barnett's Cookbook, c1969, 9 by 6in (22.5 by 15cm).
£9–10 *BFB*

M. P. Lee, *Chinese Cookery,* decorations by Chiang Yee, published by Faber & Faber, 20thC, 7½ by 5in (17.5 by 12.5cm).
£2–3 *BFB*

Robin McDouall, *Clubland Cooking,* published by Phaidon Press, 1974, 9 by 5in (23 by 12.5cm).
£8–10 *BFB*

Ambrose Heath, *Dining Out,* c1936, 7 by 4½in (17.5 by 11.5cm).
£3–4 *BFB*

BOOK ENDS

A pair of plaster owl book ends, 20thC, 5in (12.5cm) high.
£25–35 *ARE*

A pair of 'Mouseman' book ends, late 20thC, 6in (15cm) high.
£200–250 *APO*

A pair of French bronze book ends, by Moilet, with ivory faces, on marble bases, early 20thC, 7½in (19cm) high.
£800–900 *ARE*

CALENDARS

The connection of scantily-clad women with cars is a long-established, if not particularly enlightened, tradition and is epitomised by the pin-up calendar. The Pirelli calendar, the most famous of the genre, was launched in 1964. With high quality 'tasteful' photographs and deliberately limited circulation, it rapidly became a status symbol, spawning many imitators.

Calendars can be collectable on account of the photographer, the subject matter or the product they advertise. Although prices are currently low, they could well rise in the future.

A Pentax calendar, by GuyBourdin, 1980.
50p–£3 *PC*

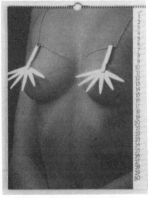

A VW-Audi calendar, 1978.
50p–£3 *PC*

A Pentax calendar, by Sam Haskins, 1975.
50p–£3 *PC*

A Pentax calendar, by Helmut Newton, 1976.
50p–£3 *PC*

A Pentax calendar, by Sam Haskins, 1981.
50p–£3 *PC*

A Unipart calendar, by Patrick Lichfield, 1991.
50p–£3 *PC*

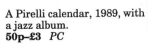

A Pirelli calendar, 1989, with a jazz album.
50p–£3 *PC*

A Unipart calendar, by Patrick Lichfield, 1992.
50p–£3 *PC*

CAMERAS

A Lancaster mahogany camera, with tailboard, red square cut bellows, International patent, c1885–1905.
£150–180 *HEG*

A quarter-plate camera, with Aldis lens, focal plane shutter, red bellows, dark slides and case, c1900, 8½in (21cm) long.
£120–140 *HEG*

An early falling plate camera, with Ilex shutter, brass and mahogany interior, c1900.
£60–80 *HEG*

A half-plate hand and stand camera, with red bellows, 1890.
£120–150 *HEG*

A Continental hand and stand walnut plate camera, with revolving back, IDD slide, possibly Swiss, c1900, 11in (28cm) wide.
£120–180 *WAG*

A Kodak folding pocket camera, No. 1, 1908, 7in (17.5cm) high.
£20–25 *HEG*

The Kodak folding pocket camera, No. 0, for 105 film, double finders behind leather covered front, red bellows, 1902–06.
£25–30 *HEG*

A Sanderson quarter-plate camera, with red bellows, slides and plate changer back, 1900, 9in (23cm) long.
£180–220 *HEG*

The Wizard quarter-plate camera, made by the Manhattan Optical Co., NY, with red bellows, nickel trim, double pneumatic shutter, 1902.
£100–120 *HEG*

A Kodak folding pocket camera, No. 1A, 1910, 8½in (21cm) high.
£20–25 *HEG*

A Sanderson quarter-plate hand and stand plate camera, with red bellows, c1900–20.
£150–180 *HEG*

An Ensignette strut camera, No. 1, with brass back, 1½ by 2¼in roll film, 1909–30, 4in (10cm) high.
£50–55 *HEG*

An early Ensignette brass back camera, No. 2, 2 by 3in film roll, 1909–30, 5in (12.5cm) high.
£40–50 *HEG*

An Ensignette strut camera, No. 1, with aluminium back, 1912–30, 4in (10cm) high.
£40–45 *HEG*

r. A Goerz vest pocket Tenax camera, with German silver single dark slides in a leather pouch, 1909, 3½in (9cm) high.
£60–85 *HEG*

r. A Kodak VPK Autographic camera, with lazy tong struts, 127 film, 1918, 4½in (11.5cm) long.
£15–20 *HEG*

A Kodak FPK Autographic camera, No. 3, 118 film, 1914–26, 8in (20cm) long.
£20–25 *HEG*

A Kodak Autographic folding pocket camera, No. 3A, with red bellows, 1909, 9½in (24cm) long.
£30–40 *HEG*

An Auto Graflex SLR camera, 1920, 5 by 7in (12.5 by 17.5cm). **£80–100** *HEG*

A Goerz Tenax 127 camera, with Prontor F8cm lens, 1921, 5in (12.5cm) high. **£35–40** *HEG*

A Zeiss baby box Tengor camera, 1925, 3½in (9cm) high. **£20–25** *HEG*

A Coronet Midget sub-miniature black Bakelite camera, 1930, 1½in (4cm) high. **£30–40** *HEG*

A Kodak VPK Model B Autographic camera, c1930, 4½in (11.5cm) high, with original box. **£15–20** *HEG*

An Ensign John Bull promotion box camera, c1930, 6in (15cm) square, with original box. **£10–15** *HEG*

An Eljy Lumière miniature camera, in excellent condition, 1937, 3in (7.5cm) wide. **£30–40** *HEG*

An American Argus Cintor camera, with a leather case, pre-WWII, 5½in (14cm) long.
£45–50 *JUN*

An Ensign Midget miniature camera, in excellent condition, 1934–40, 3in (7.5cm) high, with original cases and box.
£40–45 *HEG*

A Kodak Jiffy VP Bakelite camera, in excellent condition, 1935, 5in (12.5cm) high, with original box.
£25–30 *HEG*

A Merlin die-cast metal sub-miniature camera, 1936, 1½in (4cm) wide.
£45–50 *HEG*

A Coronet Vogue brown Bakelite camera, for Vogue 35 film, 1937, 4½in (11.5cm) wide.
£30–40 *HEG*

A copy of an early FED Leica, made in a Russian labour camp, 1938, engraved.
£80–120 *HEG*

An Ensign black Ful-Vue camera, post-war, 4in (10cm) wide.
£4–6 *HEG*

A Paillard Bolex H16 Reflex 16mm movie camea, with 3-lens turret, c1950.
£200–300 *HEG*

A Purma Plus three-speed camera, with metal body, 127 film, gravity shutter speeds, 1951, 6½in (16.5cm) wide.
£20–25 *HEG*

An Ensign Selfix 20 Popular FPK, 6 by 9cm on 120 film, c1950, 6in (15cm) wide.
£15–20 *HEG*

A Russian Contax II copy of a Kiev IV Rangefinder camera, 1958, 5½in (14cm) wide.
£50–60 *HEG*

An Exacta VX 1000 camera, with bayonet fit lens, instant return mirror, 1967, 6in (15cm) wide.
£65–70 *HEG*

A Nemrod Silvro underwater camera, for 120 film, with lead weights inside back, front valve to pressurise interior, 1960–62.
£50–85 *HEG*

An EXA 500 camera, with 35mm Exacta Bayonet mount f2.8, 50mm Domiplan lens, 1967, 5in (12.5cm).
£25–30 *HEG*

An Olympus Pen EES half frame 30mm Automatic camera, 1962–68, 4½in (11.5cm) wide.
£25–30 *HEG*

Miscellaneous

r. A hand-cranked pathescope projector, c1930.
£15–25 *HEG*

A brass and tin magic lantern, with a box of electric illumination slides, c1900.
£60–95 *HEG*

l. A tin lantern slide projector, brass lens, with slides, c1900, 17in (43cm) long.
£70–80 *HEG*

CERAMICS

Ceramics are, without doubt, one of the most popular collectables, offering something for every taste and every pocket. For easy reference, the ceramics section is organised alphabetically by period, factory and collecting field, e.g. Animals, Art Deco ceramics, and Bristol. Condition is all important in this fragile field. Look out for repairs, cracks and chipped decoration. Always handle ceramics carefully. Pick up pots by placing hands inside or around the body rather than by the handle, and be particularly gentle with lids and applied decoration. Items should be washed with lukewarm soapy water or wiped with a damp cloth, and do not use unprotected metal plate hangers.

Three carpet bowls, coloured pink and green, pink sponged and tartan, 19thC.
£40-50 each *WAG*

A table centrepiece, depicting a boudoir with a group of girls in conversation at a dressing table, gilded and flower encrusted overall, 15in (38cm) high.
£400–500 *LF*

A grey stoneware embossed jug decorated with grape vines, bacchante and satyrs, 19thC, 9in (23cm) high.
£100–160 *LF*

A feeder cup, 19thC, 3in (7.5cm) high.
£15–20 *LF*

Two embossed gilt, blue and white leaf and flower decorated dishes, 19thC, 11 and 10in (28 and 25cm) diam.
£125–200 *LF*

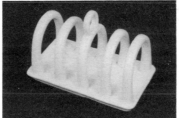

A white toast rack, c1890, 5in (12.5cm) long.
£12–15 *AL*

A pair of vases, possibly Bevington, c1860, 7½in (19cm) high.
£90–110 *WAG*

A Gustavsberg Argenta vase, by Wilhelm Kåge, decorated with a sea dragon, early 20thC, 6½in (16.5cm) high.
£300–350 *KAC*

A Delft Dutch house pastille burner, 20thC, 5in (12.5cm) high.
£40–50 *OCA*

Animals

A soup tureen in the form of
a lamb, decorated with blue
bows, 19thC, 20in (50.5cm) long.
£300–400 *RdeR*

A pair of blanc de chine Dogs of
Fo, c1750, 10½in (26.5cm) high.
£600–800 *DAN*

A Bernard Moore flambé model
of a seated monkey, wearing an
exotic blue, green and mauve
mottled waistcoat, holding a
peach, printed mark to base,
early 20thC, 5½in (14.5cm) high.
£400–500 *P*

A Beswick horse, 'Black Beauty', with
matt finish, 20thC, 7in (17.5cm) high.
£50-55 *JDC*

A Theodore Haviland
Limoges monkey jar
and cover, designed
by Edouard-Marcel
Sandoz, decorated in
brown and pink on a
white ground, printed
factory marks and
facsimile signature,
19thC, 7in (18cm) high.
£220-320 *P*

A pair of Oriental handmade
blue and white fish wall
pockets, Meiji/Taisho period,
11in (28cm) long.
£200-300 *BKK*

A Beswick grey foal,
20thC, 3in (7.5cm) high.
£10–15 *JDC*

A Crown Devon
dog, 1930s.
£30–35 *HEW*

A Beswick palomino horse,
20thC, 8in (20cm) high.
£35–40 *JDC*

A Beswick hackney horse, gloss
finish, 20thC, 7in (17.5cm) high.
£80–85 *JDC*

A Lovatt's Langley Ware
elephant, 1930s, 4in
(10cm) wide.
£30–35 *HEW*

Art Deco

The Art Deco period offers a rich field for collectors. Works range from high quality pieces by top designers worth hundreds of pounds or more to inexpensive, factory produced tableware. It is still quite possible to buy single plates from the 1920s and '30s for under a pound from car boot sales and charity shops. A matched set of different plates from the same period not only looks attractive but is suitable for everyday use, as long as one remembers not to put them in the dishwasher, as this can destroy overglaze decoration.

Britain produced some marvellous and inventive ceramics during this period. Clarice Cliff and Susie Cooper were among the most influential designers, and factories such as Shelley and Carlton all manufactured highly distinctive wares. 'Art Deco ceramics are becoming more and more collectable,' advises specialist dealer Beverley, in London. 'Prices are on the rise, it's a healthy market and really every area is desirable and becoming more so.'

A stylised vase, c1930, 5½in (14cm) high.
£8–10 *BKK*

A Beswick Ruth jug, hand painted, c1932, 9½in (24cm) high.
£25–35 *BKK*

A selection of Arnhem pottery, c1920, jug 2½in (6.5cm) high, **£40–50,** bowl 6in (15cm) diam.
£100–110 *OO*

A Hollinshead and Kirkham hand painted cake plate, c1933, 8½in (21cm) square.
£15–20 *BKK*

A Crown Devon hand painted vase, c1932, 7½in (18.5cm) high.
£25–30 *BKK*

Two Chamelion Ware Alladin's lamps, decorated in beige and brown, c1931, 8½in and 3½in (21.5cm and 8.5cm) high.
£80–100 *BKK*

A Falcon Ware hand painted three dimensional decorative jug, c1930, 7in (17.5cm) high.
£35–45 *BKK*

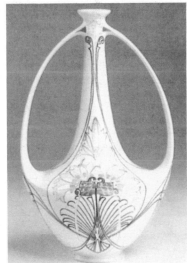

A Gypsy Ware hand painted decorative jug, c1927, 7in (17.5cm) high.
£20–25 *BKK*

A Grindley hand painted Art Deco teapot, c1932, 6in (15cm) high.
£20–25 *BKK*

A Hollinshead and Kirkham hand painted Tuliptime lustre jug, c1933, 6in (15cm) high.
£35–40 *BKK*

A Burleigh Ware Pied Piper flower jug, c1930, 8in (20cm) high.
£80–100 *BKK*

A Kensington hand painted ceramic jam pot, with chrome cover, c1934, 3½in (8.5cm).
£20–25 *BKK*

A Radford hand painted vase, c1936, 4in (10cm) high.
£55–65 *BKK*

A Royal Winton Grimwades pansy jug, c1935, 4½in (11cm) high.
£18–22 *BKK*

A Ruskin flambé glazed vase, with scattered viridian spots, dated '1933', 4in (10cm) high.
£300–350 *BKK*

An Arthur Woods Pearl lustre jug, with twisted handle, c1932, 5½in (13.5cm) high.
£35–40 *BKK*

Figures

A Shorter & Son Art Deco candlestick, c1930, 3in (7.5cm) high.
£20–25 *BKK*

A German figure of a mermaid, c1930, 4in (10cm) long.
£60–80 *BAT*

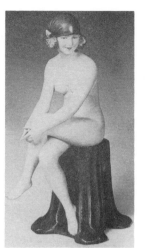

An earthenware wall mask of a lady in a hat, signed 'C & Co.', c1930.
£120–150 *HEW*

A crackleware figure, impressed Primavera, c1918, 21in (53cm).
£900–1,000 *POW*

Made in the Design Studio at Printemps which opened in 1913. Artist René Buthaud was the Technical Director of the factory from 1923–26 and developed the crackle glaze technique.

A Royal Dux figure, The Bathing Beauty, pink triangle on base, 1930s, 16in (48cm) high.
£1,200–1,500 *P*

This figure was possibly inspired by an image by Kirchner.

An English earthenware wall mask, signed 'C & Co.', c1930.
£120–150 *HEW*

A Royal Dux porcelain wall mask, 1930s.
£250–275 *HEW*

A Royal Dux porcelain wall mask, restored, c1930.
£150–175 *HEW*

A Royal Dux porcelain wall mask, 1930s.
£250–275 *HEW*

Wall Vases

A Royal Dux porcelain wall mask of a lady with a flower, 1930s.
£250–275 *HEW*

A Shorter & Son shell-shaped wall vase, c1934, 7½in (18.5cm) high.
£25–30 *BKK*

A Sadler lustre wall vase, c1933, 5in (12.5cm) high.
£25–30 *BKK*

A Lovatt's wall vase, decorated with a seagull, c1931, 8½in (21cm) high.
£20–25 *BKK*

Art Nouveau

A St. Clement faïence bowl, possibly by Gallé, coloured in pink, white, cream, blue and gilt, raised on shaped feet, signed 'St. Clement M.C.', 1920s, 16½in (41.5cm) long.
£350–450 *P*

A pair of stoneware jardinières and stands, possibly for Liberty, each oviform on short stepped cylindrical bases, moulded in relief with cartouches of irises on sinuous stems, covered in an oatmeal glaze, slight damage, 1920s–30s, 26in (66cm) high.
£800–900 *CSK*

A decorative pottery vase, c1910–30, 10in (25cm) high.
£20–30 *ACA*

Blue & White

A pair of Victorian blue and white transfer printed plates, with partridge, 'Landseer', 7in (17.5cm) diam.
£15–20 *WAG*

A blue and white mug, 19thC, 4in (10cm) high.
£40–50 *WAG*

A pair of blue and white spill vases, with a panel of classical buildings with chariots and figures, 19thC, 12½in (32cm).
£180–250 *LF*

A Victorian blue and white pint mug, decorated with hops, 4½in (11cm) high.
£20–30 *WAG*

A lazy Susan, fitted with seven Villeroy and Boch blue and white dishes, 22in (55.5cm) diam.
£90–100 *LF*

Bristol

A Bristol gurglet flask, damaged, 9½in (24cm).
£500–600 *DMa*

A Bristol figure of Andromache, weeping over the ashes of Hector, 12½in (32cm) high.
£2,500–3,000 *DMa*

- **Bristol hard paste porcelain was made c1770–78.**
- **Wreathing or spiral grooves around items is common to Bristol porcelain.**
- **There are often imperfections in the porcelain which is grey in colour as opposed to white.**

A Bristol cup, 2⅜in (6cm) high.
£140–175 *DMa*

A Bristol cream jug, Thomas Pitt service, 4½in (11cm).
£350–400 *DMa*

A Bristol cup and saucer, with green swag decoration.
£250–300 *DMa*

Carlton Ware

Carlton Ware ceramics are familiar to every collector of 1920s and '30s china. Designs include geometric pieces, exotically coloured lustreware pottery, moulded tableware and novelty items, often brightly coloured and using the form of leaves. These distinctive leaf-shaped items accounted for much of Carlton's output during this period. Although they have been considered less collectable than lustre and geometric wares, prices are certainly rising. Look out also for later products, in particular the '50s wares which are becoming ever more desirable.

A Victorian Carlton Ware dessert service, with blue and red decoration, comprising three plates and three comports.
£80–120 *LF*

A Carlton Ware honey pot, decorated with a primula handle, c1935, 3in (7.5cm).
£30–40 *BKK*

A Carlton Ware toast rack, decorated with a foxglove, c1937, 4in (10cm) long.
£50–60 *BKK*

A Carlton Ware nut dish, decorated with a squirrel, c1935, 9in (23cm) diam.
£60–80 *BKK*

A Carlton Ware jug, decorated with apple blossom, c1936, 4½in (11cm) high.
£25–30 *BKK*

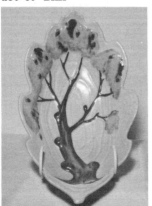

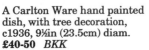

A Carlton Ware pen tray and holder, with golden pheasant decoration and lustre glaze, c1925, 7in (17.5cm) long.
£40–50 *BKK*

A Carlton Ware hand painted dish, with tree decoration, c1936, 9½in (23.5cm) diam.
£40–50 *BKK*

A Carlton Ware moulded ewer, with hand painted decoration, c1933, 10in (25cm).
£180–200 *BKK*

A Carlton Ware egg cup set, decorated with apple blossom, c1935, 8in (20cm) long.
£75–85 *BKK*

A Carlton Ware hand painted house, c1930, 2½in (6cm) high.
£100–120 *BKK*

A Carlton Ware vase, with poppy and daisy decoration, c1930, 5in (12.5cm).
£140–180 *BKK*

Cruets

A Carlton Ware tomato shaped cruet, c1938, 8in (20cm) long.
£20–25 *BKK*

A Carlton Ware fruit-shaped cruet, c1940, 9in (23cm) long.
£20–25 *BKK*

A Carlton Ware vegetable cruet, c1936, 9in (23cm) long.
£25–30 *BKK*

Miscellaneous

A Carlton Ware Verte Royale dish, c1930, 10in (25cm) diam.
£50–55 *BKK*

A Carlton Ware teapot, c1950, 8½in (21cm) wide.
£40–45 *HEW*

A Carlton Ware Glamour green and gold stylised plate, c1930, 9in (23cm) diam.
£65–75 *BKK*

Children's & Nursery Ware

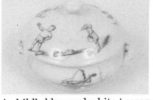

A child's blue and white tureen, early 20thC, 4in (10cm) wide.
£15–18 *WAG*

A child's mug, with transfer printed alphabet, early 20thC, 2½in (6cm) high.
£25–35 *WAG*

r. Two egg cups, with nursery transfers.
£5–6 each *HEW*

A collection of 29 mugs, each decorated with a nursery rhyme, 2½in (6cm) high.
£130–150 *LF*

Clarice Cliff

A Clarice Cliff Summerhouse pattern bowl, c1931, 7½in (18.5cm) diam.
£140–180 *BKK*

A Clarice Cliff bowl, with house and tree design, 8½in (21cm) diam.
£400–500 *HEW*

A Clarice Cliff Blue Firs pattern Biarritz plate, c1933, 9in (23cm) long.
£160–180 *BKK*

A Clarice Cliff Delecia design drip ware jug, c1930, 6in (15cm) high.
£200–220 *HEW*

A Clarice Cliff Original Bizarre sabot, c1928, 4½in (11cm) long.
£180–200 *BKK*

A Clarice Cliff Melons pattern honey pot, decorated with a bee handle, c1931, 3in (7.5cm).
£100–125 *BKK*

A Clarice Cliff Autumn Crocus pattern honey pot, shape 230, c1932, 2½in (6cm).
£80–120 *BKK*

A Clarice Cliff Windsor shape tea set, decorated in Autumn Crocus pattern, c1937, teapot 6in (15cm) high.
£200–250 *BKK*

Susie Cooper

Born in 1902, Susie Cooper is one of the most influential ceramic designers of her generation. In a career spanning from the 1920s to the present day, she pioneered new designs, shapes and techniques, supplying stylish, functional and affordable tableware to generations of customers from royalty downwards. 'When I started there was nothing available between the fine china that was extremely expensive and ordinary material that was very poor,' she explained. 'I wanted to do nice things for people who had taste, but didn't have the money to satisfy it.'

Now in her mid-90s, Susie Cooper has seen her cost-conscious china transformed into costly antiques, a fact that never ceases to amaze her. Her lustreware and geometric designs from the 1920s and '30s are her most collectable pieces, although she herself much prefers her post-war designs. 'They are far less crude', she comments crisply. Collectors are becoming increasingly interested in Susie Cooper's 1950s and '60s wares, and by the time of the second Festival of Britain in 2001, works from this period are likely to be at a premium.

A Susie Cooper orange, yellow and brown plate, for Gray's Pottery, c1928, 11in (28cm) diam.
£100–120 *CSA*

A Susie Cooper blue, green and yellow dish, for Gray's Pottery, c1928, 8in (20cm) wide.
£40–50 *CSA*

A Susie Cooper yellow, orange and gilt jug, for Gray's Pottery, c1928, 4½in (11cm) high.
£40–50 *CSA*

A pair of Susie Cooper blue and green candlesticks, for Gray's Pottery, c1928, 3½in (8.5cm) high.
£80–90 *CSA*

A Susie Cooper yellow and orange painted dessert plate, for Gray's Pottery, c1928, 6½in (16cm) diam.
£20–30 *CSA*

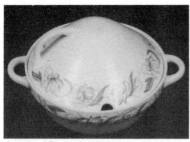

A pair of Susie Cooper vegetable tureens, in Endon pattern, c1940, 10in (25cm) wide.
£35–40 each *CSA*

A Susie Cooper soup bowl, 4½in (11cm) diam, and stand, 6½in (16cm) diam.
£18–20 *CSA*

A set of six Susie Cooper Harlequin pattern cups and saucers, c1960.
£75–85 *BKK*

Two Susie Cooper egg cups, 1½in (3.5cm).
£8–10 each *CSA*

A Susie Cooper Printemps pattern jug, c1940, 4in (10cm).
£30–35 *CSA*

A Susie Cooper 32 piece dinner service, dish 11in (28cm) wide.
£350–450 *YY*

A set of six Susie Cooper Wedgwood coffee cans and saucers, with sweet dish and original packaging, post-1966.
£75–85 *BKK*

A Susie Cooper coffee pot, cup and saucer, pot 5in (12.5cm) high.
£15–20 *PC*

A Susie Cooper dessert plate, 4½in (11.5cm) square.
£10–12 *PC*

A Susie Cooper Kestrel tea service for six, painted with bands in shades of brown, comprising teapot and cover, milk jug and sugar bowl, six cups, saucers and side plates, printed factory marks, No. 479, teapot 6½in (16cm) high, and a dinner srvice for six in the same pattern.
£340–380 *CSK*

Cruets

This selection of cruets demonstrates how one can still acquire a fascinating collection of objects for comparatively little money. The now traditional containers for salt, pepper and mustard were introduced in the 18thC. The Victorians produced decorative cruet sets in the form of figures and animals. The 1920s and '30s saw many humorous and imaginative designs and the fashion for novelty cruets continues into the present day.

Many cruets were mass-produced as promotional items to be given away or as advertising gimmicks. As a result, the manufacturer's name or date produced seldom appear on the item. The majority of objects shown here date from the 20thC. Collectors should always assess objects carefully for damage and completeness. Original matching mustard or salt spoons will enhance the value.

A fish cruet, 6in (15cm) wide.
£12–15 PC

A cruet depicting a pair of whales, 4in (10cm) wide.
£4–5 PC

A birdcage cruet, 3½in (8.5cm).
£5–6 PC

A cruet depicting three cats, coloured blue, 4in (10cm) wide.
£8–10 PC

An elephant lustreware cruet, 5in (12.5cm) wide.
£12–15 PC

A cruet depicting three dogs, c1930, 3½in (8.5cm) wide.
£15–20 PC

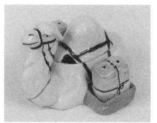

A ship of the desert cruet, 4in (10cm) wide.
£15–20 PC

A Bonzo dog cruet set, 3in (7.5cm) wide.
£10–12 PC

A cruet depicting two ducks, c1933, 4in (10cm).
£12–15 PC

A Pinky and Perky cruet, 1970s.
£8–10 PC

A cruet depicting Sooty in a car, 3⅜in (8.5cm) wide.
£12–15 *PC*

A cruet depicting three fish, 4⅓in (11cm) wide.
£5–6 *PC*

A Snoopy, 4⅓in (11cm), and Woodstock cruet, 3⅓in (8.5cm).
£8–10 *PC*

Figures

A Tetley Tea Men cruet, c1985, 4in (10cm).
£8–10 *PC*

A Staffordshire Morlors cruet, depicting elves with mushrooms, 2⅓in (6cm).
£25–30 *PC*

The Spice of Life cruet, c1970, 5⅓in (13.5cm) long.
£5–6 *PC*

A cruet depicting two pirates leaning on barrels, 2⅓in (6cm) high.
£8–10 *PC*

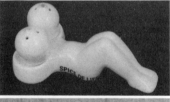

A cruet depicting two pirates and a barrel, 2⅓in (6cm).
£6–8 *PC*

Four Toby Willow pattern cruets, with red coats and yellow trousers, c1880, 6in (15cm).
£750–950 *HEY*

Household Items

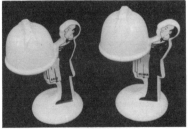

A black and white promotional cruet depicting waiters, c1935, 6⅓in (16cm).
£8–10 *PC*

A cruet depicting two telephones, 2⅓in (6cm).
£3–4 *PC*

A cruet in the form of an iron, 3in (7.5cm) wide.
£5–6 *PC*

A cruet depicting two grandfather clocks, 3½in (8.5cm).
£8–10 *PC*

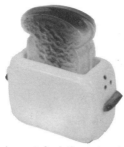

A cruet depicting a toaster and two pieces of toast, 3½in (8.5cm) high.
£5–6 *PC*

A cruet depicting two cookers, 2½in (6cm) high.
£4–5 *PC*

A cruet depicting two blue taps, 4½in (11cm).
£10–12 *PC*

A cruet depicting an electric socket, with two plugs, c1970, 5in (12.5cm) wide.
£8–10 *PC*

A cruet depicting a cooker, with kettle and pot, 3½in (8.5cm).
£6–8 *PC*

Transport

A cruet depicting two hot air balloons, and a tray, 3½in (8.5cm) high.
£8–10 *PC*

A cruet depicting a green lustre aeroplane, 6in (15cm) long.
£10–12 *PC*

A cruet in the form of an aeroplane, French, 7in (17.5cm) long.
£12–15 *PC*

A cruet in the form of an ocean liner, 5½in (13.5cm) long.
£12–15 *PC*

A cruet in the form of a galleon, 5in (12.5cm) wide.
£12–15 *PC*

A cruet shaped as a Zeppelin and clouds, 4in (10cm) wide.
£6–10 *PC*

A cruet depicting an ocean liner, inscribed 'A Present from New Brighton', 7in (17.5cm) wide.
£20–25 *JUN*

A cruet depicting a gondola,
5in (12.5cm) wide.
£8–10 *PC*

A cruet depicting a boat, inscribed 'A
present from Southend-on-Sea', 7½in
(18.5cm) wide.
£20–25 *JUN*

A cruet depicting a boat,
inscribed 'A Present from Deal',
c1950, 7in (17.5cm) long.
£15–20 *JUN*

A cruet depicting an ocean
liner, inscribed 'A Present from
Weymouth', 6in (15cm) wide.
£25–35 *JUN*

A cruet depicting an ocean liner,
inscribed 'A Present from Blackpool',
7in (17.5cm) long.
£25–35 *JUN*

A cruet in the form of of two
blue Morris Minors, 3in
(7.5cm) wide.
£6–8 *PC*

A cruet in the form of a car, 4in
(10cm) wide.
£20–25 *PC*

Miscellaneous

A cruet in the form of masks of
Tragedy and Comedy, 20thC.
£5–6 *PC*

A red cruet in the shape of a
broken heart, 3in (7.5cm) wide.
£5–6 *PC*

A cuet in the form of two sea
shells, 2½in (6cm) wide.
£3–4 *PC*

A cruet depicting the Rovers
Return Inn, from Coronation
Street, 4in (10cm).
£8–10 *PC*

A cruet in the form of two
flowers by Aynsley, in original
box, 4in (10cm) wide.
£8–10 *PC*

Denby

The Denby Pottery Company runs a visitors' centre, which includes a museum, shop, and video theatre. The museum houses a wide variety of objects ranging from 1813 to the present day and guides are happy to identify old pieces of Denby brought in by visitors. Factory tours are given daily, and in the craft room visitors can see traditional potting skills and are even given the opportunity to try their hand at potting and painting. The factory is also home to the Denby Collectors' Society.

A Denby salt glazed money box, Codnor Park Pottery, damaged, c1833, 4½in (11cm) high.
£75–85 *KES*

A Denby salt glazed apothecary's jar, with japanned lid, impressed mark, c1860, 4in (10cm).
£25–30 *KES*

A Denby salt glazed inkwell for quill pens, inscribed 'Willm Hunt Riddings November 26th 1857', 3in (7.5cm) high.
£80–100 *KES*

l. A Denby mustard jug, 19thC 3½in (8.5cm).
£18–25
r. A Denby salt glazed harvest mug, 19thC, 5½in (13.5cm).
£45–55 *KES*

A Denby jar, c1880, 4in (10cm).
£10–12
Two Denby salt glazed bottles, c1880, 5½ and 6½in (14 and 16cm).
£4–5 each *KES*

Two Bourne Denby miniature bottles, inscribed, c1880, 1in (2.5cm).
£100–120 *KES*

A Denby bottle, inscribed, c1904, 8in (20cm) high.
£8–10 *KES*

Three Denby muff warmers, c1912, 5in (12.5cm) wide.
£65–75 each *KES*

An Edwardian Denby domestic ware tea urn, lid restored, 19½in (49cm) high.
£35–45 *KES*

A Denby brown teapot, inscribed 'Great Northern Rly,Refreshment Dept.', spout damaged, early 20thC, 3½in ((8.5cm) high.
£15–25 *KES*

A Denby Orient Ware jug, early 20thC, 5½in (14cm) high.
£45–55 *KES*

A Denby dark green glazed vase, c1912, 6½in (16cm) high.
£30–35 *KES*

A Denby pastel blue Dalton vase, c1930, 8½in (21cm) high.
£75–95 *KES*

A Denby ivory and pastel bowl, 1930s, 7½in (18.5cm) diam.
£40–45 *KES*

A Denby gilded jug and mug, made for export, c1950, jug 3in (7.5cm), mug 4in (10cm) high.
£20–35 each *KES*

A Denby pastel blue delphinium jug, 1930s, 10½in (26.5cm).
£75–90 *KES*

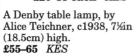

A Denby table lamp, by Alice Teichner, c1938, 7½in (18.5cm) high.
£55–65 *KES*

For further information contact: The Denby Pottery Company, Denby, Derbyshire. Tel: 01773 743641.

A Denby Tally-ho! mug,
c1949, 4in (10cm) high.
£15–20 *KES*

A Denby tube lined antique
green ashtray, c1950, 4½in
(11cm) diam.
£30–35 *KES*

A Denby sweet dish, by Glyn
College, c1950, 7in (17.5cm) diam.
£45–55 *KES*

A Denby cloisonné fruit dish,
c1958, 7½in (18.5cm) wide.
£25–30 *KES*

A Denby Tigo cruet, Clowns
design, 1960s, 9in (23cm) wide.
£25–35 *KES*

A Denby Green Wheat pattern
plate, c1960, 8in (20cm) diam.
£7–8 *KES*

Animals

In between the late 1920s and the early
'50s, Denby produced a wide range of
stoneware animals. Most popular were the
rabbits, called 'Marmaduke' (see Colour
Review) which came in a variety of sizes
and coloured glazes. The rarest and most
expensive today are those with an Orient
Ware glaze, i.e. dark blue, purple or rust.
Other animals manufactured included
various breeds of dogs, farmyard and wild
animals and birds. Donald Gilbert, son of
the great Victorian sculptor Sir Alfred
Gilbert, designed some fine animal pieces
for Denby, including the group of three
geese illustrated.

l. A Denby elephant book end, 1930–40, 5½in
(14cm) high.
£40–45
r. A Denby lamb, 1930–40, 5in
(12.5cm) high.
£25–30 *KES*

A group of Denby geese, decorated in regent
pastel, modelled by Donald Gilbert, c1930,
9in (23cm) wide.
£95–120 *KES*

A pair of Denby pastel blue
love bird book ends, c1935,
8in (20cm) high.
£100–120 *KES*

A Denby blue and
white giraffe, 1930s,
4in (10cm) high.
£25–30 *KES*

Doulton

A Doulton figure, entitled 'The Skater', HN2117, c1953–71, 8in (20cm) high.
£170–190 *YY*

A Doulton figure, entitled 'Top of the Hill', HN1937, 8in (20cm) high.
£130–150 *YY*

A Doulton figure of a Boxer dog, HN 2643, c1970.
£60–70 *YY*

r. A Doulton figure of a Boxer dog, c1970, 6in (15cm) high.
£20–30 *YY*

r. A Doulton figure, entitled 'Paisley Shawl', No. N4, c1932–45, 4in (10cm) high.
£160–170 *YY*

A Doulton figure, c1983–85, HN2981, 7in (17.5cm) high.
£60–80 *YY*

A Doulton figure, entitled 'Orange Lady', HN1953, 8in (20cm) high.
£130–150 *YY*

An enamel advertising sign, c1930, 36 by 18in (91.5 by 45.5cm).
£100–120 *PMB*

An enamel advertising sign, c1930, 18 by 12in (45.5 by 30.5cm).
£175–200 *PMB*

A tin sign, advertising Grant's Cherry Whisky, 13 by 10in (33 by 25cm).
£85–95 *JUN*

An enamel advertising sign, c1910–20.
£300–350 *PMB*

An enamel advertising sign, Birmingham Post, 28 by 18in (71 by 45.5cm).
£70–80 *PMB*

An enamel advertising sign, c1920, 20 by 30in (50.5 by 76cm).
£250–300 *PMB*

An enamel sign, advertising Spillers Shapes, 12in (30.5cm) square.
£40–45 *JUN*

An enamel advertising sign, c1930, 24 by 16in (61 by 40.5cm).
£250–280 *PMB*

An enamel advertising sign, c1930, 22 by 30in (55.5 by 76cm).
£200–220 *PMB*

An enamel advertising sign, c1930, 35 by 23in (89 by 58.5cm).
£200–250 *PMB*

An enamel advertising sign, 12 by 18in (30.5 by 45.5cm).
£90–110 *JUN*

An enamel advertising sign, c1920.
£400–450 *PMB*

A Stephenson's Furniture Cream shop display box.
£18–22 *JUN*

A Slippery Elm infant food tin, c1900.
£8–10 *JUN*

A Fry's Breakfast Cocoa shop display box, c1930, 10in (25cm) high.
£20–25 *JUN*

A Peek Frean's sample tin, 1930s, 3 by 2½in (7.5 by 6cm).
£20–25 *JUN*

An Edwardian Keen's mustard tin, 7in (17.5cm) square.
£30–35 *JUN*

A Don Confectionery Co., sweet tin, c1915, 9in (23cm) high.
£25–35 *JUN*

l. A Radiance Devon Cream Toffee tin, 1930s, 6in (15cm) high.
£20–25 *JUN*

A Mackintosh's 'Sampler' chocolates tin, 1950s, 10in (25cm) long.
£18–20 *JUN*

A Sharp's toffee tin, with pictorial story of flight, 1960s.
£12–15 *JUN*

A biscuit tin, 1930s, 7½in (19cm) diam.
£10–12 *JUN*

A tin, with mural scenes, 1920s, 7½in (19cm) high.
£18–20 *JUN*

A Stephenson's Floor Polish shop display box, 1930s, 12½in (32cm) long.
£20–25 *JUN*

A selection of cigarette packets.
£3–5 each *JUN*

Two cardboard Easter eggs,
c1950–60, 5in (12.5cm) high.
£8–10 each *CK*

A Lyle's Golden Syrup
advertisement card,
framed, 19in (48cm)
high. **£75–85** *JUN*

A framed advertisement
card for Rowntree's
Cocoa, 21in (53cm) high.
£25–35 *JUN*

An advertisement card
for Phoenix Assurance
Co., 20in (50.5cm)
high. **£35–40** *JUN*

An advertisement card for
Wright's Coal Tar soap,
21in (53cm) high.
£100–125 *JUN*

An advertising
calendar for Spencer
Matheson, 1913,
28in (71cm) high.
£20–30 *JUN*

A travel agents' plastic display model of a
Qantas Boeing 747, 38in (96.5cm) long.
£160–175 *JUN*

A model of a De Havilland
DH66 Hercules, Imperial
Airways livery, 13in
(33cm) long.
£480–580 *CSK*

A travel agents' plastic model of a
BEA Trident 3, 32in (81cm) long.
£150–160 *JUN*

A model of a Short S23
Empire 'Canopus', with
Imperial Airways livery, on
a stand, 19in (48.5cm) long.
£750–850 *CSK*

Two pattern portfolios
for model aeroplanes,
by Percival Marshall
& Co., c1912, 10½in
(26.5cm) wide.
£40–50 each *JUN*

A polyphon Musikwerke electric sailor, Leipzig, c1910.
£5,000–6,000 *DON*

An amusement machine, Le Cochon Electriseur Automatique, c1898.
£10,000–12,000 *DON*

An automatic shooting gallery, British, c1900.
£1,500–2,000 *DON*

A Player's Please Allwin type amusement machine, 27in (68.5cm) high.
£300–350 *JUN*

A cigarette vending machine, 30in (76cm) high.
£80–100 *JUN*

A two man golf game, c1899.
£10,000–12,000 *DON*

A Turban Stuffed Dates vending machine, 34in (86cm) high.
£125–150 *JUN*

A pedal car, with wooden body, 1920s, 35in (89cm) long. **£550–650** *JUN*

A Leeway pedal car, 1930s, 32in (81cm) long.
£300–400 *JUN*

A cigarette dispenser, 32in (81cm) high.
£90–110 *JUN*

A car rally plaque, 1960s.
£15–20 *COB*

A glass petrol pump globe, 18in (45.5cm) high.
£200–250 *JUN*

Theatrical Picture Book, each panel 12 by 10in (30.5 by 25cm).
£650–750 *CBS*

The Dandy Book, 1973, 11 by 7½in (28 by 19cm).
£5–6 *CBS*

The Dr Who Annual, No. 7, 1965, 10 by 7in (25 by 17.5cm).
£8–10 *CBS*

A set of five children's books, 1910.
£18–20 *CK*

Fairy Tales from the British Isles, re-told by Amabel Williams-Ellis, illustrated by Pauline Diana Baynes, published by Blackie, 1963.
£5–7 *OCS*

Richmal Crompton, *William the Superman,* 1968.
£25–35 *CBS*

Mickey Mouse Annual, 1937.
£50–60 *CBS*

Captain W. E. Johns, *Worlds of Wonder,* Children's Book Club, first edition, c1962.
£5–7 *OCS*

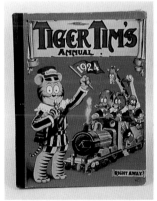

Arthur Mee's *Golden Year,* Hodder & Stoughton, 1930.
£8–10 *OCS*

Little Red Riding Hood, a Dean's Movable Book, c1857, 10 by 7in (25 by 17.5cm).
£250–300 *CBS*

Tiger Tim's Annual, 1924, 11 by 8½in (28 by 21.5cm).
£15–25 *PC*

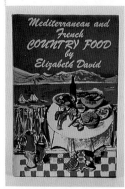

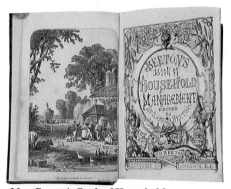

Elizabeth David, *Country Food*, published by Macdonald, c1958.
£10–15 *BFB*

Mrs. Beeton's Book of Household Management, leather bound first edition, c1861, 7 by 4½in (17.5 by 11cm).
£300–400 *HB*

Catherine Althaus and Peter Ffrench-Hodges, *Cook Now Dine Later,* c1969, 8 by 5⅓in (20 by 13.5cm).
£3–4 *BFB*

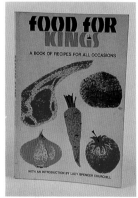

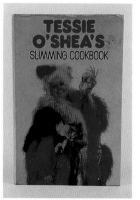

Philip Harben's Countdown Cookery, published by J. M. Dent & Son, c1971, 5½ by 9in (13.5 by 23cm).
£3–4 *BFB*

Food for Kings, signed by Lady Clementine Spencer Churchill, c1967.
£4–5 *BFB*

Tessie O'Shea's Slimming Cookbook, published by Cassell & Co., c1974.
£4–5 *BFB*

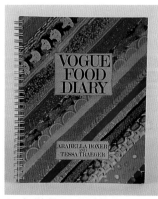

Arabella Boxer and Tessa Traeger, *Vogue Food Diary* c1977, 9 by 7½in (23 by 18.5cm).
£1–2 *BFB*

Nella Whitfield, *Fun with Food,* c1959, 10 by 7½in (25 by 18.5cm).
£3–4 *BFB*

Escoffier The Complete Guide to the Art of Modern Cookery, first published 1979, re-printed, 10in (25cm) high.
£30–35 *BFB*

A Burleigh hand decorated jug, c1930, 9½in (23.5cm) high. **£80–100** *BKK*

A Hancock's vase and charger in Lagoon pattern, c1930, charger 10in (25cm) diam. **£90–140 each** *BKK*

Three Art Deco jug-shaped vases, c1930, 7in (17.5cm) high. **£8–12 each** *BKK*

A selection of jugs by Shorter and Morley Fox, c1930, 5½in (13.5cm) high. **£15–20 each** *BKK*

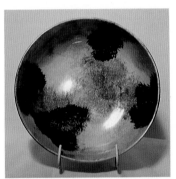

A Hollinshead and Kirkham hand painted lustre glazed bowl, c1930, 9in (23cm) diam. **£40–50** *BKK*

A Wilkinson plaque, marked, c1920, 13in (33cm) diam. **£250–300** *HEW*

l. A Blue John Pottery Art Deco jug, c1939, 10in (25cm) high. **£50–60** *BKK*

r. An Art Deco T-flow teapot, 9½in (23.5cm) wide. **£60–75** *HEW*

A Royal Venton hand painted covered dish and stand, with silver gilding, c1933. **£30–35** *BKK*

A Crown Ducal vase, 7in (17.5cm) high. **£90–120** *HEW*

An Arthur Wood's Garden Wall basket, c1933, 11in (28cm) high. **£50–60** *BKK*

A German ceramic wall mask.
£150–175 HEW

A Royal Dux porcelain wall
mask, c1930.
£250–275 *HEW*

A Czechoslovakian ceramic
wall mask, c1930.
£250–275 *HEW*

An Art Nouveau amphora
vase, 13½in (34cm) high.
£100–120 *HEW*

A Czechoslovakian ceramic wall
mask, c1930.
£250–275 HEW

A Royal Dux porcelain
wall mask.
£250–275 *HEW*

A flower vase wall plaque,
registered number for 1930,
12in (30.5cm) high.
£45–50 *BKK*

Two Royal Dux wall masks, c1930, 7in (17.5cm) high.
£220–250 each HEW

A Bristol hard paste porcelain figure of Liberty, restored, c1770–78.
£800–1,000 *DMa*

A Bristol hard paste porcelain teapot, restored, c1770–78, 6in (15cm) high.
£350–450 *DMa*

A Bristol hard paste porcelain toilet pot and cover, 3½in (9cm) high.
£400–500 *DMa*

A Carlton Ware dish, with Foxglove pattern, c1937, 9½in (24cm) diam.
£35–40 *BKK*

A Carlton Ware butter dish, with Buttercup pattern, c1934, 7½in (19cm) long.
£100–120 *BKK*

A Carlton Ware hand painted chinoiserie bowl, c1900.
£150–180 *BKK*

A Carlton Ware lustre jug, 7in (17.5cm) high.
£200–250 *HEW*

A set of three Carlton Ware hand painted Rouge Royale dishes, c1930, 5 to 10½in (12.5 to 27cm) diam.
£25–55 each *BKK*

A Carlton Ware jam pot, No. 754901, c1930, 4in (10cm).
£45–50 *BKK*

A Carlton Ware egg cup set, c1934, 8in (20cm) long.
£45–50 *BKK*

Three ceramic toothbrush holders, c1920, 4 to 6in (10 to 15cm) high.
£20–30 each *PC*

A Mason's Ironstone child's plate, c1950, 9in (23cm) diam.
£40–45 *HEW*

A Clarice Cliff double handled lotus jug, Autumn Crocus pattern, c1933, 12in (30.5cm).
£280–350 *BKK*

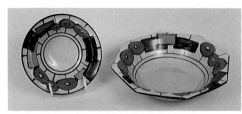

A Clarice Cliff dessert set, comprising a bowl and 6 plates, bowl 9½in (23.5cm) diam.
£350–400 *HEW*

A Clarice Cliff bowl, Aurea pattern, c1935, 8in (20cm) diam.
£230–250 *BKK*

A Clarice Cliff wall mask, 15in (38cm) high.
£1,200–1,400 *HEW*

A Clarice Cliff biscuit barrel, Gay Day design, 5in (12.5cm) high.
£350–380 *HEW*

A Clarice Cliff Athens jug, Summerhouse design, 8in (20cm) high.
£500–520 *HEW*

A Coalport coffee can, c1810, 2⅜in (6cm) high.
£60–90 *LIO*

A Susie Cooper cup and saucer, The Homestead pattern, the saucer 5½in (13.5cm) diam.
£200–220 *HEW*

A Clarice Cliff Athens jug, Petunia design, 8in (20cm).
£450–500 *HEW*

A Susie Cooper plate, 7in (17.5cm) diam.
£5–6 *CSA*

A Susie Cooper Art Nouveau 22-piece coffee service, c1970, pot 8in (20cm) high.
£100–120 *BKK*

A Susie Cooper plate, for Gray's Pottery, marked, c1928, 10⅜in (26.5cm) diam.
£125–150 *CSA*

A submarine condiment set, inscribed 'A present from Margate', 7in (17.5cm) long.
£20–30 *JUN*

An ocean liner condiment set, inscribed 'A present from Margate', 7in (17.5cm) long.
£25–35 *JUN*

A lady in a crinoline dress cruet, 20thC, 5in (12.5cm) high.
£30–35 *PC*

An aeroplane condiment set, inscribed 'Welsh Costume', 7in (17.5cm) long.
£35–45 *JUN*

A golf club cruet, 20thC, 4½in (11cm) high.
£10–15 *PC*

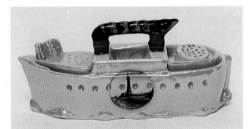

An ocean liner condiment set, inscribed 'A Present from Blackpool', 8in (20cm) long
£25–35 *JUN*

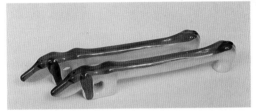

A ceramic dachshund cruet, unmarked, 20thC, 9½in (23.5cm) long.
£15–20 *PC*

A Goebels cruet of three monkeys, 20thC, 5½in (13.5cm) wide.
£35–50 *PC*

A lustre cruet, 20thC, 4in (10cm) high.
£10–15 *PC*

A Carlton Ware promotional cruet, 20thC, 5½in (13.5cm) high.
£15–20 *PC*

A condiment set, inscribed 'A Present from Ryde', 7in (17.5cm) long.
£15–18 *JUN*

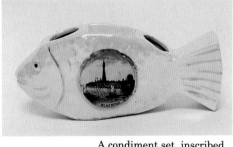

A condiment set, inscribed 'A Present from Blackpool', incomplete, 6in (15cm) long.
£10–14 *JUN*

A three part cruet, in the form of a lighthouse, 5½in (14cm) high.
£12–20 *PC*

A condiment set, inscribed 'Sands Looking South, Mablethorpe', 7in (17.5cm) long.
£35–45 *JUN*

A Humpty Dumpty cruet, 20thC, 4in (10cm) high.
£10–15 *PC*

A mouse and cheese cruet, 20thC, 3½in (9cm) high.
£6–10 *PC*

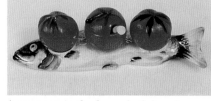

A cruet set, in the form of a fish and tomatoes, 20thC, 6in (15cm) long.
£8–12 *PC*

A cruet set, in the form of jazz singers, 20thC, 3in (7.5cm) high.
£6–10 *PC*

A Humpty Dumpty cruet, unmarked, 20thC, 3in (7.5cm) long.
£15–20 *PC*

A cruet, in the form of a clown riding a pony, 20thC, 3in (7.5cm) high.
£25–30 *PC*

A ceramic cruet set, in the form of hamburgers, 20thC, 2in (5cm) high.
£6–8 *PC*

Three Denby Reform cordial bottles, of Queen Victoria, Lord Grey and Daniel O'Connell, c1840, 8½in (21cm) high.
£200–400 each *KES*

A Denby tube-lined two-handled vase, Totley pattern, 5in (12.5cm) high.
£45–55 *KES*

Two Denby plant tallies, made for the Great Exhibition, c1851, 12in (30.5cm) high.
£85–110 each *KES*

A Denby two-handled vase, Elton pattern, 10in (25cm) high.
£50–65 *KES*

A Denby frog mug, with greyhound handles, c1896, 4in (10cm). **£60–75** *KES*

A Denby Byngo novelty ashtray, and a spill vase, c1930.
£30–45 each *KES*

A Denby pastel blue Kirkstone vase, 6in (15cm) high.
£50–65 *KES*

A Denby lamp base, by Glyn College, c1950, 8in (20cm) high.
£75–85 *KES*

A pair of Denby terrier dog book ends, c1935, 6½in (16cm) high.
£95–110 *KES*

A Denby dish, by Glyn College, c1950, 8in (20cm) diam.
£45–50 *KES*

A collection of six Denby rabbits, 1½in (3.5cm) to 6½in (16cm) high.
£10–55 each *KES*

A Denby jug, by Glyn College, 8in (20cm) high. **£50–65** *KES*

A Royal Doulton vase, designed by Charles Pritchard, c1922, 10in (25cm).
£120–140 *BKK*

A Doulton figure, 'The China Repairer', 1983–88.
£140–180 *LIO*

A Doulton figure, 'Judith', 1952–59.
£120–140 *LIO*

A Doulton figure, 'Midinette', 1952–65.
£170–200 *LIO*

A Drioli ceramic miniature liqueur bottle, designed as a tipsy cat, Italian, c1950–70, 5in (12.5cm) high.
£8–15 *JTA*

A Drioli ceramic miniature liqueur bottle, designed as a gondola, Italian, c1950–70, 5in (12.5cm) high.
£10–15 *JTA*

A Doulton character jug, 'Mine Host', c1950.
£60–75 *LIO*

A bottle, in the form of a 'barrel man', c1960, 8in (20cm) high.
£50–75 *CRA*

A Drioli liqueur bottle, 5in (12.5cm) high.
£5–10 *JTA*

A Drioli abstract design, liqueur bottle, c1950–70.
£5–8 *JTA*

A set of Italian liqueur bottles, of Snow White and five dwarfs, c1950, 5in (12.5cm) high.
£90–100 *HEW*

A Florentine china shoe, inscribed 'Oldham', c1920. **£5–6** *LIO*

A Gray's hand painted dish, c1933, 5½in (13.5cm) diam. **£18–24** *BKK*

A Foley Intarsio jug and bowl set, c1897–99, jug 13½in (34cm) high, bowl 17in (43cm) wide. **£950–1,100** *AJ*

A Hummel figure, 'Be Patient', c1948, 4in (10cm). **£70–90** *JDC*

A Hollinshead & Kirkham Viola pattern jug, c1935, 6in (15cm) high. **£50–60** *CSA*

A Gray's plate, c1930, 10½in (26cm) diam. **£200–220** *HEW*

A bowl, designed by James Kent, c1930, 9in (23cm) diam. **£90–120** *HEW*

A Mason's Ironstone plate, in Muscovy Duck pattern, c1835, 10in (25cm) diam. **£100–125** *PC*

A Mason's Ironstone dessert dish, early crown mark, c1820. **£180–220**
A Mason's Ironstone inkstand with lids. **£850–900** *JP*

A Hancock Rubinsware hand painted plate, Pomegranate pattern, 9in (23cm) diam. **£30–40** *CSA*

A Hancock ware hand painted vase, 8in (20cm) high. **£60–70** *CSA*

A Moorcroft MacIntyre
Florian ware vase,
c1900, 8in (20cm) high.
£700–800 *LIO*

A Walter Moorcroft Leaf and
Berry design teapot and cover,
c1949, 4½in (11.5cm) high.
£300–400 *RUM*

A Moorcroft MacIntyre
Cornflower design jug,
c1902, 5½in (14cm).
£300–400 *LIO*

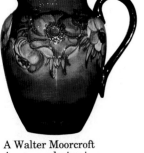

A Walter Moorcroft
Anemone design jug,
c1949, 10in (25cm) high.
£300–350 *RUM*

A Moorcroft Flamminian vase,
c1905, 5½in (14cm) high.
£400–500 *LIO*

A William Moorcroft
Eventide Landscape
vase, c1925, 6in (15cm).
£650–850 *RUM*

A Walter Moorcroft Bougainvillaea
design plate, c1955, 10in (25cm) diam.
£200–300 *RUM*

A William Moorcroft Moonlit
Blue Landscape design vase,
c1925, 4in (10cm) high.
£500–700 *RUM*

A Moorcroft vase,
c1972, 11in (28cm).
£500–600 *LIO*

A Myott's flower jug,
c1932, 8½in (21cm).
£50–60 *BKK*

A Myott's hand painted
vase, c1932, 7½in (19cm).
£35–45 *BKK*

A Noritake dish,
5½in (14cm) wide.
£40–50 *WTA*

Drioli

The following selection of hand painted miniature ceramic liqueur bottles were produced by Drioli in Italy between the 1950's and '70s. Prices range from £5 for an abstract design to £20 for a piece from a set of musicians.

A Drioli miniature Curaçao liqueur bottle, depicting an artist and pin-up portrait, 5in (12.5cm) high.
£10–15 *JTA*

A Drioli unopened miniature liqueur bottle, in the form of a native girl, 5in (12.5cm) high.
£5–8 *JTA*

A Drioli miniature liqueur bottle, designed as an Oriental lady, 5in (12.5cm) high.
£8–10 *JTA*

Two Drioli miniature apricot liqueur bottles, each in the form of a native girl, with label, 5in (12.5cm) high.
£10–15 each *JTA*

A Drioli miniature liqueur bottle, designed as a singing cowboy, 5in (12.5cm) high.
£5–10 *JTA*

A Drioli miniature liqueur bottle, designed as a sultan, 5in (12.5cm) high.
£5–10 *JTA*

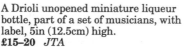

A Drioli miniature liqueur bottle, in the form of a comic character, 5in (12.5cm) high.
£10–15 *JTA*

A Drioli unopened miniature liqueur bottle, part of a set of musicians, with label, 5in (12.5cm) high.
£15–20 *JTA*

A Drioli unopened miniature apricot liqueur bottle, with abstract design and label.
£5–6 *JTA*

Foley

A Foley Intarsio jardinière, c1897, 16in (40.5cm).
£475–500 *AJ*

A Foley Intarsio bowl,
Second Series pattern,
signed 'Walter Slater',
c1912, 10in (25cm) diam.
£350–400 *AJ*

A Foley Intarsio vase,
c1897, 9in (23cm) high.
£200–250 *AJ*

MAKE THE MOST OF MILLERS

Price ranges in this book reflect what you should
expect to *pay* for a similar example. When selling,
however, you would expect to receive a lower figure.
This will fluctuate according to a dealer's stock and
saleability at a particular time. It is always advisable,
when selling a collectable, to approach a reputable
dealer or an auction house which has specialist sales.

Frog Mugs

These humorous mugs were popular during
the Georgian and Victorian periods. The
frog or toad was placed crouching on the
base, or climbing the sides of the vessel
and, depending on its size, a mug could
contain up to three frogs. Before 1800, the
frogs were hand-modelled, on later
examples the bodies were cast by industrial
potters. Subsequent refinements included
producing hollow frogs with open mouths,
so that when the mug was raised liquid
spurted all over the drinker's face!

A frog mug, decorated
with a panel of a sailor
on a rocky shore, with
copper base, 19thC,
5in (12.5cm) high.
£225–300 *LF*

A pair of pink lustre frog
mugs, inscribed 'Cast
Iron Bridge over the
River Wear', c1900, 5in
(12.5cm) high.
£450–500 *LF*

Two orange lustre frog
mugs, with inscriptions,
'The Sailor's Farewell'
and 'The Agamemnon
in a Storm', early
19thC, 4 and 5in
(10 and 12.5cm) high.
£250–300 *LF*

Two orange lustre frog mugs,
inscribed 'Ancient Order of
Foresters', and 'True Love from
Hull', 19thC, 5in (12.5cm) high.
£150–200 *LF*

A pair of pink lustre frog mugs,
with inscriptions, 'The Sailor's
Farewell' and 'The Sailor's
Return', 19thC, 5in (12.5cm) high.
£320–350 *LF*

A memorial frog mug, with
printed inscription, 19thC,
6in (15cm) high.
£180–200 *LF*

Goss & Crested China

Goss and Crested China was fashionable in Victorian and Edwardian times. Cheap, cheerful and decorated with the coats-of-arms of English towns and seaside resorts, it was purchased by day trippers as souvenirs, the ceramic equivalent of a stick of rock.

Today it is a well established collectable with prices ranging from under £5 for a simple pot to £1,000 for the rarest Goss cottages. The majority of examples illustrated date from the late 19thC to the early 1920s.

Goss

A Goss crested Swiss milk bucket, 2in (5.5cm).
£12–14 *G&CC*

A Goss Bagware jug, decorated with sprays of forget-me-nots, 4in (10.5cm).
£20–25 *G&CC*

A collection of Goss figures, c1930, *left to right:*
Balloon seller, 3½in (8.5cm).
£125–160
Bell Lady, 3½in (8.5cm).
£90–125
Lady Betty, 6½in (16cm).
£200–225
Bridesmaid, 5½in (14cm).
£200–250
Peggy, 5in (12.5cm).
£80–110 *CCC*

A Goss lobster trap, inscribed 'Epsom', 2in (5cm).
£15–20 *G&CC*

Two Goss lighthouses:
l. Beachy Head Lighthouse with matching crest, 5in (12.5cm). **£70–80**
r. Longship's Lighthouse, Land's End, 5in (12.5cm).
£30–40 *G&CC*

r. A Goss Exeter goblet, decorated with the Flags of the Allies, 5in (13cm).
£25–30 *G&CC*

A Goss circular plaque, c1860, 13½in (34cm) diam.
£200–250 *CCC*

A Goss crested Swiss vinegar bottle, inscribed, 3in (7.5cm).
£12–15 *G&CC*

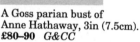

A Goss parian bust of Anne Hathaway, 3in (7.5cm).
£80–90 *G&CC*

A Goss parian model of the Lincoln Imp, 4½in (11.5cm).
£65–75 *G&CC*

Goss Cottages

A Goss model of Dove Cottage, Grasmere, the home of Wordsworth, slight wear, printed marks, inscribed to base, 4in (10cm) wide.
£350–400 *CSK*

A Goss model of Charles Dickens house, Gad's Hill, Rochester, slight wear, printed marks, inscribed to base, 2½in (6cm) wide.
£140–180 *CSK*

A Goss model of Prince Llewelyn's House, Beddgelert, printed marks, titled to base, slight wear, 2½in (6cm) wide.
£100–150 *CSK*

A Goss model of Manx Cottage, glazed, printed marks, titled to base, 2½in (6cm) wide.
£75–100 *CSK*

Above. A Goss model of Shakespeare's house, 3in (7.5cm). *Below.* Anne Hathaway's cottage, 2½in (6cm) wide, with Second Period black printed marks and inscriptions.
£150–200 *CSK*

A Goss model of the Goss oven, 3in (7.5cm).
£300–350 *G&CC*

A Goss model of Ye Old Market House, Ledbury, titled, printed mark, slight wear, 3in (7.5cm) wide.
£320–380 *CSK*

A Goss model of Lloyd George's home, Second Period black printed mark and inscription, 4in (10cm) wide.
£110–150 *CSK*

A Goss model of Ellen Terry's house, Tenterden, Kent, some damage, printed marks, inscribed to base, 3in (7.5cm).
£150–200 *CSK*

A Goss model of a Window in Thrums, Second Period black printed mark and inscription, 2in (5cm) wide.
£100–125 *CSK*

A Goss model of Wordsworth's birthplace, Cockermouth, Second Period black printed mark and inscription, 3in (7.5cm) wide.
£200–250 *CSK*

A Goss model of The Castle, Newcastle-upon-Tyne, printed marks, titled and inscribed to base, slight wear, 3½in (9cm).
£400–500 *CSK*

Crested China

A Carlton sundial, 4½in (12cm).
£12–15 *G&CC*

A Podmore bag of black coal, 2in (5cm).
£18–20 *G&CC*

A Savoy bathing machine, 2½in (6cm).
£12–15 *G&CC*

An Arcadian grandfather clock, 4in (10cm).
£18–20 *G&CC*

A crested china pillar box, British, 3in (7cm).
£12–15 *G&CC*

An Arcadian coaching hat, 1½in (4cm).
£8–10 *G&CC*

Animals

A Willow Art crested china dog, wearing a blue Glengarry.
£10–12 *G&CC*

A Grafton figure of a wallaby.
£65–75 *G&CC*

A collection of crested china cats.
£12–45 each *CCC*

A collection of crested china animals.
£20–65 each *CCC*

l. A W and R crested china cat, with a blue bow.
£20–25 *G&CC*

A collection of crested china buildings.
£30–80 each *CCC*

Buildings

A Carlton model of Hastings Castle ruins.
£30–35 *G&CC*

A Saxony model of Skegness Clock Tower.
£8–10 *G&CC*

Four crested china buildings, c1920, *left to right:*
An Arcadian model of Morpeth Castle, 3½in (8.5cm).
£70–95
A Carlton model of Keswick Town Hall, 3½in (8.5cm).
£100–125
A Grafton model of Tonbridge Castle, 3in (7.5cm).
£35–48
A Carlton model of Micklegate Bar, 4½in (11.5cm).
£45–55 *CCC*

Figures

An Arcadian model of
a sailor, 3in (8cm).
£50–55 *G&CC*

Two Grafton models of a girl and boy playing
on the beach, 3 and 3½in (7.5 and 8.5cm).
£120–125 each *G&CC*

A Kingsway Art model of a
Dutch girl, 3in (7.5cm).
£10–12 *G&CC*

WWI Crested China

A Corona tank.
£20–25 *G&CC*

A Rita bust of Lloyd George,
c1916, 8in (20cm).
£100–150 *CCC*

A crested china bathing belle,
made in Germany, 3in (7.5cm).
£50–55 *G&CC*

A collection of ships and
submarines, *left to right:*
A ship inscribed 'The Great War
1914–18 The German Fleet
Surrendered'.
£95–100
A ship inscribed 'Model of
Torpedo Boat Destroyed'.
£180–200
Two models of submarines.
£30–35 each *CCC*

A collection of crested china
war memorials.
£100–275 each *CCC*

Hollinshead & Kirkham

An H & K Viola pattern jug, by R. Grocott, c1935, 3in (7.5cm). **£35–40** *CSA*

An H & K hand painted Viola pattern side plate, by R. Grocott, c1935, 4½in (11cm) diam. **£20–25** *CSA*

An H & K hand painted Tulip Time pattern quaiche, by R. Grocott, c1935, 7½in (19cm) wide. **£25–30** *CSA*

An H & K hand painted Viola pattern dish, by R. Grocott, c1935, 4½in (11cm) diam. **£20–25** *CSA*

An H & K hand painted Viola pattern jug, by R. Grocott, c1935, 5½in (14cm) high. **£45–50** *CSA*

An H & K Tulip pattern quaiche, by R. Grocott, c1935, 7in (17.5cm) wide. **£35–40** *CSA*

Hummel

At the Leipzig fair in 1935 W. Goebel introduced a series of figurines based on the childhood caricatures created by Franciscan Sister M. I. Hummel. Many of the original releases are still in production today, although the different backstamps will give an indication of the date of manufacture. The small 3in (7.5cm) high figurines are the most common and least expensive.

A Hummel figure of a boy and a bird, Singing Lesson, No. HUM 63, introduced 1937, 3in (7.5cm) high. **£60–70** *JDC*

A Hummel figure of a girl, Little Shopper, No. HUM 96, introduced 1937, 4½in (11cm) high. **£60–70** *JDC*

A Hummel figure of a boy, Home From Market, No. HUM 198, c1948, 5in (12.5cm). **£60–70** *JDC*

Five Hummel miniature figures, *left to right:* Little Sweeper, No. 66940/02/4, Apple Tree Boy, No. 66940/08/1, Schoolboy, No. 66940/16/4, Goosegirl, No. 66940/18/0, and Waiter, No. 66940/09/9, each 1in (2.5cm) high. **£50–80 each** *JDC*

Lustreware

A Hummel resin covered ceramic miniature marketplace with hotel, 5½in (14cm) wide, and a village with figurines, 8½in (21.5cm) wide.
£100–110 each *JDC*

A lustre jug, decorated in mauve with the 'Death of Punch' by T. Rowlandson, from the Dr. Syntax series, early 19thC, 9in (23cm) high.
£200–250 *TVM*

A lustre jug, decorated in blue, purple and green on a white ground, with raised classical chariots drawn by lions, inscribed 'Ann Jenkins, Whittan, born May 16th 1819', 5in (12.5cm) high.
£300–350 *TVM*

A silver lustre jug, transfer printed with Heddon Grange, Petersfield, on a buff ground, inscribed 'JK 1814', 5in (12.5cm).
£150–200 *TVM*

A copper and pink lustre jug and goblet, late 19thC, 4½in and 5in (11 and 12.5cm).
£85–125 each *LF*

A two-handled lustre vase, painted by Joe Juster, decorated in red with exotic birds and foliage, on a white crackled ground, signed on base in blue 'W. de Morgan & Co. Fulham 2154 J.J.', late 19thC, 10in (25cm).
£950–1,250 *P*

A lustre asparagus dish, by Roger Michell, the cover in the form of two naked crouching female figures, the base moulded with asparagus, painted mark, dated '79', 13½in (34cm) wide.
£125–175 *DN*

A German pink lustre souvenir mug, with a view of Staplehurst Church, Kent, c1900, 3in (7.5cm).
£12–15 *JMC*

Mason's Ironstone

A Mason's Ironstone jug, by Ashworth's, with Ironstone mark, c1870, 25in (63.5cm).
£120–140 *AMH*

A Mason's Ironstone two-handled tyg, decorated in blue and gilt, c1815–25, 8in (20cm) high.
£300–330 *WAG*

A Mason's Ironstone Brown Velvet pattern teapot, 19thC, 8in (20cm) high.
£35–45 *LF*

Meissen

A Meissen brown tabby cat, c1850, 6in (15cm) long.
£700–800 *DAV*

A Meissen braying donkey, No. R218, 6in (15cm) high.
£40–60 *DAV*

First modelled by Erich Hösel in 1943.

A Meissen panther washing himself, No. G242, c1921, 7in (17.5cm) high.
£250–350 *DAV*

Minton

A Minton part tea service, in multi-coloured Oriental design, comprising 20 pieces, 19thC, saucer 6in (15cm) diam.
£70–100 *LF*

A Minton candlestick, painted by James Edwin Dean, c1910, 7in (18cm) high.
£160–170 *AMH*

Two early Minton painted tiles, black on white, late 19thC, 4in (10cm) square.
£35–45 each *WAG*

A Minton plate, by Christopher Dresser, c1878, 10in (25cm) diam.
£270–290 *AMH*

A pair of Minton menu holders, c1874, 4½in (11cm) high.
£100–110 *AMH*

Moorcroft

From 1898, William Moorcroft (1872–1945) headed the Art Pottery department of MacIntyre & Co., at Burslem, and in 1913 he opened his own pottery.

One of the most influential figures in British Art Nouveau ceramics, Moorcroft is perhaps most celebrated for his Florian ware, characterised by slender shapes, symmetrical floral designs and tube lined decoration.

A Moorcroft Pomegranate vase, c1920, 4in (10cm).
£250–300 *LIO*

A Moorcroft banded Pomegranate vase, c1926, 3½in (9cm) high.
£250–300 *RUM*

A Moorcroft powder blue panel vase, c1915, 7in (17.5cm) high.
£200–250 *LIO*

A Moorcroft moonlight blue Tree pattern Tudric vase, signed, c1928, 7in (17.5cm).
£550–650 *BKK*

r. A Moorcroft powder blue vase, with floral panels, c1916, 5½in (14cm) high.
£600–800 *RUM*

A Moorcroft salt glazed banded vase, decorated with Honesty design, c1935, 6in (15cm).
£600–800 *RUM*

A Moorcroft blue ground coffee pot, Waving Corn design, c1935, 8in (20cm) high.
£300–400 *RUM*

A Moorcroft salt glazed pot, decorated with a Leaf and Berry design, c1932, 4in (10cm).
£150–200 *LIO*

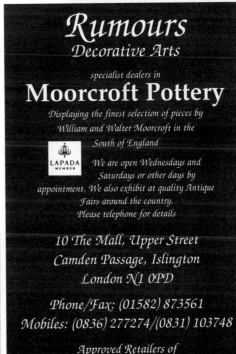

A Moorcroft salt glazed plate, decorated with pink toadstools, c1930, 5½in (14cm) diam.
£100–150 *LIO*

A Moorcroft caramel coloured shallow dish, decorated with Waving Corn design, c1935, 8in (20cm) diam.
£300–400 *RUM*

A Moorcroft salt glazed vase, decorated with Anemone design, c1935, 5in (12.5cm).
£600–700 *RUM*

Myott & Son

A Myott hand painted Art Deco flower jug, c1930, 8in (20cm).
£40–50 *BKK*

A Myott hand painted Bow Tie decorative jug, c1935, 5½in (14cm) high.
£50–60 *BKK*

Pot Lids

Two pictorial pot lids of Shakespeare's House and the Chapel Royal, Savoy, 19thC, 4½in (11cm) diam.
£60–80 each *LF*

Pottery & Porcelain Lids

Three porcelain lids:
Top left. Sèvres, peacock blue and gilt enamelled, 4½in (11cm) diam.
Top right. English, probably Worcester, with rose finial, 4in (10cm) diam.
Bottom. Worcester, decorated in puce, orange, and gilt, 5in (12.5cm) diam.
£5–25 each *BHA*

Two pot lids by F. & R. Pratt, each with printed pictures of the interior of Shakespeare's birthplace and Anne Hathaway's residence, within scrolling foliate borders, 19thC.
£225–300 *CSK*

Top. A Mason's Ironstone tureen lid, decorated in orange and blue, marked, 19thC, 5in (12.5cm) wide.
Bottom. A Coalport tureen lid, decorated in orange, blue, green and gilt, 19thC.
£5–25 each *BHA*

Powder Bowls

Three porcelain lids, 19thC:
Top left. Sèvres, peacock blue and gilt enamelled, 4½in (11cm) diam.
Top right. English, probably Worcester, with rose finial, 4in (10cm) diam.
Bottom. Worcester, decorated in puce, orange, and gilt, 5in (12.5cm) diam.
£5–25 each *BHA*

An Art Nouveau black and white powder bowl, unmarked, c1920, 5½in (14cm) high.
£20–25 *PC*

Two ceramic powder bowls, unmarked, 20thC, 5½ and 6½in (14 and 16cm) high.
£15–25 each *PC*

An Art Nouveau powder bowl, unmarked, c1920, 4in (10cm) diam.
£15–25 *PC*

Three ceramic powder bowls, unmarked, c1930, 4½ to 6in (11 to 15cm) high.
£10–20 each *PC*

A powder bowl, unmarked, 20thC, 8in (20cm) high.
£30–35 *PC*

> **MAKE THE MOST OF MILLERS**
>
> Price ranges in this book reflect what you should expect to *pay* for a similar example. When selling, however, you would expect to receive a lower figure. This will fluctuate according to a dealer's stock and saleability at a particular time. It is always advisable, when selling a collectable, to approach a reputable dealer or an auction house which has specialist sales.

A ceramic powder bowl, 20thC, 7½in (19cm) high.
£40–50 *PC*

This powder bowl was produced to promote Yardley Lavender.

A ceramic powder bowl, 1930s, 7in (17.5cm) high.
£15–25 *PC*

A Dutch lady powder bowl, 1930s, 5in (12.5cm) high.
£18–20 *PC*

A crinoline lady powder bowl, 1930s, 4in (10cm) high.
£15–25 *PC*

A ceramic powder bowl, 1930s, 6in (15cm) high.
£25–30 *PC*

Two ceramic powder bowls, unmarked, 20thC, 6 and 7in (15 and 17.5cm) high.
£20–30 each *PC*

> **Miller's is a price GUIDE not a price LIST**

A Crown Ducal Charlotte Rhead plaque, Peony pattern, c1935, 17½in (44cm) diam.
£500–600 *CSA*

A ceramic powder bowl, 1930s, 5in (12.5cm) high, with a swansdown puff.
£20–25 *PC*

Charlotte Rhead

A Charlotte Rhead octagonal bowl, Rhodian pattern, c1935, 8in (20cm) diam.
£300–350 *WTA*

A Charlotte Rhead Bursley Ware powder bowl, decorated with stencilled slip stylised carnations, c1954, 4½in (11cm) diam.
£50–60 *CSA*

A great many wares in this pattern were exported to North America.

A Charlotte Rhead Bursley Ware bowl, with stencilled slip pattern, c1954, 6½in (16cm) wide.
£30–40 *CSA*

Sarreguemines

In the late 18thC, three Strasbourg tobacconists founded a ceramic factory in Sarreguemines, a small town in Eastern France. The pottery began by producing cream-coloured earthenware in the style of Wedgwood. In the 19thC tableware was produced with printed decoration, and in the 1860s Sarreguemines launched its famous majolica. Extremely popular, these items ranged from monumental pieces, from grandiose fountains to novelty character jugs. They were of high quality, distinguished by their bold and often humorous moulded shapes and bright colours. Production peaked between the 1890s and 1914 when Sarreguemines was one of the most important potteries of its kind in Europe. Majolica was manufactured until the 1930s.

A Sarreguemines advertising spill vase, No. 1845, c1880, 12in (30.5cm). **£500–600** *PC*

A Sarreguemines 'Young Prince' jug, No. 3300, c1902, 7in (17.5cm). **£150–200** *PC*

l. A fake Sarreguemines double-headed jug, with motto written in English, c1992, 9in (23cm) high. **£8–10**
r. A Sarreguemines double-headed jug, No. 2313, c1901. **£160–180** *PC*

A Sarreguemines green majolica tobacco jar and lid, No. 87, c1870, 13in (33cm). **£400–500** *PC*

A Sarrguemines advertising jug, inscribed 'W^m. Green Glasgow Whisky', c1902, 6in (15cm) high. **£100–120** *PC*

Advertising jugs were exported to Britain where they were overprinted. Collectors of advertising items have increased the value of these jugs, but the wording on them must be clear.

A Sarreguemines 'Dog' jug, No. 4024, c1902, 7in (17.5cm). **£140–160** *PC*

A Sarreguemines advertising 'Farmer' jug, for Stodart's Whisky, No. 3181, c1902, 7in (17.5cm) high. **£200–250** *PC*

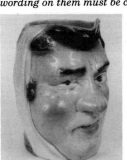

A Sarreguemines 'Toothache' jug, No. 3321, c1903, 7in (17.5cm). **£130–150** *PC*

r. A Sarreguemines 'Staring Eyes' jug, No. 3258, c1902, 8in (20cm) high. **£100–120** *PC*

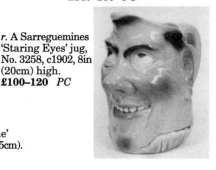

A Sarreguemines 'Lady with a Bonnet' jug, No. 3319, c1903, 7in (17.5cm) high.
£150–175 *PC*

A Sarreguemines 'Man with a Monocle' jug, No. 3466, c1903, 6in (15cm) high.
£85–100 *PC*

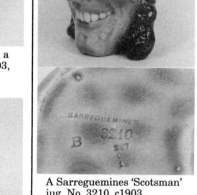

A Sarreguemines 'Scotsman' jug, No. 3210, c1903, 8in (20cm) high.
£100–120 *PC*

A pair of Sarreguemines jugs, 'Punch', No. 3431, and 'Judy', No. 3430, Dec. 1904, 13 and 12½in (33 and 32cm).
£350–450 *PC*

A Sarreguemines 'Pelican' jug, No. 8529, impressed mark, c1904, 8in (20cm).
£80–90 *PC*

A Sarreguemines muffin dish, No. 4514, c1920, 8in (20cm) diam.
£75–85 *PC*

A Sarreguemines Art Deco 'Dutch Lady' jug, No. 1752, c1920, 9in (23cm).
£250–350 *PC*

A Sarreguemines 'Lion' jug, No. 4020, post-1920 mark, 6½in (16cm).
£100–150 *PC*

Two Sarreguemines jugs, 'Puck', No. 653, c1901, 7in (17.5cm) high.
£100–150 each *PC*

Sarreguemines jugs are normally turquoise inside, but these were a special order and have pink interiors.

Shelley

A Shelley Mabel Lucie Attwell figure, 'I's Shy', c1930, 6½in (16cm) high.
£380–420 *BKK*

A Shelley 21-piece tea set, Regent shape with Brown Swirls pattern, c1934.
£150–200 *BKK*

A Shelley lustre charger, signed Walter Slater, 20thC, 14in (35.5cm) diam.
£250–285 *AJ*

A Shelley Flamboyant vase, c1914.
£120–150 *AJ*

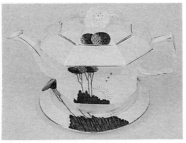

A Melba teapot and stand, copy of a Shelley design and pattern, 20thC.
£25–30 *PC*

A Shelley Melody teapot, c1948, 6in (15cm) diam.
£100–140 *BKK*

A Shelley teapot, **£90–100** and a bread and butter plate, 1930s.
£30–40 *YY*

A Shelley Art Nouveau floral decorated part tea service, comprising 21 pieces, early 20thC.
£300–350 *PCh*

Staffordshire

Staffordshire figures became popular during the early Victorian period, and by 1845 they were being mass produced. The figures provide a 'potted history' of the period, with subjects including royalty, military and political heroes, theatrical and sporting stars and, on a macabre note, famous murderers of the day. Fictional characters, in particular from Shakespeare and Dickens, were another common theme, along with anonymous romantic and narrative groups such as 'The Jealous Rival', 'The Sailor's Return' and, of course, animals, with dogs being a perennial favourite. Although many of the pieces were originally sold for pennies at fairgrounds and markets, today they can command high prices. Value depends on rarity, quality and condition. Earlier figures are often of a higher standard than later models, with crisp moulding, good decoration and fine detail.

Miller's is a price GUIDE not a price LIST

Animals

A Staffordshire group of two spaniels with a barrel, c1860, 8in (20cm) high.
£90–140 *LF*

A Staffordshire figure of a peacock alighting her nest, 19thC, 7in (17.5cm) high.
£200–250 *TVM*

A pair of Staffordshire figures of dogs, 19thC.
£450–480 *TVM*

A pair of Staffordshire figures of horses, decorated as zebras, c1850, 8in (20cm).
£400–450 *RWB*

A pair of Staffordshire spill vases, modelled as zebras being pursued by foxes over a bridge and stream, c1860, 9in (23cm).
£500–550 *RWB*

A pair of Staffordshire figures of seated whippets with dead hares, c1860, 12½in (32cm).
£630–680 *RWB*

A pair of Staffordshire spill vases, modelled as a ram and ewe, c1825, 6½in (16cm).
£650–700 *RWB*

A pair of Staffordshire figures of dalmatians, c1840, 7in (17.5cm).
£500–550 *RWB*

Figures

A pair of Staffordshire figures, a boy with a cow and a girl with a cow, c1860, 6in (15cm) high.
£300–400 *LF*

A Staffordshire figure of a horseman, c1860, 15in (38cm) high.
£90–140 *LF*

A Staffordshire group of young women reading with a boy, and a cradle, c1860, 6½in (16.5cm) high.
£100–150 *TVM*

A Staffordshire spill vase, with the figure of an artist decorating a Grecian vase, 19thC, 8in (20cm).
£200–250 *TVM*

A Staffordshire group of a maiden and a youth in an arbour, 13in (33cm) high.
£60–80 *LF*

A Staffordshire group
of a Scots boy with
sheep, c1860, 8in (20cm).
£120–160 *LF*

A Staffordshire untitled
group of La Polka, c1845,
8in (20cm).
£260–280 *RWB*

A pair of Staffordshire figures of reclining
Turks, he smoking a hookah, she playing a
mandolin, c1835, 5½in (14cm) long.
£360–400 *RWB*

Historical

A pair of Staffordshire untitled figures of
John Solomon Rarey, and horse Cruiser,
c1860, 9in (23cm) high.
£250–280 *RWB*

A pair of Staffordshire inkwells,
modelled as the Royal children with
spaniels, c1850, 6in (15cm).
£500–550 *RWB*

A selection of miniature Staffordshire figures:
l. to r. Victoria and Albert, Wellington, Garibaldi,
Farmer George and Napoleon, early 19thC,
3 to 5in (7.5 to 12.5cm).
£120–180 each *TVM*

A Staffordshire group of
Burns and Mary, c1860.
£50–60 *LF*

A Staffordshire bust of John
Wesley, c1820, 11½in (29cm).
£400–450 *RWB*

r. A pair of Staffordshire figures of the
Prince of Wales and Prince Alfred,
c1858, 10½in (26cm) high.
£600–650 *RWB*

Literary

r. A Staffordshire group spill vase, possibly Lear and Cordelia, 19thC, 7in (17.5cm).
£250–350 *TVM*

Religious & Mythological

A Staffordshire figure portraying Mazeppa, from Byron's *Mazeppa's Ride*, as performed by Astley's Circus, c1864.
£650–700 *TVM*

A Staffordshire figure, possibly Flora, holding a basket of flowers, early 19thC, 6in (15cm) high.
£100–150 *TVM*

A pair of Staffordshire figures of St. John as a boy, with a lamb, c1855, 6½in (16cm) high.
£280–300 *RWB*

A Staffordshire figure of St. George and the dragon, c1860, 4in (10cm) high.
£300–400 *TVM*

A Staffordshire pearlware figure of the goddess Diana, on a square base, c1860, 8in (20cm) high.
£250–300 *TVM*

A Staffordshire figure of Neptune, with overglaze enamel painted decoration, c1825, 9½in (23.5cm) high.
£160–180 *RWB*

SylvaC

SylvaC has been growing increasingly collectable. The name was first coined in 1935 by the Shaw and Copestake factory, Longton (founded 1894). Although the factory produced a wide variety of items, perhaps the most distinctive SylvaC products are the range of animals and figures first developed in the pre-war period. Matt glazes were introduced with green being by far the most popular colour and it remains so with collectors of today although blue matt glaze items can command higher prices because of their rarity. So successful were these novelty cats, dogs, rabbits, etc., that the factory continued to produce them until its closure in 1982.

A SylvaC boot with kittens, glossy glaze, No. 4977, 4½in (11cm) long.
£20–25 *JDC*

A SylvaC comical cat, biscuit coloured, No. 5299, 5in (12.5cm).
£25–30 *PC*

Animals

A SylvaC figure of a cat, with long neck and embossed flowers, white matt glaze, No. 3392, 12½in (31.5cm).
£40–50 *JDC*

A SylvaC scared cat, green glaze, No. 1046, 6in (15cm) high.
£25–35 *PC*

A SylvaC figure of a Siamese cat, with glossy glaze, No. 5111, 8½in (21cm) high.
£30–40 *JDC*

A SylvaC kitten sitting on a hat, light brown glaze, No. 477, 4in (10cm) high.
£25–35 *PC*

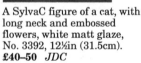

A SylvaC dog, green glaze, c1930, 4in (10cm).
£30–35 *HEW*

A SylvaC sheepdog, biscuit coloured glaze, No. 5302, 5½in (13.5cm) high.
£20–25 *PC*

A SylvaC dog, green glaze, No. 1205, 5in (12.5cm).
£20–25 *PC*

A SylvaC dog, beige glaze, c1930.
£30–35 *HEW*

A SylvaC comical dog, green glaze, No. 1646, 5in (12.5cm) long.
£30–40 *PC*

A SylvaC dog with paw in a sling, green glaze, No. 1433, 3½in (8.5cm) high.
£20–25 *PC*

A SylvaC dog with toothache, cream glaze, No. 3093, 4in (10cm) high.
£30–35 *PC*

A SylvaC dog, brown and green glaze, No. 1122, 6in (15cm) long.
£25–30 *PC*

A SylvaC camel, brown satin glaze, No. 5230, 5in (12.5cm) long.
£35–40 *JDC*

A SylvaC elephant, black cellulose finish, No. 771, 1930s–'40s, 8½in (21cm) high.
£30–40 *JDC*

A SylvaC rabbit teapot, pale blue, 1930s, 7in (17.5cm) high.
£80–90 *CSA*

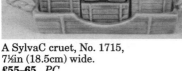

A SylvaC cruet, No. 1715, 7½in (18.5cm) wide.
£55–65 *PC*

Difficult to find complete and undamaged.

A pair of SylvaC horses' heads book ends, matt glaze, No. 2521, 4in (10cm) high.
£50–60 *JDC*

Tableware & Vases

A SylvaC fox ashtray, brown glossy glaze, No. 2517, 6½in (16.5cm) diam.
£10–15 *JDC*

A SylvaC jug, with a squirrel handle, matt fawn glaze, No. 1959, 8½in (21cm) high.
£35–45 *JDC*

A SylvaC asparagus dish, green glaze, No. 528, 12½in (31.5cm).
£15–20 *JDC*

A SylvaC jug, with a squirrel handle, dark green glossy glaze, No. 1993, 3in (7.5cm) high.
£12–18 *JDC*

A SylvaC barrel mug, cream glaze, c1920, 3½in (8.5cm).
£3–4 *AL*

A SylvaC teddy nursery egg cup, No. 3788, 3in (7.5cm) diam.
£4–6 *JDC*

A SylvaC vase, Moselle range with cupid, white matt glaze, No. 2626, 8½in (21cm) high.
£40–50 *JDC*

A SylvaC vase, pale green and pink glaze, No. 684, 5in (12.5cm) high.
£8–10 *JDC*

l. A SylvaC beetroot pot, No. 4553, 5in (12.5cm) diam. **£15–20**
r. A SylvaC beetroot pot, No. 5127, 3½in (8.5cm) diam. **£25–30** *JDC*
The smaller pot is rarer and, therefore, more expensive.

A SylvaC pot for tartare sauce, No. 4915, 4in (10cm) diam.
£40–50 *JDC*

A SylvaC pot for bread sauce, No. 4551, 5in (12.5cm) diam.
£25–30 *JDC*

A SylvaC vase, with scroll handles, mottled green satin glaze, No. 1346, 10½in (26.5cm).
£25–30 *JDC*

Szeiler

A Szeiler fawn coloured chipmunk and squirrel, c1951–85, 2in (5cm) high.
£8–12 each *JDC*

A Szeiler fawn coloured seated teddy bear, c1951–85, 3in (7.5cm) high.
£12–16 *JDC*

A Szeiler black and white sleeping cat, c1951–85, 1in (2.5cm) high.
£5–6 *JDC*

A Szeiler fawn coloured foal, c1951–85, 2in (5cm) high.
£10–12 *JDC*

A Szeiler fawn coloured seated cat, c1951–85, 2in (5cm) high.
£10–15 *JDC*

A Szeiler cat with a bucket, coloured fawn and blue, c1951–85, 3in (7.5cm) high.
£10–15 *JDC*

A Szeiler blue duck, c1951–85, 3in (7.5cm) high.
£10–15 *JDC*

A Szeiler lamb, 1in (2.5cm), and fawn, c1951–85, 2in (5cm) high.
£10–12 each *JDC*

A Japanese eggshell china part tea and coffee service, comprising 51 pieces.
£40–60 *LF*

According to ceramics expert Henry Sandon, Japanese eggshell services are amongst the most common items brought in to the BBC Antiques Roadshow. Most, he explains, were probably given as wedding presents in the 1920s and '30s. Because they tended to be kept in display cabinets rather than be used, an enormous number have survived and their value is correspondingly modest.

Teapots

A Wedgwood teapot, c1875–80, 6in (15cm) high.
£275–300 *AMH*

A La Coutille hand painted teapot and cover, cornflower pattern, repaired, c1790, 6in (15cm) high.
£130–150 *BKK*

Toby Jugs

Three character jugs, depicting Clarice Cliff, Susie Cooper and Young Peggy (Davies), limited editions of 350.
£80–85 each *ZKF*

A Toby jug, unmarked, late 19thC, 9½in (23.5cm).
£25–35 *LF*

Two Toby jug topers, late 19thC, 8½in (21cm).
£80–120 *LF*

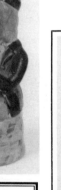

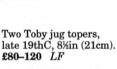

Two Toby jug topers, 8½in (21cm) high.
£80–120 *LF*

A blue and white snuff taker Toby jug, 20thC, 11in (28cm) high.
£100–125 *WAG*

A Wedgwood 'Jailer' toby jug, early 20thC, 6in (15cm) high.
£60–70 *AnE*

Troika

Troika Pottery was founded in St. Ives in 1963 by sculptor Leslie Illsley, potter Benny Sirota and architect Jan Thompson. Although the local crafts establishment estimated that the venture would collapse in three months it in fact lasted 20 years, selling innovative domestic and decorative ceramics to Heal's, Liberty's and leading stores throughout the world.

Typical of its period, Troika pottery is noted for its distinctive moulded shapes and sculptural, abstracted style. The artists were not afraid to experiment. Clay was mixed in a second-hand bakery dough mixer, and shapes were devised so as to pack the kiln as solidly as possible. Inspiration for design, colour and texture came from sources as varied as Paul Klee and the Cornish landscape, and reflected developments in contemporary art. No matter how large or small a piece, how cheap or expensive, each individual pot was conceived as a sculptural work of art.

Two Troika pottery ashtrays, made for Heals, 4½in (11cm) square.
£75–85 each *NCA*

Two Troika pottery double egg cups, 3½in (8.5cm) high.
£40–45 each *NCA*

Two Troika pottery mugs, c1966, 4½in (11cm) high.
£30–35 each *NCA*

A Troika pottery chimney, by Sue Bladen, 8in (20cm) high.
£60–70 *NCA*

A Troika pottery spice jar, by Jane Fitzgerald, 6in (15cm) high.
£30–40 *NCA*

A Troika pottery charger, by
Brian Illsley, 10in (25cm) diam.
£200–250 *NCA*

Three Troika pottery cylinder
vases, 5½in (13.5cm) high.
£40–50 each *NCA*

A Troika pottery marmalade jar,
by Ann Long, 3½in (9cm) high.
£40–50 *NCA*

A Troika pottery vase, c1965.
£200–220 *NCA*

A Troika pottery vase, made for
Heal's, 4½in (11cm) high.
£50–60 *NCA*

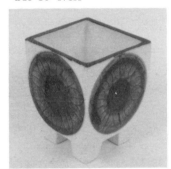

A Troika pottery vase, made for
Heal's, 4in (10cm) high.
£70–80 *NCA*

Two Troika pottery storage jars,
by Avril Bennett, 8in (20cm) high.
£40–50 each *NCA*

A Troika pottery apple,
2½in (6cm) diam.
£200–250 *NCA*

*Leslie Illsley made a pottery
apple to send to his idol, John
Lennon, at the Abbey Road
Studios. Illsley continued to
make the apples, and some were
put on ashtrays. Surviving
examples are rare.*

A selection of Troika marks.

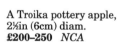

FURTHER READING:
Troika – Exhibition Catalogue,
New Century, 69 Kensington
Church Street, London W8, 1994.

Victorian & Edwardian

A William Alsager Adderley coffee cup and saucer, with a transfer of Balmoral Castle, c1876–85, 4½in (11cm) diam.
£30–40 *OCA*

A basalt jug, c1850, 3in (7.5cm).
£20–25 *SAD*

A Copeland and Garrett ring tree, c1835, 3in (8cm) diam.
£90–100 *AMH*

Miller's is a price GUIDE not a price LIST

A.T. Goode & Co., Copeland dessert set, with royal blue and gilt border, comprising one comport and seven plates, some damage, late 19thC, 9in (23cm) diam.
£100–140 *LF*

A Berlin plaque of a young girl, c1855, 8in (20cm) diam.
£900–1,000 *AMH*

A Copeland two-handled vase, c1851–85, 5in (12.5cm).
£160–180 *AMH*

A Royal Crown Derby miniature jug and basin set, c1917.
£100–120 *PCh*

A Crown Derby pot pourri vase, c1890, 7½in (19cm) high.
£500–550 *AMH*

A Cork, Edge & Malkin two-handled loving cup, with red and gold Holly Berry pattern, late 19thC, 4½in (11cm) high.
£30–40 *WAG*

A richly gilded dessert service, with royal blue and orange decoration in the Derby manner, comprising 12 plates and five comports, c1900, comport 13in (33cm) diam.
£450–550 *LF*

A set of six Royal Doulton napkin rings, including Sam Weller, Mr. Micawber, and the Fat Boy, 19thC.
£600–700 *AAV*

A Thomas Dimmock & Co., jug and basin, c1828–59, basin 15in (38cm) diam.
£300–350 *AMH*

r. An Elsmore & Forster ale jug, depicting the clown The Great Cashmore, inscribed 'William Williams, Salt Brook Inn 1864', 9in (23cm) high.
£500–575 *BHA*

l. A Royal Doulton fruit bowl, The Gipsies, 10in (25cm) diam.
r. A Royal Doulton dish, Sedan Chair, 9in (23cm) diam., both 19thC.
£60–80 *LF*

A Worcester Flight, Barr & Barr cup and saucer, c1815–20, cup 4in (11cm) high.
£250–270 *AMH*

An Elsmore & Forster pottery puzzle jug, the baluster body transfer decorated with two masked jesters and three cock fighting scenes, decorated in polychrome enamels, with gilt initials, dated '1867', 8in (20cm) high.
£350–450 *WIL*

A Hill Pottery bottle vase, with a dragon handle, 5in (12.5cm).
£80–100 *BKK*

The Hill Pottery factory ran from 1861–67.

A Maling vase, with stork decoration, early CTM mark, c1910, 8in (20cm) high.
£70–80 *BKK*

A J. Jamieson & Co., comport, with brown and white Bosphorus pattern transfer, c1840, 9in (23cm) wide.
£25–30 *CSA*

A Continental majolica comport, c1880.
£350–400 *WAG*

A pair of Spode baskets and stands, decorated with Castle pattern, c1820, 11in (28cm) wide.
£1,100–1,200 *AMH*

A Victorian transfer printed mug, 2⅜in (6cm) high.
£50–70 *CA*

A John Marshall & Co., pottery plate, with brown and white Bosphorus pattern transfer, c1840, 9in (23cm) diam.
£15–20 *CSA*

A Spode soup tureen, decorated with Castle pattern, c1820, 12in (31cm) high.
£425–475 *AMH*

A Victorian mug with turquoise decoration on white ground, 3in (7.5cm) high.
£10–15 *WAG*

A Martin Brothers unglazed grotesque, modelled as an open-mouthed creature with two prominent jaws, its body of fan shaped layers terminating with a scroll tail, incised 'Martin Bros. London Southall 11-1894' 5in (12.5cm) long.
£750–900 *P*

A Victorian transfer painted mug, 3½in (8.5cm) high.
£30–35 *WAG*

A Martin Brothers stoneware jardinière, with undulating rim, incised with bold grotesque fish swimming amid aquatic foliage, heightened in black, brown, white and blue against a brown ground, damaged, base signed 'Martin Brothers, Southall 7-1885', 16in (40cm) diam.
£1,250–1,500 *P*

An English ceramic tile, with
grey printed pattern, 6in
(15cm) square.
£10–12 *TER*

A Vienna ginger jar, and
sweetmeat dish, c1850,
11in (28cm) wide.
£120-130 *PC*

Worcester

A Worcester polychrome
leaf-shaped dish, decorated
with flowers, late 18thC, 10in
(25cm) wide.
£220–250 *PCh*

A Royal Worcester plate,
painted by Rushlon, c1933,
9in (23cm) diam.
£100–120 *TVM*

A Worcester figure, Monday's
Child, No. 3257, date mark for
c1956, 6½in (16cm) high.
£110–135 *ORA*

A Worcester blue and white
sauceboat, decorated with
Rearing Rock Island pattern,
late 18thC, 9in (23cm) long.
£180–220 *PCh*

A Royal Worcester bamboo
pattern double vase, 19thC.
£130–150 *HCH*

A Royal Worcester figure,
Friday's Child, No. 3261,
c1954, 7in (17.5cm) high.
£100–125 *ORA*

A Royal Worcester figure,
Monday's Child, No. 3519,
c1959, 7½in (18.5cm) high.
£110–135 *ORA*

A Worcester figure, Friday's
Child, No. 3523, date mark for
1959, 6in (15cm) high.
£125–150 *ORA*

CLOCKS, WATCHES & TIMEKEEPERS

A German musical alarm clock, excellent condition, early 20thC.
£80–85 *TRU*

l. An early Victorian wall clock, the rosewood case with shaped ears, 8-day movement with heavy brass plates, 8in (20cm) painted dial indistinctly signed, 13in (33cm) high.
£450–550

r. A wall clock, by A. Brugger & Co., 19 High Holborn, London, the mahogany case with moulded front bezel, 8-day movement, 10in (25.5cm) painted dial, early 19thC.
£400–500 *CAG*

A French onyx and brass cased four glass clock, with 8-day movement, mercury compensated pendulum, c1900, 11in (28cm) high.
£300–350 *TRU*

A Swiss miniature pendulum clock, c1920, 3in (7.5cm) high.
£100–120 *BER*

An Arts & Crafts copper clock garniture, the clock with a white dial within a square panel with blue enamelled corners, the face embossed with three leaf and flower motifs, 1920s–30s, 12½in (31.5cm) high, and a pair of candlesticks, 11in (28cm) high.
£600–700 *P*

A green lacquer cased mantel clock, with Swiss 8-day platform movement, 1920s.
£45–50 *TRU*

A French marble clock garniture, with chiming movement, marked Paris, c1926, 8½in (21cm) high.
£250–280 *BKK*

l. A silver cased 30-hour bedside clock, Birmingham 1923, 3½in (9cm) diam.
£125–150 *TRU*

A Swiss miniature pendulum clock, c1920, 3in (7.5cm) high.
£100–120 *BER*

A pair of French clocks, each in a ceramic panel shaped as an artist's palette, on brass easels, 19thC, largest 18in (46cm).
£250–350 each *LF*

A pocket watch, in a boulle case, c1880, 2in (5cm) high.
£450–500 *DUN*

A ceramic kitchen clock, by Emes, with winding key, c1930, 9in (23cm) wide.
£35–40 *AL*

A gold half hunter watch, by D. & J. Wellby, London, the case hallmarked 18 ct, c1897.
£3,250–3,750 *S*

A nickel plated and Bakelite press for unbreakable watch 'crystals', c1940.
£20–25 *TRU*

A Blick factory time clock, early 20thC, 39in (99cm) high.
£225–250 *JUN*

A 'clocking-in' machine, c1920, 35½in (91cm) high.
£75–125 *WAB*

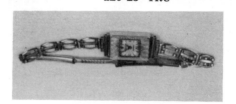

A lady's gold wristwatch, c1930.
£80–100 *ASA*

A watchmaker's lathe, with accessories, 19thC.
£150–175 *TRU*

A double-sided clock, with GNR plate, 20thC, 30in (76cm) diam.
£350–400 *JUN*

A stopwatch, c1960.
£10–20 *WAB*

COMMEMORATIVE WARE

The 19thC saw a great expansion in commemorative ware. Queen Victoria's popularity and longevity provided innumerable excuses for decorative celebration, culminating in the Diamond Jubilee of 1897. The development of new manufacturing techniques and a national system of railways and canals gradually enabled mass-produced objects to be brought to the mass market. Today an appealing and accurate image contributes towards an item's desirability.

As Eric Knowles explains in *Miller's Club News,* 'rarity is all important' - for instance, a slipware charger bearing a naive portrait of Charles I, could be worth £30,000 or more. Far more affordable are the colour transfer printed mugs, plates and jugs mass produced for most Royal events, such as Queen Elizabeth II's Silver Jubilee, which sell for only a few pounds.

Military & Naval

Exhibitions

A bevelled glass casket, souvenir of the Imperial International Exhibition, London, c1909, 3in (7.5cm) wide.
£20–25 *TRU*

A Grafton pin tray, commemorating the British Empire Exhibition, 1924, with the City of London crest, 2½in (6.5cm) diam.
£20–30 *CRO*

A Cauldon dish, commemorating the British Empire Exhibition, Wembley, April to October 1924, 5in (12.5cm) square.
£20–30 *CRO*

A pair of Baxter prints, of Sir Robert Peel and Lord Nelson, in gilt frames, c1860, 8½ by 7in (21 by 18cm).
£400–420 *TVM*

A Staffordshire jug, showing Lord Wellington and General Hill, in Prattware traditional colours of red, black and yellow, c1860.
£300–360 *TVM*

A Sunderland jug, celebrating joint forces with France in the Crimean War, with a coat-of-arms and motto in English and French, the 'Sailor's Return' on reverse, c1860, 8in (20cm) high.
£450–550 *TVM*

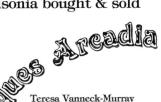

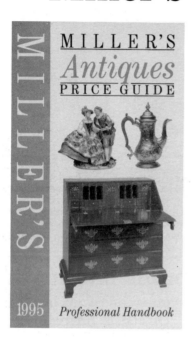
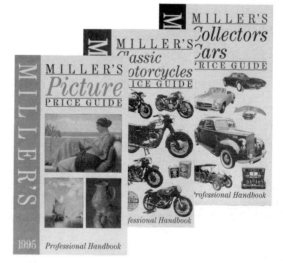

Boer War

The Boer War (1899–1902) was responsible for the most amazing variety of ornaments, keepsakes and commemorative pieces, notes expert Pieter Oosthuizen. The conflict captured public imagination across the globe, partly because of the enormous riches of the gold and diamond fields of South Africa, because troops were involved from many different countries and because of the drama of events and characters, extensively chronicled by the press.

The following memorabilia provides a fascinating picture of the period.

Three plates, each with transfer prints of Field Marshal Lord Roberts VC in a medallion, 8½in (21.5cm) diam.
£30–35 each *OO*

Ceramics

A pair of porcelain egg cups, with titled portraits of Lord Kitchener and General Sir G. White.
£95–120 *TVM*

A Staffordshire figure of 'French' on a horse facing right, and a figure of 'Roberts', on a horse facing left, 14½in (37cm).
£200–250 *OO*

A lustreware cup and saucer, the cup with a picture of Queen Victoria, and the saucer with pictures of 'Lieutenant-General J. D. P. French, General Right Hon. Sir Redvers H. Buller and Lieutenant-General Sir G. White.'
£95–110 *OO*

A tea set was produced depicting different generals.

FURTHER READING:
Boer War Memorabilia, The Collectors Guide Pieter Oosthuizen, Alderman Press, 1987.

Two Staffordshire figures, one marked 'Baden-Powell', the other 'De Wet', 17in (43cm) high.
£250–350 each *OO*

The Staffordshire potters produced the same figure to honour two different generals.

An earthenware biscuit barrel with a picture of General Sir Redvers Buller in the uniform of the Colonel Commandant of the 60th Rifles, unmarked, 69in (175cm) high.
£100–120 *OO*

l. A brown glaze milk jug, with various war scenes and inscribed 'South African War', 'They beat their swords into ploughshares' and 'Peace declared June 10 1902', unmarked, 6in (15cm).
£100–120
r. A brown glaze teapot with pictures of various generals, and inscribed, 'Though it cost the best of our British blood there is no turning back', unmarked, 6in (15cm) high.
£150–180 *OO*

Coins & Medals

A bronze pendant medallion,
inscribed 'Field Marshal
Roberts of Kandahar.'
£30–35 *OO*

A bronze medallion, inscribed,
2½in (6cm) diam.
£80–90 *OO*

An inscribed bronze medallion
showing 'M. T. Steijn, State
Pres. of the Orange Free State'.
£70–75 *OO*

l. A pair of carved stone
medallions showing Queen
Victoria and President Kruger,
inscribed on the reverse, 1901.
£100–120 *OO*

A collection of coin cut-outs and
engraving on coins from the
POW camps.
£5–25 each *OO*

Three medals, each 1in (3cm):
l. A Boer with gun, inscribed 'Alles zal recht kom',
1899–1900.
c. A bronze medal inscribed
'S. J. P. Kruger, Staatspresident der
Z. A. Republiek 1883–1900'.
r. A Dutch medal with a burning Boer
farmhouse inscribed '1899–1901 De Engelschen
in Zuid Afrika' 'Dan voor een geveinsde vrede te
worden bedrogen.
£70–75 each *OO*

Metalware

l. A pewter salt cellar, decorated with maps of the
Transvaal and the Orange Free State, inscribed 'The
Late Boer Republics', 3½in (8.5cm) high.
£30–40 and
r. A flat lead figure of a mounted soldier inscribed
'Boer War' and '1899-1900', 3in (7.5cm) high.
£15–20 *OO*

c. A picture frame decorated
with soldiers and arms,
10½in (26.5cm) high.
£120–140
l. & r. Two brass figures of
'A Gentleman in Khaki'
and 'The Handyman',
3½in (8.5cm) high.
£20–25 each *OO*

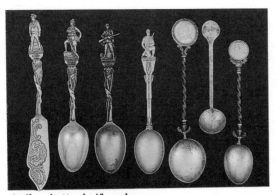

A silver butter knife and a collection of silver spoons, some inscribed and dated.
£20–45 each *OO*

Miscellaneous

A collection of Ogden's cigarette cards.
£4–5 each *OO*

A collection of mounted and inscribed wooden items from HMS 'Terrible', including a cannon fragment, bullets and shell casings.
£20–40 each *OO*

A coach carved from bone, drawn by horses carved from wood, with a carved figure of President Kruger on the back seat, the door of the coach inscribed and dated '1902', 12in (30.5cm) long.
£300–350 *OO*

A collection of Boer War period advertisements.
£3–5 each *OO*

A wristband or napkin ring, made from beef bone, 3½in (8.5cm diam).
£25–30
An inscribed beef bone brooch, 1½in (3.5cm) diam.
£40–45 *OO*

A skill game, called 'Get the Last Nail in Old Kruger's Coffin', the cardboard box with a glass top, 4½in (11cm) long.
£40–45 *OO*

Statuettes & Busts

l. A spelter bust of Lord
Kitchener, on a wooden base,
inscribed, 7in (17.5cm) high.
£40–45
c. A bronze bust of Lord
Roberts, on a marble base,
8in (20cm) high.
£100–130
r. A spelter bust, on a wood
base, inscribed 'Lord Roberts'.
£40–45 *OO*

l. A bust of Lord Kitchener,
inscribed, maker's mark '1209',
5in (12.5cm) high.
£25–30
r. A parian ware bust of Lord
Kitchener, with a white glazed
base, inscribed 'W. G. Lawton
Scul (ptor), Copyright', 6½in
(16cm) high.
£40–50 *OO*

A parian ware figure of Lord
Roberts, inscribed on the base
'Lord Roberts VC, CGB',
marked on the back 'W. C.
Lawton Sculptor, August 31st
1900, Copyright', 11in (28cm).
£200–250 *OO*

Royal

Victoria & Albert

A commemorative plate,
decorated with a portrait of
Queen Victoria, c1897, 10in
(25cm) diam.
£50–60 *LIO*

l. A dish to commemorate the
Diamond Jubilee of Queen
Victoria, 1897, 10in (25cm) wide.
£50–75 *LIO*

A Foley breakfast cup and saucer, to commemorate
the Diamond Jubilee of Queen Victoria 1897, saucer
6½in (16cm) diam.
£95–150 *CRO*

A Victoria and Albert cup and
saucer, with coloured and pink
lustre decoration, c1850, saucer
5½in (14cm) diam.
£150–230 *CRO*

Edward VII & Alexandra

A Doulton Edward VII and Queen Alexandra commemorative beaker, 1902, with silver rim 5in (12.5cm).
£150–250 *CRO*

A framed pot lid, showing a marriage picture of King Edward VII and Queen Alexandra, St. George's Chapel, Windsor, 1863, 4½in (11cm) diam.
£75–150 *CRO*

This lid is of the late edition – early editions lack the Greek key border.

> **Miller's is a price GUIDE not a price LIST**

An Edward VII porcelain egg cup, inscribed 'Osborne'.
£35–45 *TVM*

A commemorative plate, showing portrait of King Edward VII, 8½in (21cm) diam.
£70–130 *CRO*

A pair of cups and saucers to commemorate the Coronation of Edward VII and Queen Alexandra, 1902, saucers 5½in (14cm) diam.
£300–400 *CRO*

A commemorative lattice border plate, with a portrait of Queen Alexandra, 8½in (21cm) diam.
£25–35 *LIO*

A Queen Alexandra gift box for the troops, 1915, 3 by 4in (7.5 by 10cm).
£10–40 *CRO*

The boxes, presented to her own regiments, were personally paid for by the Queen.

Two lithographs of invitations on the occasion of the visit by The Duke and Duchess of Cornwall and York to New Zealand, June 1901, 11 by 14in (28 by 36cm).
£20–50 each *CRO*

George V & Queen Mary

A Royal Doulton Art Deco sugar bowl and cover, commemorating the Silver Jubilee of King George V and Queen Mary, 1935, with sepia portraits, gold handles and finial, 4½in (11cm).
£100–150 *CRO*

A Shelley pot and cover, commemorating the Silver Jubilee of King George V and Queen Mary, 1935, 4in (10cm).
£20–30 *LIO*

A brass door knocker, shaped as the head of King George V, to commemorate his Silver Jubilee, 1935, 6½in (16cm).
£30–60 *CRO*

A lattice border dish, commemorating the coronation of King George V & Queen Mary, 1911, 10½in (26cm) wide.
£50–75 *LIO*

A Copeland Spode gin flask, commemorating the coronation of George V and Queen Mary, 1911, top missing, 8½in (21cm).
£80–100 *CRO*

Edward VIII

A mug, to commemorate the visit by the Prince of Wales to Johannesburg, 1925, 3in (7.5cm).
£100–150 *CRO*

A Thorne's toffee tin, with colour portrait of the Prince of Wales, c1925, 4 by 3in (10 by 7.5cm). **£10–40** *CRO*

A memorial mug for the Duke and Duchess of Windsor, by A. C. Wilton, inscribed 'Duke Born 1894, Abdicated 1936, Died 1972, Duchess Born 1896, Married 1937, Died 1986', 3in (7.5cm) high.
£50–100 *CRO*

George VI & Queen Elizabeth

A Wedgwood mug, commemorating the coronation of George VI and Queen Elizabeth, 1937, designed by Keith Macaroy, 5in (12.5cm).
£90–160 *CRO*

A matchbox case, to commemorate the coronation of George VI and Queen Elizabeth, 1937, for Bryant & May's matches, 2 by 1½in (5 by 4cm).
£20–40 *CRO*

Queen Elizabeth II & The Duke of Edinburgh

A Chad Valley Princess Elizabeth doll, with velvet body, stiffened felt head and glass eyes, original mohair wig, 1938, 18in (46cm) high.
£400–500 *CK*

FURTHER READING:
Miller's Royal Memorabilia, Reed Consumer Books Ltd., London, 1994.

A Paragon Ware tankard, with Prince Philip's crest on the front and his yacht on reverse, 1960s, 5in (12.5cm) high.
£50–100 *CRO*

A bone china miniature plaque, commemorating Elizabeth II's Royal Tour, 1953–54, 1½in (4cm) wide.
£35–75 *CRO*

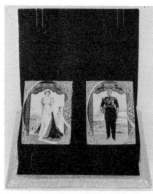

An unopened double pack of playing cards to commemorate the coronation of Queen Elizabeth II & The Duke of Edinburgh 1953, by de la Rue, with maroon and gold box, 5½ by 6½in (14 by 16cm).
£100–150   CRO

A Wedgwood mug, designed by Eric Ravilious, commemorating the coronation of Elizabeth II, 1953, 4in (10cm) high.
£120–130   CSA

r. An engraved brass bell commemorating the coronation of Queen Elizabeth II, 1953, 2½in (6cm) high.
£7–8   COL

A glass cup commemorating the coronation of Elizabeth II, 1953, 2½in (6cm) high.
£1–2   COL

The Prince & Princess of Wales

A Mason's Ironstone plate commemorating the marriage of Prince Charles and Lady Diana Spencer, 1981, 8in (20cm) diam.
£8–10   COL

A ceramic bell to commemorate the marriage of The Prince of Wales and Lady Diana Spencer, 1981, 4in (10cm) high.
£4–5   COL

A ceramic ashtray by Adams to commemorate the marriage of The Prince of Wales and Lady Diana Spencer, 1981, 3½in (9cm) diam.
£5–6   PC

COSMETICS

Demand for cosmetics began to expand at the turn of the century. In 1908 Helena Rubinstein and Max Factor opened their beauty salons, followed two years later by Elizabeth Arden. During WWI, whilst men were at the front, women were in the factories, many earning money for the first time to spend on cosmetics and other feminine luxuries. It was after the war that the industry really took off. A major influence was Hollywood, with new stars such as Pola Negri, Theda Bara and Clara Bow encouraging women to experiment with eye make-up, lipstick and powder. Products were created for every pocket, and amongst the compacts displayed here some originally retailed at Woolworths for 6d (2½p). Compacts capture in miniature the flavour of their period, both in design and even in scent, many still containing traces of their original powder.

Three powder compacts, each with foil pictures of dancers and skaters, 1930s, 2 to 2½in (5 to 6cm) wide.
£8–10 each *PC*

A combined loose powder compact with cigarette case, and a smaller metal compact, 1930s.
£8–10 each *PC*

Compacts

Three powder compacts, with foil pictures of crinoline ladies by Gwenda, 1930s.
£7–10 each *PC*

These compacts were sold at Woolworths for 6d (2½p).

Three Art Deco metal powder compacts, the one in the centre with original box, c1930.
£15–20 each *PC*

l. A Bakelite compact with gold decoration, 1930s.
£5–6 *PC*

Three metal powder compacts, decorated with dogs, 1930s–50s, 2½ and 2in (6 and 5cm) square.
£6–10 each *PC*

Three metal loose powder compacts, 1930s.
£5–6 each *PC*

Three butterfly wing powder compacts, 1930s.
£20–25 each *PC*

These were given away or sold on board cruise ships.

Four souvenir powder compacts, 1930s, 2 to 3in (5 to 7.5cm)
£3–5 each *PC*

A tartan covered powder compact, 1950s.
£4–5 *PC*

A powder compact, with a foil picture of birds, 1930s.
£5–6 *PC*

Two metal powder compacts, one styled as an envelope, c1930, 2½ by 3in (6 by 7.5cm), the other with Blackpool Tower, 2½ by 2in (6 by 5cm).
£15–20 each *PC*

A metal powder compact, decorated with marcasite, 1950s, 3in (7.5cm) long.
£6–8 *PC*

Two powder compacts, decorated with cross stitch pictures, 1950s, 4in (10cm) wide, and 3in (7.5cm) diam.
£5–8 each *PC*

An Art Deco powder compact, 1936, 2in (5cm) square.
£6–8 *PC*

A powder compact, with cross stitch pattern and zip, 1950s, 4in (10cm) wide.
£3–4 *PC*

A Bakelite powder compact, with gold decoration, 1950s, 2in (5cm) diam.
£3–4 *PC*

A metal powder compact, decorated with transfer printed butterflies, 1930s, 3 by 3½in (7.5 by 9cm).
£5–6 *PC*

A BOAC powder compact, 1950s, 3in (7.5cm) diam.
£3–4 *PC*

A plastic powder compact, with a picture of Virginia Mayo, 1950s.
£4–5 *PC*

Two metal commemorative powder compacts, 1930s.
£20–25 each *PC*

A metal souvenir powder compact, from Polperro, 1930s, 2in (5cm) square.
£3–4 *PC*

Cosmetic Accessories

A glass bottle, with rosewood case, c1880, 5½in (14cm) high.
£40–60 *DUN*

A silver mounted cut glass jar, c1892, 3⅛in (8cm) high.
£40–50 *DUN*

Two ceramic bottle holders, in the shape of ladies in crinoline dresses, 20thC, 4 and 4⅜in (10 and 11cm) high.
£15–20 each *PC*

Two Victorian shoe horns/ buttonhooks, 9 and 11in (23 and 28cm) long.
£5–8 each *PHay*

A cylinder-shaped glass container, with owl's head top, 20thC, 10in (25cm) high.
£50–60 *LF*

Vanity Cases

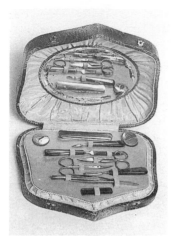

A lady's travelling vanity manicure case, c1910.
£100–180 *MCh*

An Edwardian travelling vanity case, with 18ct gold and blue porcelain fittings.
£500–800 *MCh*

A gentleman's travelling vanity case, 1920s.
£180–220 *MCh*

A lady's travelling manicure case, c1900.
£120–180 *MCh*

MAKE THE MOST OF MILLERS

Condition is absolutely vital when assessing the value of any item. Damaged pieces appreciate much less than perfect examples. However, a rare, desirable piece may command a high price even when damaged.

l. A leather collar box, c1910, 8in (20cm) wide.
£30–35 *DUN*

A leather collar box, c1930, 7in (17.5cm) diam.
£25–30 *DUN*

A lady's travelling vanity case, 1950s.
£60–85 *MCh*

COSTUME

One of the joys of collecting costume is that in many instances you can wear your collectables, although they should be treated with respect. Old and delicate fabrics need careful handling. Be careful when wearing rings and bracelets not to catch a thread and cause damage. People in the past were smaller than we are today – if something is too tiny, do not try and squeeze into it, and if an article is really too fragile it is better looked at rather than worn. Old and delicate pieces should be professionally cleaned. Padded hangers and covers should be used for storage, and wrap articles in acid free tissue paper or a clean white cotton sheet. Many museums have costume collections, the two most prestigious being at the Victoria and Albert Museum in London and the Museum of Costume in Bath, which also houses a Fashion Research Centre, open to the general public by appointment.

Bags & Purses

A French beaded purse, with silver plated frame, decorated with semi-precious stones, c1850.
£90–120 *JPr*

A beaded and silk embroidered evening bag, with velvet ribbons, c1835–50.
£18–20 *JPr*

A Victorian beaded purse, with tortoisehell fastener, 10½in (26.5cm) long.
£50–60 *TOM*

l. A beaded purse, with gilded frame, c1820, 3in (7.5cm) wide.
£25–35 *JPr*

An enamelled chain metal purse, silk lined, c1900, 5in (12.5cm) long.
£10–20 *JPr*

l. A beaded drawstring purse, c1910, 8in (20cm) long.
£45–55 *JPr*

PERIOD STYLES

Date	Period
1558–1603	Elizabethan
1603–1625	Jacobean
1625–1649	Carolean
1649–1660	Cromwellian
1660–1689	Restoration
1689–1694	William & Mary
1694–1702	William III
1702–1714	Queen Anne
1714–1727	Early Georgian
1727–1760	Georgian
1760–1812	Late Georgian
1812–1820	Regency
1820–1830	Late Regency
1830–1837	William IV
1837–1860	Early Victorian
1860–1901	Late Victorian
1880–1900	Arts & Crafts
1870–1920s	Art Nouveau
1901–1910	Edwardian
1910–1930s	Art Deco

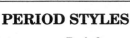

A metal and beaded machine-knitted purse, 1930s, 7in (17.5cm) long.
£30–40 *JPr*

Three chain purses, c1900, 3in (7.5cm) long.
£35–45 each *LB*

Miser's Purses

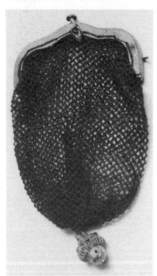

A selection of handbag clasps, c1930–40.
£1–2 each *LB*

Museum of Costume,
Assembly Rooms,
Bennett Street, Bath,
BA1 2QH.
Tel: 01225 461111.

Victoria & Albert Museum,
Cromwell Road, London
SW7 2RL.
Tel: 0171-938 8500

Three miser's purses, 19thC, largest 12in (30.5cm) long.
£20–30 each *LB*

A knotted sovereign purse, with a gilt tassel, c1820, 4in (10cm).
£20–25 *JPr*

A miser's purse, navy blue crochet with steel beads and trimming, c1830–70, 13in (33cm) long.
£15–30 *JPr*

Two miser's purses, with steel beads and trimmings, steel sliders, 19thC, largest 12in (30.5cm) long.
£12–25 each *JPr*

Boots & Shoes

A pair of leather and felt military or naval magazine boots, 1914–18.
£35–55 *WAB*

A pair of Victorian black leather button boots.
£50–70 *TOM*

A pair of leather field boots, with trees, 1930s, 18in (46cm) high.
£80–120 *MSh*

Two pairs of baby's leather shoes, 1920s.
l. **£35–40**
r. **£18–25** *WAG*

An Edwardian mahogany boot jack, c1910.
£70–100 *MSh*

A slipware boot warmer, 19thC, 8in (20cm) long.
£150–200 *TVM*

A pair of Victorian black leather lady's shoes, with jet decoration.
£50–60 *LB*

A pair of Victorian child's leather button boots, 5½in (14cm) long.
£50–65 *CK*

A collection of shoe heels, c1920-30, 3in (7.5cm) high.
£5–15 per pair *BAT*

r. A pair of children's leather shoes with straps, c1920.
£40–50 *CK*

Dress

A Victorian gown, with 'leg-of-mutton' sleeves, c1890.
£90–120 *TOM*

A bridal gown, c1920.
£150–180 *TOM*

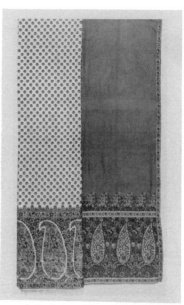

l. An ivory silk and wool shawl, woven with a sprigged field, the ends with floral cones reserved in ivory, c1825, 50 by 112in (127 by 284.5cm).
£500–600
r. A raspberry pink silk stole, woven with end borders of leaf based cones, possibly Norwich, 19thC, 30 by 100in (76 by 254cm).
£120–180 *CSK*

A day dress, of white muslin printed with emerald green stripes and simulated moiré pattern, green and white braid trimming, printed shawl cloth bodice, c1870.
£180–200 *CSK*

A child's dress, of sky blue wool, embroidered with a border of yellow flowers, trimmed with pink scalloped edges, late 19thC.
£60–80 *CSK*

A mushroom striped taffeta dress, with deep brown striped border, V-shaped bodice trimmed with fringing, pagoda sleeves, and two tiered skirt, 1860s.
£180–200 *CSK*

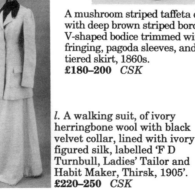

l. A walking suit, of ivory herringbone wool with black velvet collar, lined with ivory figured silk, labelled 'F D Turnbull, Ladies' Tailor and Habit Maker, Thirsk, 1905'.
£220–250 *CSK*

An Edwardian black velvet evening cape, embroidered with pale blue diamanté, French.
£125–180 *TOM*

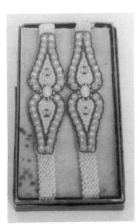

A young boy's suit, bottle green facecloth with cut steel buttons, with scarlet wool waistcoat, jacket labelled 'Peter Robinson', late 19thC, and a young girl's scarlet velvet dress.
£80–100 *CSK*

A pair of Edwardian garters, probably bridal, decorated with pearls and diamanté, boxed.
£50–70 *TOM*

An aubergine and sage green shot silk dress, woven with posies of flowers, the sleeves and skirt front of green satin trimmed with borders of beadwork, 1895.
£220–250 *CSK*

Fashion Prints & Patterns

Four Parisian fashion prints, c1820, 7½ by 5in (19 by 12.5cm).
£20–25 each *STA*

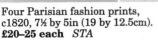

Four French fashion prints, c1820, 7 by 4½in (17.5 by 11cm), unframed.
£40–45 each *STA*

Two Vogue patterns, 1949.
£4–5 each *COL*

Two patterns, one for hat, neckpiece and muff, the other for gloves, 1949.
£4–5 each *COL*

A Vogue pattern, designed by Balmain, c1950.
£4–5 *COL*

1950s Fashions

Fifties clothes are readily available, easy to wear and enormous fun. Perhaps the most evocative pieces are the printed cotton skirts and dresses, decorated with everything from cabbage roses, to kitchen equipment or city scenes. With their bright colours and swirling shapes they summon up the spirit of the period and like many fifties fabrics seem very underpriced in the curret market, with prices beginning for as little as £5 for a skirt. Better still for any fifties fan they are comfortable to wear, often machine washable and the fabric weight means that they can often be hung up to dry rather than ironed – a user-friendly collectable.

A cotton dress, with pink and grey flowers.
£10–20 *PC*

A handmade cotton skirt, with orange, black, yellow and green geometric design.
£20–30 *PC*

A black and white check cotton dress, with floral panels on the skirt.
£10–20 *PC*

A white cotton skirt, with pink and yellow flowers.
£5–10 *PC*

This skirt has been cut down from a dress.

A white cotton dress, with red printed flowers.
£15–30 *PC*

Miller's is a price GUIDE not a price LIST

A Gor-ray cotton and linen skirt, coloured black, yellow, red and green, with stiffened underskirt.
£5–10 *PC*

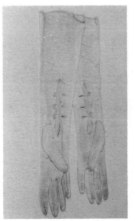

A linen and cotton dress, with grey flowers.
£10–20 *PC*

A green velvet skirt, with red roses, by T. Woodruffe WI.
£5–15 *PC*

MAKE THE MOST OF MILLERS

Condition is absolutely vital when assessing the value of any item. Damaged pieces appreciate much less than perfect examples. However, a rare, desirable piece may command a high price even when damaged.

An American 'Prom' dress, made from synthetic damask with diamanté studs.
£35–50 *PC*

A red and white cotton dress 'The Kahala', made in Honolulu for Liberty.
£10–20 *PC*

Gloves

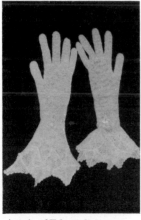

A pair of Edwardian lace gloves. **£10–15** *LB*

A pair of cream kid leather gloves, with pearl buttons, c1920, 16in (41cm) long.
£20–25 *AHL*

Handbags

A red leather handbag, with original vanity mirror, c1930.
£5–10 *PC*

Hats

A Victorian black bonnet, made from lace with chiffon flowers on straw, pink and mauve ribbon and flowers.
£30–45 *TOM*

A Victorian black bonnet, with ostrich feathers, lace, silver thread, and beaded decoration.
£30–50 *TOM*

A silver sequinned net evening cap, 1920s.
£18–20 *TOM*

A brown felt hat, with pink swansdown pompom, c1930.
£15–25 *TOM*

A black beaded cap, with diamanté decoration, c1960.
£50–60 *TOM*

A net cap, decorated with sequins and diamanté, trimmed with lace, 1920s.
£50–75 *TOM*

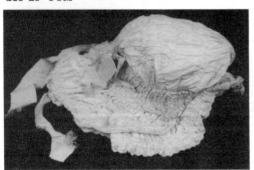

A child's bonnet, 19thC.
£35–55 *LB*

Three silk baby's bonnets, c1900.
£25–40 each *LL*

A bonnet, with Ayrshire work crown, 19thC.
£35–50 *LB*

An Eton rowing boater, highly decorated, 1890s.
£100–140 *MSh*

A cotton baby's cap, with quilted border, c1920.
£20–25 *LB*

A school or college cap, dated '1959–60'.
£40–60 *MSh*

Hat Pins

A selection of paste, brass and mother-of-pearl hat pins, 1900–20.
£10–18 each *VB*

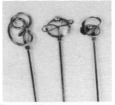

Three silver hat pins, by Charles Horner, 1900–15.
£20–35 each *VB*

Three hat pin holders, c1900.
£14–20 each *VB*

Lace

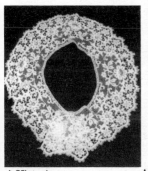

A Victorian needlepoint collar.
£50–70 *LB*

An appliquéd lappet, c1900, 46in (116.5cm).
£20–25 *LL*

A Maltese lace collar, c1900.
£15–25 *LL*

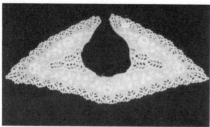

A cutwork collar, 1920.
£12–20 *LB*

A lace maker's adjustable pillow stand, 18thC.
£250–300 *PAR*

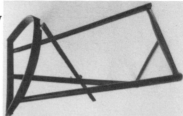

An Ayrshire palarine, 1840.
£30–32 *LL*

CRAFTS

Contemporary crafts in Britain can be exciting, varied and of extremely high quality. Prices are often surprisingly reasonable, with 'art' pieces generally retailing for far less than paintings or sculpture, whilst handmade domestic and functional wares will cost you no more than many factory made mass-produced items. Craft galleries flourish around the country and many of their wares will undoubtedly become the collectables of the future.

A recycled fish, made from tin cans, forks and a shoe stretcher, by Anne Carrington.
£100–200 *PC*

A ceramic bowl, decorated with birds, by Jill Fanshaw-Cato, 14in (36cm) diam.
£300–320 *NEW*

r. A metal and wood mechanical toy, 'Fabulous Animals', by Neil Hardy.
£30–40 *NEW*

A square metallic clock, by Jane Adam, 9in (23cm).
£100–110 *NEW*

A ceramic form sculpture, by Martin Booth.
£230–260 *NEW*

A ceramic teapot and mug, in Blue Fish pattern, by Chris Lewis, 7 and 4in (17.5 and 10cm) high.
Teapot £45–55
Mug £6–8 *NEW*

A blue mug, decorated with gold fish, by Robert Goldsmith, 4in (10cm) high.
£19–21 *NEW*

A wenge wood cat, by John
Mainwaring, 8½in (21cm).
£35–40 *NEW*

A dessert bowl, by Pauline
Zelinski, 6in (15cm) diam.
£18–22 *NEW*

A glass vase, engraved and
hand painted with gold leaf
and enamel, by Liz Lowe,
5½in (14cm) high.
£200–240 *NEW*

A copper, brass and tin lion,
by Joanna Ryding.
£35–40 *PC*

A ceramic teapot, decorated
with female nude, by Julia
Quigley, 4in (10cm) high.
£40–45 *NEW*

A hexagonal ceramic
plate, by Charles
Spacey, 14in
(36cm) diam.
£100–120 *NEW*

A mini Troubadour wooden
upright clock, by Ben Simons,
19in (48cm) high.
£140–160 *NEW*

A ceramic vase,
by Sue Mundy,
18in (46cm) high.
£100–130 *NEW*

A ceramic form,
by Kris Rice,
4in (10cm) high.
£20–25 *NEW*

DOLLS

We have categorised our dolls section by the medium from which the head is made, i.e. bisque, celluloid, china, etc. Antique dolls have grown enormously in popularity in recent years and amongst the most valuable are 18thC examples made from wood and 19thC bisque dolls, which can fetch thousands of pounds at auction.

Age, rarity and condition are all important. Period clothes can greatly enhance the value of a doll, as can the presence of the original box, which can double the value of, for example, an early Barbie. Despite rising prices, there is still an enormous variety of dolls available to those without a fortune to spend, in particular examples from the post-war period. There is always the option of laying down contemporary dolls as future collectables, perhaps concentrating on items which have enjoyed a particular craze amongst today's children, such as Polly Pocket and her paraphernalia – see page 473.

Bisque – General

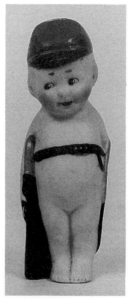

A bisque Foreign Legion doll, with roguish eyes, c1920, 4in (10cm) high.
£30–40 *CK*

A rigid bisque Red Indian doll, with roguish eyes, c1920, 3in (7.5cm) high.
£15–20 *CK*

A bisque bonnet doll/pudding doll, with jointed arms, c1900, 3½in (9cm) high.
£30–35 *CK*

A bisque bonnet doll, with jointed arms, and blue boots, c1890–1900, 4½in (11.5cm) high.
£30–40 *CK*

A rigid bisque baby doll, with roguish eyes, jointed arms and starfish hands, dressed in original ribbons, c1920, 2½in (6.5cm) high.
£18–25 *CK*

A bisque dolls' house doll, with cloth body, bisque lower limbs, and painted eyes, original clothes, c1880, 4in (10cm) high.
£80–100 *CK*

A bisque-headed child doll, with blue eyes, heavy brows, pierced ears, brown wig and jointed wood and papier mâché body, dressed in contemporary clothes, some damage, impressed '5', mid-19thC, 21in (53cm) high.
£800–900 *CSK*

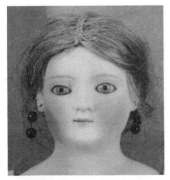

A bisque shoulder-headed lady doll, with closed mouth, fixed bright blue eyes, pierced ears, blonde hair wig, stuffed body and bisque arms, impressed '7', mid-19thC, 20in (51cm) high.
£550–650 *CSK*

German Bisque

A bisque shoulder-headed doll, with moulded hair ornament, stuffed body with bisque limbs, the legs with flat-heeled painted boots, c1870, 16½in (42cm) high.
£325–400 *CSK*

A bisque flapper doll, with painted eyes and moulded top-knot, mid-19thC, 4½in (11.5cm) high.
£150–180 *CK*

A doll with a kid body, bisque lower arms, marked 'S', original condition, c1890, 16in (41cm) high.
£450–500 *CK*

An early Armand Marseille doll, marked 'AM', c1890, 28in (71cm) high.
£850–900 *CK*

An Armand Marseille Red Indian doll, with rigid limbs, original clothes, c1900, 10in (25cm) high.
£125–155 *CK*

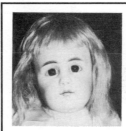

An Armand Marseille doll, 'My Dream Baby', marked 'AM351', with open mouth, c1925, 24in (61cm) high.
£180–200 *CK*

An Armand Marseille baby doll, with soft body, celluloid hands, closed mouth, marked 'AM341', 1920–25, 15in (38cm) high.
£275–300 *CK*

A doll with blonde ringlets, marked 'AM390', c1910, 22in (55.5cm) high.
£200–250 *PC*

A Gebrüder Knock doll, marked with cross-bones, original condition, c1900, 14in (36cm).
£250–280 *CK*

A blonde bisque doll, with stuffed body and bisque lower arms and legs, possibly by C. F. Kling & Co., c1880, 10in (25cm) high.
£150–175 *CK*

A Cuno & Otto Dressel shoulder-headed doll, on a stuffed body with composition lower arms, bright blue eyes, stamped with Minerva helmet mark, c1900, 19in (48cm) high.
£325–365 *CK*

A Bähr & Pröschild doll, with human hair wig pulled through silk backing, marked '273', c1890, with later clothes, 28in (71cm) high.
£875–900 *CK*

A Cuno & Otto Dressel doll, with kid body, bisque lower arms, mohair wig, original clothes, marked 'COD 1896', 18in (46cm) high.
£400–450 *CK*

A Kaiser character baby doll, with jointed limbs, c1900, 11in (28cm) high.
£350–400 *CK*

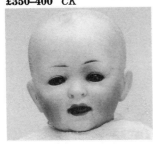

A child doll, with bisque head, blue sleeping eyes, pierced ears, blonde mohair wig, jointed wood and composition body, impressed 'Heinrich Handwerck Simon & Halbig 7', late 19thC, 33in (84cm) high.
£1,600–2,000 *CSK*

A character baby doll, by Hertel, Schwab & Co., with open/closed mouth, blue sleeping eyes, moulded hair with paint strokes and bent limbed composition body, damaged, impressed '3 142', late 19thC, 12in (30.5cm) high.
£450–550 *CSK*

A Käthe Kruse boy doll, with painted eyes, hair wig original white sailor suit and odd slippers, c1920, 20in (50.5cm) high.
£1,500–1,800 *CSK*

The boy doll of this mould, by Igor von Jakimow, was called Friedebald as it was modelled from Käthe Kruse's eight year old son, and was the only doll in the range designed as one of her own children.

J. D. Kestner

A Kestner bisque boy doll, with glass eyes, jointed head and limbs, original clothes, marked '31', c1890, 5½in (14cm) high.
£175–200 *CK*

A Kestner bisque boy doll, with rigid limbs, glass eyes, in original clothes, c1890, 4in (10cm) high.
£200–225 *CK*

A pair of Kestner bisque dolls, with rigid limbs, glass eyes, and original clothes, c1890.
£325–350 *CK*

A Kestner doll, with original mohair wig, contemporary clothes, marked '136', c1890, 28in (71cm) high.
£900–1,000 *CK*

A Kestner all bisque doll, with rigid limbs, glass eyes, original clothes, c1890, 4½in (11.5cm) high.
£150–185 *CK*

A bisque character doll, by J. D. Kestner, with open closed mouth, weighted brown eyes, blonde wig over plaster pate and curved limb composition body, in original costume, together with wooden trunk, c1912, 15in (35.5cm) high.
£800–1,000 *S(S)*

A Kestner doll, with trousseau of original clothes, marked '192', c1890, 12in (30.5cm) high.
£500–600 *CK*

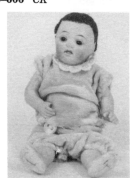

A Kestner bisque character boy doll, with jointed head and limbs, skin wig and sleeping eyes, c1920.
£300–325 *CK*

A Kestner French type boy doll, with jointed arms and legs, in original silk sailor's outfit, blue shoes, and glass eyes, c1890, 4in (10cm) high.
£200–250 *CK*

A Plymouth mug, restored,
c1770, 5in (12.5cm) high.
£500–600 *DMa*

A Plymouth salt, restored,
c1770, 8½in (21cm) wide.
£1,100–1,350 *DMa*

r. A Plymouth
figure, restored,
c1770, 6in
(15cm) high.
£350–450 *DMa*

A Poole Pottery jug, 7½in
(18.5cm) high.
£220–250 *HEW*

An Oriental lady ceramic
powder bowl, c1930, 6½in
(16.5cm) high.
£25–30 *PC*

A Pratt Ware pot lid, The Fishmarket.
£60–70 *LIO*

A ceramic powder bowl,
1920s, 7in (17.5cm) wide.
£20–25 *PC*

A crinoline lady
powder bowl, 20thC,
9in (23cm) high.
£20–30 *PC*

A Pratt Ware pot lid,
Fording the Stream.
£70–80 *LIO*

An Art Deco ceramic powder
bowl, c1930, 5½in (13.5cm).
£10–15 *PC*

A grey lustre ceramic
powder bowl, c1930.
£25–30 *PC*

A German powder
bowl, 20thC.
£15–25 *PC*

A ceramic woodpecker
powder bowl, 20thC.
£15–20 *PC*

A pair of majolica
Sarreguemines jugs,
c1875, 10in (25cm).
£700–800 *PC*

A Charlotte Rhead Crown Ducal
vase, c1935, 8½in (21cm) diam.
£90–100 *CSA*

A Radford jardinière,
6in (15cm) diam.
£70–80 *WTA*

A Sarreguemines game tureen,
No. 4451, c1900, 14in (35.5cm) long.
£300–400 *PC*

A Sarreguemines Toby
jug, No. 3429, c1904,
13in (33cm) high.
£160–200 *PC*

A Sarreguemines plate,
No. 3424, c1904, 9½in
(24cm) diam.
£100–125 *PC*

A Sarreguemines 'Farmer'
jug, No. 3181, c1904, 8in
(20cm) high.
£100–120 *PC*

Two Sarreguemines jugs,
l. 'Monkey', No. 3322.
£150–200
r. 'Pig', No. 3318.
£100–120 *PC*

A Sarreguemines 'Clown'
jug, No. 4639, 6½in
(16.5cm) high.
£250–300 *PC*

A Sarreguemines
'Popeye' jug, No. 8715,
6in (15cm) high.
£75–100 *PC*

A Sarreguemines comport,
with blue interior, No. 5121,
c1920, 9½in (24cm) diam.
£175–185 *PC*

A moustache cup and saucer, inscribed
'The Irish Jaunting Car'.
£50–60 *CRA*

A Staffordshire pottery spill vase, with reclining lion, 19thC.
£200–220 *TVM*

A pair of Staffordshire pottery figures of deer, with flowered bocage, c1830, 7in (17.5cm) high.
£400–450 *RWB*

A Staffordshire pottery figure of 'The Poet', 19thC.
£125–160 *TVM*

A Staffordshire pottery tithe group, 19thC, 9in (23cm) high.
£900–1,250 *TVM*

A Staffordshire pottery figure of a woman 'who found her gold piece', 6in (15cm) high.
£160–180 *TVM*

A Staffordshire pottery group of 'Scuffle', with flowered bocage, c1820, 8in (20cm).
£400–450 *RWB*

A rare Staffordshire pottery figure of Bloomer Lady, c1850, damaged.
£120–160 *LIO*

A pair of Staffordshire figures of Venus and Neptune, c1830, 9in (23cm) high.
£200–300 *LIO*

A pair of Staffordshire pearlware figures of a 'Shepherd' and 'Shepherdess', 5½in (14cm) high.
£400–450 *TVM*

A SylvaC cat, with long neck, No. 3457, 12in (31.5cm) high.
£45–55 *JDC*

A SylvaC coleslaw pot, No. 4750, 5in (12.5cm) diam.
£35–45 *JDC*

A SylvaC ketchup pot, No. 4751, 5in (12.5cm) diam.
£35–40 *JDC*

A Swineside Ceramics limited edition 'Ritzy' teapot, 20thC, 5in (12.5cm) high.
£50–60 *BKK*

A SylvaC jardinière, Aurora range, No. 4331, 7in (17.5cm) wide.
£6–8 *JDC*

Two Szeiler donkeys, 5 and 2in (12.5 and 5cm) high.
£10–25 each *JDC*

A Sadler racing car teapot, with registration mark 'OKT 42', 20thC, 7in (17.5cm) long.
£100–130 *AAV*

A SylvaC vase, with stylised lamb, c1934, 4⅓in (11cm) high.
£25–30 *BKK*

A SylvaC musical tankard, inscribed with German rhyme, playing an English tune, 7½in (19cm) high.
£150–200 *CRA*

A SylvaC jug, depicting William Shakespeare, 20thC, 3in (7.5cm) high.
£15–25 *PC*

A pair of Torquay Pottery vases, c1910, 9in (23cm) high.
£150–200 *JO*

A Troika vase, by Penny
Broadribb, 12in (31cm).
£100–120 *NCA*

A Troika pottery medium
wheel vase, by Hilary Cox,
6½in (16.5cm) high.
£90–150 *NCA*

A Troika pottery vase of
Newlyn construction, by Alison
Brigden, marked, c1960–70,
9in (23cm) wide.
£100–200 *NCA*

Two Troika coffin vases, by
Alison Brigden, 7in (17.5cm).
£30–40 each *NCA*

A Wedgwood jug, c1880,
6½in (16.5cm) high.
£80–100 *LIO*

A German porcelain tray,
with the painted head and
shoulders of Ophelia, c1880,
14in (35.5cm) high.
£200–250 *WAG*

l. A pair of cabinet
plates, c1825, 5in
(12.5cm) diam.
£30–40 *LIO*

A Studio pottery dish, made for
Liberty's by Robyn Wilkinson,
c1992, 12in (30.5cm) diam.
£30–40 *PC*

A Royal Worcester figure,
Tuesday's Child, No. 3534,
c1959, 8in (20cm) high.
£150–175 *ORA*

A Royal Worcester figure
Wednesday's Child, No.
3259, c1954, 7in (17.5cm).
£100–120 *ORA*

A Smiths wooden cased electric clock, 1936, 7in (17.5cm) high. **£25–35** *BKK*

A marble clock garniture, with spelter decoration, movement by Smiths, c1928, 28½in (73cm) long. **£150–180** *BKK*

A Foley Intarsio clock, by Frederick Rhead, c1900, 9½in (24cm) high. **£350–500** *CSA*

A plate commemorating the coronation of Edward VII and Queen Alexandra, 1902, 9½in (24cm) diam. **£40–50** *LIO*

A Queen Alexandra commemorative lady's metal notebook case, 3in (7.5cm). **£40–80** *CRO*

A tile, depicting the head of Gladstone, 19thC, 6in (15cm) square. **£15–20** *LIO*

A Pratt Ware framed pot lid, depicting Prince Albert, 1861, lid 4in (10cm) diam. **£70–100** *CRO*

A pair of bell pulls, with porcelain roundels, and enamelled portraits of Admiral Lord Nelson, c1800. **£3,000–5,000** *TVM*

A Mason's jug, by Cyril Shingler, for the Silver Jubilee of King George V and Queen Mary, 1935. **£150–300** *CRO*

A mug, showing King George VI and Queen Elizabeth, made in South Africa, 3in (7.5cm). **£80–150** *CRO*

A Thorne's toffee tin, showing HRH Prince of Wales, Duke of York and Prince Henry, c1925. **£20–40** *CRO*

A Royal Crown Derby dish, 1953, 4in (10cm). **£20–40** *CRO*

Four powder compacts, with foil pictures of birds, by Gwenda.
£7–10 each *PC*

A powder compact, depicting Sleepy, by Gwenda, 1930s.
£6–7 *PC*

Two powder compacts:
l. decorated with a lizard and beads,
r. with floral decoration.
£6–8 each *PC*

A selection of powder compacts, with foil pictures, c1930.
£5 –10 each *PC*

r. A swan's-down powder puff, with Barbola handle, 1920s, 12in (30.5cm) long.
£10–12 *TOM*

l. An Art Deco combined compact and cigarette case, 6in (15cm).
r. Two Art Deco painted compacts.
£8–10 each *PC*

An Art Deco enamelled souvenir compact, c1930.
£5–8 *PC*

A collection of pill boxes, with agate, enamelled or metal lids, c1900–30.
£7–22 each *VB*

A collection of glove buttonhooks, with various metals and semi-precious stone handles, c1900.
£12–28 each *VB*

A motorist's travelling grooming case, by Sirrain Ltd., 1950s.
£60–80 *MCh*

A lady's travelling vanity case, with silver and enamelled brushes, comb and mirror.
£300–400 *MCh*

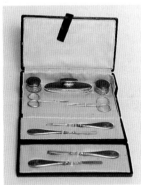

An 18ct gold, blue porcelain and enamelled lady's manicure set, 1923.
£450–550 *MCh*

A beaded bag, the gilt frame with enamel and stones, 11in (28cm).
£130–180 *JPr*

An Austrian petit point purse, c1920, 6in (15cm) square.
£40–50 *JPr*

A beaded bag, with a silver plated frame, c1840, 8in (20cm) long.
£70–90 *JPr*

A beaded purse, with scrollwork silver frame, 9in (23cm) long.
£120–150 *JPr*

A beaded drawstring purse, c1880, 7in (17.5cm) long.
£30–40 *JPr*

A beaded bag, slight damage, late 18thC, 7in (17.5cm) long.
£150–190 *JPr*

A beaded tobacco pouch, lined with kid leather, c1850–70, 7in (17.5cm) long.
£50–60 *JPr*

r. A silver framed beaded purse, c1800, 4in (10cm) long.
£25–35 *JPr*

A French beaded framed purse, c1800–20, 5½in (14cm) long.
£50–60 *JPr*

A silver and gold coloured metal evening bag, c1930, 8in (20cm) long.
£20–30 *JPr*

A Victorian beaded purse, 8½in (21.5cm) long.
£50–85 *TOM*

Simon & Halbig

A Simon & Halbig child doll, with a box containing her trousseau and a lamb, impressed 'DEP 0', c1890, 10in (25cm) high.
£700–800 CSK

A Simon & Halbig rigid limbed doll, all original, marked 'DEP', c1890, 7in (17.5cm) high.
£225–275 CK

A Simon & Halbig jointed doll, in original shift, c1890, 8in (20cm) high.
£225–250 CK

A Simon & Halbig jointed doll, with original mohair wig, and contemporary clothes, marked 'No. 1079', c1890, 10½in (27cm) high.
£300–350 CK

A Simon & Halbig doll, fired black, original knotted wig, marked 'No. 1079', c1890, 25in (63.5cm) high.
£950–1,000 CK

A Simon & Halbig doll, marked 'No. DEP 1900', 9in (23cm) high.
£275–300 CK

l. A Simon & Halbig doll, marked 'DEP 1079', red Wimpern stamp, c1900, 17in (43cm).
£450–480 CK

Two Simon & Halbig dolls, marked 'DEP 1079', all original, c1900–10, 17in (43cm) high.
£450–500 each *CK*

A Simon & Halbig or Kestner bisque doll, with glass eyes, in modern clothes, c1910.
£175–200 *CK*

Two character 'Poppy' boy dolls, heads made by Simon & Halbig for Cuno & Otto Dressel, with closed mouths, stuffed cloth bodies and composition lower arms, and flocked mohair hair, all original, c1910, 14 and 13in (35.5 and 33cm) high.
£475–500 each *CK*

China

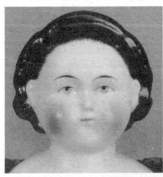

An early china-headed doll, with painted features, moulded black hair swept back into a bun, stuffed body with china limbs, painted pink garters and black flat boots, dressed in red woollen frock and underwear, hand damaged, c1840, 19in (48cm) high.
£800–900 *CSK*

A German china-headed doll, with cloth body, jet necklace, all original, unmarked, c1870, 16in (41cm) high.
£350–375 *CMF*

A china-headed doll, c1870.
£100–120 *PC*

A china-headed autoperipatetikos, with blue painted eyes and black moulded hair coiled round her head into a bow, in contemporary brown silk and lace dress, c1865, 10in (25cm).
£500–600 *CSK*

A china shoulder-headed doll, pink cheeks and stuffed body, c1880, 22in (55.5cm) high.
£220–300 *CSK*

A china-headed doll, with forehead curls, a moulded band and ringlets at the back of her head, stuffed body and china limbs, c1880, 16½in (42cm) high.
£375–425 *CSK*

A china dolls' house doll, with black hair, bisque lower arms and legs, in original clothes, c1880.
£50–60 *CK*

A German autoperipatetikos walking doll, with china shoulder head, painted features, moulded black hair, leather arms, in original blue silk dress with lace edging over conical cardboard skirt containing key-wind mechanism causing the metal boots to walk, damaged, 19thC, 10in (25cm) high, with original cardboard box.
£800–1,000 *S(S)*

Composition Dolls

A composition Scootles doll, with blue painted eyes, moulded curls, original blue printed shorts and jacket and white shoes, with swing ticket reading 'Scootles Rose O'Neill a Cameo Doll', c1925, 13½in (34.5cm) high.
£250–350 *CSK*

A Cuno & Otto Dressel doll, with cloth body and composition head, arms and legs, in original silk dress, and yellow high-heeled shoes, c1900, 14in (35.5cm) high.
£250–280 *CK*

A German jointed doll, with rigid limbs, dressed in original regional outfit, 1920–30, 5in (12.5cm) high.
£15–20 *CK*

Fabric Dolls

A rag doll, with embroidered eyes, painted nose and mouth, c1920, 15in (38cm) high.
£18–22 *WAG*

A Chad Valley moulded felt-headed doll, designed by Mabel Lucie Attwell, with brown side glancing eyes, brown mohair wig and stuffed velvet body, dressed in original orange cotton romper suit and felt shoes, marked with Chad Valley button under its arm, with swing ticket, 1930s, 16½in (42cm) high, in original box.
£680–800 *CSK*

A stockinette doll, dressed as a fairy, c1930, 10in (25cm) high.
£40–45 *CK*

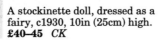

Miller's is a price GUIDE not a price LIST

A Norah Wellings felt doll, in original outfit, mohair wig, marked on wrist, 1930s, 23in (58.5cm).
£150–165 *CK*

A 'mammy' rag doll, 1920s–30s, 23in (59cm) high.
£50–55 *LF*

Papier Mâché

A papier mâché-headed doll in original clothes, with moulded ringlets, stuffed body, wooden limbs, and pink cotton dress with pantalettes and net over-skirt, c1837, 11½in (29cm) high.
£480–580 *CSK*

Three papier mâché ventriloquist's dummies:
top. Modelled as a parson, with eye and mouth movement, dressed in black wool suit and dog collar, 33in (84cm) high.
£250–300
left. Dressed as a boy in a tweed suit, with jaw movement, 32in (81.5cm) high. **£150–200**
bottom. A doll with a moulded bonnet, 17in (43cm) high.
£150–200 *CSK*

Plastic & Celluloid

Doll dealer Maureen Anne Stanford told Miller's that hard plastic dolls have become increasingly collectable due to rising prices in the doll market and the effects of recession. Look out for 1950s dolls which are growing ever more popular.

A hard plastic Pedigree doll, 'Elizabeth', in original dress, 1950s, 18in (46cm) high.
£50–60 *CMF*

A Pedigree hard plastic walking doll, with original dress, 1950s, 28in (71cm).
£125–150 *CMF*

A Pedigree 'Flirty-Eye' black walking doll, slight damage, 1950s, 22in (56cm) high.
£85–95 *CMF*

A Pedigree black toddler doll, 1950s.
£100–115 *CMF*

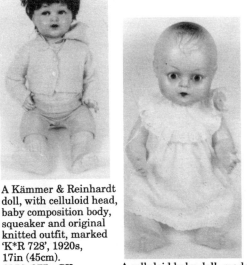

A Kämmer & Reinhardt doll, with celluloid head, baby composition body, squeaker and original knitted outfit, marked 'K*R 728', 1920s, 17in (45cm).
£250–275 *CK*

A celluloid baby doll, made in Hong Kong, 1950s, 18in (46cm) high.
£30–35 *CMF*

Stiffened Mask

A Dean's mascot doll, with cloth body, c1938, 41in (104cm) high.
£150–185 *CK*

A Dean's doll, with a cloth body, and rayon hair, c1940, 18in (46cm) high.
£100–120 *CK*

A Pierotti poured wax doll, wearing contemporary outfit, c1880, 16½in (42cm) high.
£450–500 *CK*

Wax Dolls

A shoulder-headed girl doll with blonde hair ringlets, fixed blue glass eyes, fabric limbs, wearing a crinoline skirted lace frock with sequins, and floral headdress, 19thC, 23in (58.5cm) high, in a mahogany framed glazed display cabinet.
£450–550 *AH*

A wax over composition doll, all original, c1915, 8½in (21cm) high.
£250–275 *CMF*

A pair of wooden figures, probably foreign gifts, 1970s, 16in (40.5cm) high.
£10–12 each *LF*

Wooden Dolls

A Russian Babushka wooden doll, c1950.
£10–12 *CMF*

Puppets

Boxes greatly enhance the value of all toys, especially puppets, and can also provide a helpful guide to dating an item. The box accompanying the Pelham witch is typical of the 1940s, made from brown cardboard with a blue front. A closed yellow box was used in the 1950s and 60s (see Colour Review), and a yellow box with a cellophane window in the 1960s and 70s. Boxes illustrated with Disney characters can be collectable in their own right.

A Pelham puppet, 'Figaro', Pinocchio's cat, 1960s, unboxed.
£24–28 CMF

Cross Reference:
Soft Toys - Glove puppets

A Pelham puppet, 'Minstrel', 1970s, boxed.
£40–48 CMF

A Pelham puppet, 'The Witch', c1940, boxed.
£40–45 CMF

Dolls' Clothes

A doll's handmade white cotton lawn dress, 1860–70.
£40–45 CK

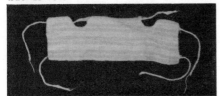

A doll's flannel pink and white striped corset, c1890.
£8–10 CK

A three-piece set of doll's clothes, with felt shoes, c1950.
£25–35 *CK*

A doll's handmade white cotton lawn dress, 1860–70.
£40–45 *CK*

A doll's floral cotton dress, with tape decoration, c1810.
£70–80 *CK*

A pair of doll's red leather Oriental sandals, c1910, 3½in (9cm) long.
£50–60 *CK*

A doll's white cotton corset, with brass eyelets, c1900, 4in (10cm) long.
£25–30 *CK*

A pair of doll's white cotton combinations, c1900, 12in (30.5cm) long.
£10–12 *CK*

Dolls' Accessories

A Victorian tortoiseshell brush and comb set, 2½in (7cm) long.
£40–45 *CK*

A French metal doll's cot, c1900, 6½in (16cm) long.
£30–40 *WAG*

Dolls' Houses

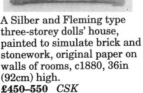

A Silber and Fleming type three-storey dolls' house, painted to simulate brick and stonework, original paper on walls of rooms, c1880, 36in (92cm) high.
£450–550 *CSK*

A mock Tudor 'Amersham' house, all original, c1930.
£550–600 *CK*

A two-storey dolls' house, painted to simulate brick front and slate roof, panelled front door, with four large rooms, c1860, 47in (119cm) high.
£550–700 *CSK*

A painted wooden butcher's shop, with carved and painted joints, three butchers, the upper storey with potted plants, windows with painted curtains, the hand written inscription reads 'This is an exact replica of a shop in South London in 1870, carved by C. Jones finished in 1878', 28 by 20in (71 by 51cm) in glazed case.
£3,750–4,500 *CSK*

Dolls' House Furniture

A Tri-ang dolls' house, 1950s.
£75–85 *CMF*

l. A grandfather clock, wireless set and hot water bottle, 1950s.
£5.50–8 each *CMF*

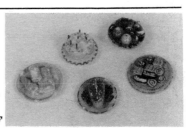

r. A selection of dolls' house food, 1950.
£1.50–10 each *CMF*

A Kleeware plastic baby on a swing, and a pram c1950.
£5.50–8.50 each *CMF*

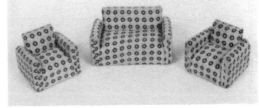

A three-piece dolls' house suite, 1950s.
£10–12 *CMF*

l. A plastic TV with hologram.
£3–3.50
r. A wooden TV, 1960s.
£10–12 *CMF*

A cream painted wooden kitchen set, 1950s.
£18–22 *CMF*

Miniatures

These jointed pewter miniatures, often collected by doll enthusiasts, are made in the Scottish Highlands by Hantel Ltd. Inspired by Victorian illustrations, these contemporary models have grown increasingly popular inspiring Hantel to found their own collectors' society.

A selection of hand painted jointed pewter miniature figures of characters from *Alice in Wonderland*, Hantel limited edition, 1990s, 1¼in (3cm) high.
£13–20 each *TMN*

A selection of miniature characters from *Alice in Wonderland,* by Thos. Chislett, 1990s.
£25–40 each *TMN*

A Hantel Punch and Judy theatre set, with hand painted jointed pewter miniature figures, 1990s, 1 to 2½in (3 to 6cm) high.
£9–15 each *TMN*

Three Wiener bronze miniatures of Beatrix Potter characters, 1990s, 1 to 1½in (3 to 4cm) high.
£50–70 each *TMN*

Four hand painted jointed pewter figures, made by Hantel for Society members only, 1990s.
£60–70 *TMN*

DRINKING

Corkscrews

Prominent among drinking collectables are corkscrews. The features necessary to make a corkscrew collectable include novelty, for example an unusual working mechanism, rarity, a maker's signature or an advertiser's name. Ivory or silver handled examples are likely to be more expensive than wooden models. Corkscrews dating from before the middle of the 18thC are extremely rare, and the first corkscrew patent was taken out in 1795. The Victorian age saw the development of an extensive variety of mechanical corkscrews, and many innovative designs have been produced in our own century.

A named Lund lever two-part cast steel cork drawer, with bronzed copper finish, c1870.
£30–50 *CS*

A Charles Hull 1869 patent Le Presto ratchet type corkscrew.
£400–500 *CS*

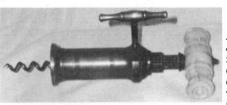

A bone handled King's screw type corkscrew, with brass barrel, 19thC.
£150–170 *HCH*

A brass Farrow & Jackson type wing nut mechanical corkscrew, with centre cut tapered worm, c1850.
£60–90 *CS*

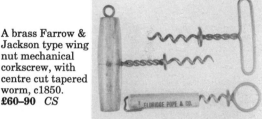

Cross Reference
Glass

l. A French cast steel Perrile side wind rack-and-pinion corkscrew, c1880.
£60–80
r. An English 'Wolfruna' Plants patent, c1884.
£20–40 *CS*

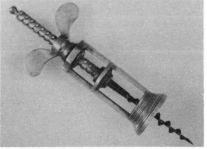

Three one-piece twisted wire corkscrews, American invention of 1875.
£10–15 each *CS*

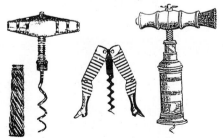

A Norwegian silver corkscrew, with double helix, early 20thC.
£150–200 *CS*

Decanters

A chrome and Bakelite decanter, in the form of a Mercedes radiator, c1950, 7½in (19cm) high.
£75–85 *PC*

> **Cross Reference:**
> Automobilia

A chrome and Bakelite decanter, in the form of a Jaguar radiator, c1950, 7½in (19cm) high.
£75–85 *PC*

Two brass figural corkscrews, depicting William Shakepeare and the three-legged crest of the Isle of Man, c1920–30.
£12–20 each *CS*

A chrome and Bakelite decanter, in the form of a Bentley radiator, c1950, 8in (20cm) high.
£125–150 *PC*

Flasks

A glass bottle, in a boxwood case, c1870, 9in (23cm) high.
£40–60 *DUN*

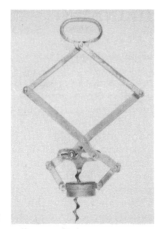

An all steel HD Armstrong 1902 patent concertina corkscrew, with bladed worm.
£25–40 *CS*

A chrome and Bakelite decanter, in the form of a Rolls-Royce radiator, c1950, 8in (20cm) high.
£125–150 *PC*

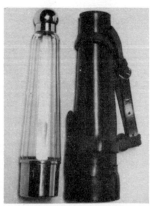

A glass and silver plated flask, in a leather case, c1920.
£70–100 *DUN*

Mugs and Tankards

A pair of engraved glass tankards, c1890.
£70–90 *DUN*

A glass beer mug, advertising Barclay's London Lager, c1930, 3½in (8.5cm) high.
£8–10 *AL*

A pewter tankard, with straight sides, plain glass base, inscribed 'Marjorie 1931', and another half pint hammered pewter tankard, 4½in (11.5cm) high.
£15–20 *LF*

Wine Related Antiques

A Verwood pottery Dorset owl bottle, early 19thC, 10in (25cm) high.
£120–140 *IW*

A pewter Customs & Excise measure, 1826, 5in (12.5cm).
£60–65 *PC*

A tyg, excavated in Burslem in 1937, rim ground down, 17thC, 4½in (11.5cm) high.
£60–80 *IW*

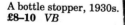

A bottle stopper, 1930s.
£8–10 *VB*

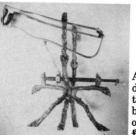

A silver plated port decanting cradle, in the form of vine branches and bunches of grapes, c1840.
£350–450 *CS*

EPHEMERA
Autographs
Entertainment

A signed photograph of Ursula
Andress, 1960s, 8 by 10in (20 by
25cm), excellent condition.
£20–30 *VS*

A signed photograph of
Josephine Baker, dated 1936,
3½ by 5½in (8.5 by 13.5cm).
£80–120 *VS*

A signed and inscribed
photograph of Errol Flynn,
very good condition, 8 by 10in
(20 by 25cm).
£400–500 *VS*

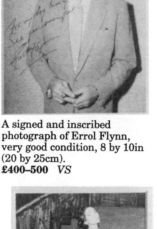

A signed and dated photograph
of Maria Callas, 3½ by 5½in
(8.5 by 13.5cm).
£200–300 *VS*

A signed reproduction
photograph of Lauren Bacall
and Humphrey Bogart, framed
and glazed, 1940s, 14 by 20in
(35 by 50.5cm).
£300–400 *VS*

A signed and inscribed concert
programme of Miles Davis, 1960
Tour of Great Britain, very
good condition.
£120–150 *VS*

A signed photograph of
Fred Astaire, 3½ by 5½in
(8.5 by 13.5cm).
£40–50 *VS*

A signed postcard of Will Hay,
very good condition.
£80–100 *VS*

A reproduction photograph of Audrey Hepburn, signed in later years, excellent condition, 8 by 10in (20 by 25cm).
£150–180 *VS*

A signed colour photograph of Arnold Schwarzenegger, from *Terminator*, excellent condition, 8 by 10in (20 by 25cm).
£80–100 *VS*

A signed photograph of Vivien Leigh, in costume as Scarlet O'Hara from *Gone with the Wind,* good condition.
£550–650 *VS*

A signed postcard of Laurence Olivier, in costume as Hotspur, excellent condition.
£60–100 *VS*

A signed photograph of River Phoenix, excellent condition, 8 by 10in (20 by 25cm).
£140–160 *VS*

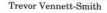

l. A signed photograph of Steven Spielberg, 8 by 10in (20 by 25cm).
£100–120 *VS*

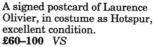

Political

A photograph of Nelson Mandela with signed card, dated 11th October 1993, excellent condition, 8 by 13in (20 by 33cm). **£140–180** *VS*

A colour photograph of the entrance to Number 10 Downing Street, signed by Lord Home, Harold Wilson, James Callaghan, Edward Heath, Margaret Thatcher and John Major, very good condition, 10 by 8in (25 by 20cm). **£200–250** *VS*

Sporting

Two signed photographs, 4½ by 5½in (11 by 14cm): *l.* Jack Hobbs. **£60–80** *r.* Tom Hayward. **£100–150** *VS*

A signed colour photograph of Brian Lara, 8½ by 12in (21 by 30.5cm). **£30–40** *VS*

A photograph and signed letter from James Corbett, picture 7½ by 12in (18.5 by 30.5cm). **£400–500** *VS*

A signed photograph of W. G. Grace, 3½ by 5½in (8.5 by 14cm). **£150–200** *VS*

A signed and inscribed colour photograph of Mohammed Ali, c1959, 8 by 10in (20 by 25cm). **£80–100** *VS*

A signed photograph of Helen Shapiro, Sugar Ray Robinson, and Terry Downes, 10 by 8in (25 by 20cm). **£80–120** *VS*

A signed and inscribed photograph of Jack Johnson, 3½ by 5½in (8.5 by 13.5cm). **£400–600** *VS*

Cigarette Cards

First produced in America in the 1880s, cigarette cards soon came over to England with the major British tobacco companies issuing high quality coloured lithographed sets to advertise their wares. Early cards from the 1880s to c1905 in good condition command the highest prices. Large numbers of cards were produced in the 1920s and '30s, enabling today's collectors to acquire sets at affordable prices. Cigarette cards are ever growing in popularity and tend to have maintained their values throughout the recession.

According to dealer Janet Wooster, certain subjects such as golf will always attract a premium, whereas others are comparatively unappreciated. Natural history sets, she suggests, are currently under-valued and could be a good area for consideration by collectors.

John Player & Sons, Animals of the Countryside, set of 50, c1939. **£11–22** *ACC*

John Player & Sons, Butterflies and Moths, set of 50, c1904. **£85–170** *ACC*

Animals & Wildlife

John Player & Sons, Aviary and Cage Birds, set of 50, c1933. **£38–76** *ACC*

John Player & Sons, Wild Animals' Heads, set of 50, c1931. **£24–48** *ACC*

l. John Player & Sons, Curious Beaks, set of 50, c1929. **£25–50** *ACC*

John Player & Sons, Doncella, British Mammals, set of 30, c1983. **£11–13** *ACC*

John Player & Sons, Doncella, British Butterflies, set of 32, c1984. **£8–10** *ACC*

John Player & Sons, Dogs, set
of 50, c1931.
£32–64 *ACC*

John Player & Sons, Dogs, set
of 20, c1926.
£42–84 *ACC*

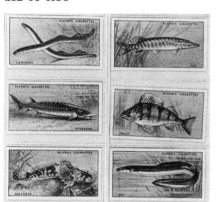

John Player & Sons, Freshwater
Fishes, set of 50, c1933.
£38–76 *ACC*

John Player & Sons,
Miniatures, set of 25, c1923.
£9–18 *ACC*

Beauties

Franklyn Davey, Beauties
(CERF), set of 12, c1905.
£650–1,300 *ACC*

John Player & Sons,
Famous Beauties,
set of 25, c1937.
£40–70 *ACC*

John Player & Sons, Bygone
Beauties, set of 25, c1914.
£30–60 *ACC*

A selection of South American
cards, with different
borders, c1900.
£3–5 each *ACC*
*These cards were produced by a
variety of companies, and were
often not catalogued.*

Cartoons & Caricatures

Carreras Ltd., Amusing
Tricks and How to do Them,
set of 50, c1937.
£24–40 *ACC*

Ardath Tobacco Co. Ltd., Figures
of Speech, set of 50, c1936.
£40–80 *ACC*

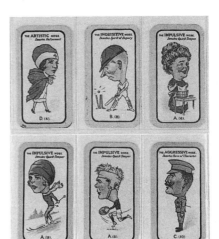

Carreras Ltd., The Nose Game,
set of 50, c1927.
£15–30 *ACC*

> **Miller's is a price GUIDE
> not a price LIST**

Film, Theatre & Music

W. D. & H. O. Wills, Cinema
Stars, set of 50, c1931.
£70–140 *ACC*

John Player & Son, Film Stars,
set of 50, c1938.
£32–64 *ACC*

Carreras Ltd., Film Stars,
set of 54, c1937.
£36–70 *ACC*

Godfrey Phillips, Actresses,
set of 50, c1916.
£180–210 *ACC*

W. D. & H. O. Wills, Musical
Celebrities, set of 50, c1911.
£110–250 *ACC*

John Player & Sons, Gilbert &
Sullivan, set of 50, c1925.
£50–100 *ACC*

Literature

Fine & Decorative Arts

Carreras Ltd., Old Staffordshire
Figures, set of 24, c1926.
£36–56 *ACC*

John Player & Sons, Characters
from Dickens, set of 50, c1923.
£70–140 *ACC*

W. D. & H. O. Wills,
British School of Painting,
set of 25, c1927.
£30–60 *ACC*

Carreras Ltd., Alice in
Wonderland, set of 48, c1930.
£55–110 *ACC*

Maritime

W. D. & H. O. Wills, Naval
Dress & Badges, set of 50, c1909.
£95–205 *ACC*

John Player & Sons, Ships'
Figureheads, set of 25, c1912.
£24–54 *ACC*

John Player & Sons, Life on
Board a Man of War in 1805
and 1905, set of 50, c1905.
£90–180 *ACC*

Military

John Player & Sons, Old
England's Defenders, series of
50, c1898.
£750–1,500 *ACC*

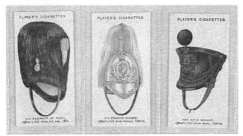

John Player & Sons, Military
Head-dress, set of 50, c1931.
£42–84 *ACC*

John Player & Sons, Army Life,
set of 25, c1910.
£36–72 *ACC*

Craven A, Military Uniforms, set of 50, c1976.
£3–5 *ACC*

Sporting

W. D. & H. O. Wills, British
Sporting Personalities, set of
48, c1927.
£30–60 *ACC*

Alexander Boguslavsky, Turf
Cigarettes, Sports Records, set
of 25, c1925.
£21–42 *ACC*

Stephen Mitchell & Son, Sports,
set of 25, c1907.
£275–550 *ACC*

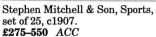

W. A. & A. C. Churchman,
Boxing Personalities, set
of 50, c1938.
£100–200 *ACC*

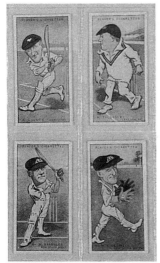

John Player & Sons,
Cricketers Caricatures by RIP,
set of 50, c1926.
£70–140 *ACC*

Godfrey Phillips, Famous
Cricketers, set of 32, c1926.
£125–135 *ACC*

FURTHER READING
*The Guide to Cigarette Card
Collecting, Current Values,*
Albert's (20th Edition), 1995.
*The Catalogue of British and
Foreign Cards;
Cigarette Card News and Trade
Card Chronicle;
Catalogue of Trade Card Issues,*
The London Cigarette Card Co.
Ltd., Somerton, Somerset.
Cigarette Card Values,
Murray Cards (International)
Ltd., 51 Watford Way, Hendon,
London NW4. 1994.

John Player & Son,
Cycling, set of 50, c1939.
£32–64 *ACC*

Godfrey Phillips, Footballers
(Pinnace), issued on a
continuous basis during 1924.
80p–£1.50 each *ACC*

John Player & Sons, Association
Cup Winners, set of 50, c1930.
£62–124 *ACC*

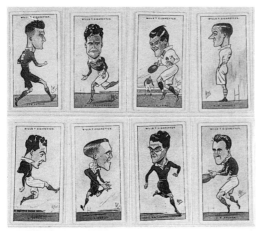

W. D. & H. O. Wills, Rugby
Internationals, set of 50, c1929.
£48–96 *ACC*

Franklyn Davey & Co.,
Hunting, set of 25, c1925.
£24–48 *ACC*

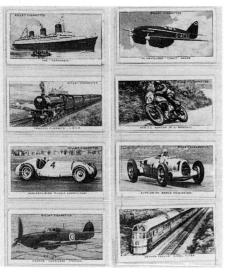

W. D. & H. O. Wills, Speed, set
of 50, c1938.
£12–24 *ACC*

W. A. & A. C. Churchman,
Kings of Speed, set of 50, c1939.
£30–60 *ACC*

John Player & Sons, Speedway
Riders, set of 50, c1937.
£58–116 *ACC*

John Player & Sons, Tennis, set
of 50, c1936.
£32–64 *ACC*

Miscellaneous

Carreras, Notable MPs, set of
50, c1929.
£35–70 *ACC*

John Player & Sons, Coronation
Series, set of 50, c1937.
£12–24 *ACC*

W. & F. Faulkner, Policemen of
the World, set of 12, c1899.
£360–720 *ACC*

W. D. & H. O. Wills, Railway
Engines, set of 50, c1936.
£40–80 *ACC*

African Tobacco
Manufacturers,
Cape Town, Houses
of Parliament,
set of 33, c1923.
£100–165 *ACC*

Trade Cards

As cigarette cards become harder to find and consequently more expensive, more dealers and collectors now specialise in trade cards, produced by companies such as Brooke Bond, Oxo and Texaco.

A & BC Gum trade cards, Batman, c1966.
75–85p each *ACC*

J. Bibby & Sons trade cards, Good Dogs, set of 25, c1955.
£40–45 *ACC*
For Tirex Club members.

> **Miller's is a price GUIDE not a price LIST**

Brooke Bond Tea trade cards, Tropical Birds, set of 50, c1961.
£3–4 *ACC*

Brooke Bond Tea trade cards, Freshwater Fish, set of 50, c1960.
£3–4 *ACC*

Brooke Bond Tea trade cards, Wild Flowers, set of 50, c1959.
£3–4 *ACC*

Whitbread trade cards, Maritime Inn Signs, set of 25, c1974.
£5–6 *ACC*

Comics

Comics have been growing increasingly in popularity and value and one collector recently spent a less than comical £80,000 on the first comic in which Batman appeared in 1939. Celebrity enthusiasts such as David Bowie, Bill Wyman and Jonathan Ross have served to raise the profile of comic collecting in Britain. It is a huge business in the United States, where first editions introducing such heroes as Batman and Superman can now fetch thousands of pounds. Although American publications are by far the most expensive, early examples of British comics such as the Eagle and Beano are rising in value.

Four *Beano* comics, Christmas 1947, No. 325, and New Year 1953, No. 546, **£8–10 each**
April 1st 1955, No. 663, and November 1st 1955, No. 695.
£6–8 each *NOS*

A selection of *Dandy* comics, 2d, c1955.
£8–10 each *NOS*

Dandy comic No. 295, June 23 1945, 2d, with Keyhole Kate on the cover instead of Korky the Cat.
£20–25 *NOS*

Batman, No.38, 6d, c1952.
£4–5 *NOS*

Master Comics, No. 83, published by L. Miller & Sons Ltd., a Fawcett Production reprint, c1946.
£8–10 *NOS*

San Diego Comiccon Comics, 1992, only available at Conventions, rare mask appearance.
£8–10 *NOS*

Strange Adventures, No. 180, c1965, featuring the first appearance of Animal Man.
£60–65 *NOS*

Super Thriller Comic, No. 27, c1953, 6d, one of only a few US sized comics.
£3–4 *NOS*

Mickey Mouse, Christmas Issue, December 15th, 1945.
£14–15 *NOS*

Rainbow, No. 1678, February 9th 1952.
£3–4 *NOS*

Master Comics, No. 49, a two-colour, 16 page comic, 1946.
£8–10 *NOS*

Darker Image, No. 1, with the first appearance of Maxx and Death Blow, limited foil edition, c1993.
£12–15 *NOS*

Whiz Comics, No. 65, 1950, 6d, an oversize reprint.
£4–5 *NOS*

The Young Marvelman, volume 2, No. 210, 1957, 6d, featuring updated 1940s character with name change.
£4–5 *NOS*

A WWII issue of *The Wizard,* No. 976, August 16th 1941, 2d.
£8–10 *NOS*

A Toys 'Я' Us limited edition *X-Men,* No. 1, 1993, not available at UK branches.
£6–8 *NOS*

Comic Characters

A Topps uncut card sheet.
£2–3 *NOS*

A Manga character uncut
card sheet.
75p–£1 *NOS*

A *Creators Universe* uncut
card sheet.
£1–2 *NOS*

The *Comic Book Price Guide for
Great Britain,* by Duncan
McAlpine, 1993/94 edition.
£9–10 *ALI*

Dark Dominion, an uncut
card sheet.
75p–£1 *NOS*

Two Warner uncut card sheets
for US store promotion.
75p–£1 *NOS*

Postcards

Vulgar humour is much-loved by the British, and has been celebrated in music hall, the Carry-On films and, of course, the comic postcard. The printer, James Bamforth has been the main producer of comic postcards in Britain throughout the 20thC, including all the following examples. The Holmforth-based firm introduced its first artist-drawn comic postcards in 1910, and by 1960 Bamforth's was the largest producer of 'saucy' postcards in the world. Arnold Taylor (employed 1926–87) was the company's most celebrated artist and his original naughty designs are now highly collectable.

Seven postcard designs, by Brian Fitzpatrick, pen, black ink and watercolour heightened with white, signed, 5½ by 8½in (14 by 21cm).
£200–250 *CSK*

Holmfirth Postcard Museum
47 Huddersfield Road
Holmfirth, West Yorks
HD7 1JH
Tel: 01484 682231

Seven postcard designs, by Brian Fitzpatrick and Arnold Taylor, pencil, pen, black ink and watercolour, signed, 6 by 9in (15 by 23cm).
£475–575 *CSK*

Five postcard designs, by Arnold Taylor and Brian Fitzpatrick, signed, pen, brown ink, watercolour and bodycolour, 6 by 9in (15 by 23cm).
£350–450 *CSK*

Nine postcard designs, by Arnold Taylor, signed, pencil, pen and brown ink heightened with white, 9 by 6in (23 by 15cm).
£475–575 *CSK*

MAKE THE MOST OF MILLERS

Price ranges in this book reflect what you should expect to *pay* for a similar example. When selling, however, you would expect to receive a lower figure. This will fluctuate according to a dealer's stock and saleability at a particular time. It is always advisable, when selling a collectable, to approach a reputable dealer or an auction house which has specialist sales.

A postcard design, by Arnold Taylor, pencil, pen and brown ink, watercolour and bodycolour, signed, 6 by 9in (15 by 23cm).
£150–200 *CSK*

Four postcard designs, by Arnold Taylor and Brian Fitzpatrick, signed, watercolour and bodycolour, 8½ by 5½in (21 by 14cm).
£750–900 *CSK*

Eight postcard designs, by Arnold Taylor, Brian Fitzpatrick and others, signed, pen, brown ink and watercolour heightened with white, 5½ by 8½in (14 by 21cm).
£300–400 *CSK*

Eight postcard designs, by Arnold Taylor and others, signed, pencil, pen, brown ink and watercolour, 6 by 9in (15 by 23cm).
£225–325 *CSK*

Six postcard designs, by Arnold Taylor, Charles Griggs and Brian Fitzpatrick, signed, pen, black ink and watercolour, 9 by 6in (23 by 15cm).
£225–325 *CSK*

Five postcard designs, by Arnold Taylor, signed, watercolour and bodycolour, 6 by 9in (15 by 23cm).
£425–525 *CSK*

Posters
Aviation 1920s–40s

Waddon Aerodrome, Change Cars at West Croydon, a colour poster on board, published by London Tramways, 1923, 25½ by 20in (65 by 51cm).
£150–200 *ONS*

Civil Air Display, Brooklands, 1930s, 30 by 20in (76 by 51cm).
£300–400 *ONS*

The Civil Air Display with Royal Air Force Assistance Saturday May 20th at Brooklands, 1930s, 30 by 20in (76 by 51cm).
£300–400 *ONS*

London to Paris Daily by Handley Page, mono photographic and letterpress, 1930s, 30 by 20in (76 by 51cm).
£600–800 *ONS*

A poster of a Lancaster bomber ready for take off, by Holmes, 1944.
£40–60 *ONS*

A poster by Walker, 'Trust your Instruments – Not your Senses', 1945.
£40–60 *ONS*

Rock & Pop Memorabilia

Beatles

Ringo inside The Fantasy Mansion, 'Yellow Submarine', 1968, gouache on full celluloid applied to a graphite, coloured pencil and watercolour background, 13 by 15½in (33 by 39cm), framed.
£800–1,000 *CSK*

An autographed note from John Lennon to his housekeeper, c1966, 4½in (11cm) diam., mounted with a machine-print portrait photograph, overall 11 by 9in 28 by 23cm), framed.
£450–650 *CSK*

A piece of paper signed in ink by all four Beatles, in common mount with a colour reproduction of the group dressed as Sgt. Pepper's Lonely Hearts Club Band, 1960s, overall 14½ by 11in (37 by 28cm), framed.
£850–1,000 *CSK*

A Dandie Fashions double-breasted jacket of black striped worsted with black satin lapels and pocket flaps, labelled, c1968.
£120–200 *CSK*

According to an employee of Dandie Fashions, John Lennon had an identical jacket to this.

A piece of paper signed in blue ink by each member of the Beatles, c1964, 3 by 4in (7.5 by 10cm), in common mount with a concert programme and ticket for Another Beatles Christmas Show, January 14th, 1965, an early Parlophone Records publicity postcard, and three newspaper cuttings, overall 12 by 16in (30.5 by 41cm), framed.
£675–800 *CSK*

A presentation gold disc, 'Let It Be', RIAA certified, strip plate format, presented to Cooper Distributors, 1960s, 17 by 13in (43 by 33cm), framed.
£500–700 *CSK*

> **Cross Reference**
> Record Covers

A concert ticket for The Beatles Show, 4th December, 1965, City Hall, Newcastle, signed on reverse by Paul McCartney, and a colour photograph, 15 by 8½in (38 by 21cm), framed.
£250–350 *CSK*

A film poster, 'Help', UA, 1965, British Quad, 30 by 40in (76 by 101.5cm), framed.
£200–300 *CSK*

A photograph, signed by all four Beatles, 1960s, 12 by 10in (30.5 by 25cm).
£600–800 *VS*

A Capitol Records 30th anniversary commemorative pack, comprising: a gold single, 'I Want to Hold Your Hand' 13 by 10in (33 by 25cm), a corresponding single and CD single, with modern reproductions of the original picture sleeve, and a red sweatshirt, the front with printed design incorporating a portrait of the Beatles, the back with the Capitol Records logo.
£600–800 *CSK*

A page from a souvenir concert programme, signed and inscribed in black biro by all four members of the group, creased and torn, c1963, 10 by 8in (25 by 20cm).
£900–1,100 *CSK*

A collection of fourteen unused concert and film première tickets and fan club letters, various concert venues, 1963–66.
£400–500 *CSK*

Miscellaneous

The Rolling Stones, an EP single cover 'Time Is On My Side', Decca, 1964, signed on the front in black biro by each member of the group, 7in (17.5cm) square, framed.
£350–450 *CSK*

A Beatles talcum powder tin, 1960s, 7½ by 4½in (19 by 11cm).
£80–120 *VS*

A piece of paper signed and inscribed in blue biro 'Jimi Hendrix EXP', in common mount with a black and white machine-print photograph, overall 11½ by 6½in (29 by 16cm).
£600–800 *CSK*

A presentation platinum single disc, Frankie Goes to Hollywood, 'Two Tribes', presented to Tony Pope, BPI certified, c1984, 14½ by 10½in (36 by 26cm), framed.
£350–450 *CSK*

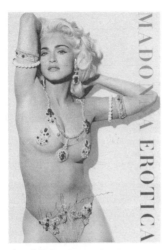

A black satin stage bra, labelled 'Dolce & Gabbana' and signed on the label 'Madonna', and a letter of authenticity from WEA records, 1990s.
£800–1,000 *CSK*

A publicity poster for the Madonna album 'Erotica', signed in black felt pen 'Love Madonna', 1990s, 38 by 26in (96.5 by 66cm), framed.
£550–750 *CSK*

Two metal funfair tokens, embossed 'I Love you Chan Signed Bird' and 'I Love Chan My Darling', both 1in (3cm) diam.
£600–700 *CSK*

Five signatures in an autograph book, including Jimi Hendrix, Noel Redding, Engelbert Humperdink and Cat Stevens, 1967.
£800–1,000 *CSK*

An Ibanez Silver Cadet steel string acoustic guitar, model No. SZW 300TS, the body signed in black felt pen by Simon and Garfunkel, c1970.
£650–750 *CSK*

Two shirts once owned by Mick Jagger, one labelled 'Silka, New York, London, Paris', the other labelled 'Mr Fish, 17 Clifford Street, London W1', with letters of authenticity.
£450–550 *CSK*

An early colour machine-print photograph of The Yardbirds, signed in different coloured inks by Eric Clapton, Keith Relf, Paul Samwell-Smith, Chris Dreja and Jim McCarty, 1960s, 9½ by 13½in (24 by 34cm), framed.
£500–600 *CSK*

A Remo Weather King drumskin, signed and inscribed 'To John Best Wishes Roger Taylor', 18½in (47cm) diam.
£275–350 *CSK*

An Ampex Golden Reel Award, for Roger Taylor, Duran Duran 'Seven and the Ragged Tiger', 1980s, 17 by 13in (43 by 33cm).
£175–225 *CSK*

FANS

Fans have been in use since the earliest times and the ancient civilisations of the East produced a wide range of personal fans. The Chinese were probably the first to use painted decoration on the leaf and during the 7th Century AD the Japanese invented the folding fan. In the 16thC, visiting merchants brought back these Oriental luxuries to the courts of Europe with fans becoming fashionable in the West, and continuing into the 1930s. Most fans on the market today date from the 18thC to the 20thC. Examples can be found in every style and material, ranging from early printed and painted examples, to Art Deco advertising fans and flapper's ostrich feathers, with prices varying accordingly.

A painted leaf fan, the carved ivory sticks pierced, chinoiserie decorated, mother-of-pearl guardsticks, repaired, c1740, 11in (28cm). **£400–500** *CSK*

A Brussels lace fan, the blonde sticks carved and pierced with putti, c1890, 13½in (34cm), in glazed fan-shaped case. **£850–1,000** *CSK*

Two Victorian fans, one with black watered silk effect paper leaves, the other with black lace mounted on white organza. **£15–25** *LF*

A mid-Victorian papier mâché face screen. **£75–125** *TOM*

Two Edwardian fans, one organza with black spines, decorated with silver sequins, the other a small black Oriental fan, 9½ and 7in (24 and 17.5cm). **£15–25** *LF*

An unmounted fan leaf, painted with a view of Naples from the west, with Vesuvius beyond and a carriage, monks and a gondola in the foreground, inscribed, c1770, 19½in (49cm), framed and glazed. **£1,600–2,000** *CSK*

The Fan Museum
12 Crooms Hill, Greenwich
London SE10 8ER
Telephone: 0181 858 7879

A coloured lithographed fan with mother-of-pearl spines and guards, mid-19thC, 10½in (26cm). **£75–125** *LF*

An Edwardian ostrich feather fan, with tied ends. **£50–100** *PC*

A silk leaf fan, painted with birds, applied with featherwork and flowers decorated with straw-work, with steel plinths and spangles, the ivory sticks pierced and silvered, c1780, 10½in (26cm).
£300–500 *CSK*

A Victorian painted georgette fan, 24in (61cm) wide.
£15–25 *PC*

Five Oriental paper fans, painted on rice paper, 20thC, 12in (30.5cm).
£20–40 *LF*

A Victorian eagle's feather and tortoiseshell fan.
£35–45 *VB*

A Victorian printed leaf fan, with open work gilt painted spines and another with party scene and musicians in a garden setting, some damage, 9½in (24cm).
£60–100 *LF*

A Victorian spangled gauze leaf fan.
£50–60 *VB*

A fawn ostrich feather fan, 20thC.
£10–20 *LF*

Electric Fans

A Limit fan, 1950s, 21in (53cm) high.
£40–50 *JUN*

An early electric fan, made by Chicago Electric Manufacturing Co., c1925, 12in (30.5cm) high.
£70–80 *BKK*

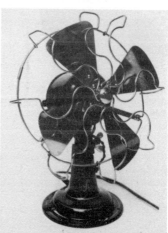

A brass electric fan, c1930, 14in (36cm) high.
£70–100 *DUN*

GLASS

The market for glass is a steady one, underpinned by faithful collectors, and has remained constant even throughout the recession. Glass from the 18thC onwards is still relatively easy to find, and this year we include a large section of early drinking glasses. Value depends on the rarity of the decoration, as well as the shape of the bowl, stem and foot. Colourful glass of the 19thC is becoming increasingly popular with collectors and is also well-illustrated in this section as well as our Colour Review.

A pair of glass salts, marked 'Varnish & Co.', c1850, 3in (7.5cm) high.
£120–140 *ARE*

A cut glass goblet, depicting footballers in action, c1920, 10in (25.5cm) high.
£400–800 *MSh*

A Victorian moulded glass chicken crock, c1890, 9in (23cm) high.
£70–90 *DUN*

A large blue witches' ball, 19thC, 16¼in (41cm) diam.
£200–250 *LF*

Animals

A Wedgwood glass elephant, marked, c1970, 4in (10cm) high.
£20–30 *SWB*

A Maltese glass sea horse, engraved 'Mdina', c1960, 6in (15cm) high.
£10–12 *SWB*

A Wedgwood glass owl, marked, c1970, 4½in (11cm) high.
£18–25 *SWB*

A Wedgwood glass frog, marked, c1970, 4in (10cm) high.
£20–30 *SWB*

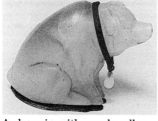

A glass pig, with ormolu collar and base, 19thC, 1½in (4cm) high.
£150–180 *DUN*

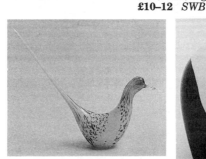

A Wedgwood glass long-tailed bird, Portland vase acid-etched mark, c1970, 9in (23cm) high.
£25–35 *SWB*

A Wedgwood glass panda, marked, c1970, 3in (7.5cm) high.
£25–35 *SWB*

Art Deco

Glass was one of the most distinctive products of the Art Deco period. While pieces by famous factories and designers such as Orrefors and René Lalique command high prices, much of the mass-produced ware from the 1920s and '30s remains comparatively inexpensive. Typically these decorative domestic wares are made from pressed glass, often frosted, using muted colours (i.e. pink, blue and green) and amber. Works are geometrical in style and favourite motifs include nudes, fish and generalised aquatic forms.

A pressed glass figure of a young girl in a pink bowl, on a plinth, made by International Bottle Co. Ltd., c1928, 13in (33cm) diam.
£55–65 *BKK*

A green pressed glass lamp in the form of a shell, with a young girl standing with angel fish, aquatic decoration to base, c1930, 8½in (21cm) high.
£120–150 *BKK*

A Lalique frosted glass sparrow, acid etched 'R. Lalique', c1935, 2in (5cm) high.
£200–250 *BKK*

A Czechoslovakian amber pressed glass fish, in a large shallow bowl, c1933, 13in (33cm) diam.
£50–60 *BKK*

An Art Deco pressed blue glass biscuit barrel and cover, c1930, 8in (20cm) high.
£12–16 *BKK*

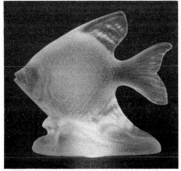

A Verlys opalescent glass angel fish, signed 'Verlys France', c1920, 4⅓in (11cm) high.
£250–300 *BKK*

A pair of Bagleys amber satin glass bamboo vases, c1935, 4in (10cm) high.
£18–20 *BKK*

A pressed glass bowl, with etched decoration, with figure of a young boy holding a fawn, on a plinth, made by International Bottle Co. Ltd., c1928, 12½in (32cm) diam.
£35–45 *BKK*

A Bagleys glass figure of Andromeda, with original blue panel bowl and plinth, c1930, 12in (30.5cm) diam.
£50–60 *BKK*

A Bagleys amber glass dressing table set, c1933.
£40–45 *BKK*

A Jobling amber glass vase, with butterfly design on base, 1930s, 9in (23cm) high.
£40–45 *HEW*

A Bagleys pink pressed glass part dressing table set, c1932.
£40–50 *BKK*

Bottles

l. A green glass sauce bottle, with gilt label inscribed 'Ketchup', gilt lozenge stopper, c1800, 3½in (9cm) high.
£180–210
r. A blue glass sauce bottle, with pouring lip and cut ball stopper, silver label inscribed 'Cayenne', c1800, 3½in (9cm) high.
£200–240 *Som*

Three blue spirit bottles, with bevelled lozenge stoppers, c1790, 7in (18cm) high.
£150–200 each *Som*

Bowls

l. An amber wrythen moulded spirit bottle, with annulated collar to neck, c1860, 11in (28.5cm) high.
r. A plain blue spirit bottle, c1840, 11½in (29.5cm) high.
£200–220 each *Som*

A pair of Bristol green glass bottles, the silver mounted neck with vine embossed decoration, 19thC, 13in (33cm) high.
£160–200 *LF*

A cut glass sweetmeat, the ogee bowl diamond cut with scalloped rim, facet cut stem with centre knop, scalloped cut foot, c1780, 6½in (16 cm) high.
£350–400 *Som*

A glass bowl, c1870, 5in (12.5cm) diam.
£40–45 *DUN*

Cross Reference:
Mirrors
Paperweights
Scent Bottles

Butter & Cheese Dishes

An Irish cut glass butter dish and cover, with band of husk decoraton and flute cutting, cut ball finial, c1810, 5in (13cm) high.
£120–150 *Som*

An Irish glass butter dish and cover, with moulded and flute cut body, the domed lid with mushroom finial, 1820, 7½in (18.5cm) high.
£550–600 *Som*

A pressed glass cheese dish and cover, c1900, 6½in (16in) high.
£20–25 *AL*

A glass butter dish and cover, c1900, 7in (17.5cm) high.
£20–25 *AL*

A pair of Czechoslovakian carnival glass candlesticks, with insect decoration to base, c1930, 8½in (21cm) high.
£60–70 *BKK*

Candlesticks

A pair of cut glass candlesticks, c1880, 12in (30.5cm) high.
£250–300 *DUN*

An opaque white candlestick, with tall, waisted and collared stem, lipped socket, on a domed foot, Bristol or south Staffordshire, c1770, 10in (25cm) high.
£400–500 *Som*

A pair of moulded glass candlesticks, c1920, 9in (23cm) high.
£70–90 *DUN*

A blue glass faceted taper stick, the fluted nozzle with fluted angles supported on a stem cut with diamond facets and terminating in a basal knop above a domed foot with geometric cutting, c1790.
£400–500 *Som*

Cranberry Glass

Cranberry glass derives its name from the United States. This transparent, reddish pink glass was produced in America and in Britain (notably at Stourbridge) from the mid-19thC. Early pieces were comparatively simple in style but later wares were often decorated with trailing, enamelling or overlay, in which the outer layer of glass is cut through to reveal the colour beneath.

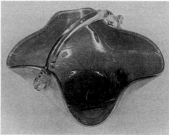

A cranberry opalescent glass basket, c1880, 4in (10cm) wide.
£100–115 *AMH*

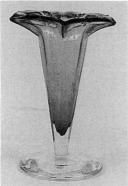

A cranberry glass vase, c1880, 5½in (13cm) high.
£75–80 *AMH*

A pair of Victorian cranberry épergne vases, c1880, 8in (20cm) high.
£140–160 *DUN*

A cranberry glass dish, c1880, 6in (15cm) diam.
£100–110 *AMH*

A cranberry heart-shaped glass dish, c1880, 8in (20cm) wide.
£140–150 *AMH*

Decanters

Two cut spirit decanters, c1820, 7½in (18cm) high.
£100–125 each *Som*

l. A tapered spirit decanter, engraved with a band of looped shamrocks and stars, lozenge stopper, c1800, 8½in (21cm) high.
£150–200
r. A spirit decanter with flute cross cut diamonds and three cut neck rings, cut mushroom stopper, c1825, 7in (19cm) high.
£125–180 *Som*

A French blue glass liqueur decanter set, 19thC, 12in (30.5cm) high.
£250–300 *WAG*

l. & r. A pair of Prussian-shaped decanters, with flute cut bases and shoulders, cut mushroom stoppers, c1810, 8½in (21.5cm) high.
£500–550
c. A flute cut spirit decanter, with target stopper, c1810, 7½in (18cm) high.
£100–125 *Som*

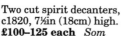

A cut glass port decanter,
c1830, 14in (35.5cm) high.
£140–165 *CS*

An Arts & Crafts pinched
decanter, with silver mount
bearing a family crest
and cut glass stopper,
9½in (24cm) high.
£80–100 *LF*

A toddy lifter, with
diamond and prism
cut body, flute cut
stem and diamond
cut neck ring, c1810,
6in (15cm) high.
£250–300 *Som*

l. An Irish glass decanter,
with diamond cut arched
panels enclosing cut stars,
flute cut base and shoulder,
three annulated neck rings
and mushroom stopper,
c1810, 8in (20cm) high.
£200–220
r. A cylindrical decanter
with broad flute cutting,
one cut neck ring and
mushroom stopper,
c1830, 8½in (21cm) high.
£50–80 *Som*

Two large green glass
decanters, with stoppers,
and a slender decanter
with cut decoration,
19thC, 13½in (34cm) high.
£70–100 *LF*

Drinking Glasses

A set of three wine
glasses, the trumpet
bowls with fruiting
vine engraving, on
stems with double
knopped multiple
spiral air-twists,
domed conical feet,
c1745, 7in (17cm).
£380–400 each *Som*

Three bonnet glasses, on plain
conical feet, c1750, 3in (7cm) high.
£50–60 each *Som*

A Masonic firing glass, with double series opaque twist stem, c1760, 4in (10cm) high.
£280–320 *Som*

Three opaque twist wine glasses, c1760, 5½in (14cm) high.
£260–280 each *Som*

A balustroid wine glass, the bell bowl on a stem with basal ball knop, folded conical foot, c1740, 6½in (16cm) high.
£300–350 *Som*

l. & r. A pair of ovoid rummers, c1810, 5in (12cm) high.
£200–225
c. A rummer, with curtain and star looped engraving, c1810, 4in (10cm) high.
£100–120 *Som*

A Masonic dram firing glass, inscribed 'Lodge of Harmony, No. 559', c1780, 3½in (9cm) high.
£300–350 *Som*

Two rummers, engraved with bands of stiff leaves and tied ribbons. c1810, 5½in (14cm) high.
£80–100 each *Som*

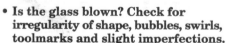

A set of eleven port glasses, c1820, 3½in (9cm) high.
£600–650 *Som*

r. A jelly glass, with hexagonal bowl and plain domed foot, c1760, 4in (10cm) high.
£100–150 *Som*

- Is the glass blown? Check for irregularity of shape, bubbles, swirls, toolmarks and slight imperfections.
- Is it lead glass? The object should feel heavy and emit a clear ring when tapped gently with a fingernail – be careful!
- Does the glass have a slight green-greyish tinge? Old glass tends to be darker and more varied in tone than modern glass.
- Are there any chips or damage? Chips to the rim or foot can be ground down leaving an angular rather than a rounded edge.

A goblet, with double series opaque white twist stem and plain conical foot, c1760, 5½in (14.5cm) high.
£400–450 *Som*

A pair of ale glasses, with diamond facet cut stems, c1780, 7in (17.5cm) high.
£300–350 *Som*

l. & r. A pair of rummers,
with petal moulded bowls
and engraved floral decoration,
c1810, 4½in (11cm) high.
£180–200
c. A rummer, with petal
moulded bowl and engraved
decoration, c1810, 4in (10cm).
£50–90 *Som*

A wine glass, with bell
bowl, on a multiple air-twist
stem and plain conical foot,
c1750, 6½in (16.5cm) high.
£250–300 *Som*

Three rummers, with petal
moulded ovoid bowls, on drawn
stems and plain feet, c1810,
5in (12cm) high.
£110–135 each *Som*

Three Masonic engraved drinking
glasses, c1810, 4½ to 7in (12 to
18cm) high.
£400–500 each *Som*

A pair of flutes, with bladed
knop stems, c1820,
6in (15cm) high.
£50–70 *Som*

Two bucket bowl rummers, with
engraved initials, c1825, 5½in
(13cm) high.
£150–200 each *Som*

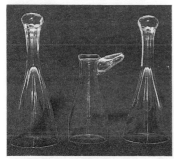

l. Two stirrup cups, the conical
bowls with flute cutting, on
short drawn ball end stems,
c1820, 5½in (13.5cm) high, and
a boot stirrup cup.
£120–140 each *Som*

A pair of heavy rummers,
with flute cut bucket bowls,
on knopped stems and plain
feet, c1830, 6in (15cm) high.
£100–150 *Som*

A pair of rummers, with lemon
squeezer feet, c1810, 7½in
(18cm) high.
£150–200 *Som*

A set of five
liqueur glasses,
c1840, 3in
(7.5cm) high.
£120–140 *Som*

A set of seven
wine glasses,
c1825, 4in
(10cm) high.
£250–300 *Som*

A pair of flutes, with trumpet bowls, flute cut knopped stems and plain feet, c1850, 6½in (16.5cm) high.
£100–150 *Som*

A matched set of 6 hock glasses, two green overlaid and slice cut, two ruby and two blue, 19thC, 8in (20cm) high.
£65–85 *LF*

A pair of rummers, with bucket bowls and bladed knopped stems, on plain feet, c1830, 5½in (13.5cm) high.
£80–100 *Som*

A set of six flute cut wine glasses, c1830, 5½in (13cm) high.
£150–180 *Som*

A set of six Bristol blue glass goblets, c1800, 5½in (14cm) high.
£60–80 *LF*

A pair of early rummers, c1830, 5in (12.5cm) high.
£50–70 *DUN*

l. Four rummers, with double ogee bowls, capstan stems and plain conical feet, c1825, 5in (13cm) high.
£65–75 each *Som*

A set of five wine glasses, with trumpet bowls and plain feet, c1840, 4½in (12cm) high.
£100–150 *Som*

l. A set of four jelly glasses, c1830, 4½in (11cm) high.
£120–140
r. Two wine glasses, with ball knopped stems, c1830, 5in (12.5cm) high.
£60–80 *Som*

A set of eight wine glasses, with prism cut bowls, on short knopped stems, c1830.
£300–320 *Som*

Jars

A glass jar and cover,
c1860, 16in (41cm) high.
£75–95 *DUN*

Two glass jars with covers,
c1820, largest 11in (28cm) high.
£50–90 each *DUN*

A large glass jar and cover,
c1870, 28in (71cm) high.
£450–550 *DUN*

Jugs

A cream jug, the baluster body
with flute and relief diamond
cutting, heavy cogwheel foot,
c1810, 5in (13cm) high.
£250–300 *Som*

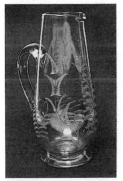

A Victorian glass ewer,
engraved with ferns,
c1870, 9½in (24cm) high.
£75–95 *DUN*

An amethyst cream jug and
sugar basin, inscribed in gold
enamel, c1800, jug 4½in
(11cm) high.
£600–700 *Som*

A glass water jug, with looped
diamond cut panels and stars
beneath a band of leaves,
scalloped rim and flute cut base,
c1825, 6in (15cm) high.
£150–200 *Som*

A Bristol blue jug and bowl,
19thC, jug 9in (23cm) high.
£70–100 *LF*

A glass water jug, c1910,
5in (12.5cm) high.
£35–45 *DUN*

A cream jug, with cut
strawberry diamonds, prism cut
bands, notched rim and star cut
base, c1815, 4in (10cm) high.
£300–350 *Som*

Three blue cream jugs:
l. Faintly wrythen moulded,
c1780, 4in (10cm) high.
£200–250
c. Plain body, c1860,
4in (10cm) high.
£100–150
r. Pear shaped body, c1800,
4½in (11.5cm) high.
£100–150 *Som*

Three blue cream jugs, c1780, 3½in (9cm) high.
£250–350 each *Som*

Three blue cream jugs,
c1800, 4½ to 5in
(11 to 13cm) high.
£200–250 each *Som*

l. An opaque white cream jug,
c1810, 5in (13cm) high.
£100–150
r. An opaque white sugar basin,
with opalescent glow, c1820,
3in (7.5cm) high.
£30–40 *Som*

Mugs

An Irish mug, with a band of
small cut diamonds below rim
and base flute cutting, engraved,
c1800, 3½in (9cm) high.
£150–200 *Som*

A pressed glass mug, by
H. Greener, with a portrait of
oarsman Edward Hanlon
seated in his boat, 1880, 4in
(10cm) high.
£100–200 *Som*

Vases

A clear glass vase, c1880,
6½in (16cm) high.
£70–90 *DUN*

An amethyst glass bucket vase,
c1890, 9½in (24cm) high.
£70–90 *DUN*

A pressed glass posy vase,
19thC, 3½in (9cm) high.
£25–30 *DUN*

A pair of 19thC vaseline posy vases.
£55–65 *DUN*

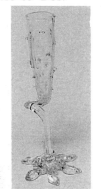

A clear glass vase,
c1890, 11in (28cm).
£100–120 *DUN*

A clear glass vase, c1900,
10in (25cm) high.
£70–90 *DUN*

A vaseline glass vase,
5in (12.5cm) high.
£65–75 *DUN*

A stag's horn vaseline
glass, c1890, 8in
(20cm) high.
£35–45 *DUN*

A vaseline glass vase,
c1880, 8in (20cm) high.
£100–120 *DUN*

A large clear glass
waisted vase, c1890,
18in (46cm) high.
£120–150 *DUN*

A Powell glass vase,
c1900, 12in (30.5cm).
£60–70 *DUN*

A large clear glass waisted
vase, c1900, 16in (41cm) high.
£150–200 *DUN*

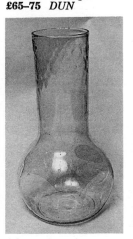

l. A WMF metal
mounted glass vase,
c1900, 7in (17.5cm).
£75–95 *DUN*

A large clear glass vase,
c1890, 16in (41cm) high.
£150–170 *DUN*

A 19thC hyacinth
vase, 7½in (19cm).
£35–45 *DUN*

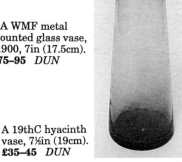

A red glass vase, with hand painted gilded decoration, c1925, 6½in (16cm) high.
£40–50 *FMN*

A large heavy blue overlaid cut glass gladioli vase, 20thC, 11in (28cm) high.
£50–70 *LF*

A blue glass hyacinth vase, c1920, 6in (15cm) high.
£25–35 *DUN*

A Malcolm Sutcliffe glass vase with dolphins, 20thC, 8in (20cm) high.
£100–130 *DUN*

A glass lily vase, c1910, 36in (92cm) high.
£70–100 *DUN*

MAKE THE MOST OF MILLERS

Price ranges in this book reflect what you should expect to *pay* for a similar example. When selling, however, you would expect to receive a lower figure. This will fluctuate according to a dealer's stock and saleability at a particular time. It is always advisable, when selling a collectable, to approach a reputable dealer or an auction house which has specialist sales.

Celery Vases

Three pressed glass celery vases, c1910, 6 to 8in (15 to 20cm) high.
£10–12 each *AL*

A Victorian cut and etched celery vase, c1890, 9½in (24cm) high.
£60–70 *DUN*

A glass celery vase, c1900, 9½in (24cm) high.
£40–50 *DUN*

Three glass celery vases, c1890, 7 to 8½in ((17.5 to 20cm) high.
£14–18 each *AL*

GRAMOPHONES

Demand for gramophones extends beyond the specialist collectors' market, so it is not only rarity that counts but also visual appeal. An original design is important and gramophones must be in working order. Among the most collectable examples are early horn gramophones, particularly those with wooden horns. Beware of fakes and watch out for 'assembled' gramophones, cobbled together from parts old and new.

A Columbia Model 112A picnic/portable gramophone, finished in green, c1930.
£75–95 *HOL*

l. An Edison Standard Model F phonograph, with Edison No. 10 Cygnet horn, two and four minute gearing, Model S reproducer, c1912.
£800–1,250 *BTA*

A Pathe coin-op 'Hill 'n' Dale', c1912, 38in (96.5cm) high.
£1,500–1,850 *HOL*

These were made for French cafés – an early form of jukebox.

r. An HMV 104 gramophone, c1932, 17½ by 13½in (44.5 by 34cm).
£80–150 *OTA*

An HMV gramophone, with oak case, original brass horn, concert soundbox and record clamp, c1898.
£1,750–2,250
A plaster and papier mâché advertising model of Nipper, the HMV trademark dog, from Hindleys gramophone shop and manufacturer, Clumber Street, Nottingham, c1920.
£600–700 *BTA*

A Columbia Model Q gramophone, c1898, 6 by 10in (15 by 25cm).
£200–250 *OTA*

A Melosonic circular cabinet gramophone, 1920s, 37in (94cm) high.
£300–350 *OTA*

An HMV 101 portable gramophone, finished in red, with No. 4 soundbox, c1920.
£75–100 *HOL*

An HMV Model 163 re-entrant tone chamber gramophone, c1930.
£400–500 *OTA*

This is the smallest of three re-entrant models,
193/194 £1,500–2,000
202/203 £7,000–8,000

A Columbia dictaphone cylinder shaver, in oak case, c1915.
£185–225 *BTA*

These machines were used for erasing phonograph cylinders which enabled them to be used for re-recording.

A Continental gramophone, with 60in (152cm) copper horn, c1910.
£850–950 *BTA*

A Decca 33 portable gramophone, 1920s, 13 by 10in (33 by 25cm).
£75–100 *OTA*

A Celebrity console gramophone, semi-circular shape, 1920s, 34in (86cm) wide.
£200–235 *HOL*

A BTH C2 loudspeaker horn, c1930, 22in (56cm) high.
£40–70 *OTA*

An Edison Fireside phonograph, complete with original horn, c1907.
£750–850 *HOL*

This phonograph plays both two and four minute cylinders.

A portable gramophone, c1965, 8½in (21cm) long.
£40–50 *HEG*

An HMV 101 portable gramophone, c1930, 16½ by 11½in (42 by 29cm).
£50–100 *OTA*

MAKE THE MOST OF MILLERS

Condition is absolutely vital when assessing the value of any item. Damaged pieces appreciate much less than perfect examples. However, a rare, desirable piece may command a high price even when damaged.

HAIR ACCESSORIES

A U-Phone small console gramophone, made by Leeds, with replacement tone arm and soundbox, 1930s.
£150–190 *HOL*

A Columbia Model 109 picnic/ portable gramophone, finished in black, c1930.
£50–65 *HOL*

An Art Nouveau tortoiseshell comb, with applied blister pearl and stylised foliate decoration.
£100–125 *CSK*

An Edwardian horn comb, 6in (15cm) long.
£18–25 *TOM*

An Edwardian tortoiseshell and diamanté hair comb, 5in (12.5cm) long.
£10–15 *TOM*

An Edwardian tortoiseshell and diamanté hair slide, 2½in (6cm) wide.
£10–15 *TOM*

An Edwardian mother-of-pearl hairpin, 3in (7.5cm) long.
£10–12 *TOM*

A black plastic three-prong comb, 4in (10cm) long.
£10–15 *TOM*

Hair Pieces

A Himalayan silver and turquoise hairpiece, mid-19thC, 2½in (6.5cm) long.
£65–110 *RAM*

A pair of Himalayan brass and turquoise hairpieces, or 'tsi-yu', worn in the hair or sometimes sewn on to a headdress, early 19thC, 1in (2.5cm) long.
£95–125 *RAM*

Three 22ct gold 19thC hairpieces, set with turquoise, 1 to 2in (2.5 to 5cm) long.
£350–550 each *RAM*

Hair Care

A gold plated on brass comb and case, c1910, 5in (12.5cm) wide.
£10–15 *FMN*

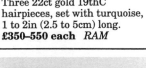

A Kaye's No. 1 Extra razor, with bone handle, in original case, 1920s.
£6–8 *JUN*

A floor standing mobile hair drier, 1930s, 67in (170cm) high.
£100–135 *JUN*

A Gotta gentleman's razor 1920–30s.
£6–8 *JUN*

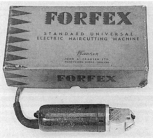

A pair of brushes in a leather case, c1900, 6in (15cm) wide.
£30–35 *DUN*

A Forfex Standard Universal Electric haircutting machine, in original box, 1950s.
£15–20 *JUN*

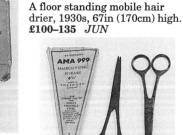

Two pairs of AMA 999 hair cutting shears, 1930s, 6½in (16cm) long, with original packet.
£6–8 each *JUN*

A set of Tantus 550 electric clippers, by John A. Fransen Ltd., 1930s, with original box.
£15–20 *JUN*

Two Vaseline Hair Cream barber's shop dispensers 1960s.
£30–35 each *JUN*

JEWELLERY

Amber

Amber is the fossilized resin from an extinct species of pine and the finest pieces come from the Baltic. Many legends surround its origin. According to various Greek myths, amber was the frozen tears of goddesses, broken bits of the sun, or drops of perspiration sweated by an overheated earth. The ancient Chinese believed amber to be the mineralised spirit of the tiger and as such symbolic of courage. Up until the early 20thC amber was used in medicinal preparations (ground and swallowed or burnt and inhaled). It was thought to be particularly resistant to the transmission of disease, hence its use in pipes and cigarette holders.

A yellow-white cabochon amber and silver ring, 1½in (4cm) long.
£70–90 *EaJ*

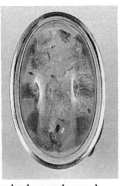

A cabochon amber and silver ring, 1½in (4cm) long.
£70–90 *EaJ*

An amber cross, 4in (10cm) long.
£100–130 *EaJ*

An amber brooch, with silver mount, 3in (7.5cm) long.
£175–200 *EaJ*

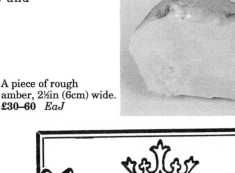

A piece of rough amber, 2½in (6cm) wide.
£30–60 *EaJ*

A cabochon amber brooch, with silver mount and decoration, 2in (5cm) diam.
£125–150 *EaJ*

A pair of yellow-white opaque amber and silver earrings, 2in (5cm) long.
£70–90 *EaJ*

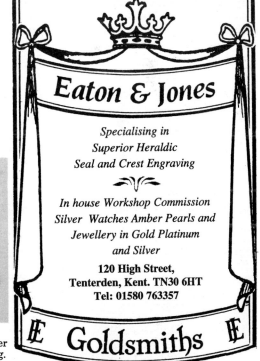

Antique Jewellery

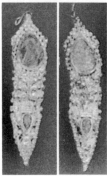

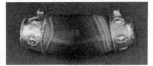

A Persian banded agate pendant, with filigree decorated thin gold end mounts with suspension loops, circa 3rd Century BC–2nd Century AD, 2in (5cm) long.
£400–500 *Bon*

A pair of Hellenistic ornate filigree decorated earrings, each set with a large and a small flat glass lozenge, 3in (7.5cm) long.
£900–1,000 *Bon*

Brooches, Buckles & Clasps

This section includes a special feature on name brooches. These were a favourite article of jewellery at the turn of the century. The names themselves, Daisy, Nelly, Edith, Lily, provide a wonderful evocation of the period, and as Victorian girls' names have come back into fashion, such brooches are often purchased today as christening presents. Some silver brooches come complete with romantic messages, for instance 'Forget Me Not', or 'Mizpah', a Hebraic word meaning 'watch tower', and signifying 'I'll watch over you'.

An opal brooch, with diamond four-stone cluster tapering shoulders.
£275–375 *CSK*

A Barkentin & Krall gem set and enamelled buckle, marked 'CK', London 1898, 4½in (11cm) wide, in original fitted case.
£950–1,200 *P*

Bracelets

A Bulgari cultured pearl, turquoise bead and mesh twist design bracelet.
£750–850 *CSK*

A millefiori glass oval panel bracelet.
£350–450 *CSK*

A Continental two-colour paving design flexible broad bracelet, with textured panels.
£750–850 *CSK*

A gold mounted carved coral bow brooch, with suspended hand pendant, 19thC.
£230–300 *CSK*

A novelty two-colour brooch, modelled as a bugle.
£400–500 *CSK*

A Victorian gold locket-back brooch, with pearl and blue enamel motif, wire and beadwork decoration, in a fitted case.
£500–600 *CSK*

A Victorian gold and opal cluster brooch, modelled as a butterfly and sword.
£400–500 *CSK*

A guilloche and painted enamel plaque, in a brooch mount, with scroll and beadwork surround, late 19thC.
£280–380 *CSK*

An Arts and Crafts enamelled and moonstone brooch, with openwork foliate mounts set with moonstone cabochons, and central green-stained chalcedony cabochon, 1½in (4cm) diam.
£600–700 *P*

A gold, pearl, citrine and enamel Celtic brooch, the central citrine with quatrefoil and circle beadwork surround, decorated with black and white enamel and half pearls, 19thC.
£420–520 *CSK*

An enamelled brooch, by George Hunt, with central pansy in a wirework mount, set with two faceted citrines, signed on reverse 'G.H. 1923', 2in (5cm) wide.
£450–550 *P*

Marcasite Brooches

A silver, marcasite and paste fox, with a garnet eye, c1920, 1½in (4cm) wide.
£35–40 *FMN*

A silver and marcasite brooch, the horse with a ruby eye, c1990, 2in (5cm) wide.
£70–80 *FMN*

Name Brooches

A silver brooch, with applied gold lettering 'Mary Jane', with Isle of Man symbol, maker J.R., Birmingham 1899, 2in (5cm) long.
£30–50 *FMN*

A silver brooch, 'Annie', with heavily engraved detailing, maker W.C.M., Birmingham 1903, 2in (5cm) long.
£60–80 *FMN*

Four white metal brooches, 20thC.
£80–85 *LF*

A silver brooch, 'Edith', with heavily engraved flowers, c1880, 2in (5cm) long.
£60–80 *FMN*

A silver brooch, with fretwork lettering, 'Louisa', c1990, 1½in (4cm) long.
£60–80 *FMN*

Silver Brooches

A silver brooch engraved with Holycross Abbey, maker C.W.H., Birmingham 1897, 1½in (4cm) wide.
£18–30 *FMN*

Many brooches were made showing bridges, churches, abbeys and castles, and are becoming popular with collectors.

A silver brooch, with engraved leaves and applied flowerhead, c1880, 1½in (4cm) diam.
£35–40 *FMN*

A silver brooch, engraved with a boat, with applied leaves, c1880, 1½in (4cm) wide.
£35–40 *FMN*

A silver brooch, engraved with leaves and berries, c1880, 1in (2.5cm) diam.
£25–30 *FMN*

A silver brooch engraved with Stratford Church, c1887, 1in (2.5cm) diam.
£35–40 *AnE*

A Victorian gold locket-back Queen Victoria Jubilee brooch, with applied enamelled Royal coat-of-arms, Union Jack and cross of St George, with two-colour foliate decoration.
£170–220 *CSK*

Cameos

l. A shell cameo, depicting Gannymede, mounted as a brooch, with engraved surround, 19thC.
£450–500 *CSK*

r. A 19thC shell cameo, depicting a classical maiden's profile, with plain and ropework surround.
£250–300 *CSK*

l. A 19thC shell cameo, depicting a kneeling child at prayer, with plain and scroll engraved surround.
£850–900 *CSK*

A 19thC shell cameo,
depicting Classical gods,
mounted as a brooch.
£475–550 *CSK*

A 19thC oval shell cameo brooch, with
plain and twist design surround.
£720–780 *CSK*

A silver pendant
on a chain, by
Emma Farquarson.
£220–240 *NEW*

Contemporary Jewellery

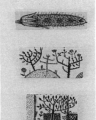

r. Two items of jewellery
by Jo Mitchell:
A silver and brass
lapel badge. **£15–17**
A pair of metal earrings.
£18–21 *NEW*

l. Three black and
white porcelain
brooches, by
Helen Smythe.

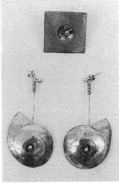

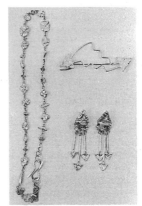

A selection of jewellery
by Holly Belsher:
Necklace. **£255–285**
Brooch. **£38–42**
Earrings. **£65–75** *NEW*

> **Miller's is a price GUIDE
> not a price LIST**

A pink tourmaline and sterling
silver with 18ct gold ring, by
Ruta Brown.
£180–200 *NEW*

An oxidised silver bangle,
by Ruta Brown.
£220–240 *NEW*

l. A sterling silver necklace, by
Ruta Brown, with aquamarine,
labradorite, topaz, citrine, and
freshwater pearls.
£1,200–1,400 *NEW*

Two bracelets made from baked
bean tins, painted, collaged and
covered with items such as clay
pipes and pottery from the
River Thames. **£25–30 each**
and a similarly made pottery
brooch, by Vicky Hawkins.
£10–20 *PC*

Cuff Links

A pair of engraved cuff links,
gold plate on brass, c1900.
£20–25 *FMN*

A pair of cuff links, gold
plate on brass, and
mother-of-pearl, c1930.
£10–20 *FMN*

A pair of cuff links, gold plate
on brass, with paste stones in
mother-of-pearl, c1940.
£10–18 *FMN*

A pair of silver cuff links,
with knot design, and faceted
semi-precious stones, c1920.
£40–50 *FMN*

A pair of hollow brass cuff
links, c1910.
£18–25 *FMN*

A pair of Japanese cuff links,
inlaid brass and silver on
ebony, c1910.
£20–30 *FMN*

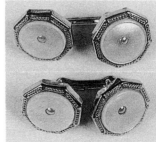

A pair of chrome cuff links, with
mother-of-pearl centred with
seed pearls, c1920.
£20–30 *FMN*

Diamonds

The diamond is the hardest natural substance known to man and many legends surround its adamantine virtues. Throughout the centuries diamonds have been regarded as a protector from illness, in particular plague and insanity, especially if they were sported on the left side of the body. Many of the most famous diamonds in history are named and have fascinating stories attached to them. The Hope diamond, now in the Smithsonian Institution, USA, was worn by both Marie Antoinette and the Princesse de Lamballe. Since both were guillotined, The Hope was long regarded as an unlucky charm. The Kohinoor diamond, set in the Queen Mother's crown, was presented to Queen Victoria in 1850. According to legend, Britain would lose India if the stone was worn by a male, and therefore it has passed down through the female line.

A lady's platinum
and diamond wrist-
watch, Swiss
17-jewel movement,
9ct white gold mesh
cordette bracelet.
£250–350 *CSK*

A red spinel and rose diamond
crescent brooch.
£250–300 *CSK*

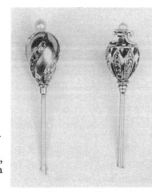

Two rose diamond and
gem hatpins, with rose
diamond, emerald and
ruby line decoration.
£500–550 *CSK*

A diamond and
ruby twin-line
crescent brooch.
£420–450 *CSK*

A diamond and baguette diamond openwork dress clip.
£450–550 *CSK*

An Art Nouveau diamond and rose diamond design openwork brooch pendant, with pearl drop.
£420–480 *CSK*

Earrings

A pair of French ear clips, the circular spiky design set with rubies.
£550–600 *CSK*

Necklaces & Pendants

A pair of Bohemian garnet cluster and drop earrings, in a later case.
£700–800 *CSK*

An Edwardian half pearl flowerhead cluster and triple swag and fringe design panel necklace, on a Prince of Wales link back chain.
£400–450 *CSK*

An Edwardian half pearl cluster foliate panel and chain link necklace, with a star brooch drop, in a fitted case.
£550–600 *CSK*

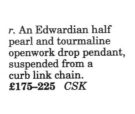

r. An Edwardian half pearl and tourmaline openwork drop pendant, suspended from a curb link chain.
£175–225 *CSK*

A solid brass pendant, with a velvet back, c1900, 2in (5cm) high.
£40–45 *FMN*

An Art Nouveau stained horn pendant, modelled as two birds with twig and foliate surround, with imitation turquoise drop and bead decoration.
£575–650 *CSK*

l. A pendant, by Bent Exner, in the form of a large flower, stamped with standard mark and 'Exner', 4in (10cm) diam., on a chain.
£185–225 *P*

A Scottish hardstone octagonal section bar link necklace.
£175–200 *CSK*

Seals

Seals were made as far back as Biblical times. The earliest forms were flat or 'stamp' seals, whilst 'cylinder' seals have the design engraved on cylindrical stones. Later, seals were mounted on signet rings or shanks. From the 16thC, seals were hung from a necklace or chatelaine, and from the 17thC men wore fob seals suspended from their watch chains. As this section shows, they were extremely popular in the 19thC.

A 19thC pinchbeck fancy cut white stone seal, engraved 'Adieu', 1in (2.5cm) high.
£60–80 *PC*

A pinchbeck cushion fob, with cornelian stone, 1½in (4cm) high.
£50–60 *PC*

A cornelian seal, with engraved gilt case, c1850, 1in (2.5cm).
£100–120 *PUR*

 (top right)

A 19thC pinchbeck embossed seal, with bevelled white transparent stone, possibly backed agate, 1½in (4cm) high.
£40–60 *PC*

l. A 19thC pinchbeck cushion fob, with faceted yellow stone, foil backed, 1in (2.5cm) high.
£50–70 *PC*

A steel seal, with a unicorn intaglio, c1830, 1in (2.5cm) high.
£150–200 *PUR*

A 19thC embossed scrolled design pinchbeck seal, with yellow faceted stone engraved 'Caroline', 1in (2.5cm) high.
£100–150 *PC*

A 19thC 9ct gold swivel pinchbeck hand engraved fob, with cornelian stone, gold backed, 1½in (4cm) high.
£100–150 *PC*

l. A pinchbeck plated swivel fob, with double oval cornelian and bloodstone, 1½in (4cm) high.
£40–60 *PC*

A grey agate and gold cased seal, c1850, 1½in (4cm) high.
£150–200 *PUR*

Two engraved stone seals.
£300–400 each *EaJ*

KITCHENALIA

Demand for kitchenalia continues to expand, with good prices being paid for the more decorative and unusual items. In this, as in every other collecting field, a tasty provenance can make all the difference. The market was stirred, shaken and sweetened by the prices fetched at the Phillips auction of kitchen equipment belonging to the late Elizabeth David. Cooks both amateur and professional crowded the saleroom hoping to buy a little of Elizabeth David's magic and such humble items as wooden spoons and biscuit moulds sold for well over their estimates. Could such results provide an indication of future trends?

Elizabeth David

A Scottish wrought iron broiler, with easel back and serpentine grids, 16in (41cm) high, a cast iron charcoal cooker, 8½in (22cm) high, and other items.
£120–150 *P*

General

A farmer's harvest barrel, 19thC, 11½in (29cm) long.
£60–65 *JUN*

A European pottery mould shaped as a heart, 10½in (27cm) long.
£150–200 *P*

A scoop-shaped sieve, with bentwood frame, and a quantity of other sieves and strainers.
£200–250 *P*

The world's oldest joint of ham, bought from Patrick Cudahy Inc., Chicago, in 1892, cured in borax and in 1932 thought to be edible, together with letters of authenticity.
£1,000–1,200 *CSK*

r. A CWS Invincible aluminium hot water bottle, c1940, 8in (20cm) diam.
£2–3 *HAC*

A stone hot water bottle, 'The Radio', 9½in (24cm) high.
£12–15 *HAC*

A green and cream tin tray, c1930, 12 by 16in (30.5 by 41cm).
£10–12 *AL*

FURTHER READING
Miller's Collecting Kitchenware, Reed International Books, September 1995.

Baking

A blue porcelain measure stand, c1930, 5in (12.5cm) square.
£6–7 *HAC*

A plastic jam jar and cover, with daisy and bee captured in the lid, 1970s.
£15–20 *HEW*

A Green's two-way sponge cake tin, c1930, 8½in (21cm) diam.
£3–4 *AL*

A patty pan, c1920, 12 by 9½in (30.5 by 24cm).
£5–6 *AL*

A Green's sponge tray, 12 by 9½in (30.5 by 24cm).
£5–6 *AL*

A set of tin pastry cutters, c1890, 1 to 3⅛in (2 to 3cm) diam.
£15–20 *AL*

A Green's sponge cake tin, c1930, 8in (20cm) diam.
£2–3 *AL*

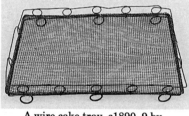

A wire cake tray, c1890, 9 by 13½in (23 by 34cm).
£10–12 *AL*

A pressed glass cake stand, c1900, 9in (23cm) diam.
£10–15 *AL*

A pressed glass cake stand, c1900, 9in (23cm) diam.
£10–15 *AL*

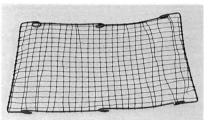

A wire cake tray, c1930, 10 by 15½in (25 by 39cm).
£5–8 *AL*

An American tin cake mixer, 'Home Cake Mixer', patented January 14th 1896, 10in (25cm) high.
£15–20 *AL*

An embroidered silk
waistcoat, 18thC.
£250–300 *CK*

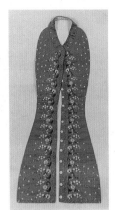

An embroidered
Spitalfields silk
front piece, 18thC.
£130–150 *CK*

An Edwardian pink
silk dress, with ecru
lace trimming.
£150–200 *TOM*

An Edwardian cut
red velvet and silk
lined smoking
jacket and cap.
£80–100 *TOM*

A hand embroidered silk
shawl, c1910–20.
£50–70 *TOM*

A Victorian woolwork
hunting waistcoat,
embroidered with foxes.
£450–500 *CK*

A velvet school or college cap, with
tassel, dated '1935' on the peak.
£40–60 *MSh*

A silk chiffon
ball gown, by
Victor Stiebel,
with matching
scarf, 1940s.
£200–250 *CSK*

A French fashion print of
German costumes,
c1800–30, 7½ by 5in
(19 by 12.5cm), unframed.
£30–40 *STA*

A fashion print of hats,
c1800–30, 7½ by 5in
(19 by 12.5cm), unframed.
£30–35 *STA*

An evening coat,
with wool, braid and
button decoration.
£60–70 *TOM*

A handmade cotton
dress, 1950s.
£10–20 *PC*

A 'California Cottons'
dress, with stiffened
petticoat, 1950s.
£25–35 *PC*

A brocade turban, with
glass and swan's-down
trimming, 1920s.
£20–40 *TOM*

A metallic thread cap.
£75–125
A beaded and
sequinned scarf.
£20–30 *TOM*

A textured cotton skirt,
decorated with roses, 1950s.
£20–30 *PC*

A 'Sportaville' cotton skirt
with stiffened lining, 1950s.
£20–30 *PC*

A pair of gold and black kid
leather shoes, 1920s.
£25–30 *TOM*

A linen skirt, decorated with
fruit and vegetables, 1950s.
£20–30 *PC*

A hat box, with floral
decoration, c1940.
£12–15 *TOM*

A Marshall & Snelgrove hat
box, c1950–60.
£10–15 *TOM*

A pair of pink beaded
garters, c1920, 7½in
(18.5cm) wide.
£25–35 *TOM*

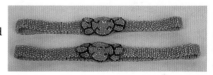

A ceramic pot, by
Nancy Angus.
£180–200 *NEW*

A glass vase, by
Martin Andrews,
12in (30.5cm) high.
£65–75 *NEW*

A ceramic mug, with
triangular design, by Harriet
Coleridge, 5in (12.5cm) high.
£25–30 *NEW*

A tulip vase and cover,
by Daphne Carnegy,
10in (25cm) high.
£100–115 *NEW*

A ceramic teapot and cup
by Sylph Baier.
Cup. **£16–18**
Teapot. **£50–60** *NEW*

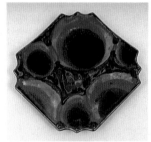

A ceramic 'Peacock' saucer,
by Dart/Tchalenko, 6½in
(16cm) square.
£14–16 *NEW*

A ceramic 'flat pot jug',
by Liz Beckenham, 11in
(28cm) high.
£70–80 *NEW*

A ceramic fish mug, by
Chris Spyer, 4in (10cm).
£15–17 *NEW*

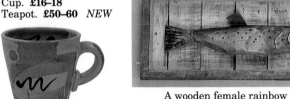

A wooden female rainbow trout
in box, by Chris Berry.
£75–80 *NEW*

A ceramic stripy mug,
by Debbie Proser, 3in
(7.5cm) high.
£15–17 *NEW*

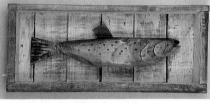

A glass bowl, with crocodile, by
Ruth Dresman, 9½in (24cm) diam.
£225–250 *NEW*

A red glass vase, by
William Shakespeare,
9½in (24cm) high.
£35–42 *NEW*

A ceramic serving platter, by Pauline
Zelinski, 14½in (37cm) long.
£95–105 *NEW*

A German celluloid
headed rattle doll,
11½in (29cm) high.
£85–95 *SP*

A Norah Wellings
doll, c1930s, 11in
(28cm) high.
£40–50 *SP*

A Kestner doll, impressed
'192', with original clothes
and wig, c1890, 18in (46cm).
£350–450 *SP*

A Shirley Temple doll,
c1930, 17in (43cm).
£250–300 *SP*

A Dean's Betty 'Oxo' doll,
c1925, 17½in (44cm) high.
£450–500 *SP*

An Armand Marseille Dream Baby,
embossed '341', with closed mouth and
hard body, c1920, 10in (25cm) high.
£150–200 *SP*

A Norah Wellings doll,
c1930, 18in (46cm) high.
£75–80 *SP*

An Armand Marseille Dream Baby,
embossed '341', closed mouth and
soft body, c1920s, 19in (48cm).
£100–150 *SP*

A Kestner Blossom
doll, c1918, 18in
(45.5cm) high.
£450–500 *SP*

A DEP mechanical
sailor doll, c1900,
15in (38cm) high.
£400–450 *SP*

A Kestner doll, with
kid body, c1880,
22½in (57cm) high.
£400–500 *SP*

A Lenci felt doll,
with original paper
label, very good
condition, 1930s.
£400–450 *CMF*

A Bähr & Pröschild
bisque shoulder doll,
No. 309, with
portmanteau, c1895.
£1,200–1,400 *WAG*

An English crock doll,
late 1940s, 20in
(51cm) high.
£30–38 *CMF*

A Simon & Halbig
bisque doll,
No. 1078, original
clothes, c1892.
£450–550 *WAG*

A hard plastic doll, probably
French, c1950, 11in (28cm) high.
£25–30 *CMF*

A pedlar doll, with
china head, made
in Sussex, 1910,
9in (23cm) high.
£500–600 *CK*

A pair of Dutch cloth dolls,
marked 'F.D.R. & Co.',
wearing original clothes,
1920s, 18½in (47cm) high.
£120–170 *WAG*

A Rosebud hard
plastic doll, original
dress, 1950s.
£50–60 *CMF*

A Roddy plastic doll,
1950s, 11in (28cm) high.
£40–45 *CMF*

A Pedigree hard plastic
boy doll, 1950s, 14in
(36cm) high.
£80–85 *CMF*

A rubber baby doll,
1940s, 12in
(30.5cm) high.
£30–40 *CMF*

A collection of bronze figures from Beatrix Potter's characters, by Wiener, c1990, 1 to 1½in (2.5 to 3.5cm). **£50–70 each** *TMN*

A limited edition set of pewter jointed miniature figures, by Hantel, 1 to 2in (2.5 to 5cm) high. **£35–45** *TMN*

l. A teddy bear's picnic revolving musical toy, c1990, 3½in (8.5cm) diam. **£195–225** *TMN*

A set of pewter miniatures, by Hantel Ltd., featuring Hey Diddle Diddle, the Cat and the Fiddle. **£65–70** *TMN*

A Noah's Ark miniature set, c1990, 3in (7.5cm) diam. **£30–35** *TMN*

A Pelham string puppet, Mr. McBoozle, boxed, c1960. **£40–45** *CMF*

A mechanical musical 'Enchanted Clock Tower', c1993. **£275–300** *TMN*

A chess set, depicting *Alice in Wonderland* characters, from a limited edition of 250, by Thos. Chislett, c1993, 2⅜in (6cm) high. **£250–275** *TMN*

A Pelham Goofy string puppet, unboxed, 1960s. **£25–30** *CMF*

A Pelham clown string puppet, boxed, 1960s. **£18–22** *CMF*

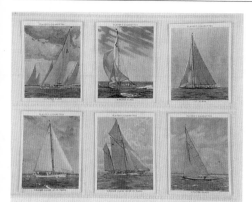

John Player & Sons cigarette cards, a set of 25 Racing Yachts, c1938.
£80–160 *ACC*

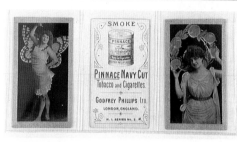

Godfrey Phillips Ltd., cigarette cards, a set of 50 Beautiful Women series, c1908.
£250–450 *ACC*

John Player & Sons cigarette cards, a set of 50, Straight Line Caricatures, c1926.
£22–44 *ACC*

Carreras cigarette cards, a set of 50 Gran-Pop series, c1933.
£18–36 *ACC*

Allen & Ginter cigarette cards, a set of 50, The World's Champions , 1st series issued 1888.
£18–20 each *ACC*

W.D. & H.O. Wills cigarette cards, a set of 40 Racehorses & Jockeys, c1938.
£55–110 *ACC*

Taddy & Co., cigarette cards, a set of 25 English Royalty series, c1903.
£475–950 *ACC*

Adventure comic, No. 1151, slim paper rationed edition, January 26, 1946, price 2d.
£4–5 *NOS*

Action Comics, No. 267, August 1960.
£28–30 *NOS*

Two copies of *Film Fun* comic, dated April 6th and October 12th, 1957, price 4d each.
£8–10 each *NOS*

Buster, with Buster's Dodger kit, dated 11th June, 1960, price 4d.
£30–35 *NOS*

The Beano Comic, dated 29th June, 1940, price 2d.
£38–40 *NOS*

A complete set of *Classic Comics*, issues 1–169, October 1941–Spring 1969.
£5,000–7,000 *CSK*

The Dandy, Halloween issue, No. 832, dated 2nd November, 1957.
£8–10 *NOS*

Detective Comics, No.359, January 1960, with first appearance of 'Batgirl'.
£28–30 *NOS*

A Mekon figure, with fibreglass head and clay on metal body, created 1977, 41in (104cm) high.
£700–900 *CSK*

Iron Man and Captain America,
No. 66, June 1965.
£20–25 *NOS*

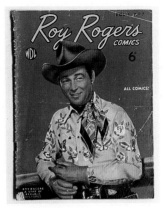

Roy Rogers Comics, Vol 1,
No. 7, 1950.
£3–4 *NOS*

Playbox, February 2nd, 1952.
£3–4 *NOS*

Samson, reprint, No. 2, 1956.
£3–4 *NOS*

Spider-Man, No. 101, Oct 1971,
first appearance of Morbius the
Living Vampire.
£65–70 *NOS*

Spider-Man and Dracula,
No. 1, July 1974.
£15–18 *NOS*

Not distributed in the UK.

Wolverine, Charleston Chew,
No. 1, half Wolverine and half
Spider-Man, 1992.
£18–20 *NOS*

Whiz Comics, No. 88, 1951.
£4–5 *NOS*

Superman's greatest rival.

Real Western Hero,
No. 120, 1956.
£3–4 *NOS*

Two postcard designs, by Arnold Taylor, pen and black ink and watercolour heightened with white, inscribed as titles, unframed, 5½ by 8½in (14 by 21cm).
£750–900 *CSK*

Six postcard designs by Arnold Taylor and Brian Fitzpatrick, pen and black ink and watercolour, inscribed.
£600–800 *CSK*

Eight postcard designs, by Arnold Taylor and Charles Griggs, pen and brown ink heightened with white, 5½ by 8½in (14 by 21cm).
£275–350 *CSK*

Six postcard designs, by Arnold Taylor, inscribed, pen and brown ink and watercolour.
£425–500 *CSK*

A collection of six postcard designs, by Arnold Taylor and Brian Fitzpatrick, pen and black ink and watercolour.
£600–800 *CSK*

Seven postcard designs, by Arnold Taylor and Charles Griggs, pen and brown ink and watercolour, inscribed, 5½ by 9in (14 by 22.5cm).
£250–300 *CSK*

Five postcard designs, by Arnold Taylor, watercolour and bodycolour, unframed.
£175–250 *CSK*

Six postcard designs, by Arnold Taylor, B. Fitzpatrick and C. Griggs, signed and inscribed as titles, unframed.
£250–350 *CSK*

An unmounted chicken skin fan leaf, painted with Bay of Naples, Vesuvius and Stromboli, c1785.
£3,000–4,000 *CSK*

A Victorian 'fan of 100 faces', with pierced bone sticks, together with fitted box.
£65–80 *VB*

A blue silk fan, with painted floral decoration, 22in (56cm) wide.
£25–30 *PC*

An Art Nouveau painted leaf fan, with decorated mother-of-pearl sticks.
£110–130 *VB*

A black chiffon fan, decorated with lilac, 25in (64cm) wide.
£20–25 *PC*

An ivory fan, with embroidery and sequin decoration, 16in (41cm) wide.
£30–40 *PC*

An ostrich feather fan, 1900–1920, 26in (66cm) wide.
£50–60 *PC*

An ivory fan, decorated with sequins, 11in (28cm) wide.
£30–50 *PC*

A set of four John Derbyshire pressed glass lions, c1875, 4in (10cm) wide.
£35–50 each *ARE*

Three Wedgwood glass mushrooms, c1970, 4in (10cm) high.
£25–30 each *SWB*

A pressed glass bowl, with three butterfly-style feet, with a satin glass lady insert, c1930.
£40–50 *BKK*

A pressed glass figure of a seated lady with parasol, c1928, 10in (25cm) diam.
£40–50 *BKK*

A pressed satin glass sailing boat, c1932, 9½in (14cm).
£40–50 *BKK*

A pink pressed glass bowl, with bird handles and cockatoo insert, c1930, 14in (36cm) diam.
£60–70 *BKK*

A Sowerby glass vase, c1932, 6in (15cm) high.
£18–20 *BKK*

A Sowerby pressed glass figure of a naked woman, in leaf pattern bowl, c1930.
£50–60 *BKK*

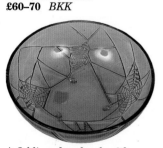

A Jobling glass bowl, with spider's web design, 8in (20cm).
£40–45 *HEW*

A Wedgwood glass duck, c1970, 4½in (11cm) long.
£20–30 *SWB*

A Wedgwood glass penguin, marked, c1970, 5in (12.5cm) .
£20–30 *SWB*

l. & r. A pair of wrythen moulded wine bottles, c1840. **£650–700**
c. A wine bottle, with spire stopper, 12in (30.5cm). **£400–450** *Som*

A spirit bottle, cut with flutes, flashed after being cut, c1820. **£300–400** *Som*

Two coloured spirit bottles, with metal mounts and stoppers, 12½in (31.5cm) high. **£180–230 each** *Som*

An onion-shaped carafe with long neck, c1840, 8⅓in (21cm) high. **£200–250** *Som*

A pair of ovoid finger bowls, with moulded vertical ribbing, c1830, 4in (10cm) high. **£200–300** *Som*

Two club-shaped spirit decanters, with plain lozenge stoppers, c1790, 8in (20cm) high. **£150–180 each** *Som*

A Victorian cranberry glass claret jug, c1860, 9½in (24cm) high. **£200–230** *ARE*

l. A pair of wrythen moulded spirit bottles, c1840. **£500–600**
A spirit flagon. **£200–220** *Som*

An enamel decorated cut glass comport, c1870, 11⅛in (29cm). **£250–300** *DUN*

A wrythen sugar basin, with everted folded rim, c1800. **£100–150** *Som*

Four hand painted scent bottles, in an ormolu and cranberry glass globe, on a marble base, 19thC. **£750–850** *WAG*

l. & r. A pair of green wine glasses, with tulip bowls, plain stems and feet, c1840. **£100–125** *c.* A wine glass with conical bowl and knopped stem, c1830, 5½in (13.5cm). **£60–80** *Som*

A glass house, filled with coloured sands from the Isle of Wight, c1920. **£9–12** *VB*

A Northwood intaglio jug, c1880, 5½in (14cm). **£650–680** *MJW*

Three North Country blue glass cream jugs, c1800, 3 to 5in (7.5 to 12.5cm) high. **£100–150 each** *Som*

Three of a set of four wine glasses, with cup bowls on hollow stems, with raspberry prunts, c1830, 4in (10cm) high. **£300–350** *Som*

Three printed glasses, c1950–60: **50p–£1 each** *PC*

An amethyst glass water jug, c1890, 5½in (14cm) high. **£45–55** *DUN*

A Nailsea flask, 6in (15cm). **£120–140** *DUN*

A Nailsea green glass flask, c1820, 8in (20cm). **£90–120** *LIO*

A Nailsea red, blue and white flask, c1820, 8in (20cm) long. **£90–120** *LIO*

A picture painted on glass, 'The Engagement', c1840–70, 12in (30.5cm) high. **£90–100** *AA*

Two Murano glass clowns, 1950s, 8½in (21cm) high. **£20–30 each** *YY*

A Bohemian enamelled cased glass vase, c1880, 10½in (26.5cm) high. **£170–220** *DUN*

Three glass rolling pins, 15in (38cm) long. **£30–40 each** *DUN*

A glass hyacinth vase, c1900, 8in (20cm) high. **£30–40** *DUN*

A Victorian glass lily vase, 10in (25cm) high. **£140–160** *DUN*

A pair of Nailsea glass bellows, 6in (15cm) long. **£100–130** *ARE*

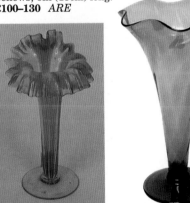

A Victorian glass vase, 7in (17.5cm). **£80–100** *ARE*

A fluted vase, by Powell & Sons, c1890, 12in (30.5cm). **£135–155** *DUN*

A wrythen glass vase, c1830, 7in (18cm) high. **£100–125** *Som*

A Loetz style three-handled vase, c1910, 3½in (9cm). **£90–100** *CSA*

An HMV Model 25 gramophone, with oak case, original red Morning Glory tinplate horn and Exhibition soundbox, c1924. **£1,000–1,250** *BTA*

A Paillard Echophone, with aluminium horn, Pathé floating reproducer, c1904. **£350–400** *BTA*

A Columbia graphophone BK, with 30in (76cm) brass horn and table stand, Lyric reproducer, c1906. **£650–750** *BTA*

A Gramophone and Typewriter Junior Monarch gramophone, oak case with Recording Angel trademark, original brass horn, Exhibition soundbox, c1904. **£1,750–2,250** *BTA*

An HMV 102 portable red gramophone, 12in (30.5cm) wide. **£150–200** *OTA*

An HMV Model 2 gramophone, with single spring motor, oak case, original oak horn, Exhibition soundbox, c1920. **£1,800–2,000** *BTA*

An HMV wind-up gramophone, for use for 78 rpm records, c1920s. **£220–240** *MCh*

An HMV Model VII Senior Monarch gramophone, oak case and horn, c1911. **£2,000–2,500** *BTA*

A horn gramophone, by Frank Snell, with mahogany case inlaid with satinwood, boxwood and ebony, c1910. **£650–750** *BTA*

Baskets

A shopping basket, c1910, 17½in (44cm) long.
£15–20 *AL*

A wicker basket, c1900, 13½in (34cm) long.
£10–15 *AL*

A deep basket, c1920, 12½in (32cm) long.
£10–15 *AL*

A shallow basket, c1920, 16in (41cm) long.
£10–15 *AL*

A wicker basket, c1920, 13in (33cm) long.
£10–15 *AL*

A round basket, c1920, 12in (30.5cm) diam.
£8–10 *AL*

A deep basket, c1920, 9½in (24cm) high.
£8–10 *AL*

A bottle basket, c1880, 10½in (26cm) long.
£20–25 *AL*

A deep wicker basket, c1920, 10in (25cm) high.
£10–15 *AL*

A cutlery basket, c1920, 14in (36cm) long.
£12–15 *AL*

A wire egg basket, c1900, 12½in (32cm) high including handle.
£18–22 *AL*

Bowls & Crocks

A set of three ceramic pudding basins, c1930, 4 to 4½in (10 to 11cm) high.
£10–12 *AL*

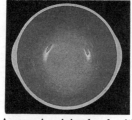

A ceramic mixing bowl, with green lining, 1960s, 11in (28cm) diam.
£10–15 *AL*

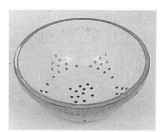

A pottery colander, c1900, 10in (25cm) diam.
£25–30 *AL*

A cream ceramic basin, with lip, c1920, 8in (20cm) diam.
£10–12 *AL*

A yellow ware crock pot, c1900, 6in (15cm) high.
£10–15 *AL*

A large ceramic crock, c1890, 11½in (29cm) high.
£30–35 *AL*

A French ceramic cook pot, 'Herbert's Cuisine', 20thC, 8½in (21cm) high.
£12–16 *AL*

A Royal Doulton crock, c1920, 7½in (19cm) high.
£10–15 *AL*

A terracotta crock, c1890, 8in (20cm) high.
£15–20 *AL*

A New Hall white ceramic pie dish, c1920, 10in (25cm) long.
£6–8 *AL*

Bread & Wooden Boards

Many bread and wooden boards come complete with carving round the rim, including floral designs, sheaves of corn, and occasionally religious or moral mottoes. Prices depend on age, condition and the quality and interest of the decoration.

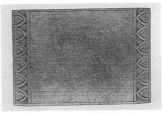

A carved bread board, c1900, 8 by 12in (20 by 30.5cm).
£10–15 *AL*

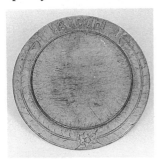

A round bread board, c1890, 11½in (29cm) diam.
£15–20 *AL*

A round bread board, 20thC, 10in (25cm) diam.
£10–12 *HAC*

A wooden chopping board, 20thC, 16 by 13in (41 by 33cm).
£15–20 *AL*

A square bread board, c1920, 10in (25cm) diam.
£10–12 *AL*

A cheese board, 20thC, 8 by 10½in (20 by 26cm).
£10–12 *HAC*

A cheese board and knife, 20thC, 7 by 6in (17.5 by 15cm).
£7–8
Butter knife, 6½in (16cm).
£4–5 *HAC*

A herb board, 20thC, 7 by 12in (17.5 by 30.5cm).
£8–10 *HAC*

A wooden garlic board, 20thC, 6½ by 8in (16 by 20cm).
£8–9 *HAC*

A small bread peel, c1890, 15in (38cm) long.
£20–25 *AL*

Bread Implements

A bread fork, with horn handle, c1880, 8in (20cm) long.
£10–12 *AL*

A dough cutter, with wooden handle, 19thC.
£5–6 *HAC*

Dairy Collectables

A terracotta 'Zerocool' butter cooler, c1920, 9in (23cm) long.
£10–12 *AL*

A terracotta butter cooler, with glass liner, 1920s, 5½in (14cm) diam.
£8–10 *AL*

A butter churn, c1930, 12in (30.5cm) high.
£25–30 *AL*

An Irish oak butter churn, with cast iron bands and paddle, 19thC, 36in (91.5cm) high.
£135–165 *CPA*

A Welsh wooden dairy bowl, c1850, 17in (43cm) diam.
£100–120 *JAC*

An Irish oak butter churn, with cast iron bands, 19thC, 36in (91.5cm) high.
£125–145 *CPA*

An 'Everston' terracotta milk cooler, c1920, 11in (28cm) high.
£10–12 *AL*

An Irish oak butter churn, with cast iron bands and paddle, 19thC, 3in (7.5cm) high.
£100–145 *CPA*

A Pontypool ware cheese coaster, early 19thC, 14½in (37cm).
£300–400 *WIL*

An Irish oak butter churn, with cast iron bands and paddle, 19thC, 36in (91.5cm) high.
£90–115 *CPA*

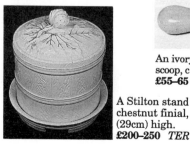

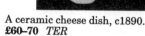

An ivory and silver plated Stilton scoop, c1880, 10in (25cm) long.
£55–65 *DUN*

A Stilton stand and cover, with chestnut finial, c1885, 11½in (29cm) high.
£200–250 *TER*

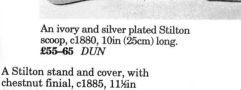

A ceramic cheese dish, c1890.
£60–70 *TER*

A French milk bottle carrier, c1920, 13in (33cm) high including handle.
£30–35 *AL*

A painted wooden egg rack, c1930, 7½ by 9in (19 by 23cm).
£8–10 *AL*

A wooden egg rack, c1990, 9in (23cm) wide.
£7–8 *AL*

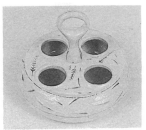

A ceramic egg cruet, c1900, 6in (15cm) diam.
£15–20 *AL*

A red painted tin egg rack, c1920, 6 by 9in (15 by 23cm).
£20–25 *AL*

l. A Tartan ware egg timer, 19thC, 3in (7.5cm) high.
£100–115
r. A Mauchline ware egg timer, 19thC, 3½in (8cm) high.
£70–80 *LBL*

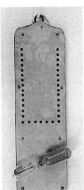

l. An egg timer, mounted on a celluloid shopping list, inscribed 'Lest you Forget', c1920, 8in (20cm) high.
£8–10 *AL*

An egg timer, mounted on a painted wooden base, c1920, 6in (15cm) high.
£10–12 *AL*

An egg cruet, damaged, c1890, 3½in (9cm) high.
£15–20 *AL*

Enamelware

An enamel flour bin with lid, 1920s–30s, 12in (30.5cm) high.
£15–20 *AL*

An enamel bread bin, with label inscribed 'Built Like a Bridge for Strength and Durability', 1920s–30s, 12in (30.5cm) high.
£10–12 *HAC*

An enamel bread bin and lid, c1900, 13in (33cm) high.
£18–20 *AL*

An enamel jug, with blue handle and rim, c1900, 6½in (16cm) high.
£10–12 *AL*

An enamel measuring jug, c1920, 6½in (16cm) high.
£6–8 *AL*

A white enamel pie dish, c1920, 13in (33cm) long.
£5–6 *AL*

An enamel one pint mug, c1900, 4⅓in (11cm) high.
£10–12 *AL*

Two white enamel mugs, with blue rims, c1900, 5 and 4in (12.5 and 10cm) high.
£5–7 each *AL*

A black enamelled kettle, c1900, 14in (36cm) high.
£15–18 *AL*

An enamel flour sifter/shaker, c1900, 4⅓in (11cm) high.
£8–10 *AL*

Two white enamel candlesticks, with blue rims, c1900, 6 and 7in (15 and 17.5cm) diam.
£6–8 each *AL*

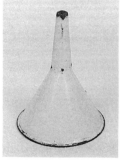

An enamel funnel, c1900, 6in (15cm) long.
£6–7 *AL*

Food Covers

A pewter food cover, c1890, 11in (28cm) long.
£20–25 *AL*

A copper food cover, c1920, 7in (18cm) diam.
£15–20 *AL*

A metal meat cover, c1890, 9in (23cm) long.
£20–25 *AL*

Jelly Moulds

Amongst the most widely collected moulds are earthenware pieces. Collectors will pay more for marked moulds and examples showing a particularly strong design. Glass moulds vary greatly in price and 19thC examples can be highly collectable. Aluminium, tin and plastic moulds remain comparatively cheap unless the subject portrayed has some specific appeal, such as a Disney character. Copper moulds can be very decorative and are expensive.

A wire mesh food cover, c1920, 16½in (42cm) long.
£10–12 *AL*

A ceramic jelly mould, with flower pattern in the base, c1860, 6in (15cm) long.
£20–22 *AL*

A ceramic jelly mould, c1880, 6in (15cm) long.
£10–12 *AL*

A ceramic jelly mould, c1860, 9in (23cm) long.
£25–28 *AL*

A ceramic jelly mould, c1880, 4in (10cm) long.
£5–8 *AL*

A ceramic jelly mould, with decorative pattern, c1860, 7in (17.5cm) long.
£10–12 *AL*

A ceramic jelly mould, c1880, 6in (15cm) wide.
£18–20 *AL*

A ceramic jelly mould, c1880, 6in (15cm) long.
£18–20 *AL*

A ceramic jelly mould, c1860,
6in (15cm) diam.
£10–12 *AL*

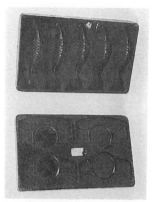

Two Bakelite moulds, with fish
and watch patterns, each 4 by
6in (10 by 15cm).
£7–8 each *HAC*

An aluminium mould, c1920,
5in (12.5cm) diam.
£1–2 *AL*

Three aluminium rabbit
moulds, c1930, 8, 7 and 4in
(20, 17.5 and 10cm).
£5–7 each *AL*

A ceramic jelly mould, with
pineapple pattern in the base,
c1850, 8in (20cm) long.
£18–20 *AL*

A plain copper mould, c1890,
3in (8cm) high.
£20–25 *AL*

One round and two oval fluted
enamel jelly moulds, c1890,
5½ (14cm) diam., 6 and 7in
(15 and 17.5cm) long.
£8–10 each *AL*

Two enamel fluted jelly moulds,
1920s, 8in (20cm) wide.
£8–12 each *CEMB*

A tin mould, c1880, 6in
(15cm) diam.
£15–20 *AL*

A copper mould, 19thC,
6½in (16cm) high.
£140–160 *DUN*

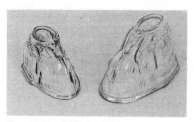

Two pressed glass rabbit
shaped moulds 20thC.
£6–8 each *AL*

A pewter mould and lid,
19thC, 6½in (16cm) high.
£30–35 *AL*

Jugs

A white pottery jug, c1880,
6½in (16cm) high.
£10–15 *AL*

Two white ceramic jugs, c1900,
5 and 5½in (12.5 and 14cm) high.
£10–12 each *AL*

A green ceramic cream jug,
with chrome lid, c1930, 7in
(17.5cm) high.
£10–15 *AL*

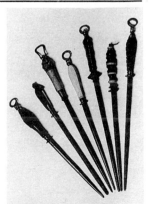

A pottery jug, with transfer
printed flowers, gilt rim and
handle, c1890, 8in (20cm) high.
£10–15 *AL*

Juicers

An Empire juice
extracter, c1930,
14in (36cm) long.
£12–15 *HAC*

A glass lemon squeezer, c1890,
6in (15cm) diam.
£3–4 *AL*

A Bakelite lemon squeezer,
c1930, 6in (15cm) wide.
£6–7 *AL*

Knife Sharpeners

An Edwardian knife
sharpener, 15in (38cm) diam.
£75–85 *JUN*

A 'Wellington'
knife polishing
board, c1900,
24in (61.5cm) high.
£10–15 *AL*

A 'Guildford' knife
board, 21in (53cm)
high, and powder
polish tin, 4½in
(11cm) high, c1900.
£10–15 *AL*

A selection of Victorian
carving steels, with ivory,
bone and wood mounts,
21in (53cm) long.
£20–200 each *DUN*

Mincers & Choppers

A National mincer, early 20thC, 9in (23cm) high.
£1–2 *HAC*

An 'Anna' mincer and grater, early 20thC, 9in (23cm) long.
£12–15 *HAC*

A No. 2 Universal food chopper, early 20thC, 10½in (26cm) high.
£3–4 *HAC*

An Enterprise tinned meat chopper, 12½in (32cm) high.
£4–5 *HAC*

Pie Funnels

Three ceramic pie funnels, c1910, 2½ to 3½in (6 to 9cm) high.
£2–3 each *AL*

Two ceramic pie funnels, one beige and one green, c1960, 3 and 2½in (7.5 and 6cm) high.
£3–6 each *AL*

A Dixon & Son herb chopper, c1880, 5½in (14cm) long.
£18–20 *AL*

r. A china pie funnel, 1930s, 3½in (9cm) high.
£2–3 *HAC*

l. A bird-shaped pie funnel, c1930, 4in (10cm) high.
£6–7 *AL*

Potato Mashers

Three wooden food mashers, c1920, 5, 6 and 8in (12.5, 15 and 20cm) diam.
£10–12 each *AL*

A selection of potato mashers, c1900, 9 to 12in (23 to 30.5cm).
£5–12 each *AL*

An Edwardian wooden potato masher, 11½in (29cm) high.
£2–3 *HAC*

Pots & Pans

An iron griddle, c1900, 11½in (29.5cm) wide.
£15–20 *AL*

Two iron saucepans, one with lid, c1880, 8½in (21cm) high.
£20–25
and 3¼in (8.5cm) high.
£6–7 *AL*

A brass preserving pan, c1880, 4¼in (11cm) diam.
£50–60 *AL*

A steel saucepan, c1890, 4½in (11cm) high.
£18–23 *AL*

A brass saucepan, c1870, 6½in (16cm) diam.
£30–40 *AL*

An iron frying pan, c1890, 9½in (23.5cm) diam.
£10–12 *AL*

A wire pan, c1920, 4½in (11cm) diam.
£8–10 *AL*

A set of kitchen scales, with brass face, c1890, 12½in (31.5cm) high.
£55–65 *AL*

A set of kitchen scales and weights, with enamel tray, c1890, 10in (25cm) wide.
£30–35 *AL*

Scales

A set of kitchen scales and weights, with a china tray, early 20thC, 13in (33cm) wide.
£25–35 *HAC*

A set of cast iron kitchen scales, with a copper tray, early 20thC, 13in (33cm) wide.
£25–35 *HAC*

A set of scales, with aluminium bowl, early 20thC, 18½in (47cm) high.
£65–75 *AL*

A set of cast iron kitchen scales
and weights, with a tin bowl,
early 20thC, 13in (33cm) wide.
£10–12 *HAC*

A set of Record enamel kitchen
scales and weights, c1920, 16in
(40.5cm) wide.
£30–35 *AL*

A set of kitchen scales and
weights, with enamel tray,
c1890, 9in (22.5cm) wide.
£30–35 *AL*

A set of Harper scales, with
aluminium tray, early 20thC,
16in (40.5cm) wide.
£10–12 *HAC*

Scissors

A pair of Victorian scissors.
£75–90 *ARE*

A set of 'Victory V' tin scales,
c1920, 16in (40.5cm) high.
£30–35 *AL*

A set of Izons kitchen scales,
c1920, 11in (28cm) high.
£30–35 *AL*

A set of kitchen balance scales,
early 20thC, 13½in (34cm) high.
£25–30 *LF*

A pair of Victorian
plated grape scissors.
£30–40 *VB*

A set of tin kitchen scales and
weights, early 20thC, 12in
(30.5cm) wide.
£5–8 *HAC*

A set of painted sweet shop
scales, with brass tray, early
20thC, 13in (33cm) wide.
£25–35 *HAC*

A set of Salter green and cream
enamel kitchen scales, c1930,
4½in (11cm) diam.
£10–15 *AL*

A set of brass weights, early 20thC.
£15–20 *NM*

Sieves & Strainers

l. A chrome tea strainer, c1930.
c. A tin coffee strainer, c1930.
r. A plated brass tea strainer, c1900.
£4–12 each *AL*

Three wire flour
sieves, c1900.
£6–8 each *AL*

r. Two hair sieves,
c1900, 9 and 10in
(22.5 and 25cm) diam.
£10–12 each *AL*

A tin strainer, c1900,
6in (15cm) long.
£8–10 *AL*

Storage Jars

Three glass storage jars, c1920,
6½ to 10in (16 to 25cm) high.
£6–12 each *AL*

A biscuit barrel and cover,
by William Goebel, 1930s,
9½in (23cm) high.
£60–80 *WIL*

Four Kleen Kitchen Ware green
and white jars, 5in and 3½in
(12.5 and 8.5cm) high, and a
sugar shaker, c1920, 5¼in
(13.5cm) high.
£4–16 each *AL*

Stoves & Ranges

A green glass biscuit
barrel, with chrome
cover, c1920, 7¼in
(18.5cm) high.
£12–16 *AL*

A white ceramic storage
jar and lid, c1890, 7in
(17.5cm) high.
£15–20 *AL*

A potbelly solid fuel stove,
late 19thC.
£200–250 *WEL*

A paraffin stove, late
19thC, 11in (28cm) high.
£20–25 *AL*

*Old paraffin stoves are not
permitted to be sold in
working order.*

A 'Modern Mistress' kitchen range, late 19thC, 36in (92cm) wide.
£320–380 *GRF*

A copper and steel gas autoclave, by Baird and Tatlock, with brass fittings, c1910–20.
£80–100 *COL*

A Victorian 'The Scottish Chief' range, with water jacket, 35in (89cm) wide.
£400–500 *RE*

A gas stove, with an iron top, c1890, 12in (30.5cm) high.
£35–40 *AL*

Tins

A Tala painted tin storage set, in a hanging rack, c1930s, 14in (35.5cm) long.
£12–15 *CEMB*

A green, black and cream painted tea tin, c1930, 5in (12.5cm) high.
£6–8 *AL*

A tea tin, c1870, 8in (20cm) high.
£10–15 *AL*

A biscuit tin, painted in orange, green and yellow on a black ground, c1950s, 8in (20cm) high.
£6–10 *AL*

Utensils

An ice knife, with blade cover, c1880, 14½in (36.5cm) long.
£10–15 *AL*

A 'Nutbrown' chromium plated kitchen saw, on original card, 20thC, 10in (25cm) long.
£1–2 *HAC*

> **Miller's is a price GUIDE not a price LIST**

A selection of kitchen tools.
From left to right.
A wine lifter, c1900, 14½in
(36.5cm) long.
A wine lifter, c1900, 11in
(28cm) long.
A Cadbury's whisk, c1900,
11½in (29.5cm) long.
A wine drainer, c1920, 16in
(40.5cm) long.
A wine ladle, c1920, 12½in
(31.5cm) long.
A slice, c1900, 9½in (23.5cm).
£3–16 each *AL*

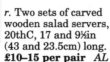

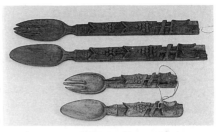

r. Two sets of carved
wooden salad servers,
20thC, 17 and 9½in
(43 and 23.5cm) long.
£10–15 per pair *AL*

A brass skimmer, late 19thC,
21in (53cm) long.
£40–50 *DUN*

A slice, c1920, 12in (30.5cm)
long, a wine scoop, c1920, 11in
(28cm) long, and a pair of
spoons, c1900, 13in (33cm) long.
£6–12 each *AL*

A selection of utensils, with
carved wooden handles, 20thC,
largest 13in (33cm) long.
£5–7 each *HAC*

A selection of slices,
and a straining ladle,
c1900, 12 to 17½in
(30.5 to 44.5cm) long.
£6–12 each *AL*

A selection of Scottish porridge
spurtles, c1890–1930, 11 to 12in
(28 to 30.5cm) long.
£8–12 each *CEMB*

A Tala icing set, in original
box, with pink plastic icing
table and metal nozzles,
20thC, box 8½in (21cm) square.
£4–5 *HAC*

A 'Nutbrown' peeler,
shredder and slicer,
on original card,
c1930–40.
£1–2 *HAC*

Washing & Cleaning

Two bundles of wooden clothes pegs, early 20thC, 4in (10cm) long.
£2–3 per bundle *AL*

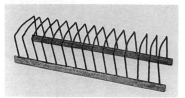

A wire plate rack, c1920, 14in (35.5cm) long.
£15–20 *AL*

A red tin dustpan, c1930, 14in (35.5cm) wide.
£10–12 *AL*

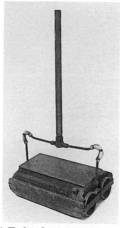

A Ewbank carpet sweeper, c1920–30.
£18–20 *JUN*

A washboard, early 20thC.
£30–35 *CPA*

A pair of laundry tongs, c1930.
£4–5 *AL*

A round drainer plate, c1890, 6½in (16cm) diam., and an oval drainer plate, c1910, 7in (17.5cm) long.
£5–7 each *AL*

Two enamel soap dishes, c1900, 5½in (13.5cm) wide.
£8–12 *AL*

A galvanised floor bucket, c1930, 9½in (23.5cm) high.
£10–12 *AL*

A green enamel soap dish, c1900, 7in (17.5cm) wide.
£8–10 *AL*

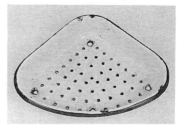

An enamel sink drainer, c1920, 8½in (21cm) wide.
£6–8 *AL*

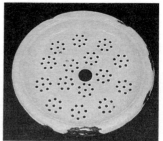

A white enamel drainer, c1920, 8½in (21cm) diam.
£6–8 *AL*

A washing dolly.
£55–65 *CPA*

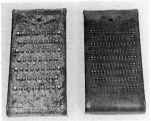

Two tin 'Wonder Shredder' soap
shredders, c1900–20, 8½in
(21cm) high.
£4–6 each *AL*

A tin wash tub, late 19thC,
21½in (54cm) wide.
£10–12 *AL*

Two flat irons, c1890,
6in (15cm) long.
£7–10 each *AL*

Two flat irons, c1880–90,
5in (12.5cm) long.
£8–10 each *AL*

Two iron trivets, one with
wooden handle, c1880–90,
7 to 9½in (17.5 to 23.5cm) long.
£12–15 each *AL*

A galvanised metal patented
non-splash dolly tub, late
19thC, 21in (53cm) high.
£15–20 *JUN*

A clothes line,
in green tin
container, c1920,
7in (17.5cm) high.
£10–12 *AL*

A 'Heludor Refinator
Water Softener', c1920,
6in (15cm) high.
£10–15 *AL*

A ceramic water filter, by
'The Berkefeld Filter Co.',
late 19thC, 18in (48cm) high.
£35–45 *JUN*

Two wooden towel holders,
c1920, 21½in (54cm) wide and
15½in (39cm) wide.
£18–20 each *AL*

Three bottle brushes, one with
brass fitting, late 19thC.
£2–12 each *AL*

LAMPS & LIGHTING

Names can be misleading. The so-called lacemaker's lamps in this section were probably too fragile and costly to have actually been used by lacemakers.

A silver plated cricketing lamp, by Elkington, marked 1851, 32½in (82cm) high.
£2,750–2,950 *Bur*

This trophy was produced by Elkington, who specialised in presentation pieces, mainly of silver plate, a process which the company invented. Elkington operated in Birmingham between 1800 and 1900, and was widely regarded as the best of its kind. This piece was possibly part of the Elkington contribution to the Great Exhibition.

A Georgian glass lacemaker's flash, 6½in (16cm) high.
£75–125 *WAB*

This flash has been filled with olives, probably by a Victorian grocer.

A lacemaker's lamp, the stem with a baluster knop, plain conical foot, c1760, 7½in (18cm) high.
£400–450 *Som*

A pair of Italian glass figural table lamps, with rectangular bodies on a domed base, c1930, 15in (38.5cm) high, with rectangular lamp shades.
£475–500 *P*

A bronze and ivory table lamp, on a Sienna marble base, by Roland, Paris, c1930, 23in (58.5cm) high.
£850–900 *SWO*

Two early wooden light switches, 19thC, 3½in (8.5cm) high.
£5–6 each *PSA*

A bronze plated spelter lamp, 'L'Amour Vagabond', by Broachon, 19thC, 21in (53cm) high.
£300–385 *WAG*

A Bakelite desk lamp, c1930, 11in (28cm) high.
£45–55 *JUN*

l. A pair of octagonal wall lamps, with fretted domes and lids, raised on scrolled branches, early 19thC, 14in (35.5cm) high.
£450–550 *B*

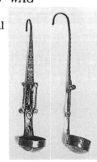

Two metal oil lamp ladles, 19thC, 14in (35.5cm) long.
£45–65 each *MofC*

LILLIPUT LANE

Two Lilliput Lane ceramic models, 'Dove Cottage', produced February 1983–December 1988.
l. 1st Version, with name embossed. **£550–600**
r. 2nd Version, name removed. **£50–60** *TP*

A Lilliput Lane ceramic model, 'Gables', produced February 1987–December 1992. **£100–120** *TP*

A Lilliput Lane ceramic model, 'Cosy Corner', produced March 1990–February 1991, a free gift for joining the collectors' club. **£60–80** *TP*

Two Lilliput Lane ceramic models, 'Sussex Mill', produced September 1982–March 1986.
l. 2nd Version. **£225–275**
r. 1st Version. **£500–600** *TP*

A Lilliput Lane ceramic model, 'Burnside', No. 41, 2nd Version, November 1982–July 1985. **£250–300** *TP*

A Lilliput Lane ceramic model, 'Gardeners Cottage', a collectors' club piece, produced March 1991–February 1992. **£100–120** *TP*

A Lilliput Lane ceramic model, 'Counting House Corner', 2nd Version, available for one day only 25th November 1993. **£700–900** *TP*

This piece was produced to commemorate the floating of Lilliput on the Stock Market, 25th November, 1993, only available to club members, 3,028 pieces only.

A Lilliput Lane ceramic model, 'Wenlock Rise', a collectors' club piece produced October 1988–September 1989. **£150–200** *TP*

A Lilliput Lane ceramic model, 'Guild Hall', produced July 1987–December 1989, only available for sale through The Association of China and Glass Retailers' Guild. **£100–150** *TP*

A Lilliput Lane ceramic model, 'St. Mary's Church', produced February 1985–December 1988.
£70–100 *TP*

A Lilliput Lane collectors' club ceramic model, 'Crendon Manor', from a 1,500 limited edition, produced November 1986–February 1989.
£300–400 *TP*

A Lilliput Lane ceramic model, 'Riverview', July 1987–July 1994.
£20–25 *TP*

A Lilliput Lane ceramic model, 'Izaak Walton', July 1987–December 1989.
£70–85 *TP*

A Lilliput Lane ceramic model, 'Honey Suckle', a 1992 anniversary piece to commemorate 10 years of the company, available for one year only.
£130–150 *TP*

A Lilliput Lane ceramic model, 'Yuletide Inn', annual Christmas Issue, December 1990–February 1991.
£120–150 *TP*

A Lilliput Lane ceramic model, 'Mayflower House', USA only, April 1989–December 1990.
£200–275 *TP*

A Lilliput Lane ceramic model, 'Adobe Church', produced October 1984–October 1985.
£350–400 *TP*

A Lilliput Lane ceramic model, 'Cliburn School', from a limited edition of 64, produced June 1983–February 1984.
£2,500–3,000 *TP*

A Lilliput Lane ceramic model, 'St. Peter's Cove', from a limited edition of 3,000, issued February 1989.
£750–900 *TP*

A ceramic model, 'Warwick Hall', 2nd Version, three versions produced.
£1,800–2,200 *TP*

A Lilliput Lane ceramic model, 'Beacon Bach', produced February 1986–July 1993.
£40–50 *TP*

McDONALD'S

McDonald's toys are certainly a contender for collectables of the future. McDonald's opened its first restaurant in California in 1937, but it was not until 1979 in the US and some ten years late in Britain, that the concept of the Happy Meal was launched. A Happy Meal consists of a hamburger, fries, drink and a plastic toy, all presented in a themed box with punch-out 3-D scenes. Toys come in sets of four, each available for a limited period only, providing a diary of juvenile culture, reflecting favourite films, toys and events.

In the United States there are already established McDonald's collectors' societies and adult enthusiasts are assembling collections of both toys and other ephemera. The earliest toys and complete sets will command a premium. Good condition is always important and the original packaging, in particular the boxes, should not be torn or grease stained.

A McDonald's store display, American, c1992, 14in (35.5cm) square.
£20–25 SBa

A McDonald's 'Ronald' character doll, c1971, 17in (43cm) high.
£15–20 SBa

A McDonald's soft toy, 'Hamburglar', c1972, 17in (43cm) high.
£25–30 SBa

A McDonald's Translite store display sign, c1991, 21½in (54.5cm) square.
£25–30 SBa

A set of 8 McDonald's Barbie dolls, with original packaging, c1993, 4½in (11cm).
£30–35 each SBa

l. A McDonald's 'Ronald' character doll, c1983, 16in (40.5cm) high.
£15–20 SBa

FURTHER READING
Tomart's Price Guide to Happy Meal Collectables, Meredith Williams

A set of McDonald's Flintstones Happy Meal toys, 1994.
£1–5 each PC

A McDonald's store display, c1992, 21½in (54.5cm) square.
£25–30 SBa

Three McDonald's 'Mac Tonight' figurines, American, c1988, 3 to 3½in (7.5 to 8.5cm).
£4–5 each
A piano, c1988, 4½in (11cm) wide.
£10–12 *SBa*

The piano plays the tune 'Mac the Knife'.

A collection of McDonald's Happy Meal toys, c1993–94.
£1–5 each *PC*

Two McDonald's Christmas ornaments, by Enesco, American:
l. c1990, 4½in (11cm) high.
r. c1992, 2½in (6cm) square.
£15–20 each *SBa*

Three McDonald's Christmas ornaments, by Enesco, American, c1991–92, 2½ to 3½in (6 to 9cm) high.
£15–20 each *SBa*

A set of four McDonald's Happy Meal promotional toys, American, c1992, 3 to 4in (7.5 to 10cm) long.
£15–20 *SBa*

A set of McDonald's Aladdin Happy Meal toys, 1993.
£1–5 each *PC*

A McDonald's bookmark, door hanger and game, 1993.
£2–3 each *SBa*

A selection of McDonald's Happy Meal toys, c1991–94, 2 to 4½in (5 to 11cm).
£2–5 each *SBa*

r. Two McDonald's die cast lorries, 1993, 7in (17.5cm).
£10–15 each *SBa*

l. Two McDonald's Christmas ornaments, by Enesco, American, c1993, 3in (7.5cm).
£15–20 each *SBa*

MAUCHLINE WARE

A Victorian Mauchline ware money box, with concealed opening, with transfer ware view of Plymouth Sound and Breakwater, 3½in (9cm) wide.
£20–25 *HAY*

A Mauchline ware clock money box, with transfer view of Tunbridge Wells, c1900, 4½in (11cm) high.
£30–40 *HAY*

A Mauchline ware sycamore watch stand box, with pictorial lid and transfer view of Southsea Beach, early 20thC, 4in (10cm) wide.
£20–25 *HAY*

A Mauchline ware sycamore kennel-shaped box, with photographic transfer, early 20thC, 4in (10cm) wide.
£30–35 *HAY*

A Mauchline ware octagonal box, with photographic transfer view of Freshwater Bay, early 20thC.
£20–25 *HAY*

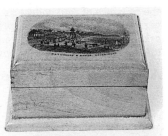

A Mauchline ware box, with transfer ware view of the Bathhouse and Sands, Dovercourt, c1900, 3in (7.5cm) wide.
£25–30 *HAY*

A Mauchline ware stamp box, with transfer view of Alloway Kirk, c1900, 2½in (6cm) wide.
£25–30 *HAY*

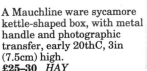

A Mauchline ware sycamore kettle-shaped box, with metal handle and photographic transfer, early 20thC, 3in (7.5cm) high.
£25–30 *HAY*

- **Mauchline Ware is a distinctive range of treen souvenir ware, usually varnished sycamore, transfer printed with colourful designs and often depicting popular views.**
- **Manufactured by A. & A. Smith in Mauchline, Ayrshire, and later in Birmingham, from c1820 until the 1930s.**
- **Objects produced include boxes, napkin rings, spill holders and other small wooden items.**

Two Mauchline ware boxes, early 20thC:
l. With a transfer view of Wales, 3½in (9cm) wide. **£18–20**
r. A ring box, with photographic ware view of Torquay, 2in (5cm).
£20–25 *HAY*

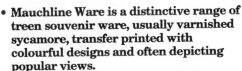

MEDALS & BADGES

The joy of commemorative medals is that you are literally holding history in your hand. Most medals tell a story – a battle lost, an agricultural prize won, or a king commemorated. As dealer Timothy Millett explains, medals first appeared in the reign of Queen Elizabeth I and became extremely popular during the Civil War, flourishing in the 19thC, when they were produced to celebrate every occasion.

Prices begin from as little as £20, and there is a wealth of material for under £200. Traditionally such medals have been the province of coin collectors, but with the variety in subject matter, price and their great historical interest, commemorative medals now appeal to a far wider audience.

l. An Australia, Hampden and Heytesbury Pastoral and Agricultural Society silver prize, by Stokes and Martin, dated '22 October 1881', 1⅜in (3.5cm) diam.
£225–245 *BAL*

r. A Warwickshire, Birmingham and Midland Counties Exhibition silver prize, by Ottley, dated '1858', 1⅜in (3.5cm) diam.
£40–50 *BAL*

Agricultural Medals

A Durham, Northumberland and Newcastle-on-Tyne Botanical and Horticultural Society silver prize, inscribed 'Instituted 1824'.
£85–95 *BAL*

A Kirton Ploughing Society silver prize, dated '2nd Jan^Y 1873', 2in (5cm) diam.
£130–145 *BAL*

A National Pig Breeders Association silver prize, 1953, 2in (5cm) diam.
£35–40 *BAL*

Livery Badges

A Cutlers' Company silver badge, inscribed on the reverse and dated 'November 9th 1829', with integral loop for suspension, 2⅜in (6cm) diam.
£200–220 *BAL*

A Turners' Company silver gilt Livery badge, inscribed and dated '25th April 1786', with loop for suspension, 2⅜in (6cm).
£245–265 *BAL*

A Fruiterers' Company silver gilt and enamelled Livery badge, decorated with the arms of the Company, Victorian hallmark, with pin for suspension on reverse, 2in (5cm) diam.
£100–115 *BAL*

Lord Mayors' Badges

A Lord Mayor's silver gilt badge, inscribed and dated '1835–6', 2in (5cm) diam.
£180–200 *BAL*

A Lord Mayor's shield-shaped silver gilt badge, inscribed and dated '1862–3'.
£200–225 *BAL*

A Lord Mayor's silver gilt badge, with ornate wreath border, inscribed and dated '1829'. with integral loop for suspension, 2½in (6cm) diam.
£200–225 *BAL*

Political

l. A Yorkshire, York Election silver ticket medal, inscribed 'Milton for Ever and 11,177', dated '1807', 2in (5cm) diam.
£165–185 *BAL*

An Abolition of Slavery white metal medal, by T. Halliday, 1834, 1½in (3.5cm) diam.
£40–50 *BAL*

A Negro Emancipation in the West Indies white metal medal, by T. Halliday, 1838, 1½in (3.5cm) diam.
£55–65 *BAL*

Military

A Nelson Crimson Oaks silver medal, probably by B. Patrick, 1808, 2½in (6cm) diam.
£250–275 *BAL*

A Montreal Taken silver medal, by J. Kirk, 1760, 1½in (4cm) diam.
£450–525 *BAL*

A Death of the Duke of Wellington silver medal, by T. R. Pinches, 1852, 2in (5cm).
£85–95 *BAL*

A Battle of Plassy bronze medal, 1758, 1½in (4cm) diam.
£45–55 *BAL*

A Shipwrecked Fishermen and Mariners' Benevolent Society white metal medal, 1839, with loop for suspension, 2in (5cm).
£40–50 *BAL*

A Battle of Cape St. Vincent white metal medal, by J. G. Hancock, 1797, 2in (5cm) diam.
£110–125 *BAL*

Royal

An Anne, Coronation official silver medal, by John Croker, 1702, 1½in (3.5cm).
£90–100 *BAL*

A Caroline, Coronation official silver medal, by John Croker, 1727, 1½in (3.5cm) diam.
£55–65 *BAL*

A Victoria Golden Jubilee silver medal, by A. Gilbert, 1887, 2½in (6cm) diam.
£1,000–1,150 *BAL*

r. An Oliver Cromwell, Elizabeth Claypole Memorial silver medal, by J. Kirk, 1658, 1½in (3.5cm) diam.
£75–85 *BAL*

Anne Claypole was the daughter of Oliver Cromwell.

l. A William IV Coronation official silver medal, by William Wyon, 1831, 1½in (3.5cm) diam.
£45–55 *BAL*

A Victoria Coronation official
silver medal, by Benedetto
Pistrucci, 1838, 1½in (3.5cm).
£40–45 *BAL*

A George IV Coronation silver
admission ticket, 1821, 1½in
(3.5cm) diam.
£85–95 *BAL*

A George IV Coronation
official silver medal, by
Benedetto Pistrucci, 1821,
1½in (3.5cm) diam.
£55–65 *BAL*

School Prizes

An Egglesfield House School
silver prize medal, by T. Wyon,
dated 'July 22 1811', 1½in (3.5cm).
£75–95 *BAL*

A Royal Belfast Academical
Institution silver medal, by
J. W. Ingram, 1810, 2in
(5cm) diam.
£110–125 *BAL*

A Grove House School, Kent
silver medal, London hallmark,
with loop for suspension, 1½in
(3.5cm) diam.
£85–95 *BAL*

Societies

A Miss Pritchard's School
silver prize medal, pierced for
suspension, dated '1809', 1½in
(3.5cm) diam.
£85–95 *BAL*

A Sensorium Club silver pass,
1715, 1½in (3.5cm) diam.
£135–145 *BAL*

*The Sensorium Club was
founded in 1715 by Sir Richard
Steele, with one hundred
members each, gentleman and
ladies 'of leading taste in
politeness, wit and learning',
who met occasionally to be
entertained with 'Music,
Eloquence and Poetry'.*

A Royal Society of Arts silver
prize, instituted 1753, by
T. Pingo, pierced for suspension,
1803, 2in (4.5cm) diam.
£65–75 *BAL*

l. A Royal Society of Arts silver
prize, instituted 1753, by
T. Wyon, 1824, 1½in (3.5cm) diam.
£85–95 *BAL*

Sporting

A Derbyshire Archers silver
prize, by B. Wyon, 1823.
£75–85 *BAL*

An Oxonian Hundred Mile Club
Championship Road Race silver
cycling prize, inscribed and
dated '1883', 1½in (3.5cm) diam.
£75–85 *BAL*

A Buccleugh Archers silver
badge, with pin for suspension
in the shape of an arrow, 1859,
1½in (3.5cm) diam.
£165–185 *BAL*

A Liverpool Race Course silver
pass, by Halliday, 2in (5cm).
£275–325 *BAL*

A white metal medal, by W.J.
Taylor, inscribed 'Hermit
Winner of the Derby May 22nd
1867', 1½in (3.5cm) diam.
£50–60 *BAL*

A Doncaster Race Course
octagonal silver pass, by Wilson,
1826, with original leather case.
£650–775 *BAL*

A Newcastle Race Course silver
admission ticket, 1800.
£275–300 *BAL*

Theatre Passes

A Her Majesty's Theatre,
Haymarket ivory pass, 1844,
1½in (3.5cm) diam.
£160–185 *BAL*

A Musical Society ivory pass,
c1850, 1½in (3.5cm) diam.
£100–125 *BAL*

An oval ivory pass, possibly
Kings Theatre and Opera,
Haymarket, c1790, 2in
(5cm) wide.
£225–250 *BAL*

*These ivory passes were the
equivalent of today's paper
tickets.*

An Opera Haymarket ivory
pass, inscribed and dated '1820',
1½in (3.5cm) diam.
£150–185 *BAL*

METALWARE
Arts & Crafts

All the following pieces are by the British Arts and Crafts metalware designer Hugh Wallis (1880–1925). Each piece is marked with his monogram.

A pewter card tray, 9½in (23.5cm) long.
£30–35 *BRD*

Two copper plates, with silver decoration, 7½in (18.5cm) diam.
£55–80 each *BRD*

r. Two copper drinks trays, largest 11½in (29cm) diam.
£60–80 each *BRD*

A hexagonal copper dish, 4in (10cm) diam.
£30–35 *BRD*

A copper bowl, 7in (17.5cm) diam.
£45–50 *BRD*

A copper dish, with silver decoration, 9½in (24cm) diam.
£90–100 *BRD*

A pewter chalice, 6in (15cm) diam.
£140–160 *BRD*

Three pewter bowls, 4 to 5½in (10 to 13.5cm) diam.
£20–30 each *BRD*

A copper fruit bowl, with pierced mistletoe pattern base, 13in (33cm) diam.
£350–400 *BRD*

r. Two oval copper trays, with silver decoration, 22in (55.5cm) wide.
£120–150 each *BRD*

Candlesticks

A pair of silver candlesticks, damaged, Birmingham 1926.
£55–65 *TRU*

A pair of Art Deco chrome plated candlesticks, c1937, 9in (23cm) high.
£35–42 *BKK*

A pair of brass candlesticks, raised on petal shaped feet, mid-18thC, 8½in (21cm) high.
£400–500 *WIL*

A miniature brass chamber stick, early 19thC.
£80–100 *JAC*

A Victorian brass 'go-to-bed', 2in (5cm) high.
£18–22 *VB*

Copper

A copper jardinière, c1880, 7in (17.5cm) high.
£40–50 *DUN*

A copper kettle, with wooden handle, c1910, 10in (25cm) high.
£30–35 *AL*

Sculptures & Figures

A Vienna bronze elephant, c1900, 2in (5cm) high.
£150–180 *DUN*

A Vienna bronze goose, c1900, 3in (7.5cm) high.
£120–150 *DUN*

A brass figure of a seated lion, 11in (28cm) long, a squirrel, 2in (5cm) high, and a cat, 4in (10cm) long.
£60–90 *LF*

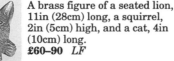

A bronze goose with a snail perched on its beak, by Edouard Marcel Sandoz, on a bronze base, 8in (20cm) long.
£480–500 *P*

A bronze and ivory figure, 'The Connoisseur' by Bruno Zach, cast and carved as a portly gentleman wearing 18thC costume, patinated in green, raised on stepped oval green onyx base, unsigned, 10in (25cm) high.
£1,350–1,500 *P*

A bronze and ivory group, cast and carved as two children, their coats patinated in red, repaired, unsigned, c1920, 8½in (21cm) high.
£950–1,200 *P*

r. A Lorenzl bronze, c1930, 9in (23cm) high.
£500–550 *HEW*

A nickel souvenir Coronation penknife, with two steel blades, 1937, 3in (8cm) long.
£12–15 *FMN*

l. An Art Deco spelter figure, 10in (25cm) high.
£350–400 *HEW*

A drama trophy, c1930, 6in (15cm) high.
£35–45 *HEW*

Silver

Silver remains one of the most popular collectables. At the top end of the market, prices for antique silver can run into many thousands of pounds, but for those with a more modest budget, there are still plenty of smaller more affordable items available, with prices beginning at under £100.

Art Nouveau

A Liberty Tudric dish, with shamrock pattern, c1910, 11in (28cm) wide.
£140–150 *CSA*

A Guild of Handicrafts silver porringer, by C.R. Ashbee, London 1901, 8in (20cm) long.
£300–400 *CSA*

Two Kayserzinn silver plates, 10in (25cm) and 7in (17.5cm).
£40–90 each *CSA*

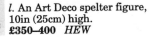

An Art Nouveau silver double struck cutlery set, 24 pieces, 800 standard.
£350–380 *TER*

Boxes

A WMF silvered pewter trinket box, 4⅓in (11cm) wide.
£80–90 *CSA*

A shagreen covered trinket box, on four silver mounted wooden feet, the lid applied with crossed Union flags, wire-work initials and dated '1807', the interior inscribed, maker's initials only on back hinge plate, 6in (15cm).
£500–600 *CSK*

A Continental silver gilt box, the sides stamped with scrolled foliage, the lid stamped with a minstrel and his lady, probably late 17thC, but with later marks, 3in (7.5cm) long.
£680–700 *CSK*

A Continental double-lidded box, the sides pierced and engraved with bird and floral studies, the top lid with similar central decoration, the base lid pierced and engraved, opening to reveal a mirrored interior, 19thC, 3½in (8.5cm) wide.
£350–400 *CSK*

Card Cases

A silver visiting card case, engraved with crest, 19thC, 3½in (9cm) long.
£85–110 *LF*

A Victorian card case, stamped with scenes on both sides, the interior with added lugs for conversion to a cigarette case, H. Mathews, Birmingham 1899, 4in (10cm) long.
£300–350 *CSK*

l. An Edwardian card case, both sides stamped with a horse-drawn cart and church within a foliate border, Joseph Gloster, Birmingham 1905, 4in (10cm) long.
£350–450 *CSK*

l. A late Victorian card case, the front stamped with a stag surrounded by scroll-work and trelliswork, Deakin and Francis, Birmingham 1900, 4in (10cm) long.
£300–350 *CSK*

MAKE THE MOST OF MILLERS

Price ranges in this book reflect what you should expect to *pay* for a similar example. When selling, however, you would expect to receive a lower figure. This will fluctuate according to a dealer's stock and saleability at a particular time. It is always advisable, when selling a collectable, to approach a reputable dealer or an auction house which has specialist sales.

l. A William IV card case, stamped with views on both sides and scrollwork, Taylor and Perry, Birmingham, 1836, 3½in (9cm) long.
£550–600 *CSK*

An amber necklace, beads 16–36mm diam, c1994, 27in (69cm) long.
£900–1,000 *EaJ*

An amber heart-shaped pendant and chain, c1994, 23in (59cm) long.
£125–175 *EaJ*

A large cabochon amber brooch, with silver mount, c1994, 3in (7.5cm) wide.
£175–200 *EaJ*

An amber pendant, with hallmarked silver mount, c1994, 3½in (8.5cm) high.
£575–625 *EaJ*

An amber and 14ct gold violin brooch, c1994.
£250–300 *EaJ*

A pair of gold top pippin amber earrings, c1993.
£100–150 *EaJ*

An amber and silver pendant, with leather collar, c1994. **£500–550** *EaJ*

An amber belt buckle, with silver mount, 1994, 2½in (6.5cm).
£500–550 *EaJ*

A silver torque, with amber pendant and silver mount, c1994. **£600–650** *EaJ*

An amber and silver filigree cigarette holder, c1900, 3⅓in (8.5cm) long.
£15–20 *DP*

Two amber cabochons, c1994, largest 1⅛in (4cm) high.
£40–70 *EaJ*

An amber and silver ring, c1994.
£80–100 *EaJ*

An amber and 14ct gold pendant, c1994.
£400–450 *EaJ*

A pair of enamel and brass cuff links, c1920.
£35–50 *FMN*

An agate seal, with pinchbeck mount, c1994, 2.5cm high.
£100–150 *EaJ*

A pair of wooden mermaid earrings, by Odyssey, c1990.
£16–18 *NEW*

A multi-coloured wooden brooch, by P. Niczewski, c1990.
£20–24 *NEW*

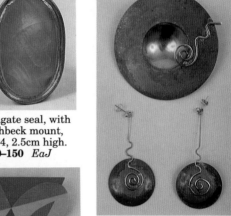

A pair of copper and brass earrings and a brooch, by Jo Mitchell, c1990.
£15–40 each *NEW*

A Georgian cameo seal ring, with gold shank, 2cm high.
£700–800 *SIG*

r. A solid brass photograph brooch, c1900, 1½in (4cm) high.
£30–40 *FMN*

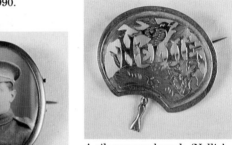

A silver name brooch, 'Nellie', with registration kite mark on reverse, c1900, 1½in (3.5cm) wide.
£60–85 *FMN*

A chrome and enamel tie pin and cuff link set, c1920.
£40–50 *FMN*

A pair of Himalayan 22ct gold and turquoise tzi-yu, late 18thC, 1¾in (4.5cm) wide.
£1,200–2,000 *RAM*

A silver seal, set with a purple 'tassie', c1860.
£85–100 *PUR*

A gilt cased seal, set with a plain cornelian, c1860, 4cm high.
£100–150 *PUR*

A gold cased seal, set with a cornelian, c1860, 3cm high.
£85–100 *PUR*

A pair of citrine cabochons, 5.18ct, c1994, 1.25cm high.
£50–70 *EaJ*

A French wooden coffee grinder, c1920–30, 6in (15cm) high.
£20–25 *CEMB*

A set of four Tala flan tins, late 1930s, moulds 4in (10cm) diam.
£10–15 *CEMB*

A French terracotta butter cooler, c1900–20, 7⅓in (18.5cm) diam.
£25–30 *CEMB*

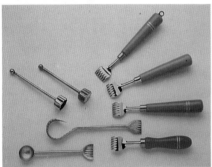

A selection of butter pat makers and curlers, c1920–50, 4½ to 6½in (11.5 to 16.5cm).
£3–8 each *CEMB*

A set of Salter household scales, 10½in (26cm) high.
£20–25 *CEMB*

Two wooden mashers, c1870.
£30–40 each *CEMB*

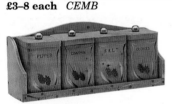

A set of spice containers, in a hand painted rack, c1950s, 11in (28cm) long.
£20–25 *CEMB*

Three Tamis cooks' sieves, c1910–50, 5½ to 9½in (13.5 to 23.5cm) diam.
£4–15 each *CEMB*

A blue painted tin egg rack, with folding handle, c1930, 7½in (18.5cm) long.
£10–15 *CEMB*

A pewter ice cream mould, c1868.
£150–200 *CEMB*

Two oak wood crushers, 18in (45.5cm) long.
£25–50 each *CEMB*

An enamel cake container, c1900–20, 5⅓in (13.5cm).
£15–20 *CEMB*

Five McDonald's character dolls, by Remco, USA, from a set of seven, 7 to 8in (17.5 to 20cm) high. **£20–25 each** *SBa*

Four McDonald's UK Happy Meal Batman toys, 1994. **£1–3 each** *PC*

A McDonald's Translite store display, American, c1992, 13in (33cm) square. **£20–25** *SBa*

A Ronald McDonald ceramic money box, c1993, 8in (20cm) high. **£15–20** *SBa*

A Ronald McDonald whistle-blowing doll, c1978, 23in (59cm) high. **£25–30** *SBa*

A McDonald's 40th Anniversary plate, by Franklin Mint, 1994, 8in (20cm) diam. **£20–25** *SBa*

A McDonald's Hamburglar soft toy, c1987, 13in (33cm). **£15–20** *SBa*

A McDonald's Translite store display, c1991, 14in (35.5cm) square. **£25–30** *SBa*

Two McDonald's Christmas ornaments, by Enesco, c1992, 3in (7.5cm) long. **£15–20 each** *SBa*

A set of six McDonald's 'Collector Series' drinking glasses, c1977, 6in (15cm) high. **£30–35** *SBa*

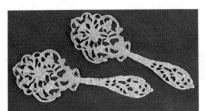

A pair of parcel gilt caddy spoons, Birmingham 1887, 5½in (13.5cm) long. **£250–275** *AMH*

Four boxed silver owl menu holders, by Sampson Mordan & Co, Chester, 1913–14. **£450–480** *RAN*

A silver gilt and enamel tea strainer, possibly Russian. **£70–90** *DEL*

A silver tea set, c1897. **£450–550** *LIO*

A pair of Sheffield silver plate fish servers, by Elkington. **£110–150** *LIO*

An Arts and Crafts copper tazza, c1900, 17½in (44.5cm) diam. **£140–180** *BRD*

A silver card case, by Deakin and Francis, c1896, 3in (7.5cm) long. **£100–140** *LIO*

A late Victorian brass and copper urn, 21in (53cm). **£250–300** *LIO*

A trailing vine pattern sifter spoon, by G. Adams, London 1863, 6½in (16cm). **£200–225** *AMH*

A cast silver gilt medal, by Nicholas Briot, depicting Charles I, with a view of London on reverse, 2in (5cm). **£1,400–1,500** *BAL*

A silver box, depicting a coronet, heart and thistle, by Hamilton and Inches, Edinburgh 1902, 4½in (11cm) wide. **£425–465** *RAN*

An alpaca two-piece part coffee service, German, pot 9in (22.5cm) high. **£150–175** *WTA*

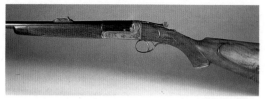

A William Evans .297/.250 boxlock ejector rook rifle, No. 15775, 14¾in (37cm) stock, weight 5lbs 10oz. **£850–1,000** *Bon*

An African knife, with wooden grip, leaf shaped blade with punched decoration, with bound hardwood sheath. **£140–150** *ASB*

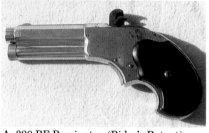

A .320 RF Remington (Rider's Patent) magazine derringer, with sheath trigger and rosewood grips, minor pitting, c1875, barrel 3in (7.5cm) long. **£550–570** *ASB*

A 92nd Regiment (Gordon Highlanders) Piper's dirk, blade 9in (22.5cm) long. **£330–350** *ASB*

Six silver teaspoons, embossed 'City Rifle Club'. **£40–50** *LIO*

A Sheffield bowie, made by Jonathon Crookes for the American market, with ivory grips, 9in (22.5cm) long. **£630–650** *ASB*

A Georgian senior Army Officer's mameluke hilted levee sword, with 'GR' monogram, c1815, blade 31in (78.5cm) long. **£1,600–1,700** *ASB*

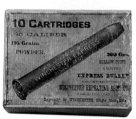

A box of .45/125 Winchester Express cartridges, c1880. **£90–100** *PC*

A box of .303 King's Norton Palma Match cartridges, c1907. **£100–125** *PC*

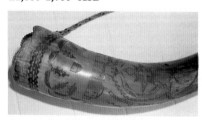

A scrimshaw decorated powderhorn, probably Peninsular War, early 19thC, 14in (35.5cm) long. **£600–700** *ASB*

Four boxes of .22 cartridges, 2⅜in (6cm) long. **£5–10 each** *PC*

Three rounds of big game rifle shotgun ammunition. **£25–35 each** *PC*

A Dresden hand painted figure of an Irish Guards Officer, 11in (28cm) high.
£370–400 *WAL*

A 2nd Lieutenant's full dress scarlet tunic of the Coldstream Guards, good condition.
£280–320 *WAL*

A Hungarian ceremonial uniform, with silk breeches, black leather boots, and mameluke hilted sword, c1900.
£1,100–1,300 *WAL*

A Piper's full dress uniform of The Black Watch, excellent condition.
£450–550 *WAL*

r. An Officer's full dress sporran of The Queen's Own Cameron Highlanders.
£750–850 *WAL*

A green cloth spiked helmet of The Duke of Cornwall's Light Infantry, post-1902.
£650–700 *WAL*

An English School portrait miniature of an Infantry officer, c1820, 4in (10cm).
£350–380 *CSK*

A cloth spiked helmet of the 8th (The King's) Regiment, c1880.
£750–800 *WAL*

A cloth spiked helmet of the 2nd Cheshire Rifle Volunteers, c1885.
£500–600 *WAL*

A group of eleven medals, to Vice-Admiral Marcel Harcourt Attwood Kelsey, mounted as worn, together with a matching set of miniatures and Certificates of Service.
£750–800 *WAL*

A German lead
money bank, c1940.
£70–80 *HAL*

Two punk money boxes,
c1970s, 5½in (13.5cm) high.
£10–15 each *YY*

A money box, depicting a Bank
of Scotland five pounds note,
3in (7.5cm) high. **£6–8** *WP*

A clock, in the form of a one pound
note, c1970, 21in (53cm) wide.
£10–15 *WP*

A Tetley Tea money box, by
Wade, c1989, 5½in (13.5cm).
£25–30 *CBa*

A Carlton Ware novelty
pirate money box, 6in
(15cm) high.
£12–18 *PCh*

l. A poster,
c1914, 20in
(50cm) wide.
£60–80 *WP*

A Crawford's biscuit
tin money box, 1920.
£80–100 *HAL*

A Midland Bank plastic
money box, c1989, 8in
(20cm) high.
£2–3 *WP*

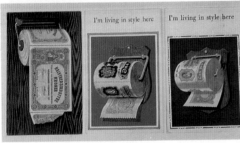

Three postcards, depicting toilet paper printed as
money, c1930. **£3–4 each** *WP*

A selection of money stickers, made in Taiwan,
c1984, 2½in (6cm) wide.
£1–2 each *WP*

A blue emergency WWII issue one pound note, 1939–45.
£6–8 *WP*

An Isle of Man five pounds note, signed by John Paul, Lieutenant Governor.
£20–25 *WP*

An error ten pounds note, the top sheet has dried on to the reverse of the sheet below during the printing process. £150–200 *WP*

A Britannia 'lion and key' five pounds note, issued in 1957.
£18–20 *WP*

An error twenty pounds note, severely miscut although issued.
£150–200 *WP*

A Central Bank of Ireland twenty pounds note, depicting Lady Lavery, 1976.
£30–36 *WP*

An error five pounds note, current issue.
£60–70 *WP*

A one pound note, known as 'Queen's Portrait' design, introduced in 1960.
£14–18 *WP*

A pair of ivory and porcelain opera glasses, with transfer printed scenes, 4in (10cm) wide.
£350–450 *ARE*

A pair of gilt and mother-of-pearl opera glasses, with enamel decoration, velvet carrying bag, 2in (5cm) high.
£450–550 *ARE*

A pair of tortoiseshell opera glasses, with handle, c1890, 3½in (8.5cm) wide.
£300–400 *ARE*

A pair of tortoiseshell opera glasses, with gauge, c1890.
£400–450 *ARE*

A pair of mother-of-pearl opera glasses, cased, c1890, 3in (7.5cm) high.
£70–80 *DP*

A pair of ivory three-draw opera glasses, c1870, 4in (10cm) high.
£120–130 *DP*

A pair of mother-of-pearl opera glasses, 4in (10cm) wide.
£350–400 *ARE*

A pair of mother-of-pearl opera glasses, with gilt fittings, c1880.
£550–600 *ARE*

A pair of stained mother-of-pearl opera glasses, by T. Armstrong & Bros., Manchester, c1880, 4in (7.5cm) high. **£80–90** *DP*

A pair of gilt opera glasses, decorated with enamel and gemstones, c1890, 4in (10cm) wide.
£350–400 *ARE*

A pair of mother-of-pearl opera glasses, cased, c1890. **£70–80** *DP*

A pair of mother-of-pearl opera glasses, with purse case, c1890, 3in (7.5cm) high.
£65–75 *DP*

A Ming Dynasty horse, partially glazed, c1300–1600, 8½in (21cm) long. **£170–250** *GHa*

A Ming Dynasty blue and white jar, 4½in (11cm) high. **£150–180** *GHa*

A Nanking Cargo Provincial bowl, unglazed, c1750, 5½in (14cm). **£100–120** *RBA*

A Ming Dynasty green glaze chest, c1300–1600, 4in (10cm) wide. **£65–100** *GHa*

A blue and white ancestor box, c1800, 4in (10cm) long. **£30–45** *GHa*

A Nanking Cargo Lattice Fence pattern plate, part of a dinner service, 9in (23cm) diam. **£450–650** *RBA*

A £2 Mercurycard, depicting A Harbour Scene,
UK–France 3 Cable, June 1989.
£20–45 *PC*

Two newspaper Mercurycards:
The Sun, £4. **£4–7**
Today, £1, sealed. **£4–6** *PC*

Four Jersey Telecom cards, 4th Issue,
Steam Locomotives.
£3–10 each *PC*

A set of four 50p Mercurycards, League of Nations.
£20–25 *PC*

Six BT advertising phonecards: Horlicks, £2. **£2–4**,
Nescafé, £4. **£5–7**, Castrol, £1. **£3–5**, Persil, 50p. **£5–8**,
Brooke Bond, 50p. **£5–10**, *Daily Mirror*. **£2–4** *PC*

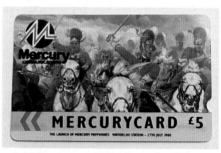

A £5 Mercurycard, The Launch of Mercury
Payphones Waterloo Station, 27 July 1988.
£8–12 *PC*

Two Telecom Eireann
Callcards.
£4–10 each *PC*

Two British Telecom Prison
Service used phonecards.
25p–75p each *PC*

An ICA 1992 £2 Mercurycard,
featuring the Orient Express.
£15–20 *PC*

A Ken Rosenfeld paperweight, with bouquet of crocuses, signed and dated '1993', 3in (7.5cm) diam.
£300–360 *MLa*

A Ken Rosenfeld lampwork paperweight, signed and dated '1993', 3in (7.5cm) diam.
£250–300 *MLa*

A Paul Ysart paperweight, 'H' cane and ring of bubbles, 1970s, 2½in (6cm) diam.
£200–225 *MLa*

A Ken Rosenfeld paperweight, signed and dated '1993', 3in (7.5cm) diam.
£300–350 *MLa*

A Ken Rosenfeld paperweight, for the 100th anniversary of the Statue of Liberty 1989, signed.
£150–200 *MLa*

A Ken Rosenfeld lampwork paperweight, signed and dated '1993', 3in (7.5cm) diam.
£300–350 *MLa*

A John Deacon cartwheel
paperweight, c1990.
£10–15 *SWB*

A green glass dump, c1860.
£120–140 *DUN*

A Perthshire 'B' series limited
edition faceted paperweight,
c1985. **£120–130** *SWB*

A Baccarat paperweight, dated
'1984', 3in (7.5cm) diam.
£300–350 *MLa*

A Whitefriars telephone
commemorative paperweight,
signed. **£275–320** *MLa*

A John Deacon pink rose on
latticinio paperweight, c1993,
2⅜in (6cm) high.
£55–65 *SWB*

A John Deacon swirl pattern
paperweight, c1993, 2⅜in (6cm).
£20–25 *SWB*

A Perthshire paperweight,
limited edition of 300, c1980.
£300–340 *MLa*

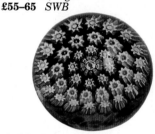

A John Deacon miniature
paperweight, c1993, 2in (5cm).
£6–8 *SWB*

A Caithness paperweight,
signed 'William Manson'.
£250–300 *MLa*

A St. Louis paperweight, limited
edition of 250, date cane '1988'.
£500–550 *MLa*

A Lundberg Studio paperweight,
signed and dated '1991'.
£250–300 *MLa*

A Perthshire paperweight, pattern No. PP2, 2⅜in (6cm).
£25–35 *SWB*

A Caithness Tawny Owl paperweight, c1989, 3in (7.5cm).
£80–90 *SWB*

A Webb Corbett paperweight, with star cut base, 3in (7.5cm).
£30–40 *SWB*

A Baccarat Princess Anne 'Sulphide' paperweight, 3in (7.5cm) high.
£75–85 *SWB*

A Murano paperweight, with typical 'cog' canes, post-WWII, 2½in (6cm) high.
£12–16 *SWB*

A Caithness 'Atlantis' paperweight, c1979, 3in (7.5cm) high.
£125–135 *SWB*

A solid copper photograph frame, with Art Nouveau design, c1900, 8 by 5½in (20 by 14cm).
£35–45 *FMN*

An Italian mosaic giltwood photograph frame, 13½ by 8½in (34 by 21.5cm).
£300–330 *HaH*

An Italian mosaic and Venetian glass photograph frame, 19thC, 12 by 8in (30.5 by 20cm).
£400–435 *HaH*

A bronze photograph frame, French, 19thC, 10½in (26.5cm) high.
£200–230 *HaH*

A champlevé enamel photograph frame, French, 19thC, 8 by 5in (20 by 12.5cm).
£160–180 *HaH*

A marbled mosaic photograph frame, with crystal stones, 20thC, 7 by 5in (17.5 by 13cm).
£100–120 *HaH*

An Italian mosaic and giltwood photograph frame, 19thC, 8½ by 6½in (21.5 by 17cm).
£225–275 *HaH*

A Victorian velvet photograph frame, with applied metalwork, 11 by 14½in (28 by 37cm) wide.
£75–85 *HaH*

An Arts & Crafts inlaid wood photograph frame, 11 by 9½in (28 by 24cm) wide. **£150–160** *HaH*

A Sorrento Ware inlaid olive wood photograph frame, late 19thC.
£175–195 *HaH*

Caddy Spoons

A silver caddy spoon, London 1862, 3in (7.5cm) long.
£220–240 AMH

A shell caddy spoon, by Matthew Lunwood, c1810, 3in (7.5cm) long.
£325–350 AMH

Three silver caddy spoons, 2½ to 5½in (6 to 14cm) long.
£30–40 each LF

Cruets

A silver cruet set, Birmingham 1865, 6½in (16cm) wide.
£500–575 AMH

A pair of silver bird cruets, 2in (5cm) high.
£200–250 PC

A pair of silver owl cruets, 2in (5cm) high.
£200–250 PC

- Early silver marks are far from uniform because the punches used for marking were handmade.
- Hallmarks should never be used as a sole guarantee of authenticity. They are easily – and frequently – faked.
- A group or set of items may have different marks, as pieces can be made at different times and even by different makers.

Menu Holders

Four silver menu holders, to commemorate the coronation of King George VI, Charringtons, London 1936, boxed.
£450–475 RAN
Probably produced for export.

Miniature Items

A silver miniature cat band, 1980–90s, 2 to 2½in (5 to 6cm) high.
£250–300 PC

Four silver animal shaped menu holders, by Hamilton & Inches, Edinburgh 1912, boxed.
£450–465 RAN

A silver miniature dog band, 1980–90s, 2in (5cm) high.
£300–350 PC

A silver vase, Sheffield 1894,
5in (12.5cm) high.
£275–300 *AMH*

A silver miniature frog band,
1980–90s, 2 to 4in (5 to
10cm) high.
£300–350 *PC*

A silver thimble bucket, London
1874, 1½in (4cm) high.
£85–100 *AMH*

Vinaigrettes

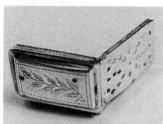

A Georgian silver vinaigrette,
engraved with fern, 1in
(2.5cm) long.
£90–110 *LIO*

A Georgian silver vinaigrette,
1in (2.5cm) long.
£90–110 *LIO*

A Georgian silver vinaigrette,
1in (2.5cm) long.
£90–110 *LIO*

Miscellaneous

A silver hat pin stand,
4½in (11cm) high.
£40–50 *LF*

A bunch of silver flowers, with a
bee, in a crystal vase, by Sarah
Jones, 1990s, 5in (12.5cm) high.
£300–350 *PC*

Four silver and mother-of-pearl
folding fruit knives, 1830–1910.
£20–40 each *VB*

A pair of Apostle spoons,
London 1887, 8in (20cm) long.
£80–90 *CSA*

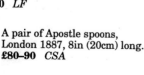

A set of six silver dessert
spoons, Dublin 1848, 5in
(13cm) long.
£90–100 *CSA*

A silver hip flask, 4in
(10cm) wide.
£150–200 *LF*

A silver gravy boat, London
1894, 6in (15cm) wide.
£120–130 *CSA*

A silver napkin ring, Mappin &
Webb, 1½in (4cm) diam., in
original box.
£75–80 *LF*

Silver Plate

A Dutch silver pickle fork,
Amsterdam 1890, 7½in
(18cm) long.
£25–30 *CSA*

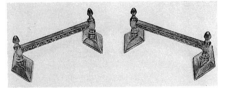

Two pairs of silver
plated knife rests,
3½ and 4in
(9 and 10cm) long.
£10–20 each *LF*

An Elkington electroplated
trefoil dish, 1890, 11in (28cm).
£70–80 *CSA*

A silver plated easel, by Asprey,
c1910, 10in (25cm) high.
£140–180 *DUN*

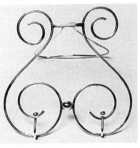

A set of six mother-of-pearl
handled knives, with
plated blades.
£25–35 *TRU*

A Victorian ornate silver plated
tea kettle on spirit stand, the
hinged lid with flower finial, the
stand with three scroll and shell
feet, 14in (36cm) high.
£220–250 *LF*

**Miller's is a price GUIDE
not a price LIST**

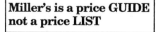

A BOAC silver plated coffee
pot, 1930s.
£20–25 *COB*

A BEA silver plated teapot, 1930s.
£20–25 *COB*

MILITARIA

'A weapon is an enemy, even to its owner', warns one Turkish proverb. As every collector knows, weapons should be treated with care. Firearms regulations must be observed, and all objects handled with circumspection. There are several specialist institutions in Britain housing magnificent collections of arms and armour as well as library facilities, where objects can be researched and advice sought by the genuine enthusiast. These include the Royal Armouries, HM Tower of London, Britain's national museum of arms and armour, the Imperial War Museum, London (20thC material), the National Army Museum, London, and the National Maritime Museum, Greenwich. For commercial advice it is best to contact specialist dealers and auction houses.

Ammunition

.303in Pomeroy explosive bullet, c1914–18.
£80–100 *PC*

This type was used against Zeppelins and intended to set fire to the fabric and hydrogen in the balloon. It was also used against aircraft.

Black powder revolver ammunition:
From left:
.476in MkIII Enfield. **£5–10**
.45in Colt model, Bennett primed, c1873.
£5–10
12mm French Perris, thick rim, c1870. **£8–12**
.500in Boxer revolver, c1870. **£8–10** *PC*

l. Big game rifle ammunition, coiled brass, black powder express with Hollands patent ratchet bullet, c1870, 3¼in.
£6–10
c. .450/400 nitro express Cogswell & Harrison Certus M16, c1885, 3¼in.
£40–50
r. .375/303in Axite, c1910, 2½in.
£6–10 *PC*

l. .5in Browning machine gun proof bullet, c1920, 4in.
£12–20
c. .55in Boyes anti-tank cartridge, c1939, 4in.
£20–30
r. .5in British Vickers heavy machine gun bullet, c1930, 3in.
£6–10 *PC*

From left:
.303in Rubin bullet, black powder, c1889. **£120–130**
.303in Rubin bullet, black powder, c1888. **£120–130**
.450in Gatling machine gun bullet, black powder, c1878.
£40–60
.402in experimental Enfield bullet, c1880, 2¼in.
£100–150 *PC*

l. Match rifle cartridge, copper covered bullet, Gibbs No.2, also used for big game, c1880, case length, 2¾in. **£25–40**
c. Gibbs No 1, c1880, 2½in.
£25–40
r. Gibbs No 3, for smaller game shooting, c1880.
£80–120 *PC*

Four automatic pistol cartridges, *from left:*
Gabbet Fairfax Mars auto pistol .450in experimental carbine cartridges, early 1900s.
£300–400
.450in, long.
£150–200
.450in, short.
£175–250
.8.5mm.
£300–500 *PC*

l. A .500/450in match rifle hexagonal cartridge, a paper patch around the nose, rifling grooves around case to take a Whitworths bullet, c1870, 2¾in.
£500–600
c. A Soper of Reading match rifle cartridge, c1870, 2½in.
£200–300
r. A Rigby match rifle cartridge, c1870, 2½in.
£40–60 *PC*

l. A cartridge for a .577in revolver, c1870.
£25–30
r. A double-barrelled pistol bullet, black powder, Howdah, c1870.
£15–20 *PC*

l. 5.45mm Russian KGB pistol bullet. **£1–2**
c. 9mm PO8 Parabellum auto pistol bullet, c1911. **£2–3**
r. .40in BSA auto pistol bullet.
£1,000–1,500 *PC*

The bullet on the left was worth £100 four years ago, before Glasnost.

A box of 50 12mm pin-fire revolver cartridges, by Eley Brothers, c1850–60.
£40–60 *PC*

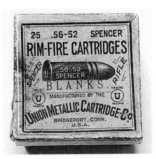

A box of 25 .56/.52in Spencer rim-fire cartridges, made in Bridgeport, Conn., USA, as used in the American Civil War, 3in (7.5cm) square.
£50–55 *PC*

top. .476in Mk III Enfield, 12 rounds, c1883.
£50–100
bottom. Adams Mk II boxer cased bullets, c1881.
£50–80 *PC*

.276in experimental P.13, ten rounds, ball, c1914.
£100–125 *PC*

A box of 50 Kynoch .350in revolver black powder cartridges, c1890.
£8–10 *PC*

A packet of .577/.450in Maxim machine gun cartridges, made by Eley for Vickers, Sons & Maxim, c1880–90.
£50–80 *PC*

top. .303in cordite Mk IV cartridges, ten rounds, ball, dated '24.11.98'.
£40–50
bottom. .303in short range Mk I practice cartridges, ten rounds, ball, dated '9.5.96'.
£50–80 *PC*

Armour

An English Pikeman's Cromwellian breastplate, with distinct medial ridge and single line incised border.
£230–270 *WAL*

A Cromwellian Officer's helmet, with two-piece skull and fixed peak deeply struck with crowned 'IR' storekeeper's mark, articulations to neck guard with ornamental rivet heads, restored.
£250–300 *WAL*

An English Cromwellian Trooper's breastplate, with distinct medial ridge, maker's initials 'HS'.
£350–400 *WAL*

A one-piece cabasset, with pear stalk finial to crown, brass rosettes around base, one original ear flap, c1600.
£240–260 *WAL*

A Cromwellian Trooper's lobster tail helmet, with triple bar face guard, ear flaps missing.
£850–875 *WAL*

A one-piece cabasset, with pear stalk finial to crown, brass rosettes around base, c1600.
£160–200 *WAL*

Edged Weapons

A Japanese cloisonné enamel mounted dagger aikuchi, enamelled koshirae against a grey pink ground depicting dragons, signed and dated '1868', blade 13in (33cm).
£1,450–1,550 *WAL*

A Persian matching khulah khud and dhal, bowl chiselled with flowers and foliage, Islamic inscriptions to border, slight damage.
£550–650 *WAL*

A Malay kris, with carved hardwood Garuda grip and wavy edged blade, in decorated hardwood sheath, blade 14in (35.5cm).
£70–80 *ASB*

A Caucasian silver niello decorated kindjal, the grip with two decorative rivets, double-edged blade tapering to needle point, the grip and scabbard decorated in niello and repoussé work, blade 11in (28cm).
£400–465 *ASB*

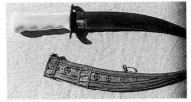

A North African jambiya, with ivory grip and curved double-edged blade, engraved and niello decorated silver sheath, blade 9in (23cm)
£200–230 *ASB*

An Indian all-steel khanjar type sword, the blade decorated with flowers, foliage, and animals, blade 26in (66cm).
£125–150 *ASB*

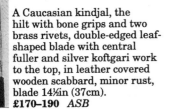

A Caucasian kindjal, the hilt with bone grips and two brass rivets, double-edged leaf-shaped blade with central fuller and silver koftgari work to the top, in leather covered wooden scabbard, minor rust, blade 14½in (37cm).
£170–190 *ASB*

A modern Cossack kindjal, with nickel silver grip decorated with wire filigree work, double-edged blade with three narrow fullers, in decorated nickel silver scabbard, blade 11in (28cm).
£120–140 *ASB*

A Japanese enamel mounted dagger aikuchi, sentoku mounts, blade 9in (23cm).
£480–520 *WAL*

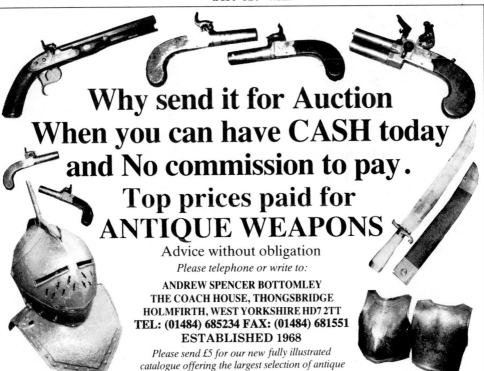

Cutlasses

l. A Continental Naval cutlass, with all-steel hilt modelled on the French cutlass of 1833, single-edged blade, mid-19thC, blade 32½in (82.5cm).
£180–220 *ASB*

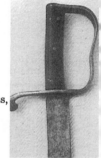

r A Naval stirrup hilted cutlass, with chequered wooden grip, single-edged blade with spear point, blade 26½in (67.5cm).
£100–120 *ASB*

A Royal Naval cutlass, with chequered iron grip, sheet iron guard, single-edged blade with crown 'GR' cypher to the forte, blade shortened and repointed, c1800, blade 20½in (52cm).
£160–190 *ASB*

r A Georgian British Naval cutlass, with figure-of-eight sheet iron guard, cast iron grip, single edged blade, blade 28in (71cm).
£180–220 *ASB*

Daggers & Dirks

A Royal Italian Navy Midshipman's dirk, by E. & F. Horster of Solingen, with brass hilt with mother-of-pearl grips, double-edged blade and brass decorated scabbard, c1890, blade 7½in (19cm).
£200–230 *ASB*

A Nazi Army Officer's dagger, with grooved ivorine grip, Nazi eagle cross guard and straight double-edged blade, 9½in (24cm).
£140–160 *ASB*

A European dagger, with round pommel, wooden grip and simple guard with rounded finials, and double-edged blade, c1530–50, blade 5in (12.5cm).
£220–240 *ASB*

Swords & Rapiers

l. A British Light Cavalry sword, similar to pattern of 1788, with iron stirrup hilt, leather covered grip, curved single-edged blade, marked 'Thos Gills Warranted', blade 32in (81cm).
£130–160 *ASB*

l. A Georgian Volunteer Officer's sword, with steel stirrup hilt, wire bound sharkskin grip, etched and gilt, curved single-edged blade, steel scabbard with twin hanging rings, c1800, blade 28in (71cm).
£225–275 *WAL*

A George VI Diplomat's small sword, with cast brass hilt, straight double-edged blade etched with royal cypher and foliage, in brass mounted black leather scabbard, with gold bullion sword knot, blade 32in (81cm).
£175–200 *ASB*

A Light Cavalry Officer's sword, possibly American, with three-bar hilt similar to the pattern of 1821, curved piped backed blade etched with foliage and military trophies, grip binding missing, blade 31½in (80cm).
£120–150 *ASB*

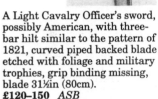

l. A Victorian Royal Artillery Officer's sword, retailed by W. Dowler & Sons, Great Charles Street, Birmingham, with steel three-bar hilt of similar type to the pattern of 1821, wire bound sharkskin covered grip, curved single-edged blade, in original steel scabbard, blade 33in (83.5cm).
£160–190 *ASB*

l. A Georgian Indian Army Light Cavalry Officer's sword, with steel hilt, langets of Indian foliate style, squared knucklebow, rounded flattened pommel, horn grip mounted with three steel rosettes, plain curved clipped back blade, c1800, blade 29in (73.5cm).
£650–700 *WAL*

l. A British Heavy Cavalry Officer's pattern 1887 sabre, retailed by Hawkes & Co., Piccadilly, London, the steel basket guard pierced with honeysuckle foliage, wire bound sharkskin covered grip, curved single-edged blade with fuller and spear point etched with cypher of Edward VII, flowers, foliage and royal arms, in brown pigskin scabbard, blade 35in (89cm).
£150–170 *ASB*

l. A French Model 1831 Gladius pattern Infantry short sword, with brass hilt and double-edged leaf shaped blade, in brass mounted black leather scabbard, blade 19in (48cm).
£120–150 *ASB*

A British Heavy Cavalry Trooper's sword, with sheet iron basket guard, grooved wooden grip and curved single-edged blade, grip binding missing, blade 36in (91.5cm).
£160–190 *ASB*

l. A British Royal Artillery Officer's Light Pattern sword, with three-bar iron hilt similar to pattern of 1821, wire bound sharkskin covered grip, curved single-edged blade with fuller and spear point, in nickel plated steel scabbard, c1870, blade 31in (78.5cm).
£100–120 *ASB*

A Nazi Army Officer's sabre, by Eickhorn Solingen, with gold anodised aluminium stirrup hilt, wire bound black plastic grip, curved single-edged blade with spear point and fuller, in black lacquered steel scabbard, blade 30in (76cm).
£190–220 *ASB*

A Royal Canadian Mounted Police commemorative sword, by Wilkinson Sword, made in the form of a 17thC Scottish claymore, with gilt brass pommel and guard, blade etched with maker's mark, RCMP badges and historical scenes, blade 34in (86cm).
£150–180 *WAL*

An Italian Cavalry Trooper's sabre, with three-bar sheet iron basket guard, chequered grip strap, plain wooden grip, and curved single-edged pipe back blade, in steel scabbard, late 19thC, blade 33in (83.5cm).
£100–120 *ASB*

r. A British Infantry Officer's pattern 1845 sword, Light Model, with brass hilt and straight blade, in steel scabbard, blade 32in (81cm).
£100–125 *ASB*

l. A Polish Cavalry sabre, the brass stirrup hilt with knuckle bow langets and short quillon, wire bound leather covered grip, curved single-edged blade with spear point and fuller engraved and etched with flowers, foliage and Polish eagle, in nickel plated steel scabbard, blade 32in (81cm).
£160–190 *ASB*

A French Napoleonic Cavalry Officer's sword, with brass 'AN IX' hilt, wire bound leather covered grip, plain curved blade with clipped back tip and traces of watered steel patterning, in black patent leather covered wooden scabbard, c1810, blade 32in (81cm).
£2,000–2,500 *WAL*

r. An Elizabeth II pattern 1897 Infantry Officer's sword, probably for a Sergeant Major, hilt with pierced basket and royal cypher, wire bound leather covered grip, straight blade etched with flowers, foliage and royal cypher, in nickel plated scabbard, Ordnance property marks, blade 32in (81cm).
£170–190 *ASB*

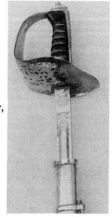

Firearms

A Continental éprouvette, with brass body, small pan for priming powder and barrel for main charge, graduated wheel bearing against a spring with indicator, the grip with animal horn scales secured by brass headed rivets, late 18thC, 6in (15cm) long overall.
£300–350 *ASB*

In the days when gunpowder was of uncertain strength or power these testers were used to determine the power of a particular batch.

A single-barrelled underlever .8in bore hammer gun, No. 17141, by C. Pryse & Co., nitro damascus barrel, border engraved patinated backlock, figured stock, barrel 34in (86cm).
£500–600 *Bon*

A flintlock insurance company guard blunderbuss, with brass barrel, breech stamped 'Memory Southwark', with London proof marks and maker's mark, lockplate signed 'Collumbell', c1765, barrel 16in (40.5cm).
£2,000–2,400 *ASB*

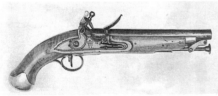

A 17 bore percussion Cavalry carbine, by Westley Richards, Birmingham, fitted with two lugs for special purpose-built bayonet at the muzzle, proof marks on breech, c1845, barrel 20in (50.5cm).
£250–300 *ASB*

Pistols & Revolvers

A .56in William IV Sea Service flintlock pistol, stocker's initials 'WG', barrel 9in (23cm).
£1,200–1,400 *WAL*

A pump-up air cane, with 140 bore rifled barrel, screwing into a 60 bore smooth bore barrel, in original oak case with brass lid escutcheon, with accessories, mid-19thC, barrel 20in (50.5cm).
£400–500 *ASB*

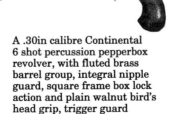

A .18in bore full stocked flintlock carriage pistol, signed 'Loader London', with three-stage brass barrel with octagonal breech and London proof marks, walnut stock with nickel silver furniture, grip cap with grotesque mask, c1760, barrel 9½in (24cm).
£1,100–1,300 *ASB*

A .30in calibre Continental 6 shot percussion pepperbox revolver, with fluted brass barrel group, integral nipple guard, square frame box lock action and plain walnut bird's head grip, trigger guard missing, c1840, barrels 4in (10cm).
£400–480 *ASB*

A 6 shot .44in bore self-cocking bar hammer percussion pepperbox revolver, by Henry Tatham, 37 Charing Cross, London, German silver frame engraved with scrollwork and maker's name and address, c1815, barrels 5in (12.5cm), in lined mahogany case, the lid engraved 'General Sir Wm. Gomm'.
£4,800–5,000 *WAL*

A .20in bore Sea Service flintlock belt pistol, regulation lock with crowned 'GR' and 'Tower', barrel 9in (23cm).
£900–1,000 *WAL*

A 6 shot .36in Savage Arms Co. self cocking second model Navy percussion revolver, carved with initials 'ACF', walnut grips, barrel 7in (17.5cm).
£850–900 *WAL*

An Enfield .38-200 No. 2 Mk I revolver, No. A8222, with walnut grips, dated '1932'.
£60–80 *Bon*

A 5 shot .54in bore double action Tranter's Patent percussion revolver, No. 17261T, Birmingham proved, engraved 'R.S. Garden 29 Piccadilly, London', barrel 6in (15cm), in lined mahogany case.
£1,800–2,000 *WAL*

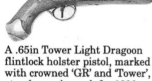

A .65in Tower Light Dragoon flintlock holster pistol, marked with crowned 'GR' and 'Tower', storekeeper's mark for 1800, barrel 9in (23cm).
£1,200–1,500 *WAL*

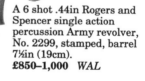

A 6 shot .44in Rogers and Spencer single action percussion Army revolver, No. 2299, stamped, barrel 7½in (19cm).
£850–1,000 *WAL*

A Steyr 7.65mm B/.32in ACP Piepers' patent semi-automatic pistol, No. 12210, bearing Austrian marks for 1910, later British proof, together with spare magazine.
£200–300 *Bon*

A pair of .28 bore brass barrelled percussion travelling pistols, by Lamb of Whitby, octagonal brass barrels, Birmingham proved, breech converted from flintlock, barrels 3½in (8.5cm), in a lined mahogany case, with Army & Navy Stores label.
£1,300–1,500 *WAL*

A Colt .380/9mm K Model 1908 semi-automatic pistol, No. 18830, with traces of original finish, c1914.
£120–160 *Bon*

l. A Webley .455in Mk VI service revolver, No. 262049, Enfield grips, bearing release marks, backstrap engraved 'J. D. Hignett', dated '1917'.
£120–160 *Bon*

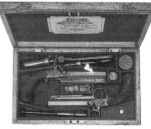

A pair of .14in bore box lock side hammer percussion belt pistols, foliate engraved frames and steel furniture, walnut butts, octagonal barrels 4in (10cm), in a lined mahogany case, with later trade label of Mortimer & Son, Edinburgh.
£1,000–1,200 *WAL*

A 5 shot .54in bore Tranters Patent double trigger percussion revolver, No. 16432T, Birmingham proved, gold inlaid top strap with coronet, barrel 6in (15cm).
£800–1,000 *WAL*

A .16in bore percussion travelling pistol, by Chapman, engraved lock and hammer, browned twist barrel 4in (10cm).
£750–1,000 *WAL*

A 5 shot .120in bore Continental copy of the 1851 Adams Patent self-cocking percussion revolver, foliate engraved frame, octagonal barrel 4in (10cm).
£400–500 *WAL*

A 6 shot .45in CF Tranters Patent presentation engraved double-action revolver, engraved 'London Armoury, Jas Kerr & Co., 54 King William St, E.C.', and with scrollwork, engraved with 'R.H.', barrel 5in (12.5cm).
£800–1,000 *WAL*

A 5 shot .38in bore 1851 model Adams self-cocking percussion Dragoon revolver, No. 1425, London proved, engraved 'Blanch & Son, 29 Gracechurch Street, London', walnut butt, barrel 7½in (18.5cm), in lined oak case.
£1,800–2,000 *WAL*

A 6 shot .80in bore single action transitional percussion revolver, by Parker Field & Sons, No. 2602, engraved, barrel 5in (12.5cm).
£1,000–1,250 *WAL*

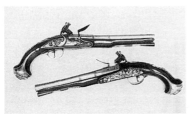

Powder Flasks

A shotgun flask, with adjustable charger and pear shaped gilding metal body, decorated overall with flutes, mid-19thC, 7½in (19cm) long.
£120–140 *ASB*

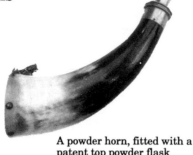

A powder horn, fitted with a patent top powder flask charger, with wooden base plug, stopper missing, 9in (23cm) long.
£100–120 *ASB*

A Swiss percussion cap dispenser, signed 'J. S. Bovy, Geneva', stamped gilded metal, tear drop form, decorated with leaves, an arrow and a hunting horn, locking catch broken, mid-19thC, 4in (10cm) long.
£175–200 *ASB*

Miscellaneous

A gun case label, framed, 12 by 10in (30.5 by 25cm).
£35–45 *TVM*

A German WWII sheepskin lined leather flying helmet, by Siemens, with throat microphone, earphones and electrical connector with plug.
£200–240 *ASB*

A Victorian Standard Bearer's gilt lace belt of the Royal Horse Guards, oak leaf pattern lace with crimson velvet edging and two central stripes, white cloth backing, heavy gilt buckle, tip and slide, the tip with 'Waterloo June 1815' and 'Peninsula'.
£425–475 *WAL*

A Georgian Officer's oval shoulder belt plate, probably for Yeomanry, engraved with a crowned strap inscribed with motto 'Pro Aris et Focis', with 'GR' cypher in the centre, original chamois liner, not hallmarked.
£120–150 *WAL*

A WWII British leather flying helmet, with chamois leather lined interior, earphones, electrical cable, oxygen mask and wireless microphone.
£170–200 *ASB*

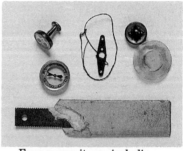

Four escape items, including a hacksaw blade in simulated chewing gum, a collar stud compass, a compass for concealment in clothing, and a simple compass hanging by cotton thread.
£70–90 *ONS*

MONEY COLLECTABLES
Ashtrays

A copper ashtray, possibly an apprentice's work, c1960, 5in (12.5cm) wide.
£15–20 *WP*

An ashtray, with a reproduction of the Fisher one pound note, c1940s, 5½in (14cm) wide.
£15–20 *WP*

A copper tray, with five pounds note design, c1960, 15½in (39cm) wide.
£10–15 *WP*

A melamine ashtray, c1970, 5in (12.5cm) square.
£3–5 *WP*

A melamine ashtray, c1980, 6in (15cm) wide.
£3–5 *WP*

A melamine ashtray, with design of a Scottish one pound note, c1980, 5in (15cm) wide.
£3–5 *WP*

An ashtray, by Fornasetti, Italy, c1970, 8in (20cm) wide.
£40–50 *WP*

Badges & Brooches

Two souvenir badges of WWI, 1½in (4cm) diam.
£10–15 each *WP*

Two souvenir badges of WWI, 1in (2.5cm) diam.
£10–15 each *WP*

An ashtray, produced by Sandhill (Bullion) Ltd., Leeds, c1980, 8in (20cm) wide.
£10–15 *WP*

Two copper coloured brooches, c1920, 1½in (4cm) wide.
£20–25 each *WP*

A gold charm, and a stick pin, c1950, c1950, pin 3in (7.5cm) long.
£10–20 each *WP*

Two Bank of England staff buttons, 3in (7.5cm) diam.
£2–4 each *WP*

Four brooches, with paper money design, c1970, 1½in (4cm) wide.
£15–20 each *WP*

Money Boxes

A Kyser & Rex Co., painted cast iron lion and monkeys bank, Double Peanut variant, slight damage.
£425–450 *CSK*

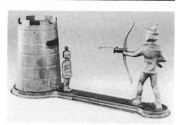

An Australian aluminium and steel gold painted William Tell bank, 14½in (35.5cm) long.
£500–600 *CSK*

A German lithographed tinplate Stollwerck 'Victoria' Savings Bank chocolate dispenser, the two-storey house printed with musicians and children receiving chocolate slabs and sweetmeats from elves, 12in (30.5cm) high.
£300–350 *CSK*

An American hoop-la money bank, c1895, 8½in (21.5cm) wide.
£425–475 *S(S)*

An American cast iron money bank, Bad Accident, repainted, c1891, 10in (25cm) wide.
£500–600 *S(S)*

A German donkey money bank, c1920, 6in (15cm) wide.
£30–40 *HAL*

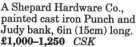

A Shepard Hardware Co., painted cast iron Punch and Judy bank, 6in (15cm) long.
£1,000–1,250 *CSK*

An HTC Japanese tinplate 'Trim-a-Tree' products Santa bank, coin and battery operated, with PVC and cloth Santa with flashing eyes and movements, in original box, c1960.
£200–250 *CSK*

A plastic money box, with money sticker, 4in (10cm) wide.
£1–2 *WP*

Two money boxes, c1970, 6½in (16.5cm) wide.
£6–8 each *WP*

A money box, c1970, 5½in (14cm) wide.
£8–10 *WP*

The only way to get money out of this box was to smash it.

A tin mechanical money bank, with the head of a minstrel, c1950, 5in (12.5cm) high.
£50–60 *HAL*

An Eiffel Tower money bank, c1908, 9in (22.5cm) high.
£100–120 *HAL*

A National Savings tin money box, 2in (5cm) high.
£6–10 *WP*

A silver plated elephant money bank, c1930, 6in (15cm) wide.
£30–35 *HAL*

A 'Hannah Beardsley' glazed pottery money bank, 1913.
£100–125 *HAL*

A German pottery head money bank, c1910, 3½in (8.5cm) high.
£20–30 *HAL*

Paper Money
British

A first-type of 'Bradbury' ten shillings note, 1914.
£200–250 *WP*

These notes were issued at the outbreak of WWI on postage stamp paper, with simple cypher watermark.

A Bank of England specimen ten shillings note, 1960–70.
£8–10 *WP*

r. A Bank of England specimen ten pounds note, issued 1964–67.
£20–25 *WP*

An emergency WWII issue mauve ten shillings note.
£20–25 *WP*

r. A Bank of England five pounds note, which succeeded the white helmeted head of Britannia, printed in blue.
£12–15 *WP*

A Bank of England specimen five pounds note, known as the 'Wellington Fiver' with portrait of the Duke of Wellington on the reverse.
£8–10 *WP*

A Bank of England specimen twenty pounds note, issued 1970–88.
£30–40 *WP*

Later issues have a window security thread and other security differences.

A Bank of England white five pounds note, signed by K. O. Peppiatt, dated '2 Sept. 1944'.
£45–50 *WP*

A second issue Fisher ten shillings note, 1922.
£80–120 *WP*

l. A Bank of England branch five pounds note, payable in Plymouth or London, dated '26 Jan'y 1920'.
£500–700 *WP*

A Bank of England trial five pounds note, c1807.
£1,500–2,000 *WP*

A provincial one pound note, issued by the Darking Bank, 1825.
£50–70 *WP*

A Bank of England one hundred pounds note, dated '29 Sept. 1936'.
£500–600 *WP*

Ireland

A Central Bank of Ireland ten shillings notes, dated '22.10.52'.
£6–8 *WP*

A one pound note issued by the Belfast Banking Company Limited, dated '9th November 1939'.
£14–16 *WP*

A Bank of England white one pound note, with hand written date, '23 August 1809'.
£800–1,000 *WP*

A Northern Bank Limited, Belfast, ten pounds note, dated '1st October 1968'.
£25–30 *WP*

A Bank of Ireland five pounds note, dated '16 Sep. 1942'.
£28–30 *WP*

Scotland

A Bank of Scotland
five pounds note,
dated '27th July 1981'.
£10–12 *WP*

A Royal Bank of Scotland
one pound note, issued to
commemorate the European
summit held in Edinburgh,
dated '8 December 1992'.
£2–4 *WP*

A National Commercial
Bank of Scotland Limited
five pounds note, dated
'2nd January 1963'.
£12–15 *WP*

Channel Islands

A five pounds interest bond,
issued by the States of the
Island of Jersey, dated '1840'.
£30–35 *WP*

A States of Guernsey
ten pounds note, signed
by Hodder.
£35–40 *WP*

A States of Jersey ten pounds
note, signed by Clennet.
£20–25 *WP*

Isle of Man

An Isle of Man ten shillings note.
£10–12 *WP*

Error Notes

A ten shillings
Peppiatt concertina
error note.
£100–150 *WP*

A ten shillings error note,
with extra paper, from
the last issue.
£100–120 *WP*

A Bank of England one pound
error note, with extra paper and
missing print.
£100–120 *WP*

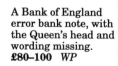

A Bank of England
error bank note, with
the Queen's head and
wording missing.
£80–100 *WP*

A Bank of England one pound error note, with 'shark's fin' extra paper.
£120–140 *WP*

A ten pounds error note, with extra paper.
£80–120 *WP*

Postcards

I'm getting through some money here!

A postcard of Bonzo tearing up money, c1920.
£5–6 *WP*

You can have it if you want it, But you've got to earn it first.

A mechanical postcard, c1925.
£6–8 *WP*

A selection of Bank of England postcards, late 19thC.
£5–8 each *WP*

Drop me a Note.

A postcard, depicting a penguin holding a ten shillings note, c1918, 5½ by 3½in (14 by 9cm).
£5–8 *WP*

A set of Reader's Digest promotional postcards, c1960.
£1–2 each *WP*

A postcard showing a toilet roll of money, c1920.
£5–6 *WP*

A selection of postcards featuring money, 1917–25.
£3–5 each *WP*

The best thing you can do is - - - send me a few.

A postcard showing money being sent in an envelope, c1940.
£3–4 *WP*

Three postcards forming a fifty pounds note, c1980, 12 by 6in (30.5 by 15cm).
£6–8 *WP*

Miscellaneous

c. A silver pill box, 2in
(5cm) diam.
£50–60
l. & r. A pair of silver plated
candlesticks, engraved
'Britannia', 4½in (11cm) high.
£45–50 *WP*

*These items were probably
produced as gifts for retiring
members of staff.*

A clock, set in the form of a
ten pound note, c1990, 6in
(15cm) wide.
£8–10 *WP*

A pack of 'Pinmoney' playing
cards, with design of money on
the backs, c1940, 3½ by 2½in
(9 by 6.5cm).
£10–15 *WP*

A metal cigarette case, designed
as a one pound note, c1950,
7in (17.5cm) wide.
£30–35 *WP*

A metal cigarette case, designed
as a one pound note, made in
Japan, 3in (7.5cm) wide.
£20–25 *WP*

A toy money tin and coins, c1910.
£5–10 *WP*

A pack of 'Robobank' playing
cards, with notes of the world
on the backs, c1980, 4 by 1½in
(10 by 6.5cm).
£10–12 *WP*

A First Day Cover,
commemorating 300 years of
the Bank of England, 1964–94,
8in (20cm) wide.
£12–15 *WP*

A silver pound clip, c1970,
1½in (4cm) high.
£15–20 *WP*

Two advertising trade
cards, c1910, smallest
4½in (11cm) long.
£4–6 each *WP*

An acrylic paperweight,
3in (7.5cm) diam.
£30–35 *WP*

An acrylic paperweight
filled with shredded
twenty pounds notes,
c1990, 3½in (8.5cm) high.
£20–25 *WP*

OPTICAL EQUIPMENT
Lorgnettes & Spectacles

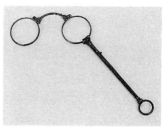

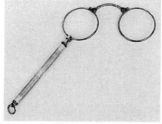

A pair of green enamel lorgnettes, c1870, handle 4½in (11cm) long.
£700–800 *ARE*

A pair of gold lorgnettes, with pink and blue handle, c1870, 3½in (9cm) long.
£850–950 *ARE*

A pair of blonde tortoiseshell lorgnettes, c1870, 6in (15cm) long.
£500–600 *ARE*

An engraved pearl monocular, c1900, 2½in (6cm) long.
£40–50 *DP*

A pair of protective goggles, c1900.
£8–10 *VB*

Opera Glasses

A pair of ivory opera glasses, by T. B. Winter, Optician, 21 Grey Street, Newcastle-on-Tyne, c1900, 4½in (11cm), with case.
£80–90 *DP*

A collection of steel framed spectacles, one in a shagreen case, a lorgnette, 3½in (8.5cm) long, and a set of optician's testing glasses, 1½in (4cm) diam.
£170–200 *LF*

A pair of ivory and a pair of gilt opera glasses, both 4in (10cm) wide.
£40–50 each *LF*

A pair of mother-of-pearl opera glasses, by Lemaire of Paris, c1880, 4in (10cm) wide.
£300–400 *ARE*

A pair of miniature opera glasses, 3in (7.5cm) wide.
£130–170 *ARE*

A pair of mother-of-pearl opera glasses, inscribed 'Lady Wolverton, 26 St James's Place', 4in (10cm) wide.
£250–350 *ARE*

A pair of pearl opera glasses, with large eyepieces, c1880, 4in (10cm) long.
£80–90 *DP*

A pair of pearl opera glasses, by Dollond, London, c1890, 4in (10cm) long, with case.
£75–85 *DP*

A pair of mother-of-pearl opera glasses, with handle, 3½in (9cm) wide.
£450–500 *ARE*

A pair of French leather covered opera glasses, c1910, 4in (10cm) long, with case.
£35–40 *DP*

A pair of gilt metal opera glasses, decorated with enamel, with ivory tops, 3½in (9cm) wide.
£250–320 *ARE*

MAKE THE MOST OF MILLERS
Condition is absolutely vital when assessing the value of any item. Damaged pieces appreciate much less than perfect examples. However, a rare, desirable piece may command a high price even when damaged.

A pair of mother-of-pearl folding opera glasses, c1900, 1½in (4cm) wide closed.
£300–400 *ARE*

A pair of pearl and gilded opera glasses, c1890, with carrying case, 3½in (9cm) long.
£100–110 *DP*

ORIENTAL WARE

A Chinese junk carrying blue and white Kangxi porcelain, blanc-de-chine and other provincial pieces foundered off the coast of Vietnam, south of Vung Tau, c1690. Some 300 years later the wreck was excavated and the finds, known as the Vung Tau Cargo, were auctioned at Christie's Amsterdam in 1992. Like the Nanking Cargo, rescued in 1985, these pieces have attracted enormous and varied interest. While the most important items were snapped up by serious Oriental porcelain collectors, non-specialist buyers have also been attracted by the romance of the story and the price range of more minor items. Some of the most appealing pieces are the so-called sculptures, formed from porcelain which has become encrusted with coral and debris from the ocean.

Vung Tau Cargo

A Vung Tau Cargo spoon, c1690, 5in (12.5cm) long.
£80–90 *DAN*

A Vung Tau Cargo blanc-de-chine tea bowl, c1690, 2½in (6cm) diam.
£70–90 *DAN*

A Vung Tau Cargo blue and white miniature vase, 1½in (4cm) high.
£150–200 *DAN*

Four Vung Tau Cargo blue and white vase lids, c1690, 1½ to 2in (4 to 5cm) diam.
£15–25 each *DAN*

A Vung Tau Cargo dish, decorated with a provincial blue and white riverscape pattern, c1690, 4½in (11cm) diam.
£80–100 *DAN*

A Vung Tau Cargo blanc-de-chine box and lid, c1690, 2½in (6cm) diam.
£220–280 *DAN*

A Vung Tau Cargo 'sculpture', covered in porcelain pieces and coral, c1690, 5in (12.5cm) diam.
£150–200 *DAN*

A Vung Tau Cargo plate, as found with coral, porcelain pieces and shells stuck to it, c1690, 5in (12.5cm) diam.
£150–200 *DAN*

A Vung Tau Cargo saucer, decorated with provincial blue and white rabbit pattern, 5in (12.5cm) diam.
£150–200 *DAN*

Chinese
Ceramics

A pair of blue and white bowls from the Hatcher Cargo Collection, in excellent condition, 3in (7 .5cm) high.
£500–550 *AnE*

These bowls were from the Hatcher cargo which was the first of the wrecks to be retrieved on a commercial scale and sold through Christie's. The cargo was originally produced for export to Europe at the end of the Ming Dynasty, known as the Transitional era. Of the three porcelain cargoes recovered (Hatcher, Nanking and Vung Tau), Hatcher is the earliest and most sophisticated in design.

Two blue and white ancestor boxes, c1800, 3in (7.5cm) wide.
£30–45 each *GHa*

Three Ming Dynasty figures, glaze worn, 6½in (16cm) high.
£50–60 each *GHa*

A Chinese export blue and white lidded mug, with European silver mounts, restored, c1710, 6½in (16cm) high.
£600–700 *DAN*

A Han Dynasty green glazed oil lamp, 6½in (16cm) high.
£200–300 *MA*

A Ming Dynasty blue and white bowl, 4½in (11cm) diam.
£45–60 *GHa*

A Ming Dynasty blue and white bowl, 4in (10cm) diam.
£40–50 *GHa*

A pair of Canton vases, c1870.
£400–500 *CAI*

A Han Dynasty bowl, with green glaze, decorated with hunting figures, circa 200 BC–200 AD, 5in (12.5cm) wide.
£65–90 *GHa*

A Ming Dynasty blue and white jar, with wooden lid, 11in (28cm) high.
£250–280 *GHa*

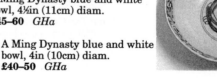

A Ming Dynasty provincial wine ewer, 14thC, 4in (10cm) high.
£140–160 *MBg*

A Chinese Liou Dynasty wine ewer, in Sancai glazes, 11thC, 6½in (16cm) wide.
£5,000–6,000 *MBg*

A Yixing miniature teapot, 18thC, 2in (5cm) high.
£150–175 *MBg*

A Ming Dynasty unglazed figure, 9½in (23.5cm) high.
£60–90 *GHa*

A Ming Dynasty green celadon glaze water dropper, in the form of a crab, 3in (7.5cm) wide.
£200–250 *MBg*

A Yixing teapot, decorated with fruit and nuts, with mushroom shaped lid, c1890, 3in (7.5cm) high.
£150–180 *MBg*

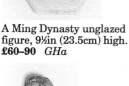

A Ming Dynasty glazed figure, 9in (22.5cm) high.
£60–90 *GHa*

A Han Dynasty figure, circa 200 BC–200 AD, 9in (22.5cm) high.
£65–100 *GHa*

A Ming Dynasty provincial blue and white wine ewer, 16thC, 6in (15cm) high.
£120–140 *MBg*

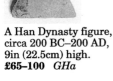

A Song Dynasty funerary jar, 900–1300 AD, 14in (36cm) high.
£60–90 *GHa*

A pair of Peking baluster-shaped vases, decorated with green relief designs depicting song birds among foliage, late 19thC, 14in (35.5cm) high.
£450–650 *HOLL*

A Yung Chêng bowl, with fish imprint on interior base, 1723–36, 5½in (13.5cm) diam.
£75–100 *GHa*

A Song Dynasty funerary jar, 900–1300 AD, 19in (48cm) high.
£60–90 *GHa*

Japanese
Ceramics

A cloisonné dish, decorated with butterflies in flight and stylised flowers, 18in (46cm) diam.
£275–350 *CSK*

An Imari pattern fluted oval bowl, c1860.
£200–300 *CAI*

A blue and white porcelain plaque, with enamel and gilt birds in flight, rocky islands and a garden, 18in (46cm) diam.
£350–450 *WIL*

A Banko bronze glazed porcelain teapot, with finger prints on external surfaces, impressed seal marks, c1890, 3in (7.5cm) high.
£220–250 *MBg*

A Satsuma earthenware bowl, the centre decorated with a crowd scene, the exterior with panels enclosing scenes of children, elders and ladies, 5½in (14cm) diam.
£2,000–2,500 *HSS*

A pair of richly gilded Imari pattern vases, c1870.
£400–600 *CAI*

A Satsuma vase, c1910, 10in (25cm) high.
£200–225 *TER*

Netsuke

An ivory netsuke, modelled
as a gamma and sennin,
18thC, 2in (5cm) wide.
£375–400 *MBg*

Ojimes

l. A Daruma
doll with Okame
face ojime,
silver inlaid with
gold, signed,
18thC, 1.5cm.
£275–300 *MBg*

An oblong silver ojime,
depicting a tiger among
bamboo, late 18thC, 1.5cm.
£250–300 *MBg*

A lacquer ojime, depicting
two faces of Okame and Okina,
19thC, 2cm.
£30–40 *MBg*

*In traditional Japanese
costume, the ojime was the bead
securing the cords between the
inro or tobacco pouch and the
netsuke. The netsuke is the
toggle attaching the cords and
pouch to the belt.*

An ivory netsuke with gamma
and senin, the eyes inlaid with
horn, signed Yoshimasa, 18thC,
2in (5cm) high.
£1,700–1,800 *MBg*

Water Droppers

A porcelain water dropper with
celadon glaze, in the form of a
parcel, late 19thC, 2⅜in (6cm).
£120–140 *MBg*

A bronze water dropper,
in the form of Daruma,
c1850, 2⅜in (6cm) high.
£230–250 *MBg*

A wooden netsuke, modelled as
a puppy, by Mansanoe, 18thC.
£575–595 *MBg*

An ivory netsuke of a shishi,
in the form of a seal, 18thC,
1½in (3.5cm) wide.
£450–475 *MBg*

A porcelain water dropper,
with prunus decoration, 3in
(7.5cm) wide.
£275–300 *MBg*

A porcelain water dropper,
with celadon glaze, 18thC,
2⅜in (6cm) wide.
£175–195 *MBg*

Miscellaneous

A carved wooden Buddha, gilded and spangled, 20in (50.5cm) high.
£200–225 *PC*

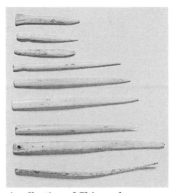

A collection of Chinese bone needles, circa 1000 BC, 3 to 6in (7.5 to 15cm) long.
£20–30 each *MA*

Three Chinese bone tools, circa 1000 BC, 4in (10cm) long.
£30–40 each *MA*

A selection of Chinese court glass bead necklaces, restrung, 18th and 19thC.
£100–150 each *MA*

A Japanese bronzed spelter elephant with rider, 19thC, 6in (15cm) high.
£40–50 *MBg*

A Japanese bronze of a stylised elephant, 19thC, 5in (12.5cm) high.
£200–250 *MBg*

A south Indian bronze figure of Narashima, 14thC, 5in (12.5cm) high.
£200–250 *MBg*

An ivory Indian god, on a wooden stand, c1845, 6in (15cm) high.
£160–165 *PC*

A north Indian bronze of Vishno, 14thC, 6in (15cm) high.
£200–250 *MBg*

A bronze table bell, c1870, 6½in (16cm) high.
£300–400 *DUN*

A Tibetan bronze of Vatuka Bhairava, 18thC, 2½in (6cm) high.
£150–175 *MBg*

PAPERWEIGHTS

Glass paperweights are beautiful collectables. As dealer Marion Langham notes, some of the finest contemporary examples are produced by individual paperweight artists in America and Scotland. 'Check for signatures,' she advises, 'on the base, on the side, or on a marked cane within the paperweight itself.' Features to look out for include clarity of glass and quality of the canes or lampwork. 'The best way of learning about paperweights is really looking at them,' she explains. 'Find a specialist dealer, and ask questions, even if you are not ready to buy.' Although paperweights can seem expensive, reports suggest they are an investment with prices rising every year, especially for limited editions. Bargains can still be found in markets and at car boot sales.

Three glass advertising paperweights, early 20thC, 4in (10cm) wide.
£8–12 each *MRT*

l. A Caithness 'May Dance' paperweight, 3in (7.5cm) high.
£35–40 *SWB*

This design was made in different colours annually from 1972.

A Caithness flower and butterfly paperweight, number 45 from a limited edition of 50, c1978, 3in (7.5cm) high.
£250–300 *SWB*

A set of Caithness 'Four Seasons' paperweights, made by William Manson, designed by Colin Terris, from a limited edition of 500, c1977, 3in (7.5cm) diam.
£900–1,000 *SWB*

A Caithness yellow and red cobra paperweight, signed William Manson, dated '1979', 3in (7.5cm) diam.
£350–400 *MLa*

This weight was produced in a limited edition of 50 in 1978, 1979 and 1980, and each year the colour of the cobra was changed.

A Whitefriars paperweight, with blue and green millefiori canes, 'White Friar' signature cane, 1978 date cane, 3in (7.5cm) diam.
£250–300 *MLa*

A Paul Ysart paperweight, with an 'H' cane, green and brown dragonfly over a blue background, signed by William Manson, c1970, 2½in (6cm) diam.
£200–225 *MLa*

A Caithness paperweight, with two fish swimming over a sandy ground, from a limited edition of 100, designed and made by William Manson, dated '1984'.
£350–400 *MLa*

A Caithness black obsidian glass paperweight, surmounted by a silver lizard, numbered 34 from a limited edition of 50, c1978, 3in (7.5cm) high.
£900–1,000 *SWB*

A Caithness paperweight, with a red octopus on a brown background, from a limited edition of 50, signed William Manson, c1978, 3in (7.5cm) diam.
£350–400 *MLa*

A paperweight with a green octopus was produced in 1979.

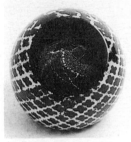

An Osiris paperweight, made at Ierston Davies Studio, Broadfield House Glass Museum, signed, c1980, 2½in (6cm) diam.
£30–35 *SWB*

A Chinese modern paperweight, 3in (7.5cm) high.
£8–10 *SWB*

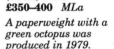

A Caithness faceted lampwork paperweight, with a white swan on a pink background, surrounded by millefiori, from a limited edition of 100, signed William Manson, dated '1979', 3in (7.5cm) diam.
£250–300 *MLa*

A glass paperweight, filled with coloured sands from the Isle of Wight, c1910.
£10–15 *VB*

An Isle of Wight paperweight, post-war, 3½in (8.5cm) high.
£15–20 *SWB*

A Mdina paperweight, Maltese, 3in (7.5cm) diam.
£12–18 *SWB*

This design is said to represent the Mediterranean Sea.

A paperweight, with aventurine sea horse in amethyst glass, with front facet, by William Manson, c1985, 3in (7.5cm) high.
£185–210 *SWB*

A Strathearn concentric millefiori paperweight, c1968, 3in (7.5cm) high.
£25–35 *SWB*

A paperweight, with a red rose on a white background, signed William Manson, from a limited editon of 250, 2½in (6cm) diam.
£200–250 *MLa*

A Perthshire star paperweight, faceted all-over with starcut base, from a limited edition of 300, signed 'P', dated 1982, 2½in (6cm) diam.
£85–100 *MLa*

A Murano glass paperweight, post-war, 3in (7.5cm) diam.
£25–35 *SWB*

A serpentine egg-shaped paperweight, c1900, 4in (10cm) wide.
£70–90 *DUN*

A Perthshire hollow blown squirrel paperweight, from a limited edition of 200, c1984, 3in (7.5cm) high.
£200–250 *SWB*

One of an annual series of hollow blown weights featuring different birds or animals.

A Chinese paperweight, with primary colours, c1930, 2½in (6cm) high.
£7–10 *SWB*

r. A Bohemian faceted paper-weight, with three flowers, c1900–20, 3½in (8.5cm) high.
£50–60 *SWB*

An Orient and Flume egg-shaped paperweight, with a yellow pansy on a black background, dated '1990', 3in (7.5cm) high.
£50–65 *MLa*

r. A Kosta paperweight, Swedish, signed, post-war, 3in (7.5cm) high.
£20–30 *SWB*

A Wedgwood glass bird, marked, c1970, 3in (7.5cm) high.
£15–20 *SWB*

PHONECARDS

Phonecard collecting, also known as fusilately or carterology, has expanded rapidly. The first phonecard was introduced in Italy in 1975 and there is now an international market for phonecards. One collector recently paid an astonishing £10,000 for a limited edition card, face value NZ$100 (£40), designed by New Zealand artist Pam Wolfe. Prices depend on rarity and condition. For example, British Telecom issued a limited edition 100 unit card to commemorate the 1987 Open Golf Championship at Muirfield. The majority of the nine hundred issued were given to journalists who used and then threw them away. Today a mint or unused card is worth around £1,000. Enthusiasts usually concentrate on cards produced by the different phone companies and also make themed collections. Specialist fairs are known as 'bourses'.

A British Telecom limited edition card, The World of Wade, No. 90 of 500, issued with *The World of Wade Book 2*. **£10–15** *PC*

A British Telecom special overprinted for Sheffield University Games 1990, World Student Games and Festival. **£25–45** *PC*

Two British Telecom 5 units Video Spa cards, 'Home Entertainments':
Spelt correctly. **£15–20**
Spelt incorrectly. **£25–30** *PC*

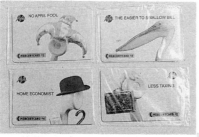

A set of four Mercurycards, £2 and £4, No April Fool, The Easier to Swallow Bill, Home Economist, and Less Taxing. **£2–15 each** *PC*

A Lufthansa £2 Mercurycard, in original folder and envelope, part of a Business Class Survey for Lufthansa. **£20–25** *PC*

A £10 Mercurycard, Associating to rebuilt Kuwait. **£15–25** *PC*

Two Mercurycards, Liverpool Airport, £2, and Stansted Airport, £1. **£5–10 each** *PC*

A First Issue No. 003 £10 Mercurycard, 1988. **£15–30** *PC*

A Ford Vending Services card, used for employee vending machines. **£5–6** *PC*

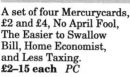

A set of three £2 Mercurycards issued in 1989, depicting:
l. A Harbour Scene, by Claude-Joseph Vernet, Dulwich Picture Gallery.
r. The Great Eastern laid the first successful Transatlantic Cable in 1866.
c. Vessels Close Hauled, by Willem van de Velde the Younger, National Gallery.
£20–25 each *PC*

A selection of off-shore oil rig phone cards.
Used **25p–50p each**
Unused **£8–10 each** *PC*

A Paytelco Mercurycard, UK International Ceramics, 50p, 1,000 issued.
£5–8 *PC*

A German programmable vending smart card.
£15–20 *PC*

A selection of Seychelles Telecom cards.
£5–15 each *PC*

A Globo reusable vending smart card.
£10–12 *PC*

A £2 Mercurycard, The Cable Ship Sir Eric Sharp, July 1989.
£20–40 *PC*

A £1 Mercurycard, 'Waterloo House'.
£8–10 *PC*

Four Mercury personal 50p cards.
£20–30 each *PC*

A set of five Mercurycards, a disc jockey series given as prizes by Capital Gold, 220 of each were issued.
£25–30 each *PC*

A British Telecom 20 units card, Forth Rail Bridge Centenary 1890–1990, 50,000 issued.
£10–15 *PC*

PHOTOGRAPH FRAMES
Bakelite

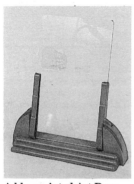

An Art Deco Bakelite photograph frame, 6in (15cm) high.
£30–35 *HEW*

A blue painted Art Deco Bakelite photograph frame, 6½in (16cm) high.
£30–35 *HEW*

Brass

A Victorian brass photograph frame, with embroidered silk mount, 12½in (31.5cm) high.
£140–160 *HaH*

A Victorian gilt metal and filigree brass photograph frame, 8½in (21cm) high.
£175–200 *HaH*

l. An Art Nouveau solid brass photograph frame, c1890, 3½in (8.5cm) high.
£25–35 *FMN*

r. A solid brass photograph frame, with impressed flower detail, c1900, 3½in (8.5cm) high.
£20–35 *FMN*

A solid brass photograph frame, c1900, 5in (12.5cm) high.
£20–30 *FMN*

> **Miller's is a price GUIDE not a price LIST**

An Indian wood photograph frame, with brass overlay, inset with two blue stones, early 20thC, 11in (28cm) high.
£60–70 *HaH*

A solid brass photograph frame, with wooden back, c1900, 7in (17.5cm) wide.
£10–18 *FMN*

A Victorian pierced gilt and silvered brass photograph frame, 10in (25cm) high.
£300–400 *HaH*

Bronze

A bronze and enamel photograph frame, with a family crest in the corners, 10in (25cm) high.
£450–480 *HaH*

Lacquer

A lacquer photograph frame, with ormolu and velvet mount, 10in (25cm) high.
£80–95 *HaH*

A Victorian lacquer photograph frame, with ivory flowers, 10½in (26cm) high.
£150–185 *HaH*

Leatherette & Cardboard

A green cardboard photograph frame, with gilt corner decoration, c1910, 8in (20cm) high.
£15–20 *FMN*

A green leatherette photograph frame, with gilt brass flower detailed edges, c1910, 5½in (13.5cm) high.
£10–15 *FMN*

Ivory

A Middle Eastern inlaid ivory mosaic photograph frame, early 20thC, 8½in (21cm) high.
£50–65 *HaH*

A red cardboard photograph frame, with brass decoration in one corner, c1910.
£8–12 *FMN*

A leatherette photograph frame, c1910, 3½in (8.5cm) high.
£5–10 *FMN*

Mosaic

A selection of Victorian mosaic photograph frames, 2 to 3½in (5 to 8.5cm) high.
£50–90 each *HaH*

Ormolu

A French ormolu photograph frame, c1880, 9in (22.5cm) high.
£140–160 *HaH*

Three triple photograph frames, 4in (10cm) wide.
£70–100 each *HaH*

A French gilt bronze photograph frame, c1866, 8in (20cm) high.
£400–440 *HaH*

An ormolu oval photograph frame, 20thC, 5in (12.5cm) high.
£120–140 *HaH*

A Victorian gilt bronze etched and pierced photograph frame, 13in (33cm) high.
£425–475 *HaH*

An Edwardian ormolu photograph frame, from Asprey's, signed on the reverse, 10in (25cm) high.
£100–145 *HaH*

Silver

Two silver photograph frames 3 and 2½in (7.5 and 6.5cm) high.
£25–50 each *LF*

An Art Nouveau silver photograph frame, embossed with chrysanthemums and leaves, wood easel back, stamped 'J. A. & S.' Birmingham 1908, 10in (26.5cm) high.
£530–580 *P*

A silver plated photograph frame, c1920, 6in (15cm) high.
£8–12 *FMN*

An Art Nouveau silver photograph frame, embossed with poppies, stems and leaves, with wood easel back, stamped with maker's marks 'E.M. & S.', Birmingham 1903, 9in (22.5cm) high.
£475–525 *P*

Tortoiseshell

An Edwardian tortoiseshell photograph frame with a brass edge, 6in (15cm) high.
£140–150 *HaH*

A tortoiseshell photograph frame, with brass edge, c1890, 6in (15cm) diam.
£150–185 *HaH*

An Edwardian tortoiseshell photograph frame, with wood back, 6in (15cm) diam.
£75–95 *HaH*

Wood

A hanging photograph frame, c1930s, 8in (20cm) diam.
£25–35 *HaH*

An Edwardian wood and alabaster photograph frame, with jade decoration, Irish, 8½in (21cm) high.
£350–385 *HaH*

A mahogany horseshoe-shaped photograph frame, 20thC, 10in (25cm) high.
£80–100 *HaH*

A wooden photograph frame, carved from an aeroplane propellor, with initials 'RAF', 1914–18, 14in (35.5cm) high.
£80–90 *Hah*

A Victorian carved wood photograph frame, 12in (30.5cm) high.
£45–55 *HaH*

An Indian carved wood photograph frame, c1940, 11½in (29cm) high.
£80–90 *HaH*

A pair of Victorian carved mahogany hanging photograph frames, 11½in (29cm) high.
£100–120 *HaH*

PIANOS & MECHANICAL MUSIC
Pianolas

An Aeolian Half Duo Art Pianola piano, No. 31587, restored, c1930, 54in (137cm) wide.
£1,400–1,500 *PIA*

A Steck reproducing piano, No. 101759, incorporating the Duo Art System of Reproduction, needs restoring, c1930, 58in (147cm) wide.
£1,500–2,000 *PIA*

The Pianola can be operated either electrically or manually. The Duo Art System of Reproduction was introduced in 1911, and was rivalled only by the more sophisticated Ampico. In a restored condition, this piano would fetch £5,500–6,500.

A Chickering Ampico Grand Electric Pianola, model 59, No. 143749, restored, c1927.
£6,000–7,000 *PIA*

Pianola Rolls

r. A Meleto standard 88 note Dance Roll, *When We're Alone,* by Janson-Burton, 1920s–30s, 12½in (32cm) long.
£2–3 *PIA*

An Ampico recording roll, *Hungarian Rhapsodie,* by Mischa Levitzki, made for an electric reproducing piano, 1920s–30s, 12½in (31.5cm) wide.
£8–10 *PIA*

Two Duo Art recording rolls, *Sleepy Valley* played by Douglas Halston, and *Always,* played by Phil Ohmans, for reproducing electric player pianos, 1920s–30s, 12½in (31.5cm) wide.
£2–3 each *PIA*

An Ampico recording roll, *The Story of Christmas,* with Christmas box, c1925, 12½in (32cm) wide.
£10–12 *PIA*

l. Two Thermodis standard rolls, *Sweet Jennie Lee* and *Second Serenade,* originally cost 1s and 1/6d.
£2–3 each *PIA*

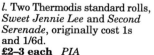

A 65 note roll, *A Little Bit of Heaven,* by E. Ball, 1920s–30s, 12½in (31.5cm) long.
50p–£1 *PIA*

A QRS Pianola new 88 note roll, *Here Comes Santa Claus*, c1993, 12½in (32cm) long.
£10–15 *PIA*

Mechanical Music
Music Boxes & Automata

A French domed automaton, by Phalbois, late 19thC, 16in (41cm) high.
£1,700–1,800 *GWe*

r. A silver musical snuff box, movement by Le Coultre, 19thC, 3½in (8.5cm) wide.
£2,000–2,200 *GWe*

A National Musical Box, by Ami Rivenc of Geneva, with 6in cylinder, the case heavily French polished, c1895, 13in (33cm) wide.
£750–850 *GWe*

A musical box, with three bells in sight, 6in cylinder, in a crossbanded rosewood case, c1895, 17in (43cm) wide.
£850–950 *GWe*

An American Regina musical box, in a golden oak case with folding cover, c1900, 28in (71cm) wide.
£7,000–7,500 *GWe*

r. A key-wind musical box, by Nicole Frères, c1840, 18in (45.5cm) wide.
£1,500–1,600 *GWe*

A singing bird musical box, in tortoiseshell case with enamelled bird lid, by Brugier, fusée drive, the bird with metal base and humming bird feathers, c1850, 3½in (8.5cm) wide.
£6,000–7,000 *GWe*

Two coin-operated singing birds in a cage, made in Paris, with wooden base, late 19thC, 21in (53cm) high.
£2,800–3,000 *GWe*

A musical snuff box with sectional comb, in composition box, c1830, 3½in (8.5cm) wide.
£700–750 *GWe*

Polyphons

A German walnut polyphon hall clock, plays 15½in diam discs, the mechanism in the trunk is activated on the hour by the clock, two finials missing, 100in (254cm) high.
£9,000–9,500 *GWe*

Symphonions

A boxed Simplex symphonion, 5½in (13.5cm) disc, c1895.
£450–550 *GWe*

Three symphonion discs, 11½in (29cm), 7½in (18.5cm) and 5½in (13.5cm) wide.
£10–20 each *GWe*

A walnut table symphonion, with inlaid decoration and interior glass lid, takes 11½in disc discs, c1895, 20in (50.5cm) wide.
£2,000–2,200 *GWe*

A rococo table symphonion, panel with picture missing from lid, with 11½in disc, c1895, 19in (48cm) wide.
£3,000–3,500 *GWe*

PINCUSHIONS

A painted velvet pear-shaped pincushion, c1830, 6in (15cm) high.
£40–75
A Regency strawberry pincushion, containing emery to polish needles, 2½in (6cm) long.
£25–30 *RdeR*

A pincushion, with an illustration of Burns' Monument, late 19thC, 2in (5cm) diam.
£50–60 *LBL*

Three Victorian silk pincushions, with shells and beads.
£12–25 each VB

A pig pincushion, early 20thC, 5½in (13.5cm) wide.
£35–40 *OCS*

A Victorian pincushion, 12in (30.5cm) high.
£175–200 *OCS*

A Victorian pincushion, with lace bobbins, 11in (28cm) wide.
£145–200 *OCS*

A brass bird pincushion, early 20thC, 2in (5cm) high.
£15–20 *OCS*

A velvet hat pincushion, c1930, 3in (7.5cm) diam.
£10–15 *OCS*

Two glass double-sided pincushions, painted with scenes of Carisbrook and Windsor Castles, c1840.
£40–50 each *VB*

An embroidered silk pincushion, late 19thC, 6½in (16cm) diam.
£35–40 *OCS*

A Victorian beaded pincushion, 7in (17.5cm) square.
£50–75 *TOM*

A silver plated shoe pincushion, early 20thC, 4in (10cm) long.
£25–35 *OCS*

A pincushion, with a porcelain head, c1920–30, 3½in (8.5cm) diam.
£40–50 *OCS*

An Art Deco half doll pincushion, with green hat, black gown decorated with pink roses, 8in (20cm) high.
£60–65 *HEW*

A black silk embroidered and beaded shoe pincushion, c1936, 4in (10cm).
£15–25 *OCS*

PRAMS

A Victorian pram, c1880.
£1,000–1,500 *MCh*

This pram is totally original, and was possibly used at Sandringham.

A doll's pram, 1930s, 34in (86cm) high.
£100–120 *JUN*

A pram, 1930s, 46in (116.5cm) high.
£100–130 *JUN*

An Edwardian pram, c1910.
£400–500 *MCh*

A Victorian pram, for two children, c1880s.
£500–700 *MCh*

A toy pram, with original paint, c1930.
£300–350 *MCh*

A French pram, c1910, 38in (96.5cm) high
£250–300 *PC*

RADIOS

As the 20thC draws to a close, interest in old technology, such as televisions, radios and gramophones, is rapidly expanding. According to Steve Harris, Director of On the Air, the broadcasting museum and shop in Chester, collectors of radios fall into two categories. One group is interested in the inner workings of the wireless and its technical history, particularly from the 1920s, whilst for the cabinet design enthusiasts, the outward appearance of a set is far more significant than its contents. Condition is all important. If a 1930s Bakelite radio has a damaged case, its value can be reduced by 50%.

Unlike modern electronics, vintage radio sets can be repaired, but unless you know what you are doing, restoration should always be carried out by a specialist, and remember this can be expensive.

A Philips 'Superinductance' radio, model 830A, c1932, 19in (48cm) high.
£300–400 *OTA*

A Brownie No. 2 crystal set, c1925, 6in (15cm) wide.
£75–120 *OTA*

r. A home-built crystal set, c1920s, 6in (15cm) square.
£40–60 *OTA*

A Graves two valve radio, 1926.
£60–65 *W*

A KB Masterpiece radio, c1930, 7¼in (18.5cm) square.
£100–150 *OTA*

This was a free gift with 500 BDV cigarette coupons.

A 'Lissen' wireless horn speaker, 1920s, 21¼in (54cm) high.
£75–85 *JUN*

A Murphy AD94 radio, 1940, 13½in (34cm) high.
£100–200 *OTA*

A Pye model MP radio, c1939, 20in (51cm) high.
£20–30 *OTA*

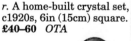

A McMichael Duplex 4 radio,
c1932, 15in (38cm) high.
£40–80 *OTA*

A Philips 364A radio, c1933.
£400–450 *W*

A Gecophone 'stork' loudspeaker,
BC 1792, c1929, 16in (41cm) high.
£80–100 *OTA*

A Gecophone BC 3300
radio, 1924.
£800–850 *W*

A Clarke's 'Atlas' table model
radio, c1935, 21in (53cm) wide.
£80–120 *OTA*

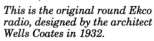

An Ekco AD65 radio, with
moulded brown Bakelite case,
on original beechwood base,
stamped 'Registered Design
No. 794465', c1934.
£950–1,250 *BTA*

*This is the original round Ekco
radio, designed by the architect
Wells Coates in 1932.*

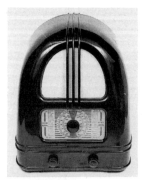

A Philco 'People's Set', model
444, c1936, 16in (41cm) high.
£250–350 *OTA*

An Art Deco fire screen radio
extension speaker, c1930s,
32in (81cm) high.
£75–95 *HOL*

A Pye MM speaker, c1932,
18½in (47cm) high.
£100–170 *OTA*

A Ferranti Constructors' AC
mains wireless set, c1932–33,
20in (51cm) wide.
£200–225 *JUN*

An Ekco AD75 Bakelite
radio, c1940.
£450–550 *BTA*

A Chakophone Junior Three,
c1927, 15in (38cm) long.
£100–120 *OTA*

An Ambassador table radio,
c1935, 18in (46cm) high.
£40–80 *OTA*

A wartime civilian receiver,
in a pine case, 1944, 13½in
(34cm) high.
£60–120 *RMV*

A Bush DAC 90A radio, c1950,
11½in (29cm) high.
£40–80 *OTA*

An Ekco AC76 radio, with
moulded brown Bakelite case,
on later stand, c1935.
£500–600 *BTA*

A Decca 'Double Decca' radio,
c1947, 12½in (32cm) high.
£20–40 *OTA*

An 8-track cassette tape player
and radio, in yellow case, 1960s,
13in (33cm) high.
£90–110 *HOL*

An Ekco AC85 Bakelite radio,
with walnut finish, c1934.
£150–250 *BTA*

A Murphy A24 radio,
c1934, 17in (43cm) high.
£50–100 *OTA*

An Ekco AD65 black and
chrome radio, c1934, 15in
(38cm) diam.
£500–700 *OTA*

A Murphy A100 Bakelite valve
radio, AC mains, 1946, 8in
(20cm) high.
£30–50 *RMV*

A K. B. FB10 'toaster' radio,
1940–50, 10in (25cm) wide.
£50–60 *TTM*

A Bush portable radio, 1950s,
13in (33cm) wide.
£25–30 *JUN*

A GEC 'Home Broadcaster',
in original display box, 7in
(17.5cm) square.
£75–85 *JUN*

An Ultra mains radio, in a red
and white plastic case, 1950s,
12in (30.5cm) wide.
£40–45 *JUN*

A Vidor 'Lady Margaret CN429'
battery/valve portable radio, in
a Rexine covered plywood case,
1954, 8in (20cm) wide.
£5–15 *RMV*

An Ekco AD 75 radio, 1945,
14in (35.5cm) diam.
£300–450 *OTA*

A Bush VHF 90 radio, c1955,
12½in (32cm) wide.
£20–30 *OTA*

A valve radio, in a pedestal
walnut case.
£25–50 *MAW*

VALUATION OF ITEMS

If you require a valuation for an item, it is advisable to
check whether the dealer or specialist will carry out this
service, and if so whether they will make a charge.

Having found a specialist who will do your valuation it is
best to send a photograph and description of the item to
the specialist together with a stamped addressed envelope
for the reply. A valuation by telephone is not possible.

Most dealers are only too happy to help you with your
enquiry, but they are also very busy people, and
consideration of the above points would be welcomed.

RAILWAYANA

A 1½in scale coal fired model of
a Wallis and Stevens road roller,
36in (91.5cm) long.
£1,500–2,000 *AH*

A fireman's stoking shovel,
43in (109cm) long.
£18–20 *JUN*

Nameplates

An LMS nameplate badge, 1930s.
£4,500–5,000 *SRA*

An LNER A3 Class
nameplate,
'Humorist', 1920s.
£4,500–5,000 *SRA*

A SR King Arthur Class cast
brass nameplate, 'Excalibur'
No. 30736, stamped '736',
ex-loco condition.
£4,500–5,000 *ONS*

A London & North Western
railway nameplate, 'Royal Oak'.
£4,250–5,000 *SRA*

A GWR Star Class No. 4060
nameplate, 'Princess Eugenie',
face restored.
£4,500–5,000 *ONS*

A GWR Saint Class nameplate and
matching brass cabside number plate,
'Twineham Court', nameplate and
face of number plate restored.
£4,750–5,250 *ONS*

A GWR King Class nameplate,
'King James II', 1920s.
£12,000–15,000 *SRA*

An LMS Patriot Class nameplate, 'The Leicestershire Regiment', 1930s.
£7,000–8,000 *SRA*

An LNER nameplate and badge, 'Lincolnshire Regiment', 1930s.
£10,000–12,000 *SRA*

An SR West Country Class nameplate set, 'Blandford Forum', 1940s.
£15,000–17,000 *SRA*

An LNER A3 Class nameplate and works plate, 'Bayardo', 1920s.
£5,000–6,000 *SRA*

A GWR Castle Class nameplate, 'Swordfish', 1940s.
£13,000–14,000 *SRA*

l. An LMS Jubilee Class nameplate, 'Canada', 1930s.
£4,250–5,000 *SRA*

Numberplates

A GWR brass cabside numberplate, '9487', with purchase invoice dated '1967'.
£350–450 *ONS*

A North Eastern Railway cabside numberplate, '537', 1887.
£2,000–2,500 *SRA*

r. A smokebox numberplate, '61660', from 'Hull City', 1950s.
£1,700–2,000 *SRA*

Works Plates

A GWR brass cabside numberplate, '9455', with purchase invoice dated '1967'.
£400–500 *ONS*

A GWR King Class King Henry VI cast iron smokebox numberplate, '6018', with bolts, inscribed pasted down paper label.
£2,500–3,000 *ONS*

A cast iron 'A & W Smith & Co.', engineers plate, dated '1880', 20in (51cm) wide.
£60–70 *JUN*

A brass Highland Railway Lochgorm Works Inverness 1879' works plate.
£2,500–3,000 *ONS*

A brass 'Vulcan Foundry No. 4756' works plate, dated '1936'.
£75–100 *ONS*

A brass 'Sharp, Stewart & Co., Atlas Works' works plate, repainted, dated '1897'.
£250–300 *ONS*

A brass 'Rebuilt St. Rollox 1900' Caledonian Railway works plate.
£1,750–2,000 *ONS*

Photographs

Two albums containing 162 bromide photographs of locomotives of the South Eastern & Chatham and Dover Railways, 1830–99, and 1899–1922, compiled by H. Dixon Hewitt, each photograph with manuscript identification, each photograph 4in (10cm) wide.
£300–400 *ONS*

Posters

A poster drawn on linen, by Constant Duval, 'Chemins de Fer de L'Etat & de Brighton', 1913.
£325–400 *ONS*

A British Railways poster, 'Cromer', 1950s.
£140–180 *SRA*

A Southern Railways poster, by Maurice Toussaint, 1932.
£175–225 *ONS*

r. A GWR coloured poster, 'The Cornish Riviera', 1920s.
£450–550 *SRA*

Signs

A GWR cast iron notice, repainted, 23½in (60cm) wide.
£600–700 *ONS*

A British Railways totem sign, 'Hykeham', 1950s.
£350–400 *SRA*

A British Railways green totem sign, 'Templecombe', 1950s.
£650–750 *ONS*

RECORDS

The rapid and recent expansion of the CD market has contrived to make all our records look antique, but what makes a collectable disc? 'Demand,' says dealer Paul Nashman simply. While records by famous artists often fetch the best prices, rare recordings by obscure or minor cult bands can be equally popular. As in any other collecting field, rarity is crucial – with collectors looking for limited edition pressings, promotional material never intended for public release, records that were withdrawn for some reason, or singles brought out privately before a band was signed up by a major label. 'Condition is more important than ever before', adds Nashman. 'There is a huge price gap between "good condition" and "mint condition", and the state of the cover and the record itself are often listed separately.' Ironically, given the nature of the subject matter, highest prices can be reserved for those rare records that come to light in 'mint unplayed condition'.

A jazz album, produced by Gene Page, Billy Page and Stanley Turrentine, 1975.
£8–10 *NAS*

A copy of a Small Faces album, on the Decca label, 1960s.
£20–25 *NAS*

A copy of a double LP, 'Sonic Youth Daydream Nation'.
£12–15 *NAS*

An Apple label sampler 7 inch EP, produced for Wall's.
£35–40 *NAS*

A promotional 12 inch single picture disc, limited edition of 1,000 copies, by Lisa Stansfield, 1990s.
£30–40 *NAS*

A David Bowie withdrawn album cover, 'The Man who Sold the World', c1971.
£170–180 *NAS*

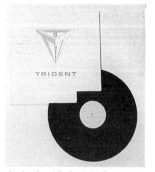

A single-sided 12 inch acetate test disc, by Ian McCulloch, the sleeve inscribed 'To Bill Drummond'.
£30–40 *NAS*

'Prince Buster on Tour', c1967.
£55–60 *NAS*

An autographed 12 inch EP, 'Inspiral Carpets Plane Crash'.
£25–40 *NAS*

A copy of 'The American Tour with Ed Rudy, Radio Pulsebeat News Disc', covering the Beatles American tour, 1965.
£80–100 *NAS*

'The Sub Plates', two promotional 10 inch discs issued to DJ's only.
£20–30 each *NAS*

A rock picture disc, 'Curved Air-Air Conditioning', 1970.
£20–25 *NAS*

These discs were often unplayable due to their poor quality.

A British progressive album 'p.m. Nite People'.
£100–125 *NAS*

Two private pressings by Therapy, 'One Night Stand' and 'Super Troupers', c1973.
£20–25 each *NAS*

A flexi disc single, 'The Senseless Things'.
£10–12 *NAS*

A sealed 7 inch single, of 'Funkadelic', 1970s.
£15–20 *NAS*

A 10 inch EP, of 'Sonic Youth', limited edition, 1990s.
£4–5 *NAS*

SCENT BOTTLES

1995 sees the launch of 'Heavenly Scent', a major exhibition organised by the Comité Français du Parfum, and chronicling the history of perfume from 2,500 BC to the present day. As well as showing a selection of rare scent bottles and related artefacts the exhibition includes such olefactory delights as an 'Odorama', a 3D experience of sound, image and smells as well as computer games to find the perfume that suits your personality.

A Baccarat cut cranberry glass scent bottle, c1900, 6in (15cm) high.
£150–200 *AA*

Two scent bottles:
l. A waisted scent bottle with blue overlay and embossed silver mount, c1870, 3in (7.5cm) long.
£200–250
r. An acorn flute cut scent bottle, with gilt brass mount and finger ring, c1870, 2in (5cm) long.
£150–180 *Som*

Two cut glass scent bottles, with silver necks, c1920, 3in (7.5cm) long.
£20–35 each *VB*

Three double-ended scent bottles, with silver mounts, c1860, 4in (10cm) long.
£150–180 each *Som*

A ruby red circular scent bottle, in a lattice work gilt brass case, with gilt brass mount and finger ring, c1880, 2½in (5.5cm) long.
£150–200 *Som*

A Victorian silver gilt cylindrical scent flask, engraved in the manner of Kate Greenaway, by Samuel Morden, London 1882, 2½in (5.5cm) high, and a fitted case.
£400–450 *CAG*

Two horn shaped clear glass scent bottles, with facet cut bodies and finger rings:
l. A vinaigrette at one end and a whistle the other, c1870, 3in (8cm) long. **£200–250**
r. With scent compartment only, 2½in (6cm) long.
£150–200 *Som*

Eight miniature scent bottles, c1860, ½ to 1½in (1.5 to 3cm) high.
£80–100 each *Som*

Three Victorian scent bottles, two with silver mounts, 2in (5cm) high.
£30–45 each *VB*

SCRIPOPHILY
Austria

A City of Vienna 4% loan certificate, 200 crowns, green and black.
£18–20 *GKR*

A City of Vienna 5% loan certificate, bond of 2,000 crowns, mauve and brown, 1921.
£18–20 *GKR*

An Austrian 4% loan certificate, 1902, pink and white.
£20–22 *GKR*

Canada

A share certificate of the San Antonio Land & Irrigation Company, facsimilie signature of F. S. Pearson, engraved by the American Banknote Co., dated '1913'.
£10–12 *SCR*

A bond certificate of the Atlantic Quebec & Western Railway Co, signed by the Earl of Ranfurley, President, c1911.
£15–18 *SCR*

A share certificate of the Canadian Mortgage Association, vignettes of farming and city scenes, brown, blue and beige, dated '1910'.
£45–55 *SCR*

China

A share certificate of the Banque Industrielle de Chine, yellow and black.
£35–42 *GKR*

This bank went into liquidation in 1920s, but was re-established as the only foreign bank allowed to operate in China under Mao, before being finally liquidated in 1960.

Estonia

A Republic of Estonia 7% bond certificate, engraved by Bradbury Wilkinson with vignette of the port of Talin, blue and black, 1927.
£50–60 *SCR*

A £100 debenture, the Levis and Kennebec Railway Company, pale blue with affixed red seal, dated '1875'.
£125–150 *SCR*

A Republic of Estonia 7% loan £100 bond, blue, with vignette of steamer on a lake, 1927.
£65–75 *GKR*

France & Belgium

A founder's share certificate of the Société des Rizeries Parisiennes, with dragon borders and factory vignettes, pink and green, issued in Paris, 1915.
£15–18 *SCR*

A bearer share certificate of the Grand Bazar du Boulevard Anspach, with vignettes of Brussels, brown and cream, dated '1927'.
£25–30 *SCR*

l. A bearer share certificate of the Baie de Mont Saint-Michel, green and blue, dated '1927'.
£175–195 *SCR*

A share certificate of Etablissements Verminck, a wine pressing and barrel manufacturer, green and blue, issued in Marseille, 1912.
£15–18 *SCR*

A founder's share certificate of the Compagnie Maritime de la Seine, depicting views of the Thames and the Seine, shades of brown, 1899.
£28–32 *GKR*

A bearer share certificate of the Compagnie Générale de Traction, blue, issued c1900.
£20–25 *SCR*

Great Britain

A share certificate for Mudie's Select Library Ltd., modelled on a British bank note, dated '1864'.
£25–30 *SCR*

A share certificate of the Newry Warrenpoint & Rostrevor Railway Company, printed on vellum with affixed red seal, dated '1846'.
£75–85 *SCR*

A share certificate of the Electric Clock Company Ltd., black on yellow, dated '1868'.
£30–35 *SCR*

A share certificate of the Pneumatic Despatch Company Ltd., dated '1860'.
£55–65 *SCR*

This company built a series of underground tubes to transport parcels for the British Post Office. The 'trains' worked on the atmospheric method (i.e. air suction) and were the earliest form of underground railway. The scheme was engineered by T. W. Rammell, and the share certificates bear his facsimile signature.

South & Central America

A share certificate of Banana du Rio Grande (Nicaragua), yellow and black, c1915.
£55–65 *SCR*

A share certificate of the Negociación Agricola 'La Sauteña', with a map of the Texas/Mexico border, green, red and black, dated '1907'.
£45–55 *SCR*

A bond certificate of the Manila Railway Company, brown/black, issued in 1907.
£15–18 *SCR*

A share certificate of the Brazil Railway Company, mauve and black.
£12–15 *GKR*

A bank bond of Banco Mercantil del Paraguay, with revenue stamp, green and black, dated '1907'.
£45–50 *GKR*

A share certificate of El Alacran Anexas, SA, with vignette of a scorpion holding a silver nugget, brown and black, dated 1920.
£12–15 *SCR*

A share certificate of the Compania Huanchaca de Bolivia, with English, French and Spanish text, issued in Valparaiso, black and purple, 1928.
£12–15 *SCR*

Spain & Portugal

A share certificate of the Companhia de Navegaçâo, depicting an elaborate harbour scene with Gothic style surround, multi-coloured, issued in Ponta Delgada, Portugal, 1920.
£85–95 *SCR*

A share certificate of Barcelona Traction, Light & Power Co. Ltd., Waterlow, engraved, red and black.
£15–20 *SCR*

A share certificate of 'Colon' Compañia Transaerea Española, depicting an airship, green and beige, dated '1928'.
£40–45 *SCR*

USA

A share certificate of the California King Gold Mines, depicting crown flanked by griffins, orange and black, c1902.
£30–35 *SCR*

A bond certificate of the Fort Wayne Rink Association, with a vignette of the rink with skaters, red, black and white.
£80–90 *SCR*

Only 200 of these $50 bonds were issued.

A bond certificate of the Cleveland Cincinnati Chicago & St. Louis Railway Co., with vignettes of harvest gatherers, brown, dated '1893'.
£20–25 *SCR*

A share certificate of the Philadelphia Bourse, with a vignette of pioneers and a ship, green and black, c1955.
£10–12 *SCR*

A mortgage bond of the La Porte Wharf & Channel Company, with affixed seal bearing imprint of Texan Star, dated '1899'.
£40–45 *SCR*

Only 400 bonds of $500 were issued.

A share certificate of the Submarine Signal Company, with a vignette of a sailing ship, c1940, 100 shares, brown.
£18–20 *SCR*

A share certificate of The Pittsburgh Youngstown & Ashtabula Railroad Company, brown and black, c1892.
£20–25 *SCR*

A share certificate of Pittsburgh Allegheny & Manchester Traction Company, with vignette of a river scene, green and black, c1895.
£12–15 *SCR*

A bond certificate of West Shore Railroad Company, with vignette of lakeside scene, red and black, c1918.
£8–10 *SCR*

A bond certificate of the Beech Creek Railroad Company, brown and black, dated '1892'.
£25–30 *SCR*

A share certificate of Cleveland & Pittsburgh Railroad Company, green and black, c1950.
£6–8 *SCR*

A share certificate of the Wagner Palace Car Company, with vignettes of trains and buildings, brown and black, c1888.
£20–25 *SCR*

A bond certificate of the Pine Creek Railway Company, signed by William K. Vanderbilt and Chauncy Depew.
£145–165 *SCR*

An unissued share certificate of 100 shares of The Columbus Southern Railway, green and black, c1890.
£6–8 *SCR*

USSR

A share certificate of Société des Ateliers & Chantiers de Nicolaïeff, dark and light green, dated '1911'.
£12–14 *GKR*

A share certificate of The Russian Tobacco Company, printed by Waterlow, green and black, c1915, 15 by 10½in (38 by 26.5cm) high.
£20–25 *GKR*

A debenture certificate of St. Petersburg Land and Mortgage Company Ltd., with a vignette of the city, blue and white, dated '1912'.
£60–65 *GKR*

SHIPPING & MARITIME
Shipping Collectables

A brass and leather bound telescope, inscribed 'Newton & Co. London, 1859', 25½in (65cm) long.
£130–170 *BAf*

A brass bound mahogany ship's wheel, 20thC, 66in (167.5cm) diam.
£750–800 *JUN*

A ship's water barrel, of splayed coopered form, with five brass bindings, circular mahogany top with brass ring centre and two side ring handles with rope mounts, signed by the maker 'P. & W. MacLellan Limited, Glasgow', 19thC, 33in (84cm) high.
£600–800 *B*

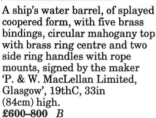

A brass compass, with oil lamp, 20thC, 8in (20cm) high.
£60–80 *BAf*

A plaster mounted crest of HMS 'Shoulton', c1970, 10in (25cm) high.
£12–18 *BAf*

An EPNS cruet set, decorated with HMS 'Rodney' crest, 1940s, 2½in (6cm) high.
£20–25 *BAf*

An Art Deco chromed condiment set, c1930, 6in (15cm) long.
£10–12 *JUN*

A finger bowl, inscribed 'Cosens & Company Limited', used on Weymouth paddle steamers, 1930s, 3in (7.5cm) diam.
£12–15 *BAf*

A Paragon Ware cup and saucer, from Cowes Yacht Club, c1960, cup 3½in (8.5cm) high, saucer 8in (20cm) diam.
£45–100 *CRO*

A mug to commemorate the first visit of 'The Mauretania' to Fishguard Harbour, August 30th, 1909, 3in (7.5cm) high.
£75–85 *WAC*

A bouillon saucer, inscribed 'White Star Line', c1910–20.
£20–40 *COB*

A nutcracker from P & O liner, SS 'Himalaya', 1950s, 7in (17.5cm) diam.
£15–20 *BAf*

A napkin ring, from the Atlas Steamship Company, 1950s.
£10–15 *BAf*

A serpentine lighthouse, with thermometer, from Cornwall, 4½in (11cm) high, and a serpentine barrel, 3in (7.5cm) high.
£20–30 each *OCA*

Globes

Demand for globes expanded during the 18thC. New lands were being charted, astronomy was a popular science, and the development of globes, both terrestrial and celestial, reflected man's exploration of the universe. Globes can appeal to both the collector of scientific instruments and the furniture specialist, notably the large library globes on elaborately carved wooden stands, which can fetch tens of thousands of pounds. At the other end of the scale, schoolroom globes, produced in the 1920s and 30s, or even earlier, can still be purchased for under £200.

A brass egg timer, from SS 'Himalaya', 1960s, 3in (7.5cm) high.
£15–20 *BAf*

An unmounted brass celestial globe, the gold painted sphere engraved with the constellations in outline, additonal stars, and other details, probably Indo-Persian, 6in (15cm) diam.
£275–350 *CSK*

A globe, on a stand, c1890, 19in (48cm) high.
£180–220 *DUN*

A globe on a bronze stand, c1870, 21in (53cm) high.
£380–420 *DUN*

A globe, covered with a set of 12 coloured lithographed gores over a turned wooden base, divided at the equator, the interior to contain a reel or ball of thread or cotton, by A. Clarke & Co., 4in (10cm) high.
£200–300 *CSK*

A miniature brass globe, engraved with lines of longitude and latitude, set in a brass meridian circle and mounted in brass stand, late 19thC, 3in (7.5cm) diam.
£450–550 *CSK*

A school orrery made up of central globe, printed in Czechoslovakian, 12 coloured lithographic gores depicting the major waterways and currents, the globe mounted on a turned wooden column and base, wooden moon ball, the sun arm supporting a candle attachment and metal reflector, by Fekl, Ferdinand and Son, 1921, globe 9in (23cm) diam.
£475–550 *CSK*

A terrestrial globe, the paper gores printed in colours with the continents and national boundaries, the oceans with steamship navigation tracks, on wooden stand, by Dr. Josef Takacs, Budapest, c1930, 15½in (39cm) high.
£150–200 *CSK*

A terrestrial globe, the printed paper gores lightly coloured, with national boundaries, oceans with named currents, steamship routes and cable tracks, on aluminium support and octagonal base, by Barrière and Thomas, Paris, c1930.
£150–200 *CSK*

A large globe globe, on wooden stand, c1938, 36in (91.5cm) diam.
£90–120 *COB*

A relief terrestrial globe, the coloured paper gores printed with the continents in relief, the oceans with depth contours, with aluminium meridian half circle, on turned oak stand, by Paul Rath, Rath's Releif-Erdglobus, Leipzig, c1950, 13in (33cm) diam.
£140–200 *CSK*

A globe, on a stand, c1926, 15in (38cm) high.
£100–120 *DUN*

Model Ships

A wood and metal model of an
Arab dhow, on a base, 20thC,
15in (38cm) long.
£65–75 *BAf*

A model sailing brig, in a glass
case, requires restoration,
20thC, 8in (20cm) wide.
£75–85 *BAf*

A wooden handmade model of a
Thames sailing barge, 20thC,
24in (61cm) long.
£350–400 *BAf*

Five metal models of German
battleships, 1935-65, 6in
(15cm) long.
£18–30 each *BAf*

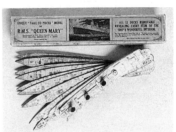

A 'Take to Pieces' model of RMS
'Queen Mary, by Chad Valley,
in original box, c1936, 13in
(33cm) long.
£85–110 *COB*

A scale model of
HMS 'Winchester Castle',
by J. S. Lindsay, c1945,
6½in (16.5cm) long.
£30–40 *BAf*

A wooden model of SS 'Bremen',
by Bassett-Lowke, 1930s,
9in (23cm) long.
£20–25 *BAf*

A wooden model of a passenger
ship, 1950s, 10in (25cm) long.
£20–30 *BAf*

Pictures & Ephemera

A gouache of the Southampton to Isle of Wight paddle steamer 'Princess Elizabeth', built 1927, by E. W. Paget Tomlinson, 1992.
£40–45 *BAf*

A P & O special sailings poster, 1927–28.
£8–10 *COB*

A gouache of the Blue Funnel MV 'Alcinous', 1952, by E. W. Paget Tomlinson, 1989, 12 by 16in (30.5 by 41cm).
£40–45 *BAf*

A watercolour of a WWI liner originally built for Canadian Pacific Line, initialled 'R.A.B.', 1916.
£120–150 *COB*

A P & O poster for summer cruises to Norway, 1927.
£8–10 *COB*

An Osborne plaque, showing RMS 'Queen Mary', c1936, 5in (12.5cm) wide.
£30–35 *COB*

A wooden jigsaw of a Cunard liner, without box, c1920, 5½ by 7in (14 by 17.5cm).
£12–15 *BAf*

A 1905 calendar, advertising The Ocean Accident & Guarantee Corporation Ltd., 15in (38cm) high.
£30–40 *COB*

A Cunard Line souvenir publication *'Eight Decades of Progress'*, by E. Keble Chatterton, with line drawings and 13 full page colour illustrations, from the British Empire Exhibition, Wembley, 1924, with original envelope.
£65–75 *CBS*

Two advertising brochures for shipping lines:
l. RMS 'Majestic' White Star Line, c1928.
r. 'Going Abroad via Cunard and Anchor Lines', c1925.
£20–30 each *COB*

A 2⅛in gauge steam model of L.M.S. 'Princess Royal' and tender, 1950s. **£1,800–2,200** *SRA*

A GWR poster, 1930s, 30 by 20in (76 by 50.5cm). **£225–325** *SRA*

A GWR Cornwall poster, 1940s, 30 by 40in (76 by 101.5cm). **£300–400** SRA

A 2in scale Burrell live steam traction engine. **£1,800–2,200** *SRA*

A vitreous enamel and gunmetal shield from SR West Country Class, No. 34040, c1969. **£4,000–4,500** *ONS*

A GWR poster, 1940s, 30 by 20in (76 by 50.5cm). **£275–375** *SRA*

An LNER Hunt Class nameplate, 1930s. **£7,250–8,000** *SRA*

r. An L&SWR platform ticket machine, c1900. **£900–1,200** *SRA*

A builder's and owner's plate, Robert Heath & Low Moor Limited, dated '1924'. **£750–850** *SRA*

A British Railways totem station sign, 1950s. **£550–650** *SRA*

A Southern Railway Lord Nelson Class nameplate, 'Sir Walter Raleigh', 1920s. **£6,000–7,000** *SRA*

A selection of early locomotive engineers' worksplates, dated 1896–1933. **£300–800 each** *SRA*

A progressive LP 'Dream Sequence' from Cosmic Eye, 1972. **£80–100** *NAS*

A live recording of 'Jazz' album, by Herbie Mann, 1967. **£12–18** *NAS*

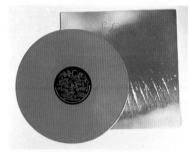

A triple LP limited edition of 'Kiss Me, Kiss Me', by The Cure, 1987. **£18–20** *NAS*

A limited edition LP 'Disintegration', by, The Cure, 1989. **£8–10** *NAS*

A picture disc, 'Dirty Old Town', by the Pogues, available by mail order only, 1985. **£12–15** *NAS*

A Prince 12in single, 'Let's Work', c1981. **£120–130** *NAS*

An LP by the Slits, 'Return of the Giants', 1981. **£8–10** *NAS*

A sealed double album, with free art print, by The Orb, 1992. **£20–25** *NAS*

Two LPs,one by Jefferson Airplane, 'After Bathing at Baxters', and the other by The Mothers of Invention, 'Freak Out!', late 1960s. **£25–35 each** *NAS*

Three shaped picture discs, Bruce Springsteen, c1980. **£15–25 each** *NAS*

A Stereolab autographed LP by Peng!, 1992. **£25–30** *NAS*

Two single sided test pressings, by Martha Reeves and The Vandellas, 1968. **£30–40** *NAS*

Three double-ended scent bottles, with
hinged silver binocular mounts, c1860–80.
£250–300 each *Som*

A cut scent bottle,
c1870, 3½in (8cm).
£75–120 *ARE*

Three double-ended scent bottles,
with silver gilt mounts, c1880.
£125–180 each *Som*

A Schuco teddy bear scent
bottle, c1930s, 4⅓in (11cm) high.
£200–250 *SP*

Two cylindrical scent
bottles, late 18thC.
£200–500 each *Som*

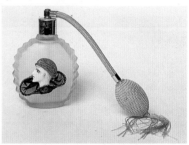

A scent bottle, decorated with the
head of an Art Deco lady, 1930s,
4⅓in (11cm) high.
£20–30 *YY*

A Schuco monkey scent bottle,
c1930, 5in (12.5cm) high.
£100–150 *SP*

Two scent bottles, with embossed
silver gilt mounts, c1840, 3 to 4in
(8 to 10cm) high.
£150–200 each *Som*

A Vasart scent bottle, with
blue, white and yellow canes,
c1970. **£300–350** *MLa*

A Perthshire scent
bottle and stopper,
c1984, 6⅓in (16cm) high.
£95–115 *SWB*

A Stourbridge satin glass scent
bottle, with silver mount, 1887.
£500–600, and an opaque scent
bottle, c1880. **£150–200** *Som*

Three single-ended scent bottles,
with embossed silver mounts, c1880,
3 to 4in (8 to 9.5cm) high.
£150–300 each *Som*

A painted cheroot
tin, c1800.
£75–90 *VB*

A pipe-shaped cigar holder, c1880,
4in (10cm) long.
£70–80 *DP*

A green glass cigar holder,
c1910, 4in (10cm) long.
£15–25 *DP*

A plastic cigarette holder, c1930,
3in (7.5cm) long.
£10–15 *DP*

A yellow striped glass cigar holder,
c1900, 2¼in (6cm) long.
£20–30 *DP*

An enamelled silver cigarette
case, c1913, 3¼in (8cm) square.
£120–140 *LIO*

An English pottery
tobacco jar, c1880,
12in (31.5cm) high.
£200–250 *RA*

An American silver vesta case,
c1880, 3⅜in (9cm) long.
£80–100 *LIO*

A mother-of-pearl cigarette holder,
stained purple, c1900, 3½in (9cm) long.
£30–40 *DP*

A set of cigarette accessories,
c1930, in original box, 9in (23cm).
£40–45 *PC*

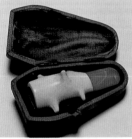

A Meerschaum and amber
cased cigar holder, c1910,
2¾in (7cm) long.
£25–30 *DP*

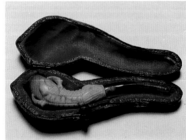

A Meerschaum bird's claw cigarette
holder, in fitted case, c1890, 4in
(10cm) long.
£30–40 *DP*

An amber and gold mounted
cigar holder, in fitted case,
c1900, 2½in (6.5cm) long.
£25–35 *DP*

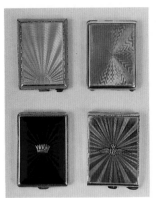

A selection of enamel on silver book match covers, c1930, 2½in (6cm) high.
£35–45 each *PC*

Three enamel on silver book match covers, c1920–30.
£35–50 each *PC*

A collection of Art Deco pearlised book match covers, c1930, 2½in (6cm) high.
£10–20 each *PC*

Two book match covers, c1920.
l. Painted floral decoration.
r. Cross stitch decoration.
£15–20 each *PC*

Three enamelled book match covers, c1920–30, 2½in (6cm) high.
£20–25 each *PC*

Three decorated and enamelled book match covers, c1930, 2½in (6cm) high.
£20–25 each *PC*

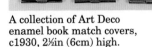

A collection of Art Deco enamel book match covers, c1930, 2½in (6cm) high.
£15–25 each *PC*

Two painted book match covers, c1930, 2½in (6cm) high.
£12–15 each *PC*

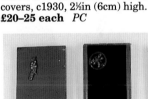

Three book match covers, with diamanté decoration, 1930–40.
£10–15 each *PC*

An American blue and silver book match cover, c1930. **£40–45** *PC*

A selection of Art Deco book match covers, c1930, 2in (5cm) high.
£5–25 each *PC*

Two book match covers, with enamelled Oriental design, c1920.
£10–15 each *PC*

Laws of Cricket, with illustrations by C. Crombie, Copyright of Perrier, London, price 5/-, c1930, 15in (38cm) wide. **£400–500** *CRA*

A Shelley jug, decorated with bears playing cricket, c1920s, 2in (5cm) high. **£15–20** *MSh*

A pair of Henry Cooper's boxing gloves, 1960s. **£350–400** *Bon*

A football programme, Scotland v. Brazil 30th June 1973. **£2–2.50** *COL*

A Milk Cup Final programme, 20th April, 1986. **£1.50–2.00** *COL*

A French plate, decorated with croquet players, c1920–30, 9in (22.5cm) diam. **£15–20** *YY*

r. An amateur football cap, 1898. **£40–60** *VS*

A cricket bat, c1845, decorated with a modern oil painting. **£60–80** *VS*

A Crown Staffordshire golfing saucer, 1960s, 6in (15cm) diam. **£8–10** *YY*

A Wembley Cup Final programme, 4th May, 1974. **£1.50–2.00** *COL*

Two football programmes, 9th May, 1951, and 25th November, 1970. **£1.50–2.00 each** *COL*

A bramble pattern golf ball, with gutta percha shell, c1905. **£60–80** *MSh*

A Grimwades 'Golf Language'
plate, c1920, 9in (22.5cm) diam.
£80–100 *MSh*

A Grimwades plate, 'The Indispensable
Caddy', c1920, 9in (22.5cm) diam.
£80–100 *MSh*

A Vienna cold painted
bronze, c1910, 6½in
(16cm) high.
£1,200–1,500 *MSh*

A Royal Doulton Series
Ware candlestick,
c1910, 6½in (16cm)
high. **£140–160** *MSh*

A Poole Pottery golf club trophy, 1972.
£100–150 *TAR*

A Royal Worcester golfing
saucer, showing Moor
Park, Sunningdale and
Wentworth, c1960, 6½in
(16cm) diam. **£8–10** *YY*

A Dunlop 31 golfing
car mascot, c1920s.
£125–150 *TAR*

A Royal Doulton Series
Ware vase, c1910,
3in (7.5cm) high.
£60–100 *MSh*

A Clifton Ware
tobacco jar, c1920,
6in (15cm) high.
£250–300 *MSh*

A porcelain cup and saucer, by W. H. Grindley
& Co., depicting bears playing golf, c1920,
saucer 5in (12.5cm) diam. **£25–35** *MSh*

A silver 'Hole in One'
golf trophy, c1900, 8in
(20cm) high.
£80–120 *MSh*

A leather trout and salmon fly wallet, with a selection of flies, 19thC, 7in (17.5cm) wide.
£100–110 *GHA*

Three perch, mounted in a setting of reeds and grasses, in a bowfronted gilt lined case, 35in (89cm) wide.
£1,400–1,700 *Bon*

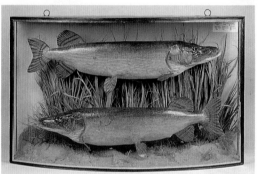

Two pike, mounted in a bowfronted gilt lined case, printed label with date '5th March, 1891', 49in (124.5cm) wide.
£2,000–2,500 *Bon*

A chub, mounted in a bowfronted case, inscribed and dated '1907', fish 18in (45.5cm) long.
£475–500 *GHA*

A Hardy 'Davy' contracted fly reel, stamped inside 'J.S.'
£525–600 *Bon*

A brass salmon reel, early 19thC, 4in (10cm) diam.
£225–250 *GHA*

A gudgeon, mounted in a bowfronted gilt lined case, inscribed and dated '11th Feb'y 1934', 13in (34cm) wide.
£3,000–4,000 *Bon*

A Royal Doulton Series Ware teapot, decorated with 'The Gallant Fishers', c1915.
£200–300 *MSh*

A Staffordshire mug, with transfer scene, 19thC, 3in (7.5cm).
£80–85 *GHA*

A Hardy Bros. brass line dryer with wooden handle, 19thC, 11in (28cm).
£225–250 *GHA*

SMOKING & TOBACCO

Although tobacco is acknowledged by many as an evil today, since its importation to Europe in the 16thC it has inspired some decorative examples of smoking paraphernalia, ranging from 18thC snuff boxes to ornate 20thC cigarette cases. From the earliest times, tobacco has also given rise to some fascinating stories. According to the Huron Indians in Canada, tobacco first appeared many centuries ago during the time of a terrible famine. The tribes met to pray to the Great Spirit for help, and heeding the cries of the hungry he sent to earth a beautiful naked squaw. She sat down, placed both hands on the ground and then disappeared into the clouds. From where her right palm rested, corn grew, and from the left, potatoes sprouted, but it was from where she had been sitting that the tobacco plant flourished.

A chrome advertising ashtray, inscribed 'Hilmor', c1930, 6½in (16.5cm) wide.
£8–10 *HEW*

An Art Deco black and green Bakelite ashtray, 3½in (8.5cm) high.
£80–95 *HEW*

An orange lustre ashtray, in the form of a pierrot, 1930, 3½in (8.5cm) long.
£30–35 *HEW*

Ashtrays

An Art Deco Bakelite advertising ashtray, inscribed 'Möbel, Wilhelm Seffers, Vohrum', 6½in (16.5cm) wide.
£20–25 *HEW*

A Meissen ashtray, printed in blue with aeroplanes, the central one with a swastika on its tail, underglaze blue crossed swords mark, impressed mark, printed date mark for 1940, 8in (20.5cm) wide.
£375–450 *P*

Cigar Collectables

A meerschaum cheroot holder, carved with a goatherd, the mount with turquoise beads and amber mouthpiece, late 19thC, 6½in (17cm) long.
£250–350 *S(S)*

A blue and white glass cigar holder, c1900, 3in (8cm) long.
£30–40 *DP*

A French cheroot case, nielloed with a chequered design surrounding an engraved shield-shaped gilt cartouche, c1930, 3½in (9cm) high.
£225–300 *CSK*

An amber cigar holder, c1900, 2½in (6.5cm) long, in a lined case.
£20–30 *DP*

A meerschaum and amber cigar holder, c1910, 3in (7cm) long, in a lined case.
£25–30 *DP*

A cigar holder, with Stanhope showing a view of Staubach, Switzerland, 5½in (13.5cm).
£40–50 *DP*

A bronze cigar cutter, in the form of a dog, c1880.
£450–500 *DUN*

Cigarette Cases

A Maki-E lacquer cigarette case, decorated with a heron on a willow branch and a full moon, signed Mitsutoshi, early 20thC, 4½in (12cm) high.
£450–500 *CSK*

A Soviet gilt lined cigarette case, one side enamelled with a study of horse's head, early 20thC, 3in (7.5cm) high.
£275–300 *CSK*

A Ronson lady's cigarette case, gold plate on brass, with mother-of-pearl, c1930, 3in (7.5cm) long.
£25–30 *FMN*

A Russian gilt lined cigarette case, polychrome cloisonné enamelled with scrollwork and stylised flowers in shades of white, blue and orange, early 20thC, 3½in (9cm) high.
£400–500 *CSK*

A Russian silver gilt cigarette case, part nielloed with a chequered design within grooved borders, Moscow 1892.
£325–350 *CSK*

A cigarette case, book match cover and notebook, c1920–30, in original box, 7½in (19cm) long.
£35–40 *PC*

A German cigarette case, the front enamelled with a female nude on a bed of feathers, early 20thC, 3½in (9cm) high.
£800–900 *CSK*

Cigar & Cigarette Holders

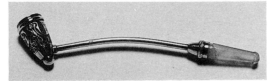

A silver pipe-shaped cigarette
holder, 1903, 4in (10cm) long.
£50–60 *DP*

A pink glass cigar holder,
c1900, 3in (7.5cm) long.
£30–40 *DP*

A glass cigar holder, in the form
of a fish, with glass 'W.S.'
initials, c1890, 4in (10cm) long.
£40–50 *DP*

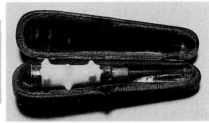

A meerschaum, silver and
amber cigarette holder, c1900,
4in (10cm) long.
£40–50 *DP*

A silver mounted antler and
cigarette holder, c1910, 5in
(12.5cm) long.
£30–40 *DP*

A silver pipe-shaped cigarette
holder, 1913, 4½in (11.5cm)
long, in lined case.
£60–70 *DP*

A red amber cigarette holder,
c1900, 6in (15cm) long, in
lined case.
£60–70 *DP*

A pink glass cigarette holder,
c1920, 8in (20cm) long.
£100–120 *DP*

A mother-of-pearl cigarette
holder, engraved with flowers,
1900, 4½in (11.5cm) long.
£120–130 *DP*

An Art Deco plastic cigarette
holder, c1930, 5in (12.5cm) long.
£5–10 *DP*

l. A twisted glass cigarette
holder, c1900, 4in (10cm) long.
£20–30 *DP*

r. A yellow plastic cigarette
holder, c1930, 3½in (9cm) long.
£5–10 *DP*

Lighters

A table lighter, c1950, 5½in (14cm) high.
£45–55 *CRA*

An Art Deco figure chrome table lighter, 7in (17.5cm) high.
£85–95 *HEW*

A Lorenzl Art Deco chrome table lighter, 10in (25cm) high.
£350–375 *HEW*

Matches: Book Match Covers

Four decorative book match covers, two in fabric, c1930.
£5–15 each *PC*

A selection of Art Deco book match covers, in Bakelite, leather and enamel.
£10–15 each *PC*

A book match cover, inscribed 'Midland Counties Airedale Terrier Club', 2 by 2½in (5 by 6.5cm), c1930.
£12–15 *PC*

Two shagreen book match covers, and one decorated with a Chinese tiger, 2 by 1½in (5 by 4cm), c1930.
£20–25 each *PC*

Three book match covers, with foil pictures of boats, late 1930s, 2 by 1½in (5 by 4cm).
£10–12 each *PC*

A book match cover, with hand painted and foil picture, in original cardboard box.
£20–25 *PC*

A selection of book match covers.
£10–20 each *PC*

Two book match covers, 2 by 2½in (5 by 6.5cm), c1930.
£15–20 each *PC*

Advertising

Two metal book match covers advertising Schweppes and J.F.G. Wines, c1930.
£5–10 each *PC*

A silver plated book match cover advertising Robertson's Dundee Whiskies, 1920s-30s, 2 by 2½in (5 by 6cm).
£10–15 *PC*

A metal book match cover advertising the stage show 'Tons of Money', c1930, 2 by 2½in (5 by 6cm).
£12–15 *PC*

Three metal book match covers advertising H.P. Sauce, Johnnie Walker and Ketton Cement, c1925.
£5–10 each *PC*

A metal book match cover advertising Simplex Conduits Ltd., Birmingham, c1930.
£12–15 *PC*

A metal book match cover advertising The Motherwell Bridge & Engineering Co. Ltd., c1930, 2 by 2½in (5 by 6cm).
£15–20 *PC*

A book match cover showing Shell-B.P. House, c1930, 2 by 2½in (5 by 6cm).
£4–5 *PC*

Two metal book match covers advertising Canadian Pacific And Elder Dempster Shipping Lines, 2½ by 1½in (6 by 4cm), c1930-40.
£15–25 *PC*

Two metal book match covers, one advertising a gentlemen's outfitters, the other with a St. Christopher medallion attached, c1930, 2 by 2½in (5 by 6cm).
£15–20 each *PC*

Commemorative

Two metal book match covers, Wembley 1924.
£15–25 each *PC*

A chromium book match cover commemorating Plymouth Navy Week, c1940.
£15–20 *PC*

Three chromium commemorative book match covers, c1937, 2 by 2½in (5 by 6cm).
£10–25 each *PC*

Leather

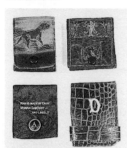

Four leather book match covers, c1940.
£10–15 each *PC*

Two leather book match covers, one with cigar cutter, c1935.
£5–10 each *PC*

A leather book match case, in original box, c1940, 2½ by 3½in (6 by 9cm).
£20–25 *PC*

A tooled leather book match cover, c1935, 2 by 2½in (5 by 6cm).
£20–25 *PC*

Silver

Three Art Deco book match covers, enamelled on silver, 2 by 1½in (5 by 4cm).
£35–40 *PC*

A Mexican silver Art Nouveau style book match cover, 2 by 2½in (5 by 6cm).
£25–30 *PC*

Four silver book match covers, hallmarked Birmingham 1921 and 1922.
£20–25 each *PC*

A selection of silver book match covers, hallmarked Sheffield, c1930.
£25–30 each *PC*

Four silver book match covers, hallmarked London, c1935.
£25–30 each *PC*

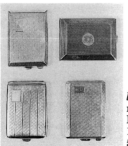

l. Four silver book match covers, marked Birmingham 1932 and 1937.
£15–25 each *PC*

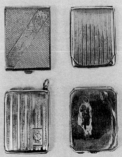

l. Four silver book match covers, hallmarked Chester, c1930.
£25–35 each *PC*

Tortoiseshell

Four tortoiseshell book match covers, c1950.
£20–25 each *PC*

r. Two tortoiseshell book match covers, with gold inlay initials.
£25–30 each *PC*

Two Scottish book match covers, one with Aberdeen coat-of-arms, the other covered in tartan fabric, c1950, 2 by 2½in (5 by 6cm).
£5–15 each *PC*

Travel & Topography

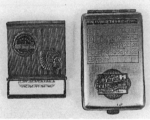

Two metal souvenir calendar book match covers, Pennsylvania and Tunbridge Wells, c1930.
£20–25 each *PC*

Two metal souvenir book match covers, Great Britain and Torquay, c1935, 2 by 2½in (5 by 6cm).
£10–15 each *PC*

A selection of brass book match covers, c1950.
£10–15 each *PC*

A silver plate book match cover, with the Cape Peninsula, c1935.
£20–25 *PC*

Two metal souvenir book match covers, Isle of Man and Stourport, c1950.
£15–20 each *PC*

A match striker, c1950, 4in (10cm) wide.
£20–30 *HEW*

Miscellaneous

A Gitanes Jumbo matchbox shop display, c1980s, 14½ by 10in (37 by 25cm).
£20–25 *WP*

Four Victorian/Edwardian vesta cases, in Bakelite, jet and metal.
£15–30 each *VB*

Pipe Smoking

An Austrian meerschaum pipe, with amber mouthpiece and carved with a successful deer hunt, c1890, 10in (25cm) long.
£100–150 *S(S)*

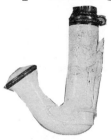

An Austrian meerschaum pipe, carved with a standing figure of Napoleon beneath trees, with silver mounts, 1814, 6½in (16cm) long, with case.
£450–500 *S(S)*

A pipe holder, c1880, 9in (23cm) high.
£300–400 *ARE*

Snuff Boxes

A German tôleware tobacco box, with painted cover, the interior with 'No. 486' and stamped 'Stobwasser's Fabrik Brunschweig' 19thC, 4in (10cm) wide.
£1,400–1,800 *CSK*

A tortoiseshell and silver mounted snuff box, the lid inset with a medal commemorating the coronation of King George II, 1727, 5in (12.5cm) long.
£350–400 *CSK*

A Georgian silver snuff box, 3in (7.5cm) long.
£150–175 *LIO*

A George III silver gilt snuff box, the lid applied with a plaque commemorating the battle victories of Wellington, with later inscription to interior, maker's initials rubbed, London 1806, 3½in (9cm) long.
£750–800 *CSK*

A French enamel and gilt copper snuff box, the cover pierced with two archers, backed with a blue enamel panel with aventurine bands, c1800, 3in (7cm) wide.
£250–300 *S(S)*

Miscellaneous

An early cigarette vending machine, c1920–30.
£200–300 *SRA*

Tobacco Jars

l. A Sarreguemines tobacco jar, the lid shaped as a fez, No. 3264, c1905, 7in (17.5cm).
£150–175 *PC*

r. A Sarreguemines tobacco jar, the lid shaped as a top hat, No. 3338, c1900, 7in (17.5cm.
£150–175 *PC*

SOUVENIRS
Butlin's

Sir William Heygate Edmund Colborne Butlin (1899-1980), better known as Billy Butlin, spent much of his youth in South Africa and Canada. He returned to England and ran a number of amusement parks, introducing Dodgem cars into this country in 1928. Inspired by his experience of Canadian summer camps he opened the first Butlin Camp in Skegness in 1936, and the original Butlin's chalet still stands there today, now a Grade II listed building! Billy Butlin opened several other sites which were taken over by the armed forces during WWII. In 1950s the holiday camps boomed and Butlin's became a national institution. As famous as the 'Wakey-Wakey' cry, which woke the happy campers, were the Butlin's badges, worn by visitors, staff and Redcoats (the Butlin's entertainers). Today, early badges such as the first Christmas badge (Clacton 1938) can be worth as much as £100, and material from all periods, in particular pre-war to the 1950s, is becoming collectable.

Badges

The first Butlin's Holiday Club badge, which cost campers 1s 0d, with blue jumper, white trousers, black boots, red labels, c1936, 1in (2.5cm) high.
£40–50 *PC*

This badge allowed holiday-makers access to the camp and bars. Butlin's was regarded as a Holiday Club until 1939.

A Christmas Tree badge, Butlin's Clacton 1938, 1in (2.5cm) high.
£75–100 *PC*

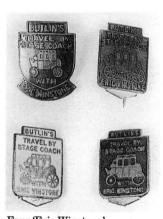

Four 'Eric Winstone' badges, c1940s and 50s:
Top l. **£20–25**
the rest **£7–10 each** *PC*

Butlin's entertainers provided their own badges.

A selection of badges issued at Butlin's, Mosney, Ireland, c1950–51, 1 to 1½in (2.5 to 4cm).
£12–15 each *PC*

A '21 Club' badge, 1in (2.5cm) high.
£12–15 *PC*

The '21 Club' was organised by Billy Butlin during WWII for the forces in Hamburg, Brussels and India, where servicemen could meet carefully vetted girls.

An advertising badge with caption 'Dicky Boy's Happy at Butlin's', 1½in (4cm) wide.
£50–55 *PC*

This badge was provided by Dicky Denny who was a bandleader.

Two Butlin's staff badges from Skegness, 1946:
l. With plain gold centre. **£10–12**
r. Enamelled badge. **£40–50**   *PC*

Two Butlin's badges from the Filey camp, 1945:
l. Holidaymakers. **£10–15**
r. Staff. **£40–50**   *PC*

*Filey was the first Butlin's camp to open
after WWII.*

Two camp Committee badges
produced until 1966 and three
hotel badges, produced until 1967.
£4–8 each   *PC*

A selection of Butlin's staff
badges, c1950s.
£20–25 each   *PC*

Two first and second issue Butlin's
Clacton badges, coloured blue, gold
and cream, 1938–39, 1in (2.5cm) high.
£20–30 each   *PC*

Five figures, available from the
Butlin's shops and a 'Wizzy's
World' badge given free.
£1–1.25 each   *PC*

A Butlin's Loyalty Club badge, 1993,
1in (2.5cm) high.
£1–2   *PC*

*Members of this club received a passport
and prizes, consisting of books filled with a
number of badges depending on how many
holidays had been taken at Butlin's.*

A selection of
Butlin's staff
and holiday-
maker's badges,
attached to a ribbon.
£1–2 each   *PC*

r. An East Anglian Motor Club Butlin's Rally badge, 1950, 1½in (4cm) high.
£20–25 *PC*

l. Two Butlin's '913 Club' badges, available in two sizes, 1 and 2in (2.5 and 5cm) diam.
50p–£1 each *PC*

This club is for nine to thirteen year olds.

Ceramics & Glass

r. A selection of Butlin's ceramic pincushions, c1970s.
£5–6 each *PC*

These were also produced without the Butlin's name.

A selection of Butlin's Manor Ware pieces, badger and hedgehog with shining eyes, c1970s.
£5–6 each *PC*

Three Butlin's plates, c1970s, 6½in (16cm) diam.
£6–8 each *PC*

Two Butlin's jugs and a soup plate, 1940s.
£5–10 each *PC*

A Butlin's ceramic owl, c1980s, 6½in (16cm) high.
£5–6 *PC*

Two Butlin's pottery jars.
£4–6 each *PC*

A selection of miniature tankards, given by Butlin's at Christmas with a tot of rum, c1953 and 1959.
£5–6 each *PC*

Dance Medals

Two *News of the World* Butlin's
Dancing Medals, 1960:
Silver. **£15–20**
Bronze. **£5–10** *PC*

A Butlin's 'Adjudicator'
badge and ribbon, 1939,
2in (5cm) diam.
£5–10 *PC*

Two *News of the World*
8th Butlin's Veleta Medals,
1952 and 1955:
Silver. **£15–20**
Bronze. **£5–10** *PC*

Ephemera

Four Butlin's rosettes, c1949.
£1–2 each *PC*

Four Butlin's Gift Vouchers,
1s 0d, 2s 6d, 5s 0d, and 10s 0d,
given as prizes at the camps.
£1–2 each *PC*

A Butlin's savings book
and stamps:
Book. **£1–1.50**
Stamps. **£5–8 each strip** *PC*
*These books of stamps were used
to save for future holidays.*

A Christmas card sent by Butlin's
to staff in the forces during WWII,
with a message that guaranteed
employment to all regular staff as
soon as possible after hostilities
cease, 4½ by 6in (11 by 15cm).
£25–30 *PC*

A Butlin's postcard, c1932.
£10–12 *PC*

Memorabilia

Three Butlin's cigarette lighters,
two designed as bullets, one a
Ronson pocket lighter, 2 and 3in
(5 and 7.5cm) high.
Ronson. £7–10
Bullets. £4–5 each PC
*The Butlin's name reduces the
value of these lighters.*

Four Butlin's tea and
biscuit tins, c1970s.
£2–7 each PC

Two Butlin's cigarette
lighters, 1990s, 2½ and 3in
(6 and 7.5cm) high.
£1–2 each PC

A Butlin's coach, by Lledo,
c1990, 5½in (14cm) long,
in mint condition and boxed.
£4–5 PC

A Butlin's brass bottle opener,
4in (10cm) long.
£10–15 PC

Two Butlin's silver plated 1pint
and ½ pint tankards, from
Clacton and Skegness, 1939.
£12–15 each PC

A Butlin's Sunshine Coach,
c1994, 5½in (14cm) long,
in mint condition and boxed.
£4–5 PC

A Butlin's 'Glamorous
Grandmother' Trophy, 1967,
10in (25cm) high.
£30–40 PC

Two Butlin's 'Beaver Club'
money boxes:
top. Made of rubber material,
5½in (14cm) high. £10–15
bottom. Ceramic, 6in (15cm) high.
£25–30 PC

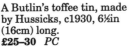

A Butlin's toffee tin, made
by Hussicks, c1930, 6½in
(16cm) long.
£25–30 PC

Sand Souvenirs

Two frog-shaped Alum Bay sand
souvenirs, 1930s, 3 and 3½in
(7.5 and 9cm) high.
£20–30 each *TAR*

Two dog-shaped Alum Bay sand
souvenirs, 1930s, 3in (7.5cm).
£15–20 each *TAR*

A Victorian Alum Bay sand
art souvenir with picture of
Carisbrook Castle, 9in
(23cm) high.
£60–80 *TAR*

*These glass souvenirs are filled
with layered, coloured sands,
and purchased from seaside
resorts from the 19thC onwards.*

Two sand souvenir paperweights,
1950s, 2½in (6cm) diam.
£8–10 each *TAR*

Two sand souvenirs shaped
as a man and a woman, 1920s,
3½in (9cm) high.
£20–30 each *TAR*

An Alum Bay sand souvenir, with
seagull, 1950s, 5in (12.5cm) high.
£10–15 *TAR*

An elephant-shaped Alum Bay
sand souvenir, 1930s, 7½in
(19cm) high.
£30–40 *TAR*

Two sand souvenirs shaped as a
lighthouse and a windmill, 1930s.
£10–15 each *TAR*

A selection of animal-shaped Alum Bay
sand souvenirs, 1930s, dog 5in (12.5cm)
long, bird 3in (7.5cm) high.
£15–30 each *TAR*

An Alum Bay sand souvenir
shaped as a fish, 1950s, 3in
(7.5cm) long.
£10–15 *TAR*

SPORTING

The market for sporting collectables continues to expand with demand often outstripping supply. Football memorabilia is growing in popularity. Bonham's recently scored with a major sale of soccer collectables, including an autograph book signed by eleven of the Manchester United 'Busby Babes' team who perished in the 1958 Munich Air Disaster. Other notable results included high prices for vintage Cup Final material. Cricketing collectables continue to do well, in particular autographed material, and tennis is another strong performer in the salerooms. The market for golf, seemingly insatiable in recent years, shows signs of becoming more selective, with the highest prices reserved only for the rarest items. Popular objects include signed clubs and early golf balls, with boxed pre-WWII rubber core golf balls fetching particularly strong prices. Fishing collectables continue to reel in the punters, with keen competition for early equipment and stuffed fish.

Badminton

A badminton set, made by the Army & Navy Stores, London, in original box, c1905.
£140–180 *MSh*

A pair of badminton shuttlecocks, made from goose feathers, cork and leather, c1860.
£40–60 each *MSh*

Boulles & Bowls

A steel boulle, c1900.
£30–40 *DUN*

Billiards & Snooker

A snooker cue tipper, 6in (15cm).
£15–20 *WAB*

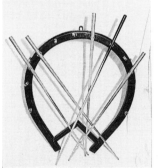

A billiard cue holder, with five cues.
£320–340 *MofC*

A boxed set of lignum vitae lawn bowls, c1900.
£80–120 *MSh*

A mahogany and brass box, containing snooker balls and triangle, c1900.
£150–200 *MSh*

Boxing

A pair of boxing gloves by Goldsmith of Cincinnati, worn by Muhammed Ali in the contest against Joe Bugner on February 14th, 1972.
£1,400–1,800 *Bon*

Cricket

A willow cricket bat, by Charles
Clapshaw, London, c1900.
£50–70 *MSh*

l. A willow cricket
bat, c1900.
£30–50 *MSh*

A 'Player's Please' proof
advertisement, 7 by 10in
(17.5 by 25cm).
£25–35 *VS*

A brass and aluminium belt
buckle, with cricket equipment
design, 1871, 3in (7.5cm) wide.
£80–100 *MSh*

A blue velvet trophy cap,
with a gold tassel, c1930.
£35–55 *WAB*

An MCC touring cap,
said to have belonged
to Geoffrey Boycott.
£200–300 *VS*

A silver plated desk set, with
model of W. G. Grace, and
glass ink bottles, c1895,
7in (17.5cm) wide.
£1,300–1,500 *Bur*

A silver plated cricketing toast
rack, by Dixon & Sons, c1890,
6½in (16.5cm) wide.
£250–300 *CSA*

A cast iron umbrella stand,
entitled 'The Burlington
Cricketer', cast from the
original of c1890, 33in
(83.5cm) high.
£220–240 *Bur*

*At the end of the 19thC there
were many designs for umbrella
stands including sporting
subjects, such as cricket, golf
and tennis. The Burlington
stand has been cast from a
Victorian original, examples of
which are now extremely rare.
The cricketer is probably based
on a portrait of Lord Harris.*

A cotton handkerchief, printed
with a portrait entitled 'Dr W.
G. Grace, Champion Cricketer
of the World', together with
biographical details and a record
of his first class centuries,
21 by 23in (53 by 59cm).
£180–230 *SWO*

Fishing

Reels

A 3¼in Hardy 'The Special Perfect', 1900–06.
£150–200 *JMG*

A 4in brass plate reel, by J. Bernard & Son, London.
£100–120 *GHA*

An Allcocks Aerial 'Popular' 4in centre pin reel, with brass feet, knarled tension adjustable disc, dual xylonite handles and line guard.
£100–140 *Bon*

A 4½in Hardy 'Perfect', with wide drum, nickel silver lineguard, 1912–17.
£80–100 *JMG*

A 2½in brass plate reel, 19thC.
£30–40 *GHA*

A 2½in Hardy Birmingham brass reel with ebonite back.
£100–180 *GHA*

A 4in brass plate reel, by the Army & Navy Stores, London.
£90–100 *GHA*

A 2⅞in Hardy 'Perfect', 1912.
£80–120 *JMG*

A Hardy 2½in all-brass
'Perfect' reel, 1896 check.
£1,000–1,200 *GHA*

A Hardy 4¼in 'Perfect' brass
salmon fly reel, with ivorine
handle and perforated foot.
£750–800 *EP*

A Hardy 4¼in 'Perfect' brass
faced salmon fly reel, with
rod and hand trademark,
ivorine handle and brass
foot, 1905 check.
£320–350 *EP*

A Hardy 4in half ebonite
salmon fly reel, with ebonite
back plate, nickel silver rims,
and horn handle.
£175–200 *EP*

A Hardy 3⅜in 'Perfect',
revarnished, post-WWII.
£60–80 *JMG*

A Hardy 2¾in 'Perfect' brass
trout fly reel, with shaded
rod and hand trademark,
ivorine handle.
£2,250–2,500 *EP*

A 3⅞in Hardy 'Perfect',
with early mechanism
inside, 1906–12.
£60–80 *JMG*

A Hardy 4in
'Perfect', wide drum,
with original leather
case, c1940.
£120–150 *JMG*

A Hardy 2⅞in 'Perfect',
narrow drum, c1920.
£60–80 *JMG*

A Hardy 3⅞in 'St. John', c1920.
£60–80 *JMG*

A Hardy 3⅞in 'St. John',
post-WWII.
£40–60 *JMG*

A Hardy 4¼in 'Silex No. 2'
casting reel, with twin ivorine
handles on fluted cups.
£110–150 *EP*

A Hardy 3in 'St. George',
post-WWII.
£50–75 *JMG*

A Hardy 3⅞in Taupo 'Perfect',
extra wide drum.
£100–140 *JMG*

*These were made mainly for
New Zealand after WWII,
and are very rare.*

l. A Hardy 3½in 'Super Silex
Multiplier' reel, c1930.
£100–130 *JMG*

A 2¾in Hardy 'Silex
Multiplier', late 1920s.
£70–90 *JMG*

A Hardy 'Perfect'
2¾in brass reel,
with ivorine handle
and rod in hand
mark, 1896 pattern.
£800–900 *GHA*

**Our Founder, Jamie Maxtone Graham, c 1924,
with a 4¾" All brass Hardy Perfect**

We are keen to buy the very best reels and rods, particularly
those made by Hardy before 1939. Other desired piscatoriana:
ingenious fly boxes and cabinets, books and catalogues; line
driers, and all the fishing gadgets - including all modern tackle.

Jamie Maxtone Graham's three books - Best of Hardy's
Anglers' guides, 210pp paperback (being reprinted, price on
application); To Catch a Fisherman (Patents) 275pp hardback
£25; Fishing Tackle of Yesterday - A Collector's Guide, 226pp
paperback £25 - are obtainable direct from Timeless Tackle.

Send £2 for our exhaustive catalogue

Write or call:
Rob Maxtone Graham's Timeless Tackle
1 Blackwood Crescent, Edinburgh, EH9 1QZ

**TEL: 0131 667 1407 or 0836 246923
FAX: 0131 662 4215**

l. A brass multiplying winch, with curved crank
handle and ivory knob.
£80–100
r. A brass multiplying winch, with brass foot
and ivory knob.
£120–140 *GHA*

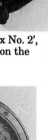

A Hardy 4in 'Silex No. 2', 2¼in brass rim on the side, 1911–21.
£40–60 *JMG*

A Hardy 3½in Silex No. 2', with brass holder on the centre, c1911.
£50–70 *JMG*

A Hardy 3½in 'Super Silex Multiplier' reel, with tapered ebonite handle, ivorine rim lever, rim regulator screw, white indicator dial and grooved brass foot.
£480–500 *EP*

General Equipment

A wooden fisherman's companion, c1870, 6in (15cm) long.
£160–200 *MSh*

A John Lyden Galway 4in all brass crank wind trolling winch, with shallow drum, horn handle and constant check.
£400–450 *Bon*

A Hardy 'Bethune' line winder with bronze frame stamped 'Hardy Bros., Makers Alnwick', curved crank with horn handle, 4 detachable arms and handle with 'W' reel fitting.
£225–275 *EP*

A big game fishing harness, 10 by 7in (25 by 17.5cm).
£25–45 *WAB*

An eel catching fork, 60in (152cm) long.
£35–65 *WAB*

Miscellaneous

A pair of canvas and leather wading boots, with hobnails.
£25–35 *WAB*

A Dartmouth Pottery dish, c1950, 9in (23cm) long.
£18–20 *CSA*

Izaak Walton, *The Compleat Angler,* colour illustrations by James Thorpe, c1911.
£45–60 *BAf*

Two bream, mounted in a gilt lined case, with 'J. E. Miller, Leeds' label, 26in (66cm) wide.
£350–450 *Bon*

A silver rose bowl, embossed with floral and foliate design on spread circular foot, engraved, London 1901, 8in (21cm) diam.
£300–400 *Bon*

An album of autographs, including those of the 1958 Manchester United team, and Tottenham Hotspur 1959–60.
£550–750 *Bon*

Football
Autographs

A photograph signed by Paul Gascoigne, 1980s, 8 by 10in (20 by 25cm).
£30–40 *VS*

> **Miller's is a price GUIDE not a price LIST**

A commemorative cover, with an unusual stamp combination, signed by Pele, 1966.
£40–60 *VS*

A commemorative cover, signed by the 1966 Uruguay football team.
£60–100 *VS*

r. A photograph showing the famous 'Hand of God' incident during the 1986 World Cup, Diego Maradona handlng the ball, signed by Peter Shilton, 8 by 10in (20 by 25cm).
£20–30 *VS*

A commemorative cover, signed by the 1966 Brazil football team.
£200–300 *VS*

r. A signed photograph of the winning 1966 World Cup England Football Team, with 11 signatures, 5 by 7½in (12.5 by 19cm).
£400–500 *VS*

An album of autographs, including those of the 'Busby Babes', the 1958 Manchester United team, many of whom died in the Munich Air Disaster of 1958, 4 by 12in (10 by 30.5cm).
£200–300 *VS*

Programmes

r. A programme for the 1920–21 F. A. Cup Final, 10 by 6in (25 by 15cm).
£400–500 *VS*

A programme for England v. Austria match at Stamford Bridge, 7th December, 1932, slightly damaged.
£80–100 *Bon*

Three programmes for Scotland v. England April 17th, 1943, April 22nd, 1944 and 'Victory International', April 13th, 1946.
£100–125 *Bon*

A Football Association complimentary programme for the England v. Scotland match at Wembley, 14th April, 1934, folded.
£100–120 *Bon*

A Football Association complimentary programme for the England v. Scotland match at Wembley, 5th April, 1930, folded.
£100–120 *Bon*

A Football Association complimentary programme for England v. Scotland at Wembley, 9th April, 1932, folded.
£125–150 *Bon*

r. An official programme for the F. A. Cup Final, Huddersfield Town v. Preston North End, 30th April, 1938, folded.
£200–225 *Bon*

A complimentary official programme for the F. A. Cup Final, Birmingham v. West Bromwich Albion, 25th April, 1931.
£250–300 *Bon*

l. Seven Arsenal home match programmes, 1929–30 season, some folded.
£225–275 *Bon*

An official souvenir programme for the F. A. Cup Final, Arsenal v. Newcastle United, corner folded, April 1932.
£260–300 *Bon*

A programme for the Wales v. England match at Wrexham, 16th November 1932.
£110–140 *Bon*

An official souvenir programme for the F. A. Cup Final, Arsenal v. Cardiff City, 23rd April, 1927, slight damage.
£350–400 *Bon*

An official souvenir programme for the F. A. Cup Final, Sheffield United v. Cardiff City, 25th April, 1925, worn.
£375–450 *Bon*

Twelve Brentford home match programmes, 1930–35, scuffed and folded.
£375–425 *Bon*

Three Brighton & Hove Albion programmes, 1932–40, two folded.
£360–420 *Bon*

Two programmes for Millwall v. Tottenham, January 31st, 1931 and The Casuals F.C. v. The Grasshoppers F.C., February 25th, 1932, folded and scuffed.
£100–125 *Bon*

A programme for the League III (Southern) match, Watford v. Queen's Park Rangers, 30th January, 1932, folded.
£60–80 *Bon*

A programme for Clapton Orient v. Charlton Athletic, Football League Division 3, (Southern Section), 2nd December 1933, folded and stained.
£120–140 *Bon*

Sixteen Chelsea home match programmes, 1930–31, scuffed and folded.
£480–550 *Bon*

Two programmes for Portsmouth v. Arsenal F. A. Cup 5th Round, February 13th, 1932 and v. West Ham, February 11th, 1939, folded and scuffed.
£140–160 *Bon*

A Tottenham Hotspur programme for 1st April 1967, and another for Manchester City, 24th September 1955.
£1.50p–2 each *COL*

Two programmes for West Ham United v. Arsenal, 1st March, 1930, and West Ham v. Leeds United, 22nd March, 1930, folded and scuffed.
£85–110 *Bon*

A Football Association complimentary programme for the F. A. Cup Final, Portsmouth v. Manchester City, 28th April, 1934, folded.
£250–300 *Bon*

Five programmes for Tottenham Hotspur home matches, 1930–31, torn and worn.
£120–140 *Bon*

Memorabilia

A pair of football boots, c1910.
£40–60 *MSh*

A book match cover, with
a picture of a footballer, c1930,
2½ by 2in (6.5 by 5cm).
£15–20 *PC*

A Wade decanter,
commemorating Wimbledon
F. C. Centenary, 1989.
£12–14 *COL*

Golf
Balls

A Fife golf ball, made by
Jefferie Malings, c1900.
£30–40 *MSh*

A gutta-percha golf ball,
by P. McEwan, c1880.
£200–300 *MSh*

A gutta-percha golf ball, c1880.
£80–100 *MSh*

A Mungo re-made gutta-percha
golf ball, c1890.
£80–120 *MSh*

A gutta-percha golf ball,
The Eureka, c1898.
£80–100 *MSh*

A gutta-percha mesh
pattern golf ball, c1890.
£50–100 *MSh*

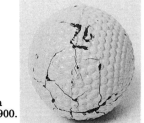

A bramble golf ball, with
damaged gutty shell, c1900.
£30–40 *MSh*

MAKE THE MOST OF MILLERS

Condition is absolutely vital when
assessing the value of any item.
Damaged pieces appreciate much
less than perfect examples. However,
a rare, desirable piece may command
a high price even when damaged.

Caddies

Clubs

An automaton golf caddy, by Bussey, c1890.
£500–600 *MSh*

A long nosed spoon golf club, by McEwan, c1860.
£2,000–3,000 *MSh*

A long nosed baffing spoon golf club, by R. Forgan of St. Andrews, c1870.
£1,600–2,600 *MSh*

A long nosed play golf club, by Alex Patrick, c1870.
£800–1,200 *MSh*

A long nosed play golf club, by T. Dunn, c1875.
£900–1,300 *MSh*

A rut iron, c1880.
£300–500 *MSh*

An Army & Navy long nosed beechwood driver, c1875.
£700–1,000 *MSh*

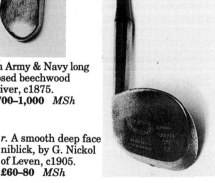

r. A smooth deep face niblick, by G. Nickol of Leven, c1905.
£60–80 *MSh*

A smooth face lofting iron, c1890.
£40–60 *MSh*

A beechwood scared head
long nosed putter, c1895.
£80–140 *MSh*

A transitional spoon
golf club, by
H. Hewitt, c1890.
£300–400 *MSh*

A Slazenger long
nosed putter, c1880.
£300–500 *MSh*

A Bussey patent
rut iron, c1880.
£150–250 *MSh*

r. A centre balance brass
headed putter, c1900,
36in (91.5cm) long.
£20–30 *MSh*

An Urquart adjustable
club, c1895.
£600–900 *MSh*

r. A Mills cleek,
MSD model,
by the Standard
Golf Co., c1910.
£80–120 *MSh*

A socket head brassie, by Simpson of St. Andrews, mint condition, c1905.
£45–65 *MSh*

A scared head driver, with leather face insert, by Hutchison of North Berwick, c1895.
£60–100 *MSh*

A Schenectady putter, dated 'March 24th, 1903'.
£80–150 *MSh*

A persimmon head putter, with brass sole plate, c1910.
£60–100 *MSh*

A vardon type putter, c1910.
£60–80 *MSh*

The Tyler ball to ball patent club, 1920s.
£120–150 *MSh*

Ceramics

A Doulton Lambeth mug, depicting golfers in relief, with silver rim, c1905, 6in (15cm) high.
£400–600 *MSh*

A Royal Doulton Kingsware golfing jug, c1935, 9½in (24cm) high.
£300–400 *MSh*

l. A Royal Doulton Kingsware golfing tankard, damaged, c1930, 5½in (14cm) high.
£200–250 *WIL*

r. A Poole Pottery Broadstone Golf Club trophy, by Donna Ridout, 1989, 8in (20cm) diam.
£45–65 *TAR*

Ephemera

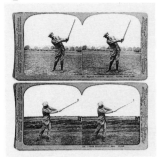

Two Edwardian stereoscopic photographs of the golfers Harry Vardon and James Braid, c1900–10, 3½ by 7in (9 by 17.5cm). **£30–40 each** *VS*

An Edwardian signed sepia print of Harry Vardon, 30 by 22in (76 by 56cm). **£800–1,000** *VS*

A playing card with a Louis Wain illustration advertisement, 1905–25, 2½ by 3½in (6 by 9cm). **£40–60** *VS*

Miscellaneous

A paper knife, with American silver handle, depicting a golfer in relief, made by Unger Bros, c1890, 10in (25cm) long. **£150–200** *MSh*

l. A silver spoon, with a double-sided figure of a golfer, 1930s, 5in (12.5cm) long. **£60–80** *MSh*

A collection of seven golfing spoons, six silver and one silver plated, various dates and makers. **£100–140** *Bon*

Sculptures & Trophies

An Italian pipe, with silver overlay of a golfer, c1930, 6in (15cm) long. **£120–140** *MSh*

A silver plated golfing inkwell, c1900, 6½in (16cm) wide. **£300–400** *MSh*

A ladies' golfing trophy, plaque with Birmingham hallmark, dated '1943', 6½in (16cm) high. **£90–100** *HEW*

A spelter golfing figure, by Zwick, c1920, 10in (25cm) high. **£400–600** *MSh*

A spelter figure of a boy golfer, on a marble base, c1920s, 10in (25cm) high. **£200–250** *MSh*

Horses & Hunting

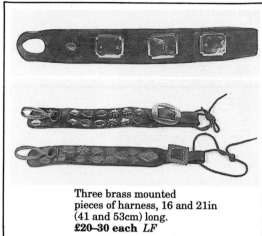

Two leather harness straps,
each holding five horse brasses,
40 and 33½in (101.5 and 85cm).
£240–300 *LF*

Three brass mounted
pieces of harness, 16 and 21in
(41 and 53cm) long.
£20–30 each *LF*

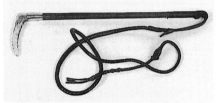

A hunting whip, c1900,
handle 18in (46cm) long.
£15–35 *WAB*

A leather harness strap, with four
horse brasses, 25in (64cm).
£50–75 *LF*

A leather harness strap, with
four brasses, 32in (81cm) long.
£75–95 *LF*

Two jockey's caps, with silks.
£80–95 each *MofC*

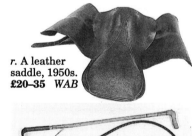

r. A leather
saddle, 1950s.
£20–35 *WAB*

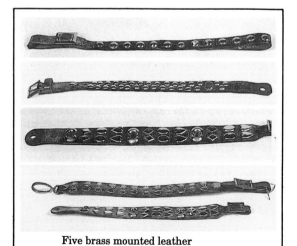

Five brass mounted leather
harness straps, 18 to 28in
(46 to 71cm) long.
£120–170 *LF*

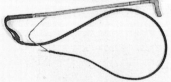

A hunting whip, with bone
handle, c1900, handle 17in
(43cm) long.
£20–35 *WAB*

A spelter horse and jockey match striker, 1900, 7in (17.5cm) long.
£200–250 *TAR*

A riding crop, c1900, 17½in (44cm) long.
£20–35 *WAB*

l. Three equestrian rosettes: Hackney Horse Society Challenge Cup, 1939, Richmond Royal Horse Show, 1932, and Royal International Horse Show Wembley, 1968.
£8–15 each *WAB*

Shooting Sticks

r. A bamboo and cane shooting stick, with brass fittings, c1910.
£110–150 *MSh*

r. A simulated bamboo shooting stick, c1910.
£60–100 *MSh*

l. An Edwardian folding stool, 28in (71cm) high.
£50–60 *JUN*

A bamboo seated shooting stick, c1890, 28in (71cm) long.
£65–95 *WAB*

Lacrosse

A lacrosse stick, 1930s, 44in (111.5cm) long.
£12–20 *WAB*

Motor Racing

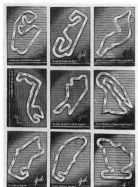

A set of Formula 1 Racing Cards, 1992, Premier Edition, including racing drivers, cars and tracks.
£20–25 *MUR*

Cross Reference
Automobilia

Rowing

A Christ Church college rowing rudder, given to the Cox as a trophy, dated '1925'.
£90–120 *MSh*

Two pewter trophies:
l. Tug of war, St John's College, 1882, 8in (20cm) high.
r. Rowing, Corpus Christi College, 1873, 6in (15cm) high.
£30–65 each *WAB*

An Acme Stentor aluminium megaphone, 18in (46cm) long.
£15–18 *JUN*

An oar trophy, 1920s, painted at a later date.
£125–150 *AHL*

A Canadian canoe paddle, c1920, 60in (152cm) long.
£20–30 *WAB*

A Victorian boathook/paddle, 60in (152cm) long.
£30–45 *WAB*

Rugby

r. A Wilson Long Gainer rugby ball, early 20thC.
£25–35 *AHL*

r. A pair of Rugby boots, The Scrum, c1930.
£30–50 *MSh*

Tennis

Rackets

l. A child's racket, made by Gremer, c1885, 24in (61cm) long.
£30–50 *MSh*

A lawn tennis racket, with horizontal double cross stringing, c1875.
£500–800 *MSh*

r. A flat top lawn tennis racket, c1885.
£120–160 *MSh*

A lob-sided lawn tennis racket, with thick stringing, by Henry Malins of Woolwich, c1880.
£500–800 *MSh*

A lawn tennis racket, the 'Zingari', by Ellison of Norwich, with cross stringing, c1880.
£500–800 *MSh*

A 'Midget Model' lawn tennis racket, made by Rollin Wilson, Memphis, USA, c1920, 20in (51cm) long.
£40–60 *MSh*

A fishtail lawn tennis racket, c1905.
£60–100 *MSh*

A lob-sided lawn tennis racket, with silver mounts, by Henry Malins, c1880.
£800–1,200 *MSh*

A Lunn's patent racket with ventilated Holdfast grip, c1900.
£150–300 *MSh*

l. A child's lawn tennis racket, c1900, 20in (51cm) long.
£40–60 *MSh*

l. A long shaped lawn tennis racket, 'The Gamage', by Gamage of London, c1905.
£70–100 *MSh*

A round headed lawn tennis racket, c1900.
£60–100 *MSh*

An aluminium lawn tennis racket, with piano wire strings, by Birmal, c1920.
£60–100 *MSh*

A lawn tennis racket, 'The Dimid', with diagonal stringing, c1920.
£80–100 *MSh*

A square head lawn tennis racket, with cork grip and replaced stringing, c1885.
£150–200 *MSh*

A pair of lady's tennis rackets, 'The Louise', c1900.
£120–160 *MSh*

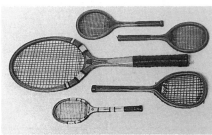

Presses

A collection of miniature tennis rackets, c1895–1940, 12, 7 and 6in (30.5, 17.5 and 15cm) long.
£40–80 each *MSh*

Miscellaneous

A mahogany tennis racket press, with brass fittings, c1900.
£80–120 *MSh*

A mahogany tennis racket press, with brass fittings, leather handle and squared top enabling it to stand, containing a fishtail racket and a pair of ladies' or junior rackets, by Spalding, c1890.
£100–150 *MSh*

A brass clock/barometer, in the form of two crossed lob-sided tennis rackets, c1880.
£600–800 *MSh*

Winter Sports

A bronze figure of a tennis player, by Anton Weinberger, dated '1912', 18in (45cm) high.
£800–1,200 *MSh*

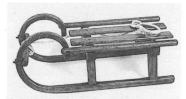

An eastern European child's sledge, 1950s, 24in (61cm) long.
£30–45 *WAB*

A signed photograph of ice skater John Curry, c1970, 10 by 8in (25 by 20cm).
£30–40 *VS*

A pair of ice skates, c1920.
£20–25 *AHL*

A pair of wooden skis, 1920s, 81in (205.5cm) long, and a pair of wooden ski poles.
£100–115 *MofC*

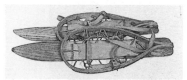

A pair of snow shoe skis, 1940s, 29in (74cm) long.
£30–40 *WAB*

A pair of Lillywhites skis and poles, c1910, skis 80in (203cm) long.
£45–85 *WAB*

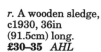

r. A wooden sledge, c1930, 36in (91.5cm) long.
£30–35 *AHL*

r. An American wooden and metal sledge, early 20thC, 51½in (130cm) long.
£70–80 *AL*

MAKE THE MOST OF MILLERS

Condition is absolutely vital when assessing the value of any item. Damaged pieces appreciate much less than perfect examples. However, a rare, desirable piece may command a high price even when damaged.

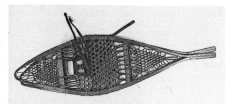

A pair of snow shoes, 1930s, 49in (124.5cm) long.
£55–85 *WAB*

r. An ice pick, with leather cover, 1930s, 33in (84cm) long.
£25–35 *WAB*

TEDDY BEARS & SOFT TOYS
Teddy Bears

The world's favourite cuddly toy owes its name to Theodore 'Teddy' Roosevelt. In 1902, the American President was invited on a bear hunt in Mississippi. To his host's embarassment, no wild bears were to be found and they were reduced to tethering a tiny bear cub to a tree – Roosevelt flatly refused to shoot the creature. The incident was celebrated by a Washington Post cartoonist, and the following year the cartoon bear was turned into a soft toy and the teddy bear was born.

Today, the teddy bear is both an essential element of childhood and a popular adult collectable. Enthusiasts are called 'arctophiles'. Early bears, dating from the 1900s, tend to fetch the highest prices, although examples from the 1950s and 60s are becoming increasingly sought after. The make affects the value, so always check for a label or a button in the ear. Condition is also important, as is the individual look and 'personality' of each bear. An appealing face can increase the value of the bear.

A Steiff beige teddy bear, with black stitched snout, black button eyes, swivel jointed body with excelsior stuffing, button missing, 19in (48cm) high.
£1,750–2,000 *S(S)*

A teddy bear with cut muzzle, glass eyes and felt pads, c1920.
£50–60 *CK*

A Steiff teddy bear, with centre seam, golden mohair, black boot button eyes, clipped snout, black stitched nose, mouth and claws, swivel head, elongated jointed shaped limbs, hump, button in ear, growler inoperative, c1908, 19in (48cm) high.
£4,000–4,500 *CSK*

A Chad Valley teddy bear, with golden mohair, amber and black glass eyes, small hump, tummy squeaker and button attached to chin, c1920s, 29in (73.5cm) high.
£625–700 *CSK*

Two teddy bears, with original clothes, makers unknown, c1914–18, 11in (28cm) high.
£70–80 each *SP*

According to the original owner, 'Edwin' and 'Harry' have always been together.

A blonde mohair teddy bear, with button eyes, felt pads, c1910–20, 11in (28cm) high.
£200–230 *CK*

A Steiff teddy bear, with centre seam, black boot button eyes, clipped snout, brown stitched nose, mouth and claws, swivel head, jointed limbs, large spoon shaped feet, hump, and button in ear, mohair was white, now cinnamon, some wear, c1908, 24in (61cm) high.
£2,250–2,750 *CSK*

A German straw filled black teddy bear, c1921.
£525–575 *CMF*

r. Twin bears by Schuco, with bells inside, 1920–30s, 13in (33cm) high.
£300–350 *CK*

A Steiff teddy bear, with pale golden mohair, brown and black glass eyes, clipped snout, remains of black stitched nose and mouth, black stitched claws, swivel head, elongated jointed limbs, hump, growler, button in ear, c1920s, 24in (61cm) high.
£1,800–2,400 *CSK*

An English teddy bear, probably Farnell, c1910, 16in (40.5cm) high.
£350–400 *CK*

An early English teddy bear, pads replaced, 20in (51cm) high.
£250–300 *WAG*

A J.K. Farnell mohair plush teddy bear, c1920, 16in (40.5cm) high.
£1,200–1,500 *BeG*

A white mohair teddy bear, possibly Farnell, very worn, one ear missing, c1920s, 12in (30.5cm) high.
£100–140 *CK*

A jointed squeeze-type musical box teddy bear, with shaggy blonde mohair, mechanism defective, c1925, 10in (25.5cm).
£120–160 *BeG*

A teddy bear, with glass eyes and black bow tie, original growler inoperative, 29in (74cm) high.
£125–150 *LF*

A multi-coloured cotton teddy bear, with red legs and jingle, c1930s.
£85–95 *CMF*

A Chiltern teddy bear, with glass eyes and a growler, excellent condition, c1930, 20in (50.5cm) high.
£200–250 *SP*

A Schuco honey coloured mohair plush wood wool stuffed teddy bear, c1935, 14in (35.5cm).
£200–250 *BeG*

An unjointed teddy bear, possibly Chiltern, c1950.
£75–85 *CMF*

A plush bear, with black and white plastic eyes, straw stuffing, possibly American, c1940s, 30in (76cm) high.
£60–80 *CK*

A German yellow mohair bear, possibly by Herman, with growler and felt pads, 12in (30.5cm) high.
£80–120 *CK*

MAKE THE MOST OF MILLERS

Price ranges in this book reflect what you should expect to *pay* for a similar example. When selling, however, you would expect to receive a lower figure. This will fluctuate according to a dealer's stock and saleability at a particular time. It is always advisable, when selling a collectable, to approach a reputable dealer or an auction house which has specialist sales.

A Herman teddy bear, pads replaced, German, early 1930s.
£350–375 *CMF*

A musical teddy bear, possibly c1940, 17in (43cm) high.
£250–300 *WAG*

A blue cotton twill teddy bear, early 1950s.
£110–125 *CMF*

A Schuco teddy bear, c1950s, 3in (7.5cm) high.
£50–60 *SP*

A teddy bear, by Le Fray, late 1950s, 36in (92cm).
£150–200 *TEM*

A Chiltern Hugmee bear, c1940s.
£200–225 *CMF*

A Schuco mohair teddy bear, with glass eyes, c1960s, 19½in (49cm) high.
£200–300 *SP*

A koala bear, c1950.
£24–28 *CMF*

A Paddington bear, c1960.
£40–48 *CMF*

A brown mohair polyester and pellet filled teddy bear, Sebastian, with shaved muzzle, long limbs and dangling legs, from a limited edition of six bears by Liz Blackwell, 1994, 16in (40.5cm) high.
£60–100 *BeG*

A butterscotch mohair pellet filled teddy bear, Mr. Murgatroyd, with ultra suede pads, 1994, 14in (35.5cm) high.
£100–150 *BeG*

Mr. Murgatroyd was made as a show special by Teresa Brookes and Barbara Percival of Appletree Bears.

A Steiff teddy bear, 'Louise', from a limited edition of 3,000, 14in (35.5cm) high.
£150–175 *TMN*

Made in 1992, these were replicas of the model made in 1911.

A Steiff brown mohair woven fur teddy bear, with growler, with button in ear, 1994, 13½in (34.5cm) high.
£45–85 *BeG*

Two teddy bears, c1990, 8 and
5in (20 and 12.5cm) high.
£8–12 *LF*

A gold crushed mohair pellet
filled teddy bear, Pendleton,
with wool felt pads, from a
limited edition of 25 bears by
Barbara-Ann Cunningham,
1994, 14in (35.5cm) high.
£60–100 *BeG*

A Wedgwood hand decorated
plate, by Jean Allen, inscribed
'Dig for Victory, Eat Well and
Live Longer', c1942, 8½in (21cm).
£80–100 *SP*

A Mother Hubbard gold mohair
pellet filled teddy bear, with
safety eyes and wool felt pads,
by Julie Hubbard, 1994, 12in
(30.5cm) high.
£40–80 *BeG*

A silver teddy bear
rattle, with bone
teething ring,
Birmingham 1910,
5½in (13.5cm) long.
£100–150 *SP*

A Steiff teddy bear, from
a limited edition of 3,000,
c1990s, 21in (53cm) high.
£245–275 *TMN*
These were replicas of the
model made in 1907.

Soft Toys

A Chad Valley toy dwarf, Bashful, from a set including Snow White and the Seven Dwarfs, c1920-30, 6in (15cm).
£20–30 *WAG*

A musical koala bear, plays 'Waltzing Matilda', 1950–60, 7in (17.5cm) high.
£10–15 *CK*

A Steiff long mohair duck, 1920s, 5in (12.5cm) long.
£40–50 *CK*

A straw-filled mooing cow, 1930s.
£34–38 *CMF*

A Merrythought lion cub, with plastic eyes, marked, 1970s, 9in (22.5cm) long.
£10–15 *CK*

A Steiff sleeping cocker spaniel puppy, with stitched eyes, c1950–60, 8in (20cm) long.
£25–35 *CK*

An organ grinder's monkey, with bald cloth body showing traces of wool burlap, felt face and ears, button eyes, c1900, 7in (17.5cm) high.
£20–25 *CK*

l. A straw filled pull-along duck, 1930s, 5½in (13.5cm) wide.
£25–30 *WAG*

A Wendy Boston Scottie dog, with tartan overcoat and sewn in plastic eyes, 1940s, 10in (25cm) high.
£10–12 *CK*

An English straw filled dog, 1940s.
£10–12 *CMF*

A Merrythought bulldog, with original label, c1960.
£50–55 *CMF*

A Felix the Cat soft toy, c1940.
£85–95 *CMF*

A lion soft toy, used as a shop
display, 1960s.
£100–120 *CK*

A Steiff tiger, with bright eyes,
c1950, 11in (28cm) wide.
£45–50 *TEM*

A mohair rabbit, possibly by
Schuco, with red plastic nose,
plastic eyes and felt ears, 1940s.
£30–50 *CK*

A Steiff sleeping cat, with
stitched eyes, 1950s, 12in
(30.5cm) long.
£35–45 *CK*

A Steiff zebra, 1950s,
5in (12.5cm) high.
£25–30 *CK*

A toy monkey, by Farnell, with
glass eyes, c1920, 15in (38cm).
£200–250 *SP*

Glove Puppets

A Sooty glove puppet, c1950s,
8½in (21cm) high.
£10–15 *CK*

A cat glove puppet, 1950s,
8in (20cm) high.
£15–18 *CK*

A teddy glove puppet, c1950.
£15–20 *CK*

A monkey glove puppet,
possibly Steiff, with glass eyes,
felt face and hands, 1950s, 9in
(22.5cm) high.
£20–25 *CK*

Nightdress Cases

A mohair nightdress case,
c1960s, 16in (40.5cm) wide.
£5–10 *SP*

A crouching Chinkie nightdress
case, with original label, c1940.
£18–22 *CMF*

Bonzo

Between the wars, Bonzo was the most popular cartoon character in Britain. Created by illustrator George Studdy (1876–1948), Bonzo first appeared in *The Sketch* newspaper in 1922 and rapidly became a star of stage, screen and advertisements, as well as books and newspapers across the world. The comic dog was also ruthlessly merchandised; innumerable postcards were produced, as well as velveteen toys, puzzles, games, ceramics and glass, Bonzos in every medium, from soaps to car mascots. All of these are much sought after by collectors.

A brass Bonzo car mascot, c1930, 5in (12.5cm) long.
£200–250 *SP*

r. A brass Bonzo bottle opener, c1925–30, 6½in (16cm) high.
£20–25 *SP*

A Chad Valley Bonzo dog, very faded, c1920–30, 9¼in (23.5cm) high.
£150–200 *SP*

Bonzo's girl friend, Ooloo, by Chad Valley, c1930, 7in (17.5cm) high.
£250–300 *SP*

A Bonzo advertising model, with articulated tail, and copyright label, c1925–30, 13in (33cm) high.
£1,500–2,000 *SP*

FURTHER READING
Bonzo - The Life and Work of George Studdy,
Paul Babb and Gay Owen, Pub. Richard Dennis 1988.

A brass Bonzo toasting fork, 1930, 19in (48cm) long.
£20–30 *SP*

r. A Bonzo game, c1930s, 4in (10cm) diam.
£60–75 *SP*

A lustre Bonzo dog, c1920–30, 6½in (16cm) high.
£15–20 *TAR*

A bisque Bonzo sweet jar, 'The Drunk', c1925–30, 5¼in (13.5cm) high.
£80–100 *SP*

Three Bonzo dog postcards, c1930s.
£4–6 each *WP*

Gollies

A felt golly, c1940s, 15½in (39cm) high.
£50–60 *SP*

A golly, c1950, not labelled, 19in (48cm) high.
£25–30 *TEM*

A golly, c1950–60, 12in (30.5cm) high.
£8–10 *SP*

A knitted golly.
£18–22 *CMF*

l. A golly, 1960s, 15in (38cm) high.
£10–15 *TEM*

l. A handmade fabric golly, 1960s.
£18–22 *CMF*

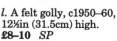

A collection of Robertson's golly badges, 1940s.
£9–14 *CMF*

l. A Roan Toy Products golly, 1970s, 35in (89cm) long.
£38–42 *CMF*

An Empire made golly, 1960s.
£20–25 *CMF*

l. A felt golly, c1950–60, 12½in (31.5cm) high.
£8–10 *SP*

TELEPHONES

An Ericsson telephone, No. 16, with line box, c1898, 11¼in (29cm) high.
£700–800 *PIA*

A candlestick telephone, without dial, by Western Electric, with bell box, c1910, 11½in (29.5cm) high.
£150–200 *PIA*

An internal system telephone, probably by Eriksson, c1900.
£100–300 *JUN*

Miller's is a price GUIDE not a price LIST

r. A 200 Series telephone, c1930.
£200–250 *BHE*

A Siemens gold telephone, 1930.
£950–1,250 *BHE*

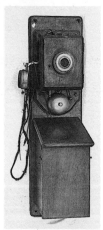

A wall mounted telephone in a wooden case, 24in (61cm) high.
£125–150 *JUN*

A police station switchboard candlestick telephone, c1940, 13in (33cm) high.
£130–150 *BHE*

r. A green 200 Series telephone, No. 232, cord replaced, c1938, 9in (22.5cm) wide.
£400–500 *PIA*

A mahogany/claret hued General Electric Company 'GECoPHONE', 1933 prototype.
£9,000–10,000 *OTW*

This extremely rare telephone is one of only three mahogany GEC telephones known to exist.

In 1933, London-Midland-Scottish Railway commissioned GEC to make telephones with a metallic silver and gold finish to complement the lavish decor of a world famous golfing hotel in the Scottish Highlands. When the hotel upgraded their telephone system in the mid-1970s, the phones were dumped in a storeroom where they were discovered ten years later, dusty but undamaged, by dealer and expert Rod Jones. When the silvery veneer was removed, he discovered that three of the phones were in a stunning mahogany wood grain Bakelite. Before black Bakelite telephones became standard issue, the Post Office is known to have issued a small number of brown Art Deco telephones, which can be worth up to £3,000. Until this discovery there was no evidence that any of these experimental brown models had been made by private companies such as GEC.

A 300 Series black Bakelite telephone, c1940–50.
£125–175 *BHE*

A 300 Series black telephone, c1940s, 9in (22.5cm) wide.
£45–65 *PIA*

A black telephone, No. 706, c1958, 9in (22.5cm) wide.
£25–30 *PIA*

A Trim Phone, c1970, excellent condition.
£30–35 *PIA*

A candlestick telephone, No. 150, c1935, 13½in (34cm) high.
£200–250 *PIA*

A No. 232 black factory boxed telephone, c1949.
£3,500–5,000 *BHE*

Miscellaneous

A telephone intercom system,
boxed, c1965.
£550–675 *BHE*

A Dictograph telephone
system, c1905.
£1,650–1,850 *BHE*

A Button A and B coin
box, with GPO locking
unit, c1935, 18in
(45.5cm) high.
£350–500 *BHE*

A telephone sign, c1935,
22in (55.5cm) long.
£450–600 *BHE*

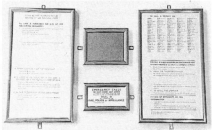

r. A selection
of public kiosk
user's notices
and a mirror,
c1936.
£125–150 *BHE*

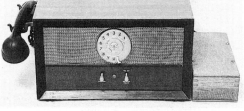

A loudspeaking telephone No. 2,
c1956, 14in (35.5cm) long.
£1,500–1,800 *BHE*

An unrestored K2
telephone kiosk, 1924.
£6,000–8,000 *BHE*

*Only 1,700 K2s were
manufactured. When
restored, it could be
worth £10,000–12,000.*

A K6 telephone kiosk,
restored with 1930s
Jubilee interior, c1936.
£5,000–6,500 *BHE*

*Unrestored, this kiosk
would only be worth
£450–600.*

Ephemera

The posters and postcards in this section are all modern reproductions of the original designs, showing the evolution of the telephone.

A selection of BT posters, reproduced from originals, 16 by 11in (40.5 by 28cm). **75p–£1.35 each** *BT*

Reproduction posters and postcards are available by mail order or from the shop only at:

'The Story of Telecommunications', BT Museum, 145 Queen Victoria Street, London EC4V 4AT.

A selection of BT Christmas and Valentine cards reproduced from originals by BT. **20p–80p each** *BT*

TELEVISIONS

The market for old televisions has sprung up with bewildering rapidity. 'A couple of years ago you could buy pre-war televisions for around £200', comments Steve Harris, dealer in broadcasting collectables, mournfully. 'Today they have shot up to £1,000 or more. I wish I'd invested...'.

'T.V. is King', a recent exhibition at Sotheby's, plenty of media coverage, and some successful auction results, have all served to increase interest and values. Nevertheless, according to Harris, few televisions are genuinely collectable, beyond pre-war models and 50s Bakelite examples. Certain design classics such as the 1970s globe-shaped televisions, based on the Apollo astronaut's helmets, and more recent oddities such as the Sinclair Microvision are always of interest. According to Harris, there are still plenty of 50s televisions available for £50 or less, but for the best advice in what is still a relatively new collecting area, consult a specialist dealer.

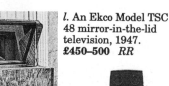

l. An Ekco Model TSC 48 mirror-in-the-lid television, 1947.
£450–500 *RR*

A Murphy television, 1940s–50s, 19in (48cm) high.
£30–40 *JUN*

A KB television, with 10in (25cm) screen, 1940s–50s, 35in (89cm) high.
£50–60 *JUN*

A Baird televisor, with alloy chassis, speaker and 24in disc, in a mahogany case, with bevelled top and sunray speaker fret, on a matching stand with hinged cover, 1940s, 56½in (143cm) high.
£9,000–10,000 *CSK*

r. A Bush TV 22, c1950, 15in (38cm) high.
£100–200 *OTA*

An Ekco TMB 272 television, c1956, 15½in (39cm) high.
£40–80 *OTA*

A Pye cabinet television, c1950s, 36in (91.5cm) high.
£40–50 *JUN*

r. A television screen magnifier, with plastic lens, fluid filled, refilled with liquid paraffin, c1950, 18in (45.5cm) wide.
£5–15 *RMV*

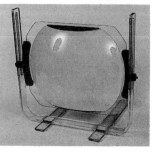

TEXTILES
Curtain Ties

A pair of Victorian curtain ties.
£100–120 *JPr*

A pair of late Victorian
French silk curtain ties.
£120–150 *JPr*

A pair of woollen curtain
ties, c1870.
£100–120 *JPr*

A pair of late Victorian
cotton curtain ties.
£80–100 *JPr*

A pair of late Victorian
cream silk tassels.
£90–120 *JPr*

A pair of French silk
curtain ties, c1900.
£80–120 *JPr*

A cream silk bell pull, c1920.
£60–90 *JPr*

A Victorian silk hand rail,
with brass fittings.
£30–50 *JPr*

A pair of French woven silk
curtain ties, c1910.
£60–80 *JPr*

A pair of French silk curtain
ties, c1920.
£55–65 *JPr*

A pair of cotton curtain ties,
early 20thC.
£60–80 *JPr*

A single silk tassel.
£45–55 *JPr*

Crochet, Cutwork & Lace

A hand crocheted and linen table-
cloth, c1880, 58in (147cm) wide.
£45–60 *LL*

A pair of frilled pillow cases,
c1890, 46in (116.5cm) wide.
£25–45 *LL*

An Edwardian nightdress case,
18in (46cm) wide.
£10–20 *LL*

An embroidered lace doyley,
c1890, 5in (12.5cm) square.
£1.50–2 *LL*

A hand crocheted and drawn
thread work mat, c1890,
28in (71cm) wide.
£15–20 LL

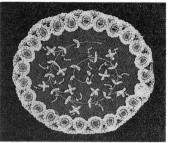

A Brussels appliqué and lace
mat, c1900, 10in (25cm) wide.
£4–5 *LL*

Cross Reference
Costume

---

r. A beaded milk jug cover,
1920s, 10in (25cm) diam.
£12–15 *LB*

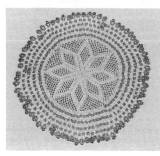

European Printed & Woven Textiles

An Italian mezzaro, printed with a man leading a camel with jungle beasts and birds, within a border of fruit and flower-filled baskets, 19thC, 102in (259cm) high.
£325–375 *CSK*

A length of Fortuny furnishing fabric, the white ground printed with a lime green damask style design, made in Italy, c1950, 58in (147cm).
£600–800 *CSK*

r. A roller printed cotton panel, with a view of the Crystal Palace, floral border, c1851, 26½in (67cm), framed and glazed.
£600–800 *CSK*

A hanging, of olive green velveteen, woven in shades of golden brown and green, with a repeating design of fruit trees within a border of trailing ivy, early 20thC, 98in (249cm) high.
£850–1,000 *CSK*

Oriental Textiles

A pair of Chinese sleeve panels in Peking stitch and gold couching, with dragonflies, butterflies and flowers, framed, c1885, 19½ by 4in (49 by 10cm).
£150–200 *PBr*

r. A pair of Chinese sleeve panels in satin stitch, framed and glazed, late 19thC, 24 by 4½in (61 by 11cm).
£150–175 *PBr*

A pair of Chinese military rank badges, worked in coloured silks in tent stitch, 19thC, 11in (28cm) square, framed and glazed.
£350–450 *CSK*

A Chinese semi-formal coat, of dark blue silk satin, embroidered in coloured silks, with flower-filled roundels and floral sprigs above a sea wave border, lined in pale blue silk damask, 19thC.
£500–600 *CSK*

A Chinese lady's sleeveless robe, of dark blue satin, embroidered in coloured silks, trimmed with ivory satin worked in coloured metal threads with emblems, lined in blue silk damask, late 19thC.
£325–425 *CSK*

A Chinese lady's coat, of dark blue silk satin, embroidered in white and shades of blue silks, the trimmings embellished with gilt thread, lined in blue silk damask, 19thC.
£650–750 *CSK*

A pair of Chinese civil rank badges, embroidered in coloured silks and metal threads, 19thC, 12in (30.5cm) wide.
£375–475 *CSK*

l. A pair of Chinese sleeve panels in Peking stitch and gold couching, with finger citron flowers and pomegranates, c1885, 25 by 5in (66 by 12.5cm).
£175–220 *PBr*

A Baluch tribal bag, West Afghanistan, made into a cushion, c1900, 28 by 25in (71 by 64cm).
£200–300 *SAM*

A pair of Chinese sleeve panels in Peking stitch, with figures and flowering foliage, framed and glazed, c1885, 23 by 6½in (59 by 16cm).
£150–210 *PBr*

A yew wood, ebony and mahogany inlaid stool, covered in a Persian kelim fragment, 18 by 15in (46 by 38cm).
£350–450 *SAM*

A pair of Chinese sleeve panels, in Peking knot and gold couching, framed and glazed, c1880–1900, 21in (53cm) long.
£155–185 *PBr*

Quilts

A broderie perse coverlet, of cream cotton applied with floral chintz cut-outs within concentric frames of taupe cotton, worn, c1800, 124 by 116in (315 by 294.5cm).
£700–800 *CSK*

A patchwork coverlet, of small print cottons in shades of brown and dark red, with central star and printed double scalloped border, c1800, 108 by 102in (274 by 259cm).
£900–1,100 *CSK*

A 'crazy patchwork' coverlet, of velvets and silks, with a crimson silk centre square, embroidered with sunflowers, and other motifs, crochet border, late 19thC, 94 by 80in (238 by 203cm).
£500–700 *CSK*

A patchwork quilt, of printed cottons in various shapes, with a central diamond and chevron border, 1840s, 80in (203cm) square.
£450–550 *CSK*

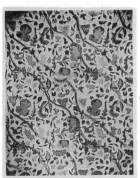

l. A crewel work coverlet, embroidered with exotic flowering and fruiting branches, early 20thC, 104 by 70in (264 by 177.5cm).
£350–450 *CSK*

A Marcella bedspread, c1900, 94 by 82in (238 by 208cm).
£60–80 *LL*

A Durham quilt, 1920s.
£200–300 *LL*

Samplers & Needlework Pictures

A sampler by Martha Freelove, worked with the Lord's Prayer, another prayer, alphabets and numerals in silks, within a stylised bud and flower border of dark blue, red, green and ivory, enclosed by a sawtooth decoration of pale blue, c1746, 16 by 10in (41 by 25cm), framed and glazed.
£675–775 *CSK*

A sampler by Isobella Marshal, worked in coloured silks with The Creed and flowers against a brown cross stitch ground, top and bottom border of stylised carnations, 18thC, 12½ by 12in (32 by 30.5cm), framed and glazed.
£450–550 *CSK*

A sampler by Maria Pearse, worked in coloured silks with a verse 'Religion Solace Sooths...', alphabets and numerals, an elegant brick house with formal garden, within a stylised floral border, 1804, 16 by 13in (41 by 33cm), framed and glazed.
£250–350 *CSK*

A sampler by Anne Cooper, worked in coloured silks with spot motifs divided by floral bands, within a honeysuckle border, 1804, 17 by 12in (43 by 30.5cm), framed and glazed.
£800–1,000 *CSK*

A sampler by Sarah Sinton, worked in coloured silks, with a verse, a house, flowering trees, plants and families of deer within railings and a gateway, surrounded by a stylised honeysuckle border and zigzag motif, 1811, 15½ by 20½in (39 by 52cm), framed and glazed.
£800–1,000 *CSK*

A sampler by Charlotte Elizabeth Gates, worked in coloured silks, with central verse, surrounded by flowers and birds, a house below with railings and a gate, 1835, 17 by 14in (43 by 36cm), framed and glazed.
£875–1,000 *CSK*

l. A sampler by Caroline Spring, worked in coloured silks on a linen ground, with a verse and the Crucifixion, surrounded by spot motifs, within a stylised floral border, 1824, 13 by 11½in (33 by 29cm), framed.
£675–800 *CSK*

A sampler by Catherine Paterson, worked in coloured silks, with alphabet, initials and crowded intricate spot motifs, 1828, 12½ by 17in (32 by 43cm), framed and glazed.
£370–450 *CSK*

A sampler by Mary Elizabeth Plant, worked in coloured silks, with short verse 'On Bliss', flanked by fritillary and lily stems, a gazebo with butterflies, stags and squirrels, dogs and an urn with carnations, within a honeysuckle border, 1822, 16 by 13in (41 by 33cm), framed and glazed.
£850–1,000 *CSK*

A sampler by Jane Alloway, worked in coloured silks, with a verse 'Honour thy Father...', surrounded by spot motifs, within a floral border, 1827, 11½ by 9½in (29 by 24cm), framed and glazed.
£325–400 *CSK*

A sampler by Mary Hall, worked in coloured wools, with two verses, an image of Solomon's Temple, surrounded by spot motifs, within a floral border, early 19thC, 20 by 14½in (51 by 37cm), framed and glazed.
£250–300 *CSK*

A sampler by Margaret Atkinson, worked in coloured silks depicting 'The Golden Pheasant' in a leafy tree, within a varied flower border, 1824, 17 by 13in (43 by 33cm), framed and glazed.
£400–500 *CSK*

A sampler by Mary Cash, worked in shades of green, cream and brown silks on a linen ground, with two verses above two houses, Adam and Eve in the centre, the Lamb of God below, within a border of stylised carnations, 1833, 25in (64cm) square, framed and glazed.
£850–1,000 *CSK*

A sampler by Ann Pringle, worked at Beattie's School Longtown, in coloured silks, with two verses, a house flanked by trees, flower vases, birds and dogs, within a border of stylised carnations, rosebuds and tulips, 1842, 18½ by 21½in (47 by 54cm), framed and glazed.
£300–400 *CSK*

l. A sampler by Elizabeth Spalding, worked in coloured wools, with alphabets, numerals, a verse, red brick house and garden with fruit trees, a band with central urn of flowers, flanked by birds, animals and trees, 1810, 15½ by 12½in (39 by 32cm), framed and glazed.
£370–450 *CSK*

A sampler by Mary Ann Atkins, worked in coloured silks, with a verse, surrounded by detailed flower stems, birds and a butterfly, within a floral border, 1844, 16½ by 15½in (42 by 39cm), framed and glazed.
£400–500 *CSK*

A sampler by Jane Pickering, worked in shades of green, brown and ivory silks, with an alphabet in buttonhole stitch, crowded spot motifs and a stylised floral border, 13in (33cm) square, framed and glazed.
£250–300 *CSK*

A Berlin woolwork sampler, in coloured wools and silks, with a wide range of stitches and decorative patterns, a witch, a military figure and the initials 'LOP', the edges bound in ivory silk, mid-19thC, 25 by 9in (64 by 23cm).
£200–250 *CSK*

l. A sampler, worked in coloured silks, with a verse 'O Jesus permit...', a band of spot motifs, a rural scene, within a floral border, 15 by 11½in (38 by 29cm), framed and glazed.
£700–850 *CSK*

A sampler, worked in coloured silks, with elaborate alphabets, central heart outline flanked by crown surmounted initials, large flowering plants below, within a blue Greek key border, late 18thC, 16½ by 19½in (42 by 49cm), framed and glazed.
£350–450 *CSK*

A piece of needlework, in contemporary carved wooden gilt frame, c1780, 2in (5cm) square.
£200–225 *PSC*

Made to wear in a pair cased verge pocket watch.

Needlework Pictures

A chenille work picture, c1820, 10½ by 14½in (26 by 37cm).
£125–150 *PSC*

An embroidered picture of Pharoah's horses, worked in ivory, black and shades of grey silks against a silk ground, late 19thC, probably Oriental for the European market, 16in (41cm) diam.
£325–375 *CSK*

A pair of embroidered pictures, worked in coloured silks, 7 by 8in (18 by 20cm), in black and gold glass mount, framed.
£370–470 *CSK*

A 'hairwork' landscape of black silk thread on a light silk background, 8 by 10in (20 by 25cm).
£150–175 *PSC*

An embroidered picture of a dog, worked in coloured silks, 11½ by 14in (29 by 36cm), framed and glazed.
£180–240 *CSK*

A stumpwork picture, with a gentleman and lady in a landscape, with many animals and insects, in applied needlework, 17thC, 13 by 18in (33 by 46cm).
£1,500–1,800 *B*

A chenille work picture, in coloured silks, with a cluster of flowers, against a cream velvet background, early 19thC, 14½ by 12½in (37 by 32cm), in black and gold glass mount, framed.
£200–250 *CSK*

A needlework picture, 20thC, 13 by 16in (33 by 41cm).
£80–120 *LB*

A needlework picture, 20thC, 12 by 9in (30.5 by 23cm).
£80–150 *LB*

An embroidered picture, in coloured wools, depicting a wounded hare lying beneath a tree, early 19thC, framed, 16½ by 19½in (42 by 49cm).
£350–400 *CSK*

MAKE THE MOST OF MILLERS

Price ranges in this book reflect what you should expect to *pay* for a similar example. When selling, however, you would expect to receive a lower figure. This will fluctuate according to a dealer's stock and saleability at a particular time. It is always advisable, when selling a collectable, to approach a reputable dealer or an auction house which has specialist sales.

An embroidered picture, worked in coloured silks and chenille threads, depicting 'Noli me tangere', with painted details, c1800, 14 by 16½in (36 by 42cm), in black and gold glass mount, framed.
£350–400 *CSK*

r. An appliqué wool picture, with a floral wreath, with silk centres and detailing, on a cream ground, framed and glazed, 25½ by 23in (65 by 59cm).
£200–250 *CSK*

TOOLS & INSTRUMENTS

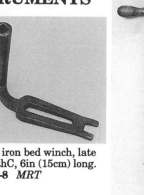

An iron bed winch, late 18thC, 6in (15cm) long.
£6–8 *MRT*

A mahogany and brass 'Waywiser', by G. Adams, No. 60 Fleet Street, London, the silvered ring with three calibrations, six-spoke wheel with iron tyre, 32in (81cm) diam, unrestored, 18thC.
£100–150 *B*

A Victorian brass water pump, 39in (99cm) high.
£80–100 *TAR*

A pair of upholsterer's steel pincers, c1900, 8in (20cm) long.
£10–12 *MRT*

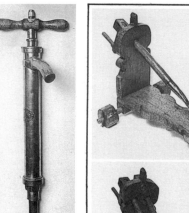

Two French cord winders, c1880, 20in (51cm) long.
£180–220 each *MofC*

Two gunsmith's turnscrews, with rosewood handles, 19thC, 5in (12.5cm) long.
£12–16 *MRT*

l. An ash handled and boxwood bodied cooper's bung borer, mid-19thC, 15in (38cm) long.
£40–45 *MRT*

A cobbler's double-headed hammer, and a leatherworker's rosewood handled crease, late 19thC.
£5–6 each *MRT*

A chocolate pick, used for breaking large blocks of chocolate, with advertisement for Cadbury's, 1920s.
£10–12 *MRT*

A pocket pruning knife, with horn handle, by Saynor, Sheffield, 19thC, 4in (10cm) long when closed.
£10–12 *MRT*

A Victorian game carrier by H. Mahillon, Brussels, 14in (36cm) long.
£50–60 *TAR*

An ebony and brass pad saw handle, 19thC, 8in (20cm) long.
£8–12 *MRT*

A 12 bore cartridge turning
tool, 1890.
£20–25 *PSC*

A lawyer's bodkin, for sewing
legal documents, late 19thC,
7in (17.5cm) long.
£6–8 *MRT*

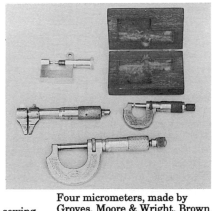

Four micrometers, made by
Groves, Moore & Wright, Brown
& Sharpe and Starratt, c1900.
£16–30 each *MRT*

An Atco petrol powered lawn
mower, c1929.
£200–250 *JUN*

A brass and ebony adjustable
mortice gauge, mid-19thC, 7in
(17.5cm) long.
£25–30 *MRT*

An insulation testing
instrument, used by electrical
wiring contractors for testing
insulation in electrical
installations, 1924.
£100–150 *RE*

A 12 gauge reloading tool
for shotgun cartridges, 4in
(10cm) high.
£40–45 *TAR*

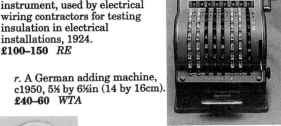

r. A German adding machine,
c1950, 5½ by 6½in (14 by 16cm).
£40–60 *WTA*

A set of bookbinder's brass
letters and numbers, 48 point
size, 19thC.
£50–60 *MRT*

r. A boxwood and brass rope
gauge, with tables for different
types of rope, 19thC.
£25–28 *MRT*

A selection of four gilder's or
bookbinder's agate burnishers,
with brass ferrules and wooden
handles, late 19thC.
£12–15 each *MRT*

A joiner's rosewood, brass and steel T-bevel, 19thC, 9in (23cm).
£10–12 *MRT*

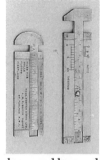

Two brass and boxwood calliper gauges, one with vernier, the other with advertising inscription, early 20thC, 4 and 3in (10 and 7.5cm) long.
£15–18 *MRT*

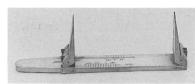

A glove maker's boxwood hand measure, for measuring width of hand, c1900.
£30–35 *MRT*

A boxwood and brass proof slide rule, from a hydrometer set, 19thC.
£12–15 *MRT*

A plumber's boxwood folding ruler, c1850, 24 to 36in (61 to 91.5cm).
£60–70 *MRT*

l. A boxwood four-fold pocket rule, brass tipped, trademark Hockley Abbey, c1920, 12in (30.5cm) long.
£15–20 *MRT*

A Routledge's engineer's two-fold rule, with brass logarithmic slide and numerous tables, by T. Bradburn, Birmingham, late 19thC, 24in (61.5cm).
£60–70 *MRT*

Planes

A cast iron panel plane, with mahogany infill, early 19thC, 14in (36cm) long.
£120–140 *MRT*

A 'stail engine' adjustable rounding plane, by Atkin & Sons, late 19thC, 11in (28cm) long.
£40–50 *MRT*

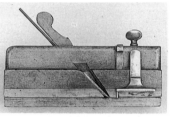

A beech and boxwood moving fillister plane, with brass fittings, by Christopher Gabriel of London, 1770–1822.
£40–45 *MRT*

Two beechwood and brass chamfer planes, late 19thC.
£35–45 each *MRT*

A steel bullnose plane, 19thC, 4in (10cm) long.
£25–30 *MRT*

A Stanley cast iron and steel adjustable compass plane, No. 113, made in U.S.A., c1914.
£50–60 *MRT*

TOYS

Prices for toys depend on maker, rarity and condition. Unnaturally well-behaved children who never damaged their cars and trains and carefully kept all the bits and boxes can certainly reap the benefits in later life. Condition is all-important to adult collectors and since toys are common compared to other antiques, they can afford to pick and choose. Stringent criteria also applies to boxes: torn tabs, splitting or graffiti will affect value and since a box can treble the worth of a toy, this has even led to reproduction, laser printed packaging .

It is important to note that when indentifying most diecast toys the catalogue number and name of manufacturer, is essential. Similarly toy trains are best identified through the manufacturer, gauge, model name and number.

Aeroplanes

A collection of aircraft toys 1930s:
A Frog Penguin plastic 49P Wellington Bomber kit, unconstructed, c1940, and a constructed Hawker Hurricane, a Warneford Moth aeroplane, Victory and other jigsaws, all in original boxes, fair condition.
£200–250 *CSK*

A *Modern Wonders* magazine MW3 Presentation Flying Model Monoplane, designed by Wallace Rigby, lightweight aluminium and card construction, with three-blade plastic propellor, instructions, leaflets, cards, oil, in original box, 1938.
£200–250 *CSK*

A Frog flying scale model Hawker Hart 2 Seat Day-going Bomber, with propeller and spinner, oil bottle, band lubricant, later model with plain unprinted engine cowling, in original plain grey box with blue and white label, 1930s, good condition.
£425–500 *CSK*

Cross Reference:
Aeronautica

A Frog flying scale model of a Hawker Hart Mark II Day Bomber, with propeller and spinner, instructions, band inserter rod, winder, oil and band lubricant, in original box, box repaired, c1934.
£600–800 *CSK*

l. Two Frog flying models:
A 23FM Mailplane, with instructions, in original box, c1940, one propellor blade missing, and a 21K Spitfire Monoplane card and balsa kit, in original box, c1940, slight wear.
£275–350 *CSK*

A scale model of a Fokker aeroplane, c1940.
£150–200 *JUN*

A Dinky Supertoys Super G Constellation Lockheed aircraft, French, c1950s, in original box, 7in (17.5cm) square.
£100–150 *HAL*

A Dinky Toys Vickers 'Viscount', French, c1950, in original box, 5in (12.5cm) square.
£80–100 *HAL*

Diecast Toys
Corgi

A Corgi Toys Ferrari 'Berlinetta' 250 Le Mans, 1960s, 4in (10cm) long, with box.
£25–35 *HAL*

A Corgi Toys No. 238 Jaguar Mark X, royal blue with red interior, with box, very good condition.
£90–125 *VMA*

A Corgi Toys Routemaster bus, with driver and clippie, in New South Wales Government Transport Dept. livery, green, cream and brown, good condition, in original box.
£600–700 *VMA*

r. A Corgi Toy Green Hornet car, 'Black Beauty', 1960s, 5in (12.5cm) long, with box.
£100–150 *HAL*

l. A Corgi Toys No. 236 Austin A60 Motor School Car, a rare pre-production version in grey with maroon side stripe and yellow plastic roof wheel, two interior figures, excellent condition, with Corgi Junior Highway Code leaflet.
£750–800 *VMA*

r. A Corgi Toys No. 230 European Mercedes - Benz 220 SE, black with lemon interior, with box.
£100–120 *VMA*

A Corgi Toys No. 322 Rover 2000 in International Rally finish, white with black bonnet, in original box, in excellent condition.
£175–250 *VMA*

A Corgi Toys No. 416S Touring Secours Land Rover, in excellent condition, with original box.
£325–375 *VMA*

l. A Corgi Toys 'Corporal' Guided Missile on Erector Vehicle, 1960s, 13½in (34cm) long.
£80–120 *HAL*

A Butlin's Dancing badge, 1964. **£20–25** *PC*

A selection of Butlin's Annual Reunion badges Royal Albert Hall, each 1in (3cm) diam: *l.* 1946. **£75–100** *lc. & rc.* 1950 and 1952. **£12–15 each**. *r.* 1949. **£20–25** *PC*

A Butlin's flask, c1975–79, 10in (25cm) high. **£5–7** *PC*

Four Butlin's Christmas badges, 1957, 1958, 1966 and 1967. **£3–4 each** *PC*

A selection of Butlin's cloth badges of various dates. **£1–10 each** *PC*

A selection of Butlin's Dancing Festival badges, Minehead, Filey and Ayr, 1950s and 60s. **£10–12 each** *PC*

Two Butlin's Juvenile Dancing Festival badges, 1957 and 1960. **£10–18 each** *PC*

Butlin's Car Club badges: *top l.* 1938. **£100–150** *r.* 1950–60s. **£20–100 each** *bottom l.* A Motorcycle Club badge, 1955. **£30–35** *PC*

A selection of Butlin's small souvenir items, 1930s–1945. **£1–2 each** *PC*

Two Butlin's Beaver Club badges, 1980s, 2in (5cm) diam. **50p–£1 each** *PC*

A Butlin's electric advertising travel agency sign, c1960. **£50–60** *PC*

A musical teddy bear,
'Jopi', c1920, 15in
(38cm) high.
£350–400 *SP*

A Chiltern teddy bear,
riding a tricycle, with
label, c1958, 12in
(30.5cm) high.
£85–95 *CMF*

A Schuco Yes/No
mohair bear, with
nodding head and
glass eyes, c1950s,
8⅓in (21cm) high.
£200–300 *SP*

A Farnell teddy bear,
c1918, 22in (56cm) high.
£300–350 *SP*

A Schuco straw filled teddy
bear, c1950s, 18in (46cm) high.
£60–80 *TAR*

A mohair teddy bear, with
glass eyes, maker unknown,
c1920, 19in (48cm) high.
£200–300 *SP*

A straw filled teddy bear,
1920s, pads damaged, 23in
(58.5cm). **£250–300** *WAG*

A Chiltern mohair teddy bear,
with glass eyes, mint condition,
c1938, 16in (40.5cm) high.
£200–250 *SP*

A Chiltern mohair 'Hugmee'
teddy bear, with glass eyes,
c1950, 17½in (44cm) high.
£150–200 *SP*

A Merrythought 'Titanic' teddy bear,
from a limited edition of 5,000, c1992,
mint condition with original box.
£40–45 *COB*

A Steiff pussy cat, 1950s,
9½in (23.5cm) long.
£40–45 *SP*

A Steiff dachsund, with label
'Hexie', 1950s, 10in (25cm) long.
£25–30 *SP*

A teddy bear, by Merrythought,
c1960s, 15½in (39cm) high.
£100–150 *SP*

A Schuco teddy bear, with compact
inside, 1930s, 3½in (8.5cm) high.
£250–300 *SP*

A Kiddieland with label
'Tubby', 'I Turn My Eyes',
c1918, 6in (15cm) wide.
£30–40 *SP*

A Dismal Desmo, made by
Dean's Rag Books, c1930s,
5in (12.5cm) high.
£100–150 *SP*

A Steiff musical Bonzo, with stud in ear, 1930.
£1,500–2,500 *SP*

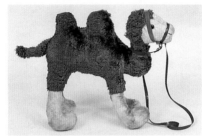

A cotton plush camel, maker unknown, c1960s, 11½in (29cm) high.
£10–15 *SP*

A Steiff pekingese dog, c1950s, 8in (20cm) long.
£25–30 *SP*

A Steiff lion, with 'Leo' label, 1950s, 9in (23cm) long.
£30–35 *SP*

An Andy Pandy rag doll, 1960s, 13in (33cm) high.
£25–35 *TAR*

A Steiff tiger, with glass eyes, 1950s, 14in (35.5cm) long.
£40–50 *SP*

A cotton plush dog, 1960s, 9in (23cm) high.
£5–10 *SP*

Mickey and Minnie Mouse, c1930–40, 7in (17.5cm) high.
£20–25 *YY*

A Continental felt covered clockwork horse, 1930s, 7in (17.5cm) high.
£40–45 *TAR*

A Japanese plush velvet lion, 1970s.
£5–10 *SP*

A Steiff boxer dog, c1950s, 5in (12.5cm) long.
£25–30 *SP*

A Pedigree golly, with label, c1960, 12in (30.5cm) high.
£28–32 *CMF*

A Robertson's Jam cut-out golly, c1950.
£12–14 *CMF*

A Chinese embroidered skirt panel, c1890, framed, 14in (35.5cm) high.
£75–120 *PBr*

A Chinese skirt panel, c1890, framed, 15in (38cm) high.
£80–120 *PBr*

A Chinese panel, early 19thC, framed, 20in (50.5cm) high.
£40–50 *STK*

A pair of Chinese sleeve panels, c1890, framed, 25in (64cm) high.
£250–350 *PBr*

A pair of mid-Victorian silk and cotton curtain tie backs.
£50–70 *JPr*

A Chinese woollen skirt panel, c1890, framed, 10½in (26cm) high.
£65–90 *PBr*

A chenille door curtain, c1930s, 84in (213cm) long.
£15–20 *TOM*

A French silk and wool single curtain tie back, c1890.
£120–140 *JPr*

A pair of French late Victorian silk curtain tie backs.
£60–80 *JPr*

Two cross stitch tapestry cushions, c1930s–40s.
£25–35 each *TOM*

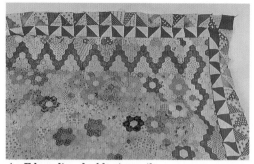

An Edwardian double size quilt,
'Grandma's Garden', incomplete.
£150–200 *CK*

An English cotton quilt, c1880.
£200–220 *CK*

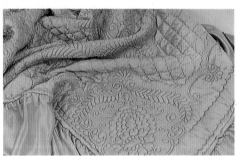

A reversible Durham 'Comfy'
quilt, machine stitched, c1900.
£50–70 *TOM*

A Victorian beadwork
slipper holder.
£80–100 *WAG*

A silk and glazed cotton multi-
coloured quilt, 1890.
£350–400 *CK*

Three reproduction stools, with handmade
kelim covers, each 17in (43cm) wide.
£80–100 each *ORG*

A quilted rayon and satin single
bedspread, 1940s.
£50–60 *CK*

Two Victorian footstools, with tapestry
needlework upholstered tops, and bun feet.
£120–140 each *PCh*

A mahogany stool, with a framed Baluch bag-
face upholstered top, 21in (53cm) wide.
£400–500 *SAM*

A Corgi Toys London Passenger Transport Set No. GS/35, including a No. 468 RM Bus, Driver and Clippie, No. 418 London Taxi, and Traffic Policeman, good condition.
£175–200 *VMA*

A Matchbox Series MB30A Ford Prefect and No 36A Austin A50, boxed.
£30–45 *VMA*

A Corgi Toys set No.21 ERF Dropside Lorry and Platform Trailer, good condition.
£125–150 *VMA*

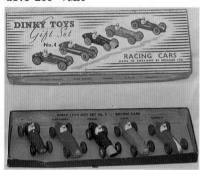

A Dinky Toys gift set No. 4 Racing Cars, with 23 series Cooper Bristol, Alfa Romeo, Ferrari, HWM, and Maserati, some damage to Cooper Bristol, box lid worn.
£275–325 *VMA*

A Corgi Toys No. 267 Batmobile, with Batman and Robin, good condition.
£200–225 *VMA*

A Dinky Supertoys No. 886 'Profileur' 100 Richier road grader, good condition.
£80–100 *VMA*

A Matchbox Series gift set No. G9, including M1B BP Petrol Tanker, MB2B Bedford York Trailer, M4A Ruston Bucyrus and M6A Pickford's Transporter, good condition.
£100–125 *VMA*

A Corgi gift set No.48 Ford Carrimore Transporter with six cars, good condition, box poor condition.
£225–275 *VMA*

A Corgi Toys gift set No. 4 Bloodhound Guided Missile, Launching Ramp, Loading Trolley, and RAF Land Rover, good condition, box lid repaired.
£160–180 *VMA*

A Dinky Toys No. 160 Mercedes 250SE, and No. 57/003 Chevrolet Impala, boxed, fair condition.
£80–100 *VMA*

A Dinky Toys No. 133 Ford Cortina and No. 171 Austin 1800, in see-through boxes, fair condition.
£60–80 *VMA*

A Tri-ang wooden milk cart, containing wooden milk bottles and 2 tin churns, 1920s–30s, 13 by 20in (33 by 50.5cm). **£100–145** *JUN*

A Chad Valley tinplate and plastic globe, c1960s, 7in (17.5cm) high. **£15–20** *FMN*

A Holiday Cruise game, by Chad Valley, c1930s, box 10 by 15in (38cm). **£15–20** *COB*

A Corgi model car, with Kermit the Frog, in poor condition, late 1970s, 3⅓in (8.5cm) long. **£4–5** *TAR*

A Spin-A-Way 'Linstom' bagatelle game, early 20thC, 14 by 23in (36 by 58.5cm). **£20–25** *JUN*

A plastic Noddy car, c1980s, 6½in (16cm) long. **£6–10** *TAR*

Two Bendy Toys Trumpton figures, c1962, 6in (15cm) high. **£15–20 each** *TAR*

A plastic Womble toothbrush holder, c1970s, 6in (15cm) high. **£8–10** *TAR*

A plastic Minnie Mouse money box, 1950s, 6½in (16cm) high. **£6–10** *TAR*

An Edwardian kaleidoscope, 11½in (29cm) long. **£10–20** *LIO*

An Airfix 1:600 model kit of HMS 'Ark Royal', c1976, box 18in (45.5cm) long. **£6–8** *COB*

A Judge Dredd 1:6 scale vinyl
kit, by Halcyon, 1994.
£45–65 *ALI*

A Dr. Who Mk3 Movie Dalek
kit, 1993. **£20–30** *ALI*

A Robocop 1 vinyl kit, by
Horizon, Japan, 1993.
£30–50 *ALI*

An Alien 3 Alien Creature plastic kit, by Halcyon
Movie Classics, USA, 1993, 9in (23cm) high.
£20–45 *ALI*

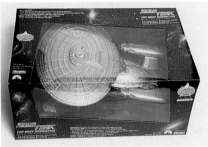

A Starship Enterprise model, by
Playmates Paramount, with box,
1994, 18in (45.5cm) long.
£100–200 *ALI*

A Batman Returns vinyl kit, by
Horizon, USA, 1993, 12in (30.5cm).
£40–65 *ALI*

A resin bust of Terminator
T800, 1993, 12in (30.5cm).
£100–150 *ALI*

A Darth Vader Star Wars
model kit, commemorative
edition, 1993, 11½in (29cm).
£15–30 *ALI*

A UFO Sky l plastic model, by
Amerang, Japan, c1970.
£7–15 *ALI*

l. A 1:8 scale vinyl model kit of
Patrick Troughton as Dr. Who,
30th Anniversay issue, 1993.
£20–40 *ALI*

A wooden and tin toy bus, 1920s, 20in (50.5cm) long.
£150–200 *TAR*

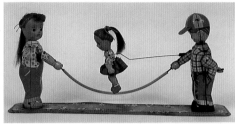

A Japanese tinplate and clockwork skipping
toy, by TPS, Japan, c1960, 12in (30.5cm) wide.
£90–110 *HAL*

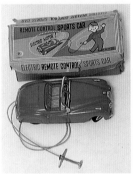

A Japanese tinplate remote
control sports car, original
box, c1960, 7½in (19cm) long.
£100–150 *JUN*

A Jetex plastic Jet
Propelled Racing Car,
1950s, with original box,
6¼in (16cm) long.
£100–135 *JUN*

A tinplate sedan, by Lehmann, c1920,
5½in (14cm) wide.
£150–200 *HAL*

A Bandai tinplate Rolls-Royce, c1950,
11in (28cm) long.
£180–200 *HAL*

A Tri-ang tinplate Transporter, c1950,
17in (43cm) long.
£50–65 *JUN*

A Hornby tinplate L&NER No. 2710 engine and
tender, 1920s, 10in (25cm) long.
£140–200 *HAL*

Three tinplate wagons each 5in (12.5cm) long, *l. to r:*
Motor Shell Spirit, c1930. **£20–40**
Fyffes Bananas, c1930, boxed. **£100–130**
Meccano, c1930. **£50–80** *HAL*

A Hornby DublO tinplate Cardiff Castle two
rail engine and tender, 1950–60s, with box,
11in (28cm) long. **£60–90** *HAL*

A Wade cottage butter dish,
c1930s, 4in (10cm) high.
£40–45 *CBa*

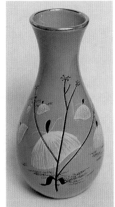

A Wade vase, with
design from the film
Fantasia, c1961, 7in
(17.5cm) high.
£25–30 *CBa*

Three Wade Hat Box Series Walt
Disney characters, c1956–65,
1½in (3.5cm) high.
£18–38 each *CBa*

A Wade cup and saucer, with
Quack-Quack design, by Robert
Barlow, c1938.
£25–30 *CBa*

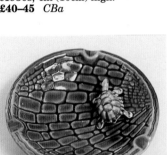

A Wade ashtray, with a tortoise in
relief, c1976–84, 6in (15cm) diam.
£10–12 *CBa*

A Wade child's night-
light, early 1930s,
3½in (8.5cm) high.
£30–35 *CBa*

A salad bowl and a
plate, stamped Wade
Heath, c1938–50.
£25–30 each *CBa*

A Wade gold coloured coffee set,
c1955–60, the pot 7in (17.5cm) high.
£200–250 *CBa*

Two Wade Teenage trinket boxes,
c1960s, 3½in (8cm) diam.
£50–60 each *CBa*

Two Mabel Lucie Attwell figures, by Wade,
c1959, 3in (7.5cm) high.
£100–120 each *CBa*

Four Whimsies by Wade, part of a set of
60 figures, c1971–84, 1½in (3.5cm) high.
£1–5 each *CBa*

Sinclair Microvision TV
model MTV1 1977.

Marconi 707 TV\Radio 1939

Baird "Lyric" TV\Radio 1946
specially finished in bird's-eye maple

Cossor Model 1210 TV\Radio 1939

Pye bakelite TV model VT2 1951

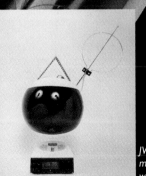

Mark III television camera 1954

JVC Videosphere "Sputnick"
model 3240 UK
with radio stand TV\Radio 1966

TV and TV related material bought and sold.

EARLY TECHNOLOGY

Tel: 0131 226 1132 Fax: 0131 665 2839 Mobile: 0831 106768

Two walnut and fruitwood gavels, 18thC.
£60–75 each *BRD*

A mahogany and mother-of-pearl studded snuff shoe, 19thC, 3⅓in (8.5cm) long.
£290–340 *JCr*

A bust of Admiral Lord Nelson, carved from ship's timber taken from the 'Duke of Wellington', c1905, 7in (17.5cm) high.
£75–80 *COB*

An Arabian wooden pestle and mortar, 19thC.
£200–250 *BRD*

An agate stamp box, with divisions, c1920–30.
£70–80 *VB*

A Victorian Tartan Ware blotter, 7½in (18.5cm) wide.
£50–75 *RdeR*

An inlaid wooden jewellery box, c1850, 8in (20cm) diam.
£400–500 *LIO*

Two Victorian beaded dip pens.
£28–35 each *VB*

l. & r. A pair of Victorian Bavarian wooden bears.
£15–20
c. A pincushion with a thimble on a stand, 5½in (13.5cm) high.
£45–50 *TAR*

A mosaic dip pen, c1900.
£25–30 *VB*

A stag's hoof, mounted as a desk trophy, 1873.
£50–70 *TAR*

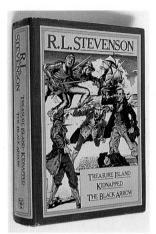

R. L. Stevenson, *Treasure Island*, *Kidnapped* and *The Black Arrow*, Book Club Associates, 1979.
£4–5 *OCS*

A Devon Pottery earthenware chamberstick, c1960, 3⅓in (8.5cm) diam.
£4–5 *CSA*

A miniature tin doll's pram, 3in (7.5cm) high.
£4–5 *SP*

A selection of baggage labels from the French Line shipping company, c1960s.
£4–5 each *COB*

A Grafton crested china shoe, inscribed 'Falmouth', c1920.
£4–5 *LIO*

A Midwinter plate, designed by Hugh Casson, 1960, and a Salad ware bowl, by Terence Conran, 1955.
£3–5 each *AND*

A British Gas promotional plastic cruet set, 20thC, 2½in (6cm) high.
£3–5 *PC*

A sailor cloth doll, 20thC.
£3–5 *COB*

Two cigarette silks, 1914–30.
£1–3 each *COL*

A selection of badges, 1970–80s.
50p – £1 each *COB*

A Susie Cooper plate, c1940, 6½in (16cm) diam.
£4–5 *CSA*

A selection of Whitbread inn signs, 3rd series, on card, 20thC.
£1.50–2.00 each *COL*

Three Mighty Morphin Power Rangers soft toys. **£17 each** *CtC* A Power Sound key chain, in original 'Try Me' packaging. **£4** *PC*

Items from children's films or television series have a short shelf-life, thus making the few that do survive in good condition highly sought after.

Bank note calculators, in original packaging, c1989, 3 by 6in (7.5 by 15cm). **£2–3 each** *WP*

A Tikkers watch 'Affections', designed by Terry Frost, RA. **£25** *RAS*

This is one of a set of 5 watches designed by Royal Academy artists.

Three wooden candlesticks, designed by David Linley, the barley twist and column-shaped candlesticks available in sycamore, oak and walnut, the spiral in just oak, each with stamped mark, 10 to 12in (25 to 30.5cm) high. **£55–70 each** *DLF*

Flintstones tissues, soap and bubble bath. **£3–5 each** *PC*

Disposable items which remain unused and intact could become collectable.

James Kelman, *How late it was, how late,* Secker and Warburg, 1994, signed first edition. **£15** *PC*

A bottle of Jean Paul Gaultier Eau de Toilette. **£35+** *COp*

The distinctive style of this scent bottle makes it a likely collectable of the future.

A *Lion King* book, book and tape set and a childs' seat belt cover/toy. **£3–5 each** *PC*

A Corgi Toys No. 1110 Bedford 'S' Type Fuel Tanker 'Shell Benzeen', in blue and white, with presentation box, excellent condition.
£2,000–2,500 *VMA*

Three Corgi Toys Bedford Vans: a 403 'Daily Express' Van, a 404M Dormobile Personnel Carrier with mechanical motor, and a 408 AA Road Service Van with split windscreen and smooth roof, in original boxes, good condition.
£125–150 *CSK*

A Corgi Toys No. 472 Public Address Vehicle, in excellent condition, 1960s, 4in (10cm) long, with original box.
£50–70 *HAL*

A Corgi Toys 1965 Rallye Monte-Carlo gift set No. 38, comprising: BMC Mini-Cooper 'S', Rover 2000 and Citroën DS19, in original box, good condition.
£500–600 *CSK*

A Corgi Toys No. 503 Chipperfield Circus Giraffe Transporter, with giraffes, with original box, 4in (10cm) square.
£40–60 *HAL*

Four Corgi Toys Bedford small Commercials: A No. 408 AA van, and three No. 404 Bedford Dormobiles, one cerise, one cream and one yellow with blue roof, in excellent condition, unboxed.
£70–90 *VMA*

Two Corgi Toys No. 464 Commer Police Vans with boxes, both good condition:
l. Dark green, opaque rear and side windows.
£330–380
r. Blue 'Rijks Politie', with blue flashing roof light, red interior, 'grilled' rear and side windows.
£190–225 *VMA*

Dinky

A Dinky Toys No. 176 Austin
A105 Saloon, grey with red
stripe and wheels, with original
box, excellent condition.
£70–80 *VMA*

A Dinky Toys Corvair Monza,
made in Hong Kong for
Meccano Ltd., c1960, 4in
(10cm) long, with original box.
£70–90 *HAL*

A Dinky Toys No. 175
Hillman Minx, grey with blue
roof and wheels, with box, in
excellent condition.
£90–110 *VMA*

A Dinky Toys No. 192 Range
Rover, with Speedwheels,
yellow, 1970s, 4½in (11cm) long,
with original box.
£45–55 *HAL*

A Dinky Toys No. 449 Chevrolet
'El Camino' Pick-up Truck,
cream and turquoise, with box,
excellent condition.
£90–110 *VMA*

A Dinky Toys No. 194 Bentley
Coupé, with gold and cream
seats, blue tonneau, with driver
and box, excellent condition.
£150–175 *VMA*

A Dinky Toys No. 231
Maserati Racing Car, 1950s,
4in (10cm) long, boxed and
in excellent condition.
£40–60 *HAL*

A Dinky Toys No. 12 Postal Set,
comprising: a Royal Mail van,
red and blue pillar boxes,
without tops, a telephone box,
a telegraph messenger,
a postman, slight damage to
van, in original box.
£350–400 *S(S)*

A Dinky Toys No. 199 Austin
Seven Countryman, 1960s,
3in (7.5cm) long, with box.
£30–40 *HAL*

A Dinky Toys red Chrysler
'New Yorker', French, c1950,
5in (12.5cm) long, with box.
£50–80 *HAL*

A Dinky Toys No. 157 Jaguar
XK120, deep yellow, with box,
very good condition.
£140–160 *VMA*

A Dinky Toys No. 260 Royal
Mail Van, c1950, 3in (7.5cm)
long, with original box.
£60–100 *HAL*

Three Dinky Toys sports cars: A 38D Alvis, green with black seats, a No. 38C Lagonda, green with dark green seats, and a No. 38A Sunbeam Talbot, dark blue and grey, all in good condition.
£55–65 *VMA*

A Dinky Supertoys No. 958 British Snow Plough, yellow, c1950–60, in original box, 8in (20cm) wide.
£100–140 *HAL*

A Dinky Supertoys No. 960, Lorry Mounted Cement Mixer with windows, 1950s, 5½in (14cm) long, with original box.
£70–100 *HAL*

A Dinky Toys No. 823 GMC Military Fuel Tanker, with filler caps, front winch, inner stand, in original box, excellent condition.
£250–300 *VMA*

A Dinky Supertoys No. 504 Foden 14 Ton Tanker, dark and mid-blue, in original box, very good condition.
£80–100 *WAL*

A Dinky Supertoys No. 948, Tractor-Trailer McLean, 1950s, 12in (30.5cm) long, with original box.
£180–250 *HAL*

A Dinky Supertoys No. 501 Foden Diesel 8 Wheel Wagon, black chassis, blue wheels, silver stripe to sides, in original box, very good condition.
£160–180 *WAL*

l. A Dinky Toys No. 153 Standard Vanguard, cream, 1950s, 4in (10cm) long, in original box, excellent condition.
£150–170 *HAL*

A Dinky Toys No. 2
Farmyard Animals and
No. 6 Shepherd Set, in
original boxes, in very
good condition.
£315–375 *CSK*

A Dinky Supertoys No. 502
Foden Flat Truck, dark green
with black chassis, green
wheels, silver stripe to sides,
in original box, very
good condition.
£160–180 *WAL*

r. Two Dinky Toys
Armoured Cars, made
in France:
l. 'AML' Panhard, boxed.
r. Half-track M3,
1950s, boxed.
£40–50 each *HAL*

A Dinky Supertoys No. 923 Big
Bedford Van, 'Heinz' red cab
and chassis, in original yellow
box, very good condition.
£1,300–1,500 *WAL*

A Dinky Supertoys No. 983
Car Carrier with Trailer, red
and grey, with box, very
good condition.
£150–175 *WAL*

A Dinky Supertoys No. 513 Guy
Flat truck with tailboard,
yellow and dark blue chassis,
with box, very good condition.
£180–200 *WAL*

A Dinky Supertoys No. 521
Bedford Articulated Lorry,
painted yellow with black wings
and wheelarches, in original
box, very good condition.
£70–100 *WAL*

Spot-On

A Spot-On AEC Mammoth
Major 8 'Shell BP' 4000 Gallon
Auto Petrol Tanker, red, green
and black livery, in original box
with paperwork and insert, very
good condition.
£275–300 *WAL*

A Spot-On ERF 68G and flat
float, with sides, red with light
grey chassis, in original box
with insert, very good condition.
£200–220 *WAL*

A Spot-On ERF 68G and flat
float, turquoise with black roof
and silver chassis, complete
with planks, in original box,
adapted lid, very good condition.
£120–150 *WAL*

A Spot-On Austin Prime Mover, with articulated flat float and MGA car in crate, the Austin in dark blue BMC livery, 'The British Motor Corporation Ltd' to cab and float sides, in original box with insert, very good condition.
£320–350 *WAL*

A Spot-On AEC Mammoth Major 8 and flat float with sides, red and silver BRS livery, unmarked, complete with optional 4-wheeled 10 ton trailer, in same livery, in original boxes, with insert for AEC, very good condition.
£320–370 *WAL*

A Spot-On Mulliner coach, silver and blue, with red flash to sides, in original box with paperwork and insert, very good condition.
£170–200 *WAL*

A Spot-On AEC Mammoth Major 8, 4000 Gallon Auto Petrol Tanker, yellow and white, with grey chassis, in original box complete with paperwork and inserts, very good condition.
£830–870 *WAL*

A Spot-On model by Tri-ang ERF 68G and flat float with sides and load of barrels, turquoise with silver load bed and chassis, in original box, good condition.
£130–170 *WAL*

Disney

A Marx Toys plastic Mickey Mouse, original, 5½in (14cm) high.
£15–20 *CK*

l. A plastic Mickey Mouse bubble bath bottle, 1980s, 9½in (24cm) high.
£8–10 *TAR*

A plastic Minnie Mouse bubble bath bottle, 1986, 5in (12.5cm) high.
£6–8 *TAR*

Games

A pair of coromandel dice shakers, early 1900s, 5in (12.5cm) high.
£100–140 *TVM*

A child's mahogany spelling box, with bone counters, by E. C. Spurn, 37 New Bond Street, London, c1900, 8in (20cm) wide.
£200–260 *CBS*

A mahogany and brass horse shoe game, c1900, 5½in (14cm) wide.
£200–250 *ARE*

A game of Beetle Drive, c1950s, 7in (17.5cm) square.
£5–7 *JUN*

A board game, entitled 'Running the Blockade', c1920, 12in (30.5cm) wide.
£10–15 *JUN*

Miller's is a price GUIDE not a price LIST

l. A Bermuda Triangle game, c1976, 20in (51cm) wide.
£6–7 *COB*

A game of Lotto, c1940s, 8in (20cm) square.
£4–5 *JUN*

A game of 'Circus Pitchem',
c1950s, 9 by 7in (21.5 by 17.5cm).
£4–5 *JUN*

A set of Dewar's White
Label Whisky 'The
Spirit of Empire'
playing cards, c1930.
£12–15 *COL*

Lead Figures

A collection of lead farmyard
accessories, by various makers,
1920–30.
£2–4 each *HAL*

A collection lead figures and animals,
by various makers, 1920–30.
£2–5 each *HAL*

A collection of lead military
figures, 1920–30, 2in (5cm) high.
£2–8 each *HAL*

Two lead figures of blacksmiths with their anvils, c1935.
£20–30 *HAL*

Today it is illegal to sell lead toys to children, as lead is a poisonous material.

Britains

A collection of Britains hunting figures, each huntsman with one moving arm, pre-WWII and post-WWII 2 to 3in (5 to 7.5cm) high.
£5–20 each *HAL*

A collection of eight Britains racehorses and jockeys, comprising one black, three grey and four bay horses, each with a jockey in coloured silks, slightly damaged.
£350–400 *S(S)*

A Britains Coronation chair, pre-WWII, boxed, 3½in (8.5cm) high.
£20–30 *HAL*

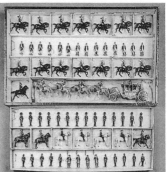

A Britains Coronation display set number 1477, in original box with interior tray and inserts, c1937, slight damage.
£1,000–1,400 *CSK*

l. A Britains pre-WWII lead figure, 'The Fat Vicar', 2in (5cm) high.
£20–25 *HAL*

Two Britains pre-WWII lead figures of village idiots, very good condition, 2in (5cm) high.
£100–130 each *HAL*

Two Britains pre-WWII lead figures, The Thin Vicar, in excellent condition, 2in (5cm) high.
£70–80 each *HAL*

A Britains lead Coronation coach, in original box, c1950, 9in (22.5cm) long.
£15–20 *HAL*

A collection of Britains lead zoo animals, pre-WWII and post-WWII, tiger 2½in (6cm) long.
£3–6 each *HAL*

Timpo

l. A collection of lead figures by Timpo and Britains, pre-WWII and post-WWII.
£3–8 each *HAL*

A Timpo detachable lead figure of Queen Elizabeth mounted on her horse, in original box, c1950s, 3½in (8.5cm) high.
£20–30 *HAL*

Meccano

A Meccano No. 1 set, pre-WWII.
£35–40 *JUN*

l. A Meccano shop display model of a windmill, with electrically operated sails and lights, 21½in (54cm) high.
£170–220 *AH*

A Meccano Accessory Outfit, No. 1A, c1950s.
£18–22 *JUN*

Pedal Toys

A metal pedal car, 'Duke', c1950s, 29in (73.5cm) wide.
£65–75 *JUN*

l. A child's tricycle, c1925, 35in (90cm) wide.
£90–100 *JUN*

A pedal aeroplane, c1930s, 46in (116.5cm) wide.
£250–300 *JUN*

A wooden Tiger Moth aeroplane, by Tiger Toys, c1950s, 25in (63.5cm) wide.
£65–75 *JUN*

A Tri-ang pedal tractor, c1950s, 30in (76cm) wide.
£200–250 *JUN*

l. A pedal car, pre-WWII, 46in (116.5cm) long.
£350–375 *JUN*

A French green and white pedal car, c1936, 46in (116.5cm) long.
£300–350 *JUN*

Rocking Horses

The rocking horse was a favourite toy in the Victorian nursery. Early 19thC examples had bow rockers, but by the late 19thC these were often replaced with trestle rockers, more stable but less elegant. Ideally, horses should look realistic and alert, with flared nostrils and pointed ears. Original paintwork and accessories will enhance value, but demand is such that modern rocking horses also command strong prices.

A corduroy covered rocking horse, c1950s, 41in (104cm) wide.
£50–60 *SIG*

Miller's is a price GUIDE not a price LIST

A rocking horse, 19thC, 55in (139.5cm) wide.
£150–200 *JUN*

A rocking horse, bridle missing, c1900, 44in (111.5cm) wide.
£500–550 *JUN*

l. A wood and plaster rocking horse, c1900.
£200–250 *OCS*

An Arts and Crafts elm rocking horse, c1880.
£250–450 *MCR*

l. A Victorian dapple grey rocking horse, with leather and corduroy saddle, leather reins, suspended on red painted frame, 62in (157cm) long.
£900–1,100 *WIL*

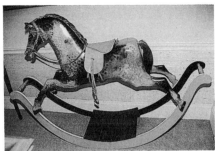

A dapple grey rocking horse, with rocker replaced, early 19thC.
£4,500–5,000 *MDI*

A Victorian carved rocking horse, requires restoring, 47in (119cm) wide.
£300–350 *SUL*

A painted rocking horse, c1930–40, 31in (79cm) wide.
£100–125 *MofC*

A dapple grey rocking horse, on trestle stand rocker, replaced mane and tail, c1880.
£1,250–1,750 *MCR*

A dapple grey rocking horse, by F. H. Ayres, with bow rocker, some original factory paint, restored and repaired, c1880.
£3,000–3,500 *APES*

A 'Nicholas Silver' rocking horse, by A. & J. Lines, with bow rocker, factory paint on body, restored and repaired, late 19thC.
£3,000–3,500 *APES*

Sci-Fi & Television Toys

The reappearance of 'Thunderbirds', 'Stingray' and 'Captain Scarlet' on British television has inspired a whole new range of children's toys. Collectors, however, are still chasing the pocket money vehicles brought out in the 1960s, which have skyrocketed in value to become very adult collectables. Gerry Anderson, creator of these cult series, has a devoted adult following who have formed their own enthusiast's society called 'Fanderson'.

A Dinky Toys UFO Interceptor, 1960s, No. 351, in excellent condition, original box, 9½in (24cm) long.
£40–60 *HAL*

A Dinky Toys Lady Penelope's Fab 1 car, No. 100, in excellent condition, with original box slightly damaged, 1960s, 6in (15cm) long.
£120–130 *HAL*

A Dinky Toys Captain Scarlet Spectrum Patrol Car, red, boxed, 1960s, 5in (12.5cm) long.
£40–70 *HAL*

A Dinky Toys Captain Scarlet Maximum Security Vehicle, in excellent condition, in original box, 1960s, 5½in (14cm) long.
£60–100 *HAL*

A completed model figure of Batman Returns 'The Penguin', made in Japan, 1:6 scale, 12in (30.5cm) high.
£45–60 *ALI*

A plastic model kit of Alien 2 Warrior, by Halcyon Movie Classics, USA, c1990, 9in (22.5cm) high.
£20–45 *ALI*

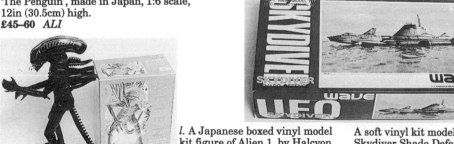

l. A Japanese boxed vinyl model kit figure of Alien 1, by Halcyon Movie Classics, c1980, 18in (46cm) high.
£45–75 *ALI*

A soft vinyl kit model of Skydiver Shado Defence, by Wave, made in Japan, c1970, 18in (45.5cm) long.
£50–75 *ALI*

A life-size vinyl model kit
of Alien 2 Face Hugger, with
Queen Alien Foetus 1:15 scale,
in misprinted box, 1990s, 54in
(137cm) wide.
£70–100 *ALI*

A Japanese PVC model kit
of Alien 1 Space Jockey,
with astronauts, 1:60 scale,
by Halcyon Movie
Classics, c1980.
£45–60 *ALI*

A plastic model kit of Robo 1
Police Car from RoboCop 2,
1:25 scale, by AMT, c1990, 12in
(30.5cm) long.
£10–15 *ALI*

A vinyl model kit of RoboCop 3,
by Horizon, 1:6 scale, c1990,
12in (30.5cm) high.
£50–75 *ALI*

A life-sive PVC model kit of
Alien 3 Dog Burster, by
Halcyon Movie Classics, c1990.
£60–100 *ALI*

A life-size PVC kit of
Alien 3 Queen Chest
Burster, by Halcyon
Movie Classics, 1990s.
£70–120 *ALI*

l. A model of Star Trek 6,
with electronic sounds,
made by AMT, c1990,
23in (58.5cm) long.
£40–50 *ALI*

A painted soft vinyl model kit of Terminator 2 T800 vs T1000, by Tsukuda Hobby Products, Japan, 1:6 scale, 12in (30.5cm) high.
£75–100 *ALI*

A coloured plastic model kit of a UFO Shado Mobile, by Amerang Ltd., Japan, c1970.
£7–15 *ALI*

A 1:8 scale plastic injection model kit of a Dalek, from Dr. Who, BBC Enterprises, by Comet, 1970s.
£20–30 *ALI*

Robots

l. A Daiya metallic blue lithographed tinplate X-70 astronaut, battery operated, with red sparking machine gun, red and yellow jet pack, slightly damaged, late 1950s, 10½in (26.5cm) high.
£150–200 *CSK*

A Nomura yellow lithographed tinplate Astronaut, with remote control, battery operated, red feet and oxygen tank, slight damage, 10½in (25cm) high, including extended aerial.
£360–400 *CSK*

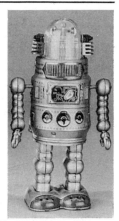

An Alps revolving and flashing gold lithographed tinplate robot, known as 'Door Robot', with battery and remote control, walking or head revolving actions, slight damage, mid-1950s, 9in (22.5cm) high.
£425–500 *CSK*

Toy Horses

A plush covered pull-along donkey, c1930s, 25in (63.5cm) wide.
£100–120 *JUN*

A French horse tricycle, hand propelled via a chain to rear axle, foot steered to front wheel, c1880.
£500–700 *MCh*

A cast iron playground horse's head.
£100–125 *JUN*

Sewing Machines

A child's sewing machine, probably German, c1895, 7in (17.5cm) wide.
£50–60 *WAG*

A German toy sewing machine, with floral decoration, c1930.
£35–40 *PC*

Tinplate

A German pulley-driven four horse carousel, finished in red, black and gold, c1900, 12½in (32cm) high.
£600–650 *CSK*

A Schuco clockwork tinplate, cloth, felt and plush roller-skating 'Rolly' Monkey, No. 7402, good condition, c1954, 8in (20cm) high.
£400–450 *CSK*

A German painted tinplate magnetic swimming toy game, with four ducks, three fish and a crayfish, paint flaking, in original red paper covered cardboard box with embossed gold lettering, c1900, 11in (28cm) wide.
£275–325 *CSK*

A Märklin painted tinplate sand mill diorama, No. 4219, with pulley driven excavator and windmill, castle above, c1910, 13in (33cm) high.
£800–900 *CSK*

Army Vehicles

A Schuco clockwork painted and lithographed Donald Duck, with orange diecast feet, hinged jaw and felt jacket, damaged, c1930, 5½in (14cm) high.
£175–225 *CSK*

A Mettoy clockwork lithographed tinplate camouflaged searchlight lorry, with four British khaki troops and battery operated searchlight, good condition, pre-WWII, 14in (35.5cm) long.
£300–350 *CSK*

A Mettoy clockwork lithographed tinplate camouflaged mobile AA gun, with four khaki troops and detachable gun, in original box, good condition, pre-WWII, 14in (35.5cm) long.
£350–400 *CSK*

Buses

A J. H. Glasman Ltd., clockwork lithographed tinplate General Transport trolley bus, red and cream, with electric lighting, good condition, slightly scratched, 10in (25cm) long.
£180–220 *CSK*

A Push-and-Go Tri-ang Minic 52M 'Routemaster' Green Line single decker bus, with cast wheel hubs, slight marks on roof, in original blue and yellow box.
£300–350 *CSK*

l. A Tri-ang Minic tinplate Green Line coach, excellent condition, with original transfers and Minic Clockwork Toys leaflet.
£190–230 *HOLL*

Cars: Pre-WWII

A Bub lithographed tinplate spring-motor four light limousine, finished in maroon over black, with chauffeur and opening rear doors, faded, one handle missing, c1912, 10½in (26.5cm) long.
£550–650 *CSK*

A Hess 1020 flywheel-driven single seat open tourer, lithographed red and black with white lining, imitation starting handle, driver dressed in brown uniform, mudguards bent, paint flaking on boot, c1920, 8in (20cm) long.
£325–375 *CSK*

A CIJ P2 Alfa Romeo clockwork racing car, finished in blue with black rubber tyres, petrol caps, handbrake and steering to front axle, paintwork scratched, 1930 20½in (52cm) long.
£1,100–1,500 *S(S)*

l. A Distler clockwork lithographed tinplate four door saloon car, registration No. JD 599, orange with light blue detailing, black roof and running board, with chauffeur, good condition, c1930, 6½in (17cm) long.
£450–500 *CSK*

Cars: Post-War

A Japanese painted and lithographed tinplate friction drive Cadillac Convertible, red with yellow and orange chequered seats, paint slightly flaking, small dent, mid-1950s, 10½in (27cm) long.
£200–250 *CSK*

A Japanese painted and lithographed tinplate Buick convertible, with yellow and orange chequered seats, good condition, mid-1950, 11½in (29.5cm) long.
£150–180 *CSK*

A Nomura battery operated Mercedes-Benz 250 SL sports car, red and black, slightly scratched, c1950, 11in (28cm) long.
£225–275 *CSK*

l. A Bandai red and dark blue painted and lithographed tinplate friction drive Ford Pick-Up, No. 353, with 'planked' load area and tailgate, excellent condition, early 1960s, in original box, 12in (30.5cm) long.
£675–800 *CSK*

Trains & Railways

A German carpet train, c1910.
£130–140 *PC*

A 5in gauge coal fired live steam 0-6-0 London, Brighton and South Coast Railway tank locomotive, 'Boxhill', finished in dark green and fawn livery, with twin internal cylinders and tubed boiler.
£1,900–2,400 *S(S)*

A Bing Gauge 0 clockwork 4-4-0 tank locomotive, No. 4201, finished in maroon LMS livery, together with two open wagons, a van and a Bing signal, slight damage.
£350–400 *S(S)*

A scratch built 5in gauge coal fired live steam 4-4-2 locomotive, 'Princess of Wales', No. 2601, finished in Midland maroon livery, with matching eight wheel tender.
£2,200–2,700 *S(S)*

A Bing for Bassett-Lowke clockwork hand painted GNR 0-6-2 condensing tank locomotive, c1922.
£700–800 *CSK*

A Bassett-Lowke clockwork hand painted LMS Mogul 2-6-0 locomotive, and matching six wheel tender, No. 2945, c1939.
£550–650 *CSK*

A Bassett-Lowke three rail electric BR 4-6-2 'Flying Scotsman' locomotive and tender, in experimental blue livery, in original box, c1950.
£1,400–1,800 *CSK*

A Carl Bub 0 gauge train set, c1920, 27in (68.5cm) long.
£85–95 *JUN*

A Bassett-Lowke steam LNER 4-6-0 locomotive and tender, No. 2871, with length of curved track, c1939.
£340–400 *CSK*

A Hornby No. 1 clockwork special
Great Western tank engine,
c1930s, 7in (17.5cm) long.
£150–250 *HAL*

A Rossignol lithographed and embossed
tinplate and lead 0-6-0 carpet train, 'Ouest'
No. 600, 9in (22.5cm) long, and a four wheel
First Class coach No. 554, c1905.
£425–500 *CSK*

l. A Hornby 0 gauge
No. 1 wagon, and
No. 0 and No. 1 milk
traffic vans, all
boxed, c1930s.
£70–80 *HCH*

A Hornby Dublo three rail engine, 'Duchess of
Montrose', with gloss paint, c1950,
12in (30.5cm) long.
£60–80 *HAL*

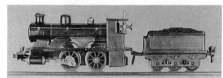

A Märklin painted tinplate
spirit fired LNER 0-4-0
locomotive, with six wheeled
lithographed tender, and bogied
plank wagon, and a Hornby
Series 'Pratts' motor spirit tank
wagon, with accessories.
£425–525 *CSK*

Cross Reference
Railwayana

A collection of Hornby Dublo loose wagons,
c1950–60, 3in (7.5cm) long.
£2–5 each *HAL*

A Märklin live steam hand painted Great
Eastern Railway 0-4-0 tank locomotive,
finished in GER dark blue livery,
damaged, c1905.
£1,800–2,200 *CSK*

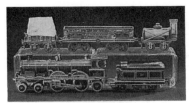

A Märklin gauge 1 electric
4-4-2 locomotive, 'La France',
No. 102, finished in black, with
matching six wheel bogey
tender, four wheel covered
wagon and tanker, with a Bing
bogie wagon, c1906.
£4,800–5,200 *S(S)*

Buildings

A Bing white and
blue painted tinplate
refreshment kiosk,
in original box, c1920s.
£225–275 *CSK*

A Wallworks Unbreakable Iron Toys
express goods train set, in original
wooden box with paper labels, c1900,
box 31in (78.5cm) long.
£400–500 *CSK*

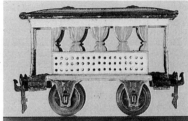

r. A Märklin hand
painted summer coach,
with perforated sides and
curtained windows, some
damage, c1904.
£950–1,200 *CSK*

r. A Märklin gauge 0 electric
4-6-2 locomotive, No.36/12920,
finished in black livery,
with matching eight wheel
bogie tender, and a Märklin
luggage car, minor damage.
£2,500–3,000 *S(S)*

A Bing blue and
white painted
tinplate newspaper
kiosk, c1920s.
£200–250 *CSK*

l. A Doll and Co.
painted tinplate
drinks dispenser
vending machine,
with two glasses
and key, c1930,
5½in (13.5cm) high.
£250–300 *CSK*

TRIBAL ART

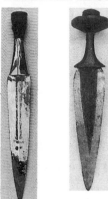

An African short sword, the hardwood grip carved in the form of a human face, decorated with geometric patterns, straight double edged blade with spear point, blade 20½in (52cm).
£275–300 *ASB*

l. An African dagger, probably from the Congo area, with carved hardwood hilt, double edged blade with decorated central portion, slight damage, 19thC, blade 12in (30.5cm).
£120–140 *ASB*

An African dagger, with leather covered wooden pommel and straight double edged blade decorated with punch marks, blade 9in (23cm).
£50–60 *ASB*

A Kissi stone head, with elongated face, open mouth showing the tongue, T-shaped nose, bulging eyes and elongated ears, half face missing, 8½in (22cm) high.
£700–1,000 *S*

An African ritual axe, with wooden stock carved in the form of a chief with a long pointed hat perching on the shoulders of one of his retainers, 24in (61cm) overall.
£140–160 *ASB*

An African knife, with kite-shaped pommel, leather bound grip and straight double edged blade, blade 5½in (14cm).
£50–60 *ASB*

A Greenland Eskimo wooden ice pail, externally decorated with encircling bands of ivory carved plaques in the form of flattened seals, perforated rectangular panels on the rim, and two North American Indian baskets, woven with zig-zag designs, the tallest 12in (30.5cm) high.
£820–875 *S*

A Lega anthropomorphic spoon, the handle in the shape of a man, dark brown patina, 6in (15cm) high.
£500–600 *S*

A Tchokwe comb, the handle incised with geometric designs and surmounted by a seated figure, brown patina, 8in (20cm) high.
£275–300 *S*

A North American argillite pipe, in the shape of a bust form Henry VIII, also decorated with floral motifs, 3½in (9cm) high.
£420–450 *S*

r. A Kissi stone head, with pointed beard, rectangular mouth, arrow-shaped nose, bulging eyes and circular ears, smooth flat forehead, dark grey patina, 5in (12.5cm) high.
£2,000–2,500 *S*

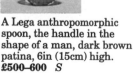

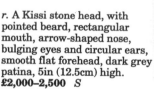

Naga Arts & Crafts

In the years before 1947, the Naga tribes of north east India came to exemplify an exotic society. These people of the hills were different in culture and beliefs from the Hindus of the plains. They were renowned for their fierce resistance to British rule and feared as head-hunters. This practice was suppressed by the British in the early 20thC but recurred during and after WWII. The thousands of small Naga villages perched on isolated hills were extremely varied, with different political systems, languages and racial characteristics. Naga crafts include weaving, dyeing, pottery and wood carving.

A Naga female wooden figure, 19thC, 9½in (24cm) high.
£150–190 *GRG*

A Naga figure with a child, 19thC, 13½in (34cm) high.
£450–500 *GRG*

A Naga basket, decorated with heads, 19thC, 12½in (32cm) high.
£600–650 *GRG*

l. A Naga belt trophy, from Burma, 19thC, 6in (15cm) high.
£100–120 *GRG*

A Naga belt, decorated with shells, 19thC.
£35–40 *GRG*

A Naga woven hat, 19thC.
£220–240 *GRG*

A Naga wooden carving of twin figures, 19thC, 5in (12.5cm) high.
£200–220 *GRG*

A Naga pipe, the bowl carved as a head, 19thC, 6½in (16cm) long.
£70–80 *GRG*

A Naga neckband, made from animals' claws, possibly anteaters, 19thC.
£460–480 *GRG*

Two Naga head-hunting trophies, 19thC, 3in (7.5cm) high.
£85–95 each *GRG*

l. A Naga neck decoration head-hunting trophy, 19thC, 4in (10cm) high.
£150–175 *GRG*

TUNBRIDGE WARE

As the name suggests, Tunbridge Ware was mainly produced in the Tunbridge Wells area of Kent. Small wooden objects, in particular boxes, were lavishly decorated with marquetry, parquetry or pictorial veneers. The image was built-up by glueing together short sticks of different naturally coloured woods, so that the ends formed the pattern. The block would then be sliced transversally, into twenty or thirty identical sheets, making a costly and labour intensive process commercially viable. Some of the more spectacular pieces of Tunbridge Ware produced for the Great Exhibition of 1851 included in excess of one hundred thousand pieces of wood. The craft flourished in the 19thC, when objects showing celebrated views were produced for the souvenir market. Some firms attached paper labels to their products but watch out for 20thC reproduction Tunbridge Ware made between the wars.

A Tunbridge Ware glove box, c1840, 10in (25cm) long.
£350–400 *AMH*

A Tunbridge Ware work box, with view of Tonbridge Castle, c1870, 11in (28cm) wide.
£700–750 *AMH*

A Tunbridge Ware bracelet, c1860, 3in (7.5cm) diam.
£190–220 *AMH*

A Tunbridge Ware paperweight, c1840, 5in (12.5cm) long.
£90–110 *VB*

A Tunbridge Ware box, bearing label 'W. Child's, Brighton', c1844–73, 4½in (11cm) long.
£160–180 *AMH*

A Tunbridge Ware rocker blotter, c1880, 7½in (19cm) long.
£220–240 *AMH*

A Tunbridge Ware inkstand, c1840, 10in (25cm) wide.
£600–675 *AMH*

r. Two Tunbridge Ware taper sticks, c1870.
£60–100 each *VB*

A Tunbridge Ware pencil box, by Edmund Nye, c1850, 9¼in (23.5cm) long.
£320–350 *AMH*

A Tunbridge Ware handkerchief box, decorated with a stag, c1870, 7in (17.5cm) wide.
£225–250 *AMH*

A Tunbridge Ware box, inscribed 'Rye', c1935, 4in (10cm) square.
£70–80 *VB*

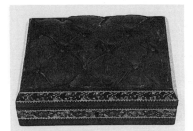

A Tunbridge Ware box, with pincushion top, c1870, 7½in (18.5cm) wide.
£140–160 *AMH*

A Tunbridge Ware inkstand, c1880.
£100–130 *VB*

A Tunbridge Ware coromandel jewellery box, with a view of Bayham Abbey ruins, c1870, 10in (25cm) wide.
£1,000–1,100 *AMH*

Two Tunbridge Ware stamp boxes, with Queen Victoria's head in tesserae, c1850.
£115–130 *VB*

A Tunbridge Ware box, c1870, 2½in (6cm) long.
£60–70 *VB*

l. A Tunbridge Ware box, c1870, 3in (7.5cm) long.
£60–70 *VB*

A Tunbridge Ware perfume bottle box, c1840, 4in (10cm) long.
£130–150 *VB*

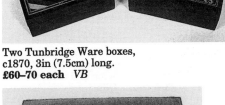

Two Tunbridge Ware boxes, c1870, 3in (7.5cm) long.
£60–70 each *VB*

A Tunbridge Ware pleat holder, by Edmund Nye, c1850, 10in (25cm) wide.
£375–425 *AMH*

WADE

Many readers will remember Wade animals from childhood, when they were popular as party gifts and cheap and cheerful children's collectables. Today Wade collecting has grown into a very adult concern. 'It is not just a hobby, it's an addiction', claims specialist Catherine Barlow. 'Over the past eight years, Wade has become increasingly popular and prices have gone up correspondingly.' At the top end of the market certain pieces can command three figure sums, although you can still pick up Wade Whimsies for about 50p from car boot sales and flea markets. Most enthusiasts begin with these familiar miniatures and then expand – moving backwards in time to seek out Wade ceramics from the 1930s and 40s, and then forwards to collect the limited edition models still being produced today.

A selection of Wade animals, made for Tom Smith's of Norwich Christmas crackers, 1½in (4cm) high.
£2–5 each *CBa*

A set of five Wade dinosaurs, c1933, 2in (5cm) wide.
£7–10 *CBa*

Animals

A Wade dog dish, with a spaniel, 4in (10cm) wide.
£20–25 *CBa*

Two Wade hares, Arthur Hare, 6in (15cm) high.
Blue. **£25–30**
Brown. **£35–40** *CBa*

These were part of a limited edition of 2,000, with the last 200 being made in 1995.

A Wade Happy Family turquoise coloured rabbit set, first edition, 1962–65, 1½in (3.5cm) high.
£40–45 *CBa*

Five different animal sets were made – Hippopotamus, Tiger, Giraffe, Rabbit and Mouse – the Tiger set being the most difficult to find.

A Wade Happy Family rabbit set, blue second edition, c1978–86, 1½in (3.5cm) high.
£12–15 each *CBa*

No tiger sets were made in the 2nd issue.

Two Wade Whoppas, from third set, 1980, 1½ to 2in (3.5 to 5cm) high.
£15–18 each *CBa*

The sets consisted of five animals, the third set being the most difficult to obtain.

l. Two Wade Whoppas, from first set, 1½ to 2in (3.5 to 5cm) high.
£3–5 each *CBa*

A selection of Wade Whimsies land animals, c1984–88, ½in (1.5cm) high.
£2–15 each   *CBa*

A collection of first edition Wade Whimsies, c1953–59, 1½in (3.5cm) high.
£10–100 each   *CBa*

There were 49 animals in a set, the Shire horse and the swan being difficult to obtain.

Birds

A Wade set of swifts, Flying Birds, No. 2, c1956–59, 3½in (8.5cm) wide.
£60–65   *CBa*

A Wade set of swallows, Flying Birds, c1956–59, 3in (7.5cm) wide.
£12–15   *CBa*

These sets were made in four different colours, blue being the most common.

A Wade hen and rooster cruet, made for German Table Ware Co., c1992, 3½ to 4½in (8.5 to 11cm) high.
£20–25   *CBa*

Bowls & Dishes

A Wade Harvest ware dish, c1947, 4in (10cm) long.
£10–12   *CBa*

A Wade butter dish, c1938–50, 5in (12.5cm) diam.
£25–30   *CBa*

A Wade poppy head bowl, c1950s, 3½in (8.5cm) diam.
£20–25   *CBa*

Buildings

A set of Wade Coronation Street houses, made for Granada TV Studios tours, c1988–89, 1½in (3.5cm) high.
£25–30   *CBa*

A Wade Whimsie In the Vale set No. 1, c1993, 1in (3cm) high.
£30–35   *CBa*

A Wade Whimsie In the Vale set No. 2, c1993, 1in (3cm) high.
£30–35   *CBa*

Disney

A Wade Donald Duck plate, cup and saucer set, c1935, plate 5in (12.5cm) diam.
£30–35 *CBa*

Door Plates

Three Wade door plates, c1960s, 4in (10cm) high.
£20–22 each *CBa*

Wade Collectors Club, Established 1989, SAE to: Mrs. C. Barlow, 14 Windsor Road, Selston, Nottingham NG16 6JJ
Telephone: 01773 860933

Three Wade figures, stamped 'My Fair Ladies', part of a set of four, c1991–92, 6¼in (16cm) high.
£100–120 each *CBa*

l. Two Wade Andy Capp figures, one with a cigarette, c1994.
£20–25 each *CBa*

Figures

A Wade figure, 'Jeanette', c1936, minor paint loss, 6in (15cm) high.
£180–220 *BKK*

A Wade figure of a butcher, c1948–58, 3½in (8.5cm) high.
£150–160 *CBa*

A Wade figure of a lady, c1927–37, 5½in (14cm) high.
£60–70 *CBa*

A Wade figure of Robin Hood, c1989, and Maid Marion, c1990, both 3in (7.5cm) high.
£15–18 each *CBa*

When completed, this will be a set of five figures.

A Wade nursery rhyme figure, 'Little Bo Peep', made for Trebor Sharps Easter eggs, c1970–71, 2½in (6cm) high.
£15–18 *CBa*

A Wade figure of a deep sea diver and a snail, part of an aquarium set of five, c1975–80, diver 3in (7.5cm) high.
Diver. **£10–12**
Snail. **£35–38** *CBa*

Five Wade figures, stamped 'My Fair Ladies', c1990–92, 3½in (8.5cm) high.
£10–45 each *CBa*

A set of twenty-four Wade nursery miniatures, made for Red Rose Tea in Canada, 1971–79, 1½in (4cm) high.
£2–30 each *CBa*

Irish Wade

Four Irish Wade character figures, part of a set of 9, c1970–86, 3½in (8.5cm) high.
£10–30 each *CBa*

An Irish Wade leprachaun, 3in (7.5cm) high.
£15–18 *CBa*

Two Irish Wade leprachauns, a cobbler and a tailor, c1956–86.
£3–5 each *CBa*

Money Boxes

A Wade money box, in the form of a dog kennel, c1987, 5½in (14cm) long.
£12–15 *CBa*

A Wade panda money box, a limited edition for National Westminster Bank customers under 7 years old, c1989.
£25–30 *CBa*

> **Miller's is a price GUIDE not a price LIST**

l. A Wade Peter polar bear money box, made for Thornton's toffee, c1988, 5½in (14cm) high.
£15–18 *CBa*

Teapots

A Wade Harvest ware pattern teapot, c1947, 5in (12.5cm) high.
£35–40 *CBa*

A Wade teapot, c1953–55, 8½in (21cm) high.
£80–100 *CBa*

WALKING STICKS

Walking sticks have provided endless opportunities for craftsmen to exercise their skill and imagination. Sticks were hollowed-out to contain glass drinking flasks, rapiers or even poachers' guns. Handles could conceal anything from watches to snuff boxes. Among the most collectable walking sticks are those with finely modelled animals' head grips – dogs were particularly popular in the Victorian period, and remain so today. At the turn of the century, walking sticks were produced in the form of golf clubs, many of which started life as actual golf clubs. These may have been made as training pieces by apprentice club makers and then transformed into walking sticks.

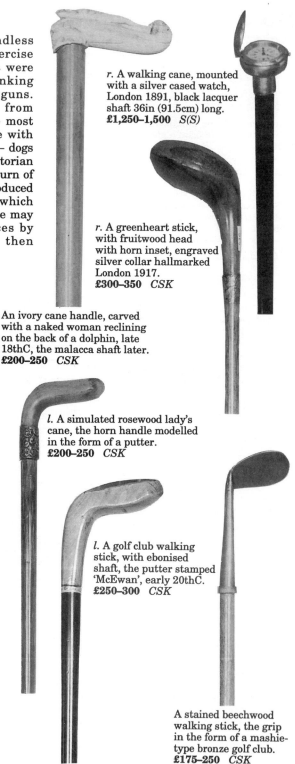

r. A walking cane, mounted with a silver cased watch, London 1891, black lacquer shaft 36in (91.5cm) long.
£1,250–1,500 *S(S)*

r. A greenheart stick, with fruitwood head with horn inset, engraved silver collar hallmarked London 1917.
£300–350 *CSK*

An ivory cane handle, carved with a naked woman reclining on the back of a dolphin, late 18thC, the malacca shaft later.
£200–250 *CSK*

l. A simulated rosewood lady's cane, the horn handle modelled in the form of a putter.
£200–250 *CSK*

l. A golf club walking stick, with ebonised shaft, the putter stamped 'McEwan', early 20thC.
£250–300 *CSK*

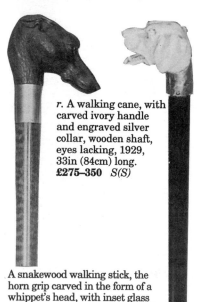

r. A walking cane, with carved ivory handle and engraved silver collar, wooden shaft, eyes lacking, 1929, 33in (84cm) long.
£275–350 *S(S)*

A snakewood walking stick, the horn grip carved in the form of a whippet's head, with inset glass eyes and white metal collar.
£450–550 *CSK*

l. A walking cane, with carved ivory handle of a whippet's head, engraved metal collar, on a lacquered shaft, one eye repaired, dated '1895', 36½in (93cm) long.
£275–325 *S(S)*

A stained beechwood walking stick, the grip in the form of a mashie-type bronze golf club.
£175–250 *CSK*

WOOD
Animals & Birds

A Swiss carved wood bear,
c1890, 7in (17.5cm) long.
£80–100 *DUN*

A pair of carved wood
elephants, 8in (20cm) high.
£20–25 *LF*

r. Three wall hanging painted
wood ducks, 1950s.
£15–25 *WAB*

A Russian cuckoo caller, 19thC,
6½in (16.5cm) high.
£50–65 *SHA*

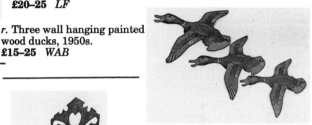

Boxes

A Victorian sewing box, inlaid with
mother-of-pearl, 10½in (26.5cm) wide.
£100–165 *AnE*

A birch ply flour box.
£40–60 *BRD*

A painted pine money box,
19thC, 11in (28cm) wide.
£60–70 *AnE*

An oak and mahogany
banded salt box, early
19thC, 20in (51cm) high.
£150–175 *WIL*

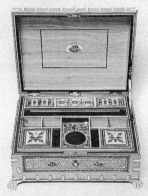

An Oriental sandalwood box,
inlaid with ivory, 19thC,
10in (25cm) wide.
£175–220 *AnE*

A walnut box, c1840,
7in (17.5cm) wide.
£80–100 *DUN*

Snuff Boxes & Shoes

A walnut and bone snuff shoe,
19thC, 3½in (8.5cm) long.
£155–175 *JCr*

A wood and bone snuff shoe,
4½in (11cm) long.
£100–175 *JCr*

A walnut snuff shoe, named and studded on the base, 19thC, 5½in (13.5cm) long.
£200–275 *JCr*

A pair of wooden snuff shoes, mid-19thC, 5in (12.5cm) long.
£550–700 *JCr*

A Continental carved wood snuff shoe, 19thC, 5in (12.5cm) long.
£200–250 *JCr*

A mahogany studded snuff shoe, with toe and heel caps, 19thC, 4in (11cm) long.
£170–200 *JCr*

A pair of Continental carved wooden snuff shoes, 19thC, 3½in (8.5cm) long.
£250–300 *JCr*

A sycamore snuff box, 18thC.
£50–55 *BRD*

A figured walnut snuff shoe, 19thC, 6in (15cm) long.
£400–500 *JCr*

A Continental carved wood and ivory snuff shoe, 3½in (8.5cm) long.
£150–170 *JCr*

A Continental oak and ivory snuff shoe, 19thC, 7in (17.5cm) long.
£230–330 *JCr*

A Continental carved wooden snuff shoe, 4½in (11cm) long.
£150–170 *JCr*

Tea Caddies

A carved wood tea caddy, c1870, 4in (10cm) high.
£80–100 *DUN*

r. A Regency mahogany tea caddy, with inlaid conch shell decoration, 7½in (18.5cm) wide.
£100–125 *WIL*

A George II Cuban mahogany tea caddy, with secret spoon drawer, c1760, 9in (23cm) wide.
£250–350 *AnE*

A Victorian coromandel tea caddy, 8in (20cm) wide.
£75–100 *AnE*

A pen work tea caddy, decorated with a picture of Melrose Abbey, inscribed, c1835, 9in (23cm) wide.
£1,200–1,500 *LBL*

A Regency mahogany tea caddy, 12in (31.5cm) wide.
£130–140 *SHA*

l. A walnut domed top tea caddy, with brass mounts, c1840–50, 9in (22.5cm) wide.
£200–300 *AnE*

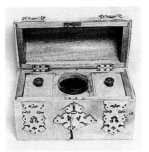

A Victorian satin birch tea caddy, in the manner of Pugin, c1860, 11in (28cm) wide.
£100–145 *SHA*

Treen

A late Victorian mahogany lazy Susan, 15in (38cm) diam.
£160–200 *WIL*

A carved and engine turned lignum vitae inkwell, 19thC.
£95–125 *BRD*

l. A treen wool winder, 19thC, 11in (28cm).
£30–35 *SHA*

> **Cross Reference**
> Boer War Memorabilia

l. A selection of treen pieces, made by prisoners of the Boer War, 1901.
Boxes and small treen items.
£35–60
Circular tobacco jar, with lid.
£90–100
A carved and inscribed gun.
£110–120 *OO*

Miscellaneous

A Victorian elm bread board,
12in (30.5cm).
£30–60 *TAR*

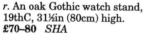

Cross Reference
Kitchenalia

A carved oak quill stand, in the
form of a Pilgrim Father, 3½in
(8.5cm) high.
£40–45 *SHA*

r. An oak Gothic watch stand,
19thC, 31½in (80cm) high.
£70–80 *SHA*

A teak clock stand, inlaid with
mother-of-pearl, with French
movement, inscribed and dated
'1894', 25in (63.5cm) high.
£600–800 *TAR*

A carved oak table cabinet for cigars,
19thC, 21½in (54cm) wide.
£375–400 *SHA*

MAKE THE MOST OF MILLERS

Condition is absolutely vital when
assessing the value of any item.
Damaged pieces appreciate much
less than perfect examples. However,
a rare, desirable piece may command
a high price even when damaged.

l. A south Indian teak figure of
a young girl from Kerela, early
19thC, 12½in (31.5cm).
£100–125 *SHA*

A Georgian wooden powder
flask, 7in (17.5cm) high.
£80–100 *SHA*

An oak Arts & Crafts carved
fire screen, 28½in (72.5cm) high.
£145–155 *SHA*

A lignum vitae sailmaker's fid,
19thC, 30in (76cm) high.
£100–135 *SHA*

A pair of carved oak griffins,
19thC, 9in (23cm) high).
£85–95 *SHA*

WRITING

The market for writing collectables is strong, with many serious collectors of fountain pens and related material. The fountain pen was first commercially developed in America in 1884 by Lewis Waterman, a salesman who had lost a commission when his pen leaked ink all over an important document, literally 'blotting his copybook'. Americans George S. Parker and Mabie Todd were working on pens at this time, and in 1901, another American, Roy Conklin, devised the innersack to suck up the ink. Pens had previously been filled with droppers or syringes.

Although pre-1945 pens are particularly desirable, rarity is far more important than age. Condition is another key factor as pens can be expensive to restore. Unusual ballpoints can command high prices, as can vintage propelling pencils.

Inkwells

An olive wood inkwell, in the form of a camel, 5in (12.5cm) wide.
£50–80 *ARE*

A late Victorian ink pot, in the form of a horse's hoof, with hinged plated mount, 3in (7.5cm) high.
£80–110 *WIL*

A metal inkwell, by Messenger & Sons, Birmingham, c1850, 6in (15cm) high.
£450–550 *ARE*

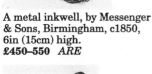

A pair of Victorian cut glass inkwells, with brass mounts 3in (7.5cm) high.
£120–140 *DEL*

A Victorian glass inkwell, with brass mount, 3½in (9cm) high.
£60–80 *DEL*

l. A glass inkwell, with a silver top, London 1890, 5in (12.5cm) high.
£450–500 *MJW*

A spelter and wood inkwell, c1880, 7in (17.5cm) high.
£300–400 *ARE*

l. A Victorian cut glass inkwell, with brass mount, 3½in (9cm) high.
£60–80 *DEL*

Two brass topped inkwells.
£20–30 each *VB*

Letter Openers

Pens & Pencils

A bronze letter opener, by Jules Moigniez, in the form of a pheasant's head holding a tail feather, signed, with a detachable seal on one end, 19thC, 15in (38cm) long, in original simulated crocodile case.
£550–650 *B*

A French blonde tortoiseshell paperknife, the blade set with marcasite, garnets and rubies in silver and gold garlands, inscribed with 'A Vous', 8in (20cm) long.
£175–225 *S(S)*

A Sharp's Toffee polished aluminium advertising paperknife, c1930, 7½in (19cm) long.
£16–18 *CSA*

A white metal and porcupine quill triple extending pencil, by S. Mordan & Co.
£90–120 *CSK*

A white metal quadruple slide action pen and pencil, by S. Mordan & Co.
£90–120 *CSK*

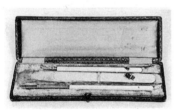

An ivory pen set, with models of insects, one missing, c1880, in original case, 8in (20cm) wide.
£300–400 *ARE*

l. A silver gilt quill pen, by J. J., London 1811, 9in (23cm) long.
£850–950 *AMH*

A display box, containing Chambers King Size 'Queen Elizabeth' souvenir pencils, c1950, 7½in (19cm) wide.
£2–3 each *COB*

A novelty slide-action pencil, with matching toothpick, in the form of a pair of duelling pistols, with foliate stamped and engraved butts, each barrel engraved 'S. Mordan, July 6th 1840', in a fitted case.
£400–500 *CSK*

l. Two Victorian hazelnut and shell propelling pencils.
£16–20 each *VB*

Fountain Pens

A Swan leverless
lady's pen, 18ct gold,
with line decoration,
London 1938.
£150–200 *S(S)*

A Conklin silver
grey Nozac
demonstration pen,
with Conklin
Cushion point nib.
£120–150 *CSK*

l. A brown striped
Mont Blanc 242
pen, with 140 nib.
£160–200 *CSK*

r. A green striped
Mont Blanc 144-G
Masterpiece, with
4810 nib.
£320–400 *CSK*

r. A Namiki Maki-E
lacquer and
mother-of-pearl
lady's pen,
decorated with a
design of round fans,
with a yellow metal
cap band, nib broken.
£400–500 *CSK*

l. A Namiki Maki-E
lacquer lady's pen,
decorated with a
heron perched on
a willow bough,
with Namiki
No. 2 nib, in
original Yamanaka
& Co. case.
£900–1,000 *CSK*

l. A Platignum Maki-E
lacquer pen, with
lever-filler, decorated
with dragons and clouds.
£400–450 *CSK*

r. A Pelikan
Tortoiseshell 140
pen, with black
ends and Pelikan nib.
£180–220 *CSK*

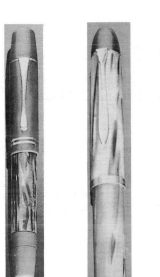

A Pelikan
Tortoiseshell
100N pen, with
brown ends
and cap, with
Pelikan nib.
£180–220 *CSK*

l. A Pelikan
Tortoiseshell DRP
pen, with brown
ends and cap, with
Pelikan nib.
£210–260 *CSK*

A Namiki Maki-E
lacquer lady's pen
decorated with
flowering lilies,
with Namiki No. 2
nib, and yellow
metal cap band.
£425–500 *CSK*

Scales

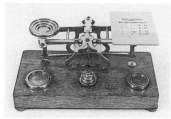

A set of letter scales, by
S. Mordan & Co., c1880,
9½in (24cm) wide.
£200–225 *AMH*

A set of letter scales, with brass
pans and weights, by S. Mordan
& Co, c1880, 11in (28cm) wide.
£250–270 *AMH*

Stationery Boxes

A coromandel stationery box,
late 19thC, 6in (15cm) high.
£120–140 *WIL*

Writing Slopes

A rosewood writing slope,
c1830, 18in (46cm) wide)
£250–275 *SHA*

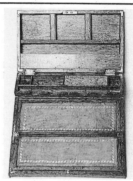

A walnut and brass banded
letter box, late 19thC, 9½in
(24cm) wide.
£150–200 *AnE*

A palm wood writing slope,
19thC, 16½in (42cm) wide.
£200–275 *AnE*

Miscellaneous

A brass letter clip, in the
form of a tennis racket,
c1880, 8in (20cm) wide.
£120–150 *DUN*

A stamp vending
machine, early 1970s,
24in (61cm) high.
£650–850 *BHE*

A pedestal letter box, c1960.
£750–950 *BHE*

COLLECTABLES UNDER £5

You don't need to be a millionaire to be a collector. The following section provides an illustration of collectables that can be purchased for under £5. Car boot sales and charity shops can provide endless opportunities for the eagle-eyed bargain hunter and many antique shops will have bargain bins of cheap or slightly damaged objects. At pocket money prices, many of these collectables could appeal to children.

Two Walt Disney badges, Donald Duck and Minnie Mouse, and a Mobil badge.
£1–2.50 each *COL*

Two button badges, advertising Bisto and Murraymints, 1950s.
£1–2 each *COL*

Badges & Pins

A selection of Butlin's badges, c1950s and '60s.
£1–2 each *PC*

Four metal badges, 20thC.
£1–5 each *CMF*

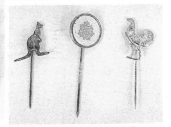

Three stick pins, 20thC:
l. Australia.
c. British Amateur Athletics.
r. The Courage cockerel.
£1–2 each *COL*

Books

Enid Blyton, *Five Go To Smuggler's Top*, The fourth adventure of the Famous Five, 1969.
£3–5 *BAf*

Three Ladybird children's books, c1960s.
£1–2 each *PC*

Cigarette Silks

A set of two cigarette silks, 1912.
£4–5 each *COL*

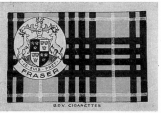

Cigarette silks, by BDV Cigarettes, issued 1922.
£4–4.50 each *COL*

l. Two cigarette silks, depicting No. 63 GP Territorial badges, and The Durham Light Infantry, 68th & 106th Foot.
£1–2 each *COL*

r. Tenth Series cigarette silks, issued 1915.
£1–1.50 each *COL*

Cruets

A toothpaste tube cruet,
3in (7.5cm) high.
£3–5 *WP*

A cruet in the shape of
a car, 4½in (11cm) wide.
£4–5 *PC*

A ham sandwich cruet,
3½in (9cm) wide.
£3–6 *PC*

A bumper car cruet, 3½in (9cm) wide.
£3–5 *WP*

A black and white cat cruet,
c1950s, 4½in (11cm) high.
£4–5 *PC*

A metal radiator cruet,
2in (5cm) wide.
£3–4 *PC*

Dolls' & Dolls' House Accessories

A Ken Roy Wringerette dolls'
mangle, with rubber feet,
c1959, 14in (35.5cm) wide.
£4–5 *HAC*

A doll's house table and chair,
table 4in (10cm) wide.
£4–5 each *SP*

Ephemera

A 'Race of Champions' Brands
Hatch programme, 1975.
£1–2 *PC*

A selection of key rings,
depicting bank notes,
c1980s and 90s.
£1–2 each *WP*

l. A selection of
Polly Pocket
miniature dolls and
accessories, 1990.
£3–5 each *HW*

A selection of hotel labels,
c1940s and '50s.
£2–5 each *COB*

Film & TV Related Toys

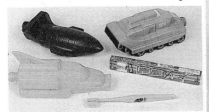

A selection of Thunderbirds and Captain Scarlet bubble bath bottles and toothbrushes.
£1–3 each *PC*

l. A collection of *Flintstones* sweet containers, note pad and pencil case, 1994.
75p–£1.65 each *PC*

Three *Jurassic Park* dinosaurs c1990.
£3–8 each *PC*

A selection of Tin Tin toys, stamped 'Hergé Bully'.
£3–4 each *PC*

Miscellaneous

A collection of promotional lead figures, made for Cadbury's by W. Britain, pre-WWII, 1½in (4cm) high.
£4–5 each *HAL*

Three bubble bath containers, The Snowman, Mickey Mouse, and Mr Blobby, 1993.
£1–3 each *PC*

A metal Magic Roundabout waste paper basket, c1971.
£4–5 *CMF*

Three Sainsbury's potted meat and paste pots, c1910, largest 3in (7.5cm) high.
£4–5 each *AL*

A Cornish serpentine lighthouse, 4in (10cm) high.
£4–5 *VB*

A 'Keep Saving' money box, with padlock and key, 7in (17.5cm) high.
£1–2 *HAC*

A collection of ceramic Coca-Cola magnets.
£1–5 each *COB*

A selection of Matchbox, Corgi and Dinky toys, all damaged, ½ to 4in (6.5 to 10cm) long.
50p–£4 each *HAL*

DIRECTORY OF SPECIALISTS

(A) Auctioneers
(A&A) Arms & Armour
(A&C) Arts & Crafts
(A&M) Arms & Militaria
(AD) Art Deco
(ADC) Art Deco Ceramics
(ADJ) Art Deco Jewellery
(Ae) Aeronautica
(AN) Art Nouveau
(Au) Automobilia
(B) Boxes
(Ba) Barometers
(BC) Baby Carriages
(BH) Button Hooks
(Bk) Books
(BM) Beer Mats
(Bot) Bottles
(BP) Baxter Prints
(Bu) Buttons
(C) Costume
(Ca) Cameras
(CaC) Card Cases
(CC) Cigarette Cards
(Ce) Ceramics
(Co) Comics
(Cns) Coins
(Col) Collectables

(Com) Commemorative
(Cor) Corkscrews
(D) Doulton
(DH) Dolls Houses
(DHF) Dolls House
    Furniture
(Do) Dolls
(DS) Display Stands
(E) Ephemera
(F) Fishing
(Fa) Fans
(G&CC) Goss & Crested
    China
(G) Glass
(Ga) Games
(GC) Greeting Cards
(Go) Golfing
(Gr) Gramophones
(H/HP) Hairdressing &
    Hat Pins
(I) Inkwells
(J) Jewellery
(Ju) Jukeboxes
(K), Kitchenalia
(L&K) Locks & Keys
(L&L) Linen & Lace
(LB) Le Blond Prints

(M) Metalware
(Ma) Matchboxes
(MB) Money Boxes
(Me) Medals
(MP) Moorcroft Pottery
(O) Oriental
(OAM) Old Amusement
    Machines
(OP) Oriental Porcelain
(P) Pottery
(Pa) Paperweights
(PaM) Paper Money
(PB) Perfume Bottles
(PF) Photograph Frames
(PH) Props Hire
(Pia) Pianolas
(PL) Pot Lids
(PM) Papier Mâché
(PMem) Police
    Memorabilia
(Po) Postcards
(R) Radios
(R&C) Rugs & Carpets
(Ra) Railwayana
(RB) Reference Books)
(Re) Records
(RH) Rocking Horses

(S) Silver
(S&MI) Scientific &
    Medical Instruments
(SC) Scottish
    Collectables (Scr)
Scripophily
(Sew) Sewing
(Sh) Shipping
(SP) Staffordshire
    Pottery (Sp) Sporting
(St) Stereoscopes
(T&MS) Tins & Metal
    Signs
(T) Textiles
(Ta) Tartanware
(TB) Teddy Bears
(Te) Telephones
(Ti) Tiles
(To) Toys
(TP) Torquay Pottery
(Tr) Treen
(TW) Tunbridge Ware
(TV) Televisions
(TVCol) TV Collectables
(W) Watches
(Wr) Writing
(WS) Walking Sticks

London

A. J. Partners (Shelley),
J28 Gray's-in-the-Mews,
1-7 Davies Mews, W1Y 1AR.
Tel: 0171-629 7034/723 5363
(ADC)

Abstract,
Kensington Church Street
Antique Centre, 58-60
Kensington Church Street,
W8 4DB.
Tel: 0171-376 2652
(ADJ)

Academy Costumes Ltd.
(Hire only),
50 Rushworth Street, SE1
0RB.
Tel: 0171-620 0771
(T, C)

Act One Hire Ltd.,
2a Scampston Mews,
Cambridge Gardens, W10.
Tel: 0181-960 1456/1494
(T, C)

Andrews, Frank,
10 Vincent Road,
N22 6NA.
Tel: 0181-889 3445
(G)

Antique Textile Company,
PO Box 2800, N1.
Tel: 0171-254 3256
(T, C)

Anything American,
33-35 Duddenhill Lane,
NW10.
Tel: 0181-451 0320
(Ju)

Baddiel, Colin,
Gray's Mews,
1-7 Davies Mews, W1Y 1AR.
Tel: 0171-408 1239/
0181-452 7243
(T)

Baddiel, Sarah,
The Book Gallery,
B12 Gray's Mews,
1-7 Davies Mews,
W1Y 1AR.
Tel: 0171-408 1239/
0181-452 7243
(Go)

Baldwin, A.H. & Sons Ltd.,
11 Adelphi Terrace,
WC2N 6BJ.
Tel: 0171 9306879/8391310
(Cns, Com, Me)

Bangs, Christopher,
P O Box 662,
SW11.3DG.
(By appointment only)
Tel: 0171-223 5676
(M)

Barham Antiques,
83 Portobello Road,
W11 2QB.
Tel: 0171-727 3845
(B)

Beverley & Beth,
30 Church Street,
NW8 8EP.
Tel: 0171-262 1576
(AD, Gl)

Boston, Nicolaus,
Kensington Church Street
Antiques Centre,
58-60 Kensington Church
Street, W8 4DB.
Tel: 0171-376 0425
(P)

Bridge, Christine,
78 Castelnau, SW13 9EX.
Tel: 0181-741 5501
(G)

British Commemoratives,
1st Floor,
Georgian Village,
Camden Passage, N1 8DU.
Tel: 0171-359 4560
(Com, G&CC)

Brittania, Stand 101,
Gray's Antique Market,
58 Davies Street,
W1Y 1LB.
Tel: 0171-629 6772
(D)

Button Queen,
19 Marylebone Lane,
W1M 5FF.
Tel: 0171-935 1505
(Bu)

Cameron, Jasmin,
Stand J6,
Antiquarius,
131-141 King's Road,
SW3 5ST.
Tel: 0171-351 4154
(Wr)

Capon, Patrick,
350 Upper Street,
Islington, N1.
Tel: 0171-354 0487/
0181-467 5722
(Ba)

Casimir, Jack, Ltd.,
The Brass Shop,
23 Pembridge Road,
W11 3HG.
Tel: 0171-727 8643
(M)

Cekay Antiques,
Gray's Antique Market,
58 Davies Street,
W1Y 1LB.
Tel: 0171-629 5130
(WS)

Chenil Galleries,
King's Road,
Chelsea, SW3.
Tel: 0171-351 5353
(T, C)

Christie's
(South Kensington) Ltd.,
85 Old Brompton Road,
London SW7 3LD.
0171 581 7611
(A)

Clark, Gerald, Antiques,
1 High Street,
Mill Hill Village,
NW7.
Tel: 0181-906 0342
(SP)

Classic Collection,
Pied Bull Yard,
Bury Place, WC1A 2JR.
Tel: 0171-831 6000
(Ca)

Classic Costumes Ltd.,
Tel: 081-764 8858/
0171-620 0771
(T, C)

Collector, The,
9 Church Street,
NW8 8DT.
Tel: 0171-706 4586
(D)

Coronets & Crowns,
Unit J12,
Gray's-in-the-Mews,
1-7 Davies Mews,
W1Y 1AR
Tel: 0171 493 3448
(Com)

Cropper, Stuart,
Gray's-in-the-Mews,
1-7 Davies Mews,
W1Y 1AR.
Tel: 0171-629 7034
(To)

David, 141 Gray's Antique
Market, Davies Street,
W1Y 1LB.
Tel: 0171-493 0208
(Cor, K, PMem)

De Fresne, Pierre,
'Beaux Bijoux',
Q9/10 Antiquarius,
135 King's Road, SW3 5ST.
Tel: 0171-352 8882
(ADJ)

Decodence (Bakelite)
(Gad Sassower), Shop 13,
The Mall,
Camden Passage, N1.
Tel: 0171-354 4473
(AD)

Dollyland, 864 Green
Lanes, Winchmore Hill,
N21 2RS.
Tel: 0181-360 1053
(Do)

Donay, 35 Camden
Passage, N1.
Tel: 0171-359 1880
(Ga)

Donohoe, L25/7, M10/12
Gray's Mews,
1-7 Davies Mews,
W1Y 1AR.
Tel: 0171-629 5633/
0181-455 5507
(S)

East Gates Antiques,
Stand G006,
Alfie's Antique Market,
13-25 Church Street,
NW8 8DT.
Tel: 0171-724 5650
(G)

Eureka Antiques,
Geoffrey Vanns Arcade,
105 Portobello Road, W11.
(Saturdays)
(Ta, CaC, J)

Fobbister, Rosemary,
Stand 28,
The Chelsea Antique
Market,
245-263 King's Road,
SW3 5HD.
Tel: 0171-352 5581
(PM)

Gallery of Antique
Costume & Textiles,
2 Church Street,
Marylebone, NW8 8ED.
Tel: 0171-723 9981
(T, C)

Gee, Rob,
Flea Market,
Camden Passage, N1.
Tel: 0171-226 6627
(Bot, PL)

Georgian Village,
First Floor,
Islington Green, N1.
Tel: 0171-226 1571/5393
(Bot)

German, Michael,
38B Kensington Church
Street, W8 4BX.
Tel: 0171-937 2771
(A&A, WS)

Goldsmith & Perris,
Stand 327, Alfie's Antique
Market, 13-25 Church
Street, NW8 8DT.
Tel: 0171-724 7051
(S)

Gosh Comics, 39 Great
Russell Street, WC1.
Tel: 0171-636 1011
(Co)

Harbottle, Patricia,
Geoffrey Vann Arcade,
107 Portobello Road, W11.
(Saturdays)
Tel: 0171-731 1972
(Cor)

Harrington Bros., The
Chelsea Antique Market,
253 King's Road, SW3 5EL.
Tel: 0171-352 1720
(Bk)

Hayman & Hayman,
M15 & L3 Antiquarius,
135 King's Road, SW3.
Tel: 0171-351 6563
(PF) (PB)

Heather's Teddys,
World Famous Arcade,
177 Portobello Road, W11.
Tel: 0181-204 0106
(TB)

Hebbs, Pam,
5 The Annexe,
Camden Passage, N1.
(TB)

Hogg, David, S141,
Gray's Antique Market,
Davies St., W1Y 1LB.
Tel: 0171-493 0208
(BH)

Horne, Jonathan,
66B & C Kensington
Church Street, W8.
Tel: 0171-221 5658
(SP)

Howard, Derek,
Chelsea Antique Market,
245-253 King's Road,
SW3 5HD.
Tel: 0171-352 4113
(S&MI)

Howard, Valerie,
2 Camden Street,
off Kensington Church
Street, W8
Tel: 0171-792 9702
(P)

Ilse Antiques,
30-32 The Vaults,
The Georgian Village,
Islington, N1.
(Ti)

Jaertelius, Monica, The
Mall, Camden Passage, N1.
Tel: 0181-546 2807
(Bu)

Jag, Unit 11, Kensington
Church Street Antiques
Centre, 58-60 Kensington
Church Street, W8 4DB.
Tel: 0171-938 4404
(ADC)

Jessops, 65 Great Russell
Street, WC1.
Tel: 0171-831 3640
(Ca)

Keith, Old Advertising,
Unit 14, 155a Northcote
Road, Battersea, SW11.
Tel: 0171-228 0741/6850
(T&MS)

King & Country, Unit 46,
Alfie's Antique Market,
13-25 Church Street,
NW8 8DT.
Tel: 0171-724 3439
(Go)

Langham, Marion, J30/31
Grays Mews, Davies
Mews, W1Y 1AR
Tel: 0171-6292511/7301002
(Ce, Pa)

Lassalle, Judith,
7 Pierrepont Arcade,
Camden Passage, N1.
Tel: 0171-607 7121
(Wed & Sat)
(RH)

Latford, Cliff, G006,
Alfie's Antique Market,
13-25 Church Street,
NW8 8DT.
Tel: 0171-724 5650, and at

Colchester
Tel: 01206 564474
(Ca)

London Silver Vaults,
Chancery House,
53-65 Chancery Lane, WC2.
Tel: 0171-242 3844
(S)

Memories,
18 Bell Lane,
Hendon, NW4.
Tel: 0181-203 1772/202 9080
(Po)

Miller, Jess,
PO Box 1461, W6.
Tel: 0181-748 9314
(F)

Moderne, Stand 5,
Georgian Village,
Camden Passage, N1.
(Bu)

Monica.
Tel: 0171-354 3125
(J)

Murray Cards
(International) Ltd.,
51 Watford Way,
Hendon Central,
NW4 3JH.
Tel: 0181-202 5688
(E, CC)

New Century Art Pottery,
69 Kensington Church
Street, W8 4DB.
Tel: 0171-376 2810
(ADC)

Noelle Antiques,
S26 Chelsea Antiques
Market, 253 King's Road,
SW3 5EL
Tel: 0171-352 5581
(BH)

Norman, Sue,
Stand L4 Antiquarius,
135 King's Road, SW3 5ST.
Tel: 0171-352 7217
(C)

Old Amusement Machines,
Tel: 0181-889 2213/
01782 680667
(OAM)

Oosthuizen, Jacqueline
First Floor,
Georgian Village,
Camden Passage, N1.
Tel: 0171-226 5393
and
23 Cale Street, SW3.
Tel: 0171-352 6071
(SP, TP)

Oosthuizen, Pieter G. K.,
1st Floor,
Georgian Village,
Camden Passage, N1.
Tel: 0171-359 3322
(A&M)

Ormonde Gallery,
156 Portobello Road, W11.
Tel: 0171-229 9800/
01424 82 226
(O)

Past and Present Toys,
862 Green Lanes,
Winchmore Hill, N21.
Tel: 0181-364 1370
(TB, To)

Past and Present,
York Arcade, Unit 5,
Camden Passage, N1.
Tel: 0171-833 2640
(ADC)

Pieces of Time,
Gray's Mews,
1-7 Davies Street,
W1Y 1AR.
Tel: 0171-629 2422
(W)

Pinchin, Doug,
Dixon's Antique Centre,
471 Upper Richmond Road
West, East Sheen, SW14
Tel: 0181-878 6788/948
1029
(D)

Powell, Sylvia,
Decorative Arts,
18 The Mall,
Camden Passage, N1 0EL.
Tel: 0171-354 2977
(Ce)

Pleasures of Past Times,
11 Cecil Court,
Charing Cross Road, WC2.
Tel: 0171-836 1142
(Bk, GC)

The Purple Shop,
Antiquarius,
135 King's Road, SW3.
Tel: 0171 352 1127
(J)

Relic Antiques,
248 Camden High Street,
NW1.
Tel: 0171-485 8072
(K)

Reubens,
44 Honor Oak Park,
Brockley, SE23.
Tel: 0181-291 1786
(S&MI)

Rotation Antiques,
Pierrepont Row
Fleamarket,
Camden Passage, N1.
Tel: 0171-226 8211
(ADC)

Rumours,
10 The Mall,
Upper Street, Camden
Passage, N1 0PD.
Tel: 01582 873561/
0836 277274
(MP)

Scripophily Shop,
Britannia Hotel,
Grosvenor Square,
W1A 3AN.
Tel: 0171-495 0580
(Scr)

Stateside Comics plc,
125 East Barnet Road, N4
Tel: 0181-449 5535
(Co)

Studio & TV Hire,
3 Ariel Way, Wood Lane,
White City, W12 7SL.
Tel: 0181-749 3445
(PH)

Thimble Society of London,
The Bees, S134 Gray's
Antique Market,
58 Davies Street,
W1Y 1LB.
Tel: 0171-493 0560
(Sew)

Top Ten Comics,
9-12 St Anne's Court,
Soho, W1.
Tel: 0171-734 7388
(Co)

Trio (Theresa Clayton).
Gray's Mews,
1-7 Davies Mews,
W1Y 1AR
Tel: 0171-629 1184
(PB)

Ursula, P16, 15 & 14,
Antiquarius,
135 King's Road,
SW3 5ST.
Tel: 0171-352 2203
(H/HP)

Vintage Cameras Ltd.,
254 & 256 Kirkdale,
Sydenham, SE26.
Tel: 0181-778 5416/5841
(Ca)

Walker, Pat,
Georgian Village,
Camden Passage, N1.
Tel: 0171-359 4560/
435 3159
(Do)

West, Mark J.,
Cobb Antiques,
39B High Street,
Wimbledon Village, SW19.
Tel: 0181-946 2811/
540 7982
(G)

Weston, David, Ltd.
44 Duke Street St James's,
SW1.
Tel: 0171-839 1051/2/3
(S&MI)

White, John,
Alfie's Antique Market,
13-25 Church Street,
NW8 8DT.
Tel: 0171-723 0449
(ADC)

Wynyards Antiques,
5 Ladbroke Road, W11.
Tel: 0171-221 7936
(Tr)

Yesterday Child, Angel
Arcade, 118 Islington High
Street, N1 8EG.
Tel: 0171-354 1601/
01908 583403
(Do)

Young, Robert, Antiques,
68 Battersea Bridge Road,
SW11.
Tel: 0171-228 7847
(P)

Yvonne, Unit 10,
Kensington Church Street
Antiques Centre, W8.
Tel: 0171 376 0425
(Fa)

Zeitgeist, 58 Kensington
Church Street, W8.
Tel: 0171-938 4817
(A&C, AN)

Avon

Barometer Shop, 3 Lower
Park Row, Bristol.
Tel: 0117 9272565
(Ba)

Bath Dolls' Hospital &
Teddy Bear Clinic,
2 Grosvenor Place,
London Road, Bath.
Tel: 01225 319668
(Do)

Bristol Dolls' Hospital,
50-52 Alpha Road,
Southville, Bristol.
Tel: 0117 9664368
(Do)

Dando, Andrew,
4 Wood Street, Bath.
Tel: 01225 422702
(P)

Great Western Toys,
Great Western Antique
Centre, Bartlett Street,
Bath.
(To)

Jessie's Button Box,
Great Western Antique
Centre, Bartlett Street,
Bath.
Tel: 0117 9299065
(Bu)

Linford, Carr,
10-11 Walcot Buildings,
London Road, Bath.
Tel: 01225 317516
(CaC)

Marchant, Nick, 13 Orwell
Drive, Keynsham, Bristol.
Tel: 0117 9865182
(M)

Nashers Music Store,
72 Walcot Street, Bath.
Tel: 01225 332298
(Re)

Pugh, Robert & Carol,
Bath.
Tel: 01225 314713
(P)

Saffell, Michael & Jo,
3 Walcot Buildings,
London Road, Bath.
Tel: 01225 315857
(T&MS)

Scott's, Bartlett Street
Antiques Centre,
Bartlett Street, Bath.
Tel: 01225 625335
(Ce)

Somervale Antiques,
6 Radstock Road,
Midsomer Norton, Bath.
Tel: 01761 412686
(G, PB)

Winstone Stamp Company,
S82 Great Western
Antiques Centre,
Bartlett Street, Bath.
Tel: 01225 310388
(CC, Ra)

Bedfordshire

Old Warden Antiques &
Collectables, Old Warden,
Tel: 01767 627201
(Col)

Sykes, Christopher,
Antiques, The Old
Parsonage, Woburn.
Tel: 01525 290259
(Cor, S&MI, M)

Berkshire

Asquiths of Windsor,
10 George V Place,
Thames Avenue, Windsor.
Tel: 01753 854954/831200
(TB)

Below Stairs, 103 High
Street, Hungerford.
Tel: 01488 682317
(K)

Boxes From Derek
McIntosh, 10 Wickham
Road, Stockcross, Newbury.
Tel: 01488 38295
(B)

Mostly Boxes, 92 & 52b
High Street, Eton, Windsor.
Tel: 01753 858470
(B, I, TW)

Specialised Auction Services,
The Coach House, Modgham
Park, Reading, RG7 5UG.
Tel: 01734 712949
(A, Com)

Buckinghamshire

Cars Only,
4 Granville Square,
Willen Local Centre,
Willen, Milton Keynes.
Tel: 01908 690024
(To)

Foster, A. & E.,
Little Heysham,
Forge Road, Naphill.
Tel: 0124 024 2024
(Tr)

Neale, Gillian A.,
The Old Post Office,
Wendover.
Tel: 01296 625335
(Ce)

Cambridgeshire

Cambridge Fine Art Ltd.,
Priest House, 33 Church
Street, Little Shelford.
Tel: 01223 842866/843537
(BP)

James Fuller & Son.
Tel: 01354 692740
(Wr)

Warboys Antiques,
Warboys, Huntingdon.
Tel: 01487 823686
(Sp)

Cheshire

Avalon, 1 City Walls,
Northgate Street, Chester.
Tel: 01244 318406
(Po)

Dé Jà Vu Antiques,
Hatters Row,
Horsemarket Street,
Warrington.
Tel: 01925 232677
(Te)

Dollectable,
53 Lower Bridge Street,
Chester, CH1 1RS
Tel: 01244 44888/679195
(Do)

Eureka Antiques,
7a Church Brow, Bowdon.
Tel: 0161-926 9722
(CaC, J, Ta)

Nantwich Art Deco &
Decorative Arts, 87 Welsh
Row, Nantwich.
Tel: 01270 624876
(AD)

On The Air, 42 Bridge
Street Row, Chester.
Tel: 01244 348468
(R)

Rayment, Derek, Antiques,
Orchard House, Barton
Road, Barton, Nr Malpas.
Tel: 01829 270429
(Ba)

Sweetbriar Gallery,
Sweetbriar House,
Robin Hood Lane, Helsby,
WA6 9NH.
Tel: 01928 723851
(Pa)

Cornwall

Millcraft Rocking Horse
Co., Lower Trannack Mill,
Coverack Bridges, Helston.
Tel: 01326 573316
(To, RH)

Cumbria

Bacchus Antiques,
Longlands at Cartmel.
Tel: 0144 854 475
(Cor)

Ceramic Restorers,
Domino Restorations,
129 Craig Walk,
Windermere, LA23 3AX
Tel: 015394 45751
(Ce)

Derbyshire

Norman King,
24 Dinting Road, Glossop.
Tel: 014574 2946
(Po)

Spurrier-Smith Antiques,
28b, 39-41 Church Street,
Ashbourne.
Tel: 01335 43669/42198
(M)

Devon

Bampton Telephone &
General Museum of
Communication and
Domestic History,
4 Brook Street, Bampton.
(Te)

Hill, Jonathan 2-4 Brook
Street, Bampton.
Tel: 01398 31310
(R)

Honiton Lace Shop,
44 High Street, Honiton.
Tel: 01404 42416
(L&L)

Taylor, Brian, Antiques,
24 Molesworth Road,
Plymouth, PL1 5LZ.
Tel: 01752 569061
(Gr)

Temeraire,
11a Higher Street,
Brixham, TQ5 8HW.
Tel: 01803 851523
(Sh)

Dorset

Books Afloat,
66 Park Street,
Weymouth, DT4 7DE.
Tel: 01305 779774
(Bk)

Chicago Sound Company,
Northmoor House,
Colesbrook, Gillingham.
Tel: 01747 824338
(Ju)

Dalkeith Auctions,
Dalkeith Hall,
Dalkeith Steps, rear of
81 Old Christchurch Road,
Bournemouth, BH1 1YL.
Tel: 01202 292905
(A, E)

Lionel Geneen Ltd.,
781 Christchurch Road,
Boscombe, Bournemouth.
Tel: 01202 422961
(O)

Mitton, Mervyn A.,
161 The Albany,
Manor Road,
Bournemouth.
Tel: 01202 293767
(PMem)

Old Button Shop,
Lytchett Minster.
Tel: 01202 622169
(Bu)

Old Harbour Antiques,
The Old Bakery,
3 Hope Square,
Weymouth.
Tel: 01305 777838
(Sh)

Yesterday's Tackle &
Books, 42 Clingan Road,
Southbourne.
Tel: 01202 476586
(F)

Essex

Basildon Baby Carriages,
83 Tyefields, Pitsea,
Basildon.
Tel: 01268 729803
(by appointment only)
(BC)

Blackwells of Hawkwell,
733 London Road,
Westcliff-on-Sea.
Tel: 01702 72248
(DHF)

East Gates Antiques,
91a East Hill, Colchester.
Tel: 01206 564474
(G)

G. K. R. Bonds Ltd.,
PO Box 1, Kelvedon.
Tel: 013765 71711
(Scr)

It's About Time,
863 London Road,
Westcliff-on-Sea.
Tel: 01702 72574
(Ba)

R. F. Postcards,
17 Hilary Crescent,
Rayleigh.
Tel: 01268 743222
(Po)

Waine, A., Tweedale,
Rye Mill Lane,
Feering, Colchester.
(ADC)

Old Telephone Co.,
The Granary Antiques
Centre,
Battlesbridge,
Nr. Wickford.
Tel: 01245 400601
(Te)

Gloucestershire

Acorn Antiques,
Sheep Street,
Stow-on-the-Wold.
GL54 1AA
Tel: 01451 831519
(Ce)

Cotswold Motor Museum,
The Old Mill,
Bourton-on-the-Water.
Tel: 01451 21255
(Au)

Lillian Middleton's
Antique Dolls Shop,
Days Stable, Sheep Street,
Stow-on-the-Wold.
Tel: 01451 31542
(Do)

Park House Antiques,
Park Street,
Stow-on-the-Wold,
GL54 1AQ.
Tel: 01451 30159
(Do, DHF, TB)

Samarkand Galleries,
2 Brewery Yard,
Stow-on-the-Wold.
Tel: 01451 832322
(R&C)

Specialised Postcard
Auctions, 25 Gloucester
Street, Cirencester,
GL7 2DJ.
Tel: 01285 659057
(A, Po)

Telephone Lines Ltd., 339
High Street, Cheltenham,
GL50 3HS.
Tel: 01242 583699
(Te)

The Trumpet, West End,
Minchinhampton,
Nr. Stroud.
Tel: 01453 883027
(Col)

Hampshire

Art Deco China Centre,
62 Murray Road, Horndean.
Tel: 01705 597440
(ADC)

Bona Arts Decorative Ltd.,
Princes Mead Shopping
Centre, Farnborough,
GU14 7TJ.
Tel: 01252 372188
(AD)

Cobwebs, 78 Northam
Road, Southampton.
Tel: 01703 227458
(Ae, Au, Sh)

Evans & Partridge
Auctioneers,
Agriculture House,
High Street, Stockbridge.
Tel: 01264 810702
(A, F)

Goss & Crested China
Ltd., 62 Murray Road,
Horndean, PO8 9JL.
Tel: 01705 597440
(G&CC)

Millers of Chelsea Ltd.,
Netherbrook House,
Christchurch Road,
Ringwood.
Tel: 01425 472062
(P)

Romsey Medal Centre,
5 Bell Street, Romsey.
Tel: 01794 512069
(A&M)

Toys Through Time,
Fareham.
Tel: 01329 288678
(Do)

Hereford & Worcester

Barometer Shop,
New Street, Leominster.
Tel: 01568 613652
(Ba)

BBM Jewellery & Coins,
(W. V. Crook), 8-9 Lion
Street, Kidderminster.
Tel: 01562 744118
(I, J, Cns)

Button Museum,
Kyrle Street, Ross-on-Wye.
Tel: 01989 66089
(Bu)

Chapman, Michael,
Tel: 01789 773897
(Au)

Platform 6 Auctions,
11a Davenport Drive,
The Willows, Bromsgrove.
Tel: 01527 871000
(A, To)

Radiocraft, 56 Main Street,
Sedgebarrow, Evesham.
Tel: 01386 881988
(R)

Hertfordshire

Ambeline Antiques,
By George Antique Centre,
St. Albans.
Tel: 01727 53032/
0181-445 8025
(H/HP)

Coombs, P.,
87 Gills Hill Lane, Radlett.
Tel: 01923 856949
(Ca)

Forget Me Not,
By George Antique Centre,
23 George Street, St. Albans.
Tel: 01727 53032/
01903 261172
(J)

Oriental Rug Gallery, 42
Verulam Road, St Albans.
Tel: 01727 41046
(R&C)

Isle of Wight

Nostalgia Toy Museum,
High Street, Godshill,
PO38 3HZ.
Tel: 01983 730055
(To)

Vectis Model Auctions,
Ward House,
12 York Avenue,
East Cowes.
Tel: 01983 292272
(To)

Kent

Amelia Dolls,
Pantiles Spa Antiques,
The Pantiles,
Tunbridge Wells. TN4 8HF
Tel: 01892 541377/
01342 713223
(Do)

Amherst Antiques,
23 London Road,
Riverhead, Sevenoak.
TN13 2BU
Tel: 01732 455047
(Tr)

Bears Galore, 8 The
Fairings, High Street,
Tenterden, TN30 6QX.
Tel: 01580 765233
(TB)

Beaubush House Antiques,
95 High Street, Sandgate,
Folkestone. CT20 3BY
Tel: 01303 49099
(SP)

Candlestick & Bakelite,
PO Box 808, Orpington.
BR5 1TB
Tel: 0181-467 3743
(Te)

Collectables, PO Box 130,
Rochester.
Tel: 01634 828767
(Col)

Dolls' House Workshop,
54a London Road,
Teynham.
Tel: 01795 533445
(DHF)

Eaton & Jones, 120 HIgh
Street, Tenterden, TN30
6HT.
Tel: 01580 763357
(J)

Falstaff Antiques Motor
Museum,
63-67 High Street,
Rolvenden, Nr. Cranbrook.
TN17 4LP
Tel: 01580 241234
(Au)

Hadlow Antiques,
P O Box 134
Tunbridge Wells. TN2 5YA
Tel: 01892 29858
(Do)

Heggie, Stuart,
58 Northgate, Canterbury,
CT1 1BB.
Tel: 01227 470422/770309
(Ca, St, R)

Kirkham, Harry,
Garden House Antiques,
118 High Street,
Tenterden, TN30 6HT.
Tel: 01580 763664
(F)

Kollectomania,
4 Catherine Street,
Rochester, ME1 2HJ.
Tel: 01634 45099
(Ma)

Lace Basket,
116 High Street,
Tenterden, TN30 6HT.
Tel: 01580 763664
(L&L, H/HP)

Lampard, Penny,
28 High Street, Headcorn,
TN27 9NE
Tel: 01622 890682
(K)

Magpie's Nest,
14 Palace Street,
Canterbury,
CT1 2DZ.
Tel: 01227 764883
(Do, DHF)

Page Angela Antiques,
Tunbridge Wells.
Tel: 01892 22217
(P)

Reeves, Keith & Veronica,
Burgate Antiques,
10c Burgate, Canterbury,
CT1 2HG.
Tel: 01227 456500/
01634 375098
(A&M)

Roses, 60 King Street,
Sandwich, CT13 9BT.
Tel: 01304 615303
(Col)

Serendipity,
168 High Street, Deal,
CT14 6BQ.
Tel: 01304 369165/366536
(Ce)

Stevenson Brothers,
The Workshop,
Ashford Road, Bethersden,
Ashford, TN26 3AP.
Tel: 01233 820363
(RH)

Strawsons Antiques,
33, 39 & 41 The Pantiles,
Tunbridge Wells,
TN2 5TE.
Tel: 01892 530607
(TW)

Sturge, Mike,
39 Union Street,
Maidstone, ME14 1ED.
Tel: 01622 654702
(Po)

Up Country,
Old Corn Stores,
68 St. John's Road,
Tunbridge Wells,
TN4 9NY.
Tel: 01892 523341
(K)

Variety Box,
16 Chapel Place, Tunbridge
Wells, TN1 1YQ.
Tel: 01892 531868
(BH, G&CC, Fa, G, H/HP,
Sew, S, TW)

Lancashire

A. S. Antiques, 26 Broad
Street, Pendleton, Salford.
Tel: 0161-737 5938
(AD)

British Heritage
Telephones,
11 Rhodes Drive,
Unsworth, Bury.
Tel: 0161-767 9259
(Te)

Bunn Roy W. Antiques,
34-36 Church Street,
Barnuldswick, Colne.
Tel: 01282 813703
(Ce, SP)

Lister Art Books,
22 Station Road, Banks,
Southport, PR9 8BF.
Tel: 01704 232033
(Bk)

Old Bakery The,
36 Inglewhite Road,
Longridge, Nr. Preston.
Tel: 01772 785411
(K)

Leicestershire

Charnwood Antiques,
Coalville, Leicester.
Tel: 01530 38530
(BP)

Jessups of Leicester Ltd.,
98 Scudamore Road,
Leicester.
Tel: 0116 2320033
(Ca)

Pooks Motor Books,
Fowke Street, Rothley,
LE7 7PJ.
Tel: 0116 2376222
(Au, Bk)

Williamson, Janice,
9 Coverdale Road,
Meadows Wiston,
Leicester.
Tel:0116 2812926
(Ce, D)

Lincolnshire

20th Century Frocks,
Lincolnshire Art Centre,
Bridge Street,
Horncastle.
Tel: 016582 7794/
016588 3638
(T)

Hayden, Peggy.
Tel: 01507 343261
(J)

Junktion, Old Railway
Station, New Bolingbroke,
Boston. Tel: 01205 480068
(To, T&MS)

Legends Rocking Horses,
Yew Tree Farmhouse,
Holme Road,
Kirton Holme, Boston.
Tel: 0120 579 214
(To, RH)

Middlesex

Albert's Cigarette Card
Specialists, 113 London
Road, Twickenham.
Tel: 0181-891 3067
(CC)

Hobday Toys,
17 Maxwell Road,
Northwood, HA6 2XY.
Tel: 01923 820115
(DH, To)

Ives, John, 5 Normanhurst
Drive, Twickenham,
TW1 1NA.
Tel: 0181-892 6265
(Bk)

Norfolk

Bluebird Arts,
1 Mount Street, Cromer.
Tel: 01263 512384/78487
(Po)

Bradbury Roger Antiques,
Church Street, Coltishall,
NR12 7DJ.
Tel: 01603 737444
(OP)

Cat Pottery, 1 Grammar
School Road, North
Walsham, NR28 9JH.
Tel: 01692 402962
(P)

Howkins, Peter,
39, 40 & 135 King Street,
Great Yarmouth.
Tel: 01493 844639
(J)

Pundole, Neville,
PO Box 6, Attleborough.
Tel: 01953 454106/
01860 278774
(ADC)

Trains & Olde Tyme Toys,
Aylsham Road, Norwich.
Tel: 01603 413585
(To)

Yesteryear Antiques,
24d Magdalen Street,
Norwich.
Tel: 01603 622908
(Ce, D)

North Humberside

Marine Art Posters
Services,
42 Ravenspur Road,
Bilton, Hull.
Tel: 01482 874700/815115
(Sh)

Northamptonshire

Aspidistra Antiques,
51 High Street, Finedon
Tel: 01933 680196/
0860 682771
(AD, AN)

Shelron, 9 Brackley Road,
Towcester.
Tel: 01327 350242
(Po)

Nottinghamshire

Breck Antiques,
726 Mansfield Road,
Nottingham.
Tel: 0115 9605263
(Ce)

Keyhole The, Dragonwyck,
Far Back Lane, Farnsfield,
Newark.
Tel: 01623 882590
(L&K)

Reflections of a Bygone
Age, 15 Debdale Lane,
Keyworth. Tel: 016077 4079
(Po)

Vennett-Smith, T.,
11 Nottingham Road,
Gotham, NG11 0HE.
Tel: 0115 9830541
(E, Po)

Vintage Wireless Shop,
The Hewarths, Sandiacre,
Nottingham.
Tel: 0115 9393138
(R, TV)

Oxfordshire

Clockwork & Steam,
The Old Marmalade
Factory, 27 Parkend
Street, Oxford.
Tel: 01865 200321
(To)

Comics & Showcase,
19-20 St. Clements Street,
Oxford. Tel: 01865 723680
(Co)

Dauphin Display (Oxford)
Ltd., Willoughby's Marsh,
Baldon
Tel: 01867 38542
(DS)

Key Antiques, 11 Horse
Fair, Chipping Norton.
Tel: 01608 3777
(M)

Manfred Schotten,
Crypt Antiques,
109 High Street, Burford.
Tel: 0199 382 2302
(Go)

R.A.T.S., Unit 16,
Telford Road, Bicester.
Tel: 01869 242161/40842
(T&MS)

Strange Peter, Restorer,
The Willows, Sutton,
Oxford.
Tel: 01865 882020
(Do)

Teddy Bears,
99 High Street, Witney,
OX8 6LY.
Tel: 01993 702616
(TB)

Thames Gallery,
Thameside,
Henley-on-Thames.
Tel: 01491 572449
(S)

Shropshire

Antiques on the Square,
2 Sandford Court,
Church Stretton.
Tel: 01694 724111
(ADC)

Expressions, 17 Princess
Street, Shrewsbury.
Tel: 01743 351731
(ADC)

Manser, F. C., & Son Ltd.,
53 Wyle Cop, Shrewsbury.
Tel: 01743 51120
(CaC, Fa, S)

Nock Deighton,
Saleroom Centre, Tasley,
Bridgnorth.
Tel: 01746 762666
(A, F)

Rocking Horse Workshop,
Ashfield House,
The Foxholes, Wem.
Tel: 01939 32335
(RH)

Scot Hay House Antiques,
7 Nantwich Road, Woore.
Tel: 0163 081 7118
(K)

Stretton Models,
12 Beaumont Road,
Church Stretton.
Tel: 01694 723737
(To)

Summers, Roger,
17 Daddlebrook,
Hollinswood, Telford.
(BM)

Tiffany Antiques, Unit 3,
Shrewsbury Antique
Centre, 15 Princess Howe,
The Square, Shrewsbury.
Tel: 01270 257425
and
Unit 15, Shrewsbury
Antique Market,
Frankwell Quay
Warehouse, Shrewsbury.
Tel: 01743 350916
(Col, K)

Vintage Fishing Tackle
Shop & Angling Art
Gallery,
103 Longden Coleham,
Shrewsbury.
Tel: 01743 69373
(F)

Staffordshire

Peggy Davies Ceramics,
28 Liverpool Road,
Stoke-on-Trent ST4 1BJ.
Tel: 01782 48002
(Ce)

Gordon,
25 Stapenhill Road,
Burton-on-Trent, DE15
9AE.
Tel: 01283 567213
(Bot)

Keystones,
Tel: 01785 566648
(P)

Midwinter Antiques,
13 Brunswick Street,
Newcastle-under-Lyme.
Tel: 01782 712483
(T)

Somerset

House, Bernard G.,
Mitre Antiques,
Market Place, Wells.
Tel: 01749 672607
(Ba)

London Cigarette Card Co.
Ltd., Sutton Road,
Somerton.
Tel: 01458 273452
(CC)

Spencer & Co., Margaret,
Dept AD, Chard Road,
Crewkerne.
Tel: 01460 72362
(RH)

Suffolk

Crafers Antiques,
The Hill, Wickham
Market,
IP13 0QS.
Tel: 01728 747347
(Ce, SP, Sew)

Hoad, W. L.,
9 St. Peter's Road, Kirkley,
Lowestoft, NR33 0LH.
Tel: 01502 587758
(CC)

Surrey

David Aldous-Cook.
Tel: 0181-642 4842
(RB)

Antiques Arcadia,
22 Richmond Hill,
Richmond-upon-Thames,
TW10 6QX.
Tel: 0181 9402035
(P)

Burns, David,
116 Chestnut Grove,
New Malden.
Tel: 0181-949 7356
(S&MI)

Childhood Memories,
The Farnham Antique
Centre, 27 South Street,
Farnham.
Tel: 01252 724475
(Do, TB)

Church Street Antiques,
15 Church Street,
Godalming, GU7 1EL..
Tel: 01483 860894
(ADC, Com)

Dorking Dolls House
Gallery, 23 West Street,
Dorking.
Tel: 01306 885785
(Do)

New Ashgate Gallery,
Wagon Yard, Farnham,
GU9 7PS.
Tel: 01252 713208
(Col)

Nostalgia Amusements,
22 Greenwood Close,
Thames Ditton.
Tel: 0181-398 2141
(Ju)

Sheppard Press, Unit 2,
Monk's Walk, Farnham,
GU9 8HT.
Tel: 01252 734347
(Bk)

Victoriana Dolls, Reigate.
Tel: 01737 249525
(Do)

West Promotions,
P O Box 257, Sutton,
SM3 9WW.
Tel: 0181 641 3224
(PaM)

West Street Antiques,
63 West Street, Dorking.
Tel: 01306 883487
(A&M)

Wych House Antiques,
Wych Hill, Woking.
Tel: 01483 764636
(K)

Sussex

Martyn Bagley.
Tel: 01825 760067
(O)

Barclay Antiques,
7 Village Mews, Little
Common, Bexhill-on-Sea.
Tel: 01797 222734
(TW)

Bartholomew, John &
Mary, The Mint Arcade,
71 The Mint, Rye.
Tel: 01797 225952
(Po)

Beech, Ron, Brambledean
Road, Portslade, Brighton.
Tel: 01273 423355
(Ce, PL)

Bygones, Collectors Shop,
123 South Street, Lancing.
Tel: 01903 750051
(Col, Po)

Chateaubriand Antique
Centre, High Street,
Burwash.
Tel: 01435 882535
(Cor, O, L&L)

Dolls Hospital,
17 George Street,
Hastings.
Tel: 01424 444117/422758
(Do)

Ginns, Ray & Diane,
PO Box 129,
East Grinstead.
Tel: 01342 326041
(SP)

Keiron James Designs,
St Dominic's Gallery,
4 South Street,
Ditchling.
Tel: 01273 846411
(TB)

Kinloch, Claire,
Bulmer House,
The Green, Sedlescombe,
TN33 0QA.
Tel: 01424 870364
(Do)

Lingard, Ann,
Rope Walk Antiques, Rye,
TN31 7NA.
Tel: 01797 223486
(K, Ti)

Old Mint House, Pevensey.
Tel: 01323 762337
(P)

Pearson, Sue, 13½ Prince
Albert Street, Brighton,
BN1 1HE.
Tel: 01273 329247
(Do, TB)

The Pianola Shop,
134 Islingword Road,
Brighton, BN2 2SH.
Tel: 01273 608999
(Pia)

Recollect Studios, Dept. M,
The Old School, London
Road, Sayers Common.
Tel: 01273 833314
(Do)

Rin Tin Tin,
34 North Road, Brighton.
Tel: 01273 672424/733689
(eves)
(Col, T&MS)

Russell, Leonard,
21 King's Avenue,
Mount Pleasant,
Newhaven.
Tel: 01273 515153
(Ce, Com)

Sporting Memories Ltd.,
5 High Street, Petworth
Tel: 01798 342377
(Sp)

Sussex Commemorative
Centre,
88 Western Road, Hove.
Tel: 01273 773911
(Ce)

Trains, 67 London Road,
Bognor Regis.
Tel: 01243 864727
(To)

V.A.G. & Co., Possingworth
Craft Centre, Brownings
Farm, Blackboys,
Uckfield. Tel: 01323 507488
(A&M)

Verrall Brian R. & Co.,
The Old Garage,
High Street, Handcross,
Haywards Heath.
Tel: 01444 400678
(Au)

Wallis & Wallis, West
Street Auction Galleries,
Lewes.
Tel: 01273 480208
(A&M, To)

Tyne & Wear

Ian Sharp Antiques,
23 Front Street,
Tynemouth.
Tel: 0191-296 0656
(Ce)

Warwickshire

Alien Enterprises,
The Antiques Shop,
30 Henley Street,
Stratford-Upon-Avon.
Tel: 01789 292485/297347
(TV Col)

Arbour Antiques Ltd.,
Poet's Arbour,
Sheep Street,
Stratford-upon-Avon.
Tel: 01789 293453
(A&M)

Art Deco Ceramics,
Stratford Antique Centre,
Ely Street,
Stratford-upon-Avon.
Tel: 01789 204351/299524
(ADC)

Bowler, Simon,
Smith Street Antique
Centre, Warwick.
Tel: 01926 400554
(O)

Central Antique Arms &
Militaria, Smith Street
Antique Centre,
7 Smith Street, Warwick.
Tel: 01926 497864
(A&M)

Jazz, Civic Hall,
Rother Street,
Stratford-upon-Avon.
Tel: 01789 298362
(ADC)

Lion's Den, 11 St Mary's
Crescent, Leamington Spa.
Tel: 01926 339498
(ADC)

Midlands Goss &
Commemoratives,
The Old Cornmarket
Antique Centre,
70 Market Place, Warwick.
Tel: 01926 419119
(Ce, Com, G&CC)

Paull, Janice,
125 Warwick Road,
Kenilworth.
Tel: 01926 55253
(P, LB)

Rich Designs,
11 Union Street,
Stratford-upon-Avon.
Tel: 01789 772111
(ADC)

Time Machine,
Paul M. Kennelly,
198 Holbrook Lane,
Coventry.
Tel: 01203 663557
(To)

West Midlands

Birmingham Railway
Auctions & Publications,
7 Ascot Road, Moseley,
Birmingham.
Tel: 0121-449 9707
(A, Ra)

Doghouse The,
309 Bloxwich Road, Walsall.
Tel: 01922 30829
(K)

Moseley Railwayana
Museum, Birmingham.
Tel: 0121-449 9707
(Ra, To)

Mr Morgan, F11 Swincross
Road, Old Swinford,
Stourbridge.
Tel: 01384 397033
(TB)

Nostalgia & Comics,
14-16 Smallbrook,
Queensway City Centre,
Birmingham.
Tel: 0121-643 0143
(Co)

Railwayana Collectors
Journal, 7 Ascot Road,
Moseley, Birmingham.
(Ra)

Sawyer, George, 11 Frayne
Avenue, Kingswinford.
Tel: 01384 273847
(Po)

Vintage & Classic
Auctions, 153 Danford
Lane, Solihull B91 1QQ.
Tel: 0121 745 5256
(A, Au)

Wiltshire

Coppins of Corsham
Repairs, 1 Church Street,
Corsham.
Tel: 01249 715404
(J)

Oxley, P. A., The Old
Rectory, Cherhill, Calne.
Tel: 01249 816227
(Ba)

Relic Antiques,
Lea, Malmesbury,
Tel: 01666 822332
(T&MS)

Wells, David, Salisbury
Antique & Collectors
Market, 37 Catherine
Street, Salisbury.
Tel: 01425 476899/01722
326033
(Po, To)

Yorkshire

Barnett, Tim,
Carlton Gallery,
60a Middle Street,
Driffield.
Tel: 01482 443954
(ADC)

British Bottle Review,
2 Strafford Avenue,
Elsecar,
Nr. Barnsley.
Tel: 01226 745156/
01709 879303
(Bot)

Camera House,
Oakworth Hall,
Colne Road, Oakworth.
Tel: 01535 642333
(Ca)

Clarke, Andrew,
42 Pollard Lane,
Bradford.
Tel: 01274 636042
(To)

Country Collector,
11-12 Birdgate,
Pickering.
Tel: 01751 477481
(ADC, P)

Crested China Company,
Station House,
Driffield, YO25 7PY.
Tel: 01377 257042
(G&CC)

Danby Antiques.
Tel: 01904 672333
(B)

Echoes, 650a Halifax Road,
Eastwood,
Todmorden,
OL14 6DW.
Tel: 01706 817505
(T)

Glance Back Bookshop,
17 Upper Church Street,
Chepstow, Gwent.
(Bk, Wr, A&M, Col)

Haley, John & Simon,
89 Northgate,
Halifax.
Tel: 01422 822148
(To, MB)

Hewitt, Muir,
Halifax Antiques Centre,
Queens Road,
Gibbet Street, Halifax.
Tel: 01442 347377
(ADC)

Holmfirth Antiques,
Halifax Antiques Centre,
Queens Road,
Gibbet Street, Halifax.
Tel: 01422 366657
(Gr)

In Retrospect,
2 Pavement,
Pocklington, York.
Tel: 01759 304894
(P)

Linen and Lace,
Halifax Antiques Centre,
Queens Road,
Gibbet Street, Halifax.
Tel: 01422 366657
(C, T)

Memory Lane,
69 Wakefield Road,
Sowerby Bridge.
Tel: 01422 833223
(TB)

National Railway Museum,
Leeman Road, York.
Tel: 01904 621261
(Ra)

Reece, Gordon, Gallery,
Finkle Street,
Knaresborough.
Tel: 01423 866219
(O, T)

Rouse, Sue,
The Dolls House,
Gladstone Buildings,
Hope Street,
Hebden Bridge.
Tel: 01422 845606
(Do)

Shaw, Izzy,
36 North Parade, Skipton.
Tel: 01756 796548
(TB)

Shaw, Jack, & Co.,
The Old Grammar School,
Skipton Road, Ilkley.
Tel: 01943 609467
(S, J)

Sheffield Railwayana
Auctions,
43 Little Norton Lane,
Sheffield, S8 8GA.
Tel: 0114 2745085
(Ra)

Sigma Antiques, Water
Skellgate, Ripon.
Tel: 01265 603163
(AD, B, P)

Spencer Bottomley,
Andrew,
The Coach House,
Thongsbridge,
Holmfirth.
Tel: 01484 685234
(A&M)

Windmill Antiques,
4 Montpelier Mews,
Harrogate.
Tel: 01423 530502
(B, M, RH)

Scotland

AKA Comics & Books,
33 Virginia Street, Glasgow
Tel: 0141-552 8731
(Co)

Black, Laurance,
45 Cumberland Street,
Edinburgh.
Tel: 0131-557 4543
(Ta)

Bow Well Antiques,
103 West Bow, Edinburgh.
Tel: 0131-225 3335
(Gr, SC)

Edinburgh Coin Shop,
2 Powarth Crescent,
Edinburgh,
EH11 1HW
Tel: 0131-229 3007/2915
(A, A&M, Cns, Me)

Edinburgh Dolls' Hospital,
35a Dundas Street,
Edinburgh.
Tel: 0131 556 4295
(TB, Do)

Golf Books, Glengarden,
Ballater, Aberdeenshire,
AB35 5UB.
Tel: 013397 55429
(Go, Bk)

Hantel Ltd.,
Bruiach House,
Kiltarlity, Inverness-shire,
IV4 7JHG.
Tel: 01463 741297
(Do)

Jay Bee Bears, 8 Whitelea
Avenue, Kilmacolm,
Renfrewshire.
Tel: 0150 587 4107
(TB)

Orcadian Company of
Bears, Rosebank Cottage,
Harray, Orkney.
Tel: 01856 76 352
(TB)

Timeless Tackle,
1 Blackwood Crescent,
Edinburgh, EH9 1QZ.
Tel: 0131 6671407
(F)

Millars,
9-11 Castle Street,
Kirkcudbright.
Tel: 01557 30236
(ADC)

Miller, Jess,
PO Box 1, Birnam,
Dunkeld, Perthshire.
Tel: 013502 522
(F)

Pastimes Vintage Toys,
140 Maryhill Road,
Glasgow.
Tel: 0141-331 1008

Stockbridge Antiques,
8 Deanhaugh Street,
Edinburgh.
Tel: 0131-332 1366
(Do, T)

Whittingham Crafts Ltd.,
8 Pentland Court,
Saltire Centre,
Glenrothes, Fife.
Tel: 01592 630433
(RH)

Wright, Tim, Antiques,
147 Bath Street,
Glasgow.
Tel: 0141 221 0364
(Ce, G, S)

Wales

A.P.E.S. Rocking Horses,
Ty Gwyn,
Llannefydd,
Denbigh, Clwyd,
LL16 5HB.
Tel: 01745 79365
(RH)

Ayers, Brindley John,
45 St. Anne's Road,
Hakin, Milford Haven,
Pembrokeshire.
Tel: 01646 678359
(F)

Biffins,
Ty Newydd,
Gwalchmai Uchaf,
Anglesey.
Tel: 01407 720550
(Po)

Corgi Toys Collectors Club,
PO Box 323,
Swansea.
Tel: 01792 476902
(To)

Doggie Hubbard's
Bookshop, Ffynnon Cadno,
Ponterwyd, Dyfed.
Tel: 0197 085224
(Bk)

Forbidden Planet,
5 Duke Street,
Cardiff.
Tel: 01222 228885
(Co)

Gibbs, Paul,
25 Castle Street,
Conwy.
Tel: 01492 593429
(BH, ADC, Ti)

Hermitage Antiquities,
10 West Street, Fishguard.
Tel: 01348 873037
(A&M, J)

Howards Antiques,
10 Alexandra Road,
Aberystwyth,
Dyfed.
Tel: 01970 624973
(P)

Watkins, Islwyn,
1 High Street/29 Market
Street,
Knighton, Powys.
Tel: 01547 520145/528940
(P)

West Wales Antiques,
18 Manselfield Road,
Murton,
Swansea.
Tel: 01792 234318
(P, Do, G, J, Col)

Williams, Paul,
Forge Antiques,
Synod Inn,
Llandysul,
Dyfed.
Tel: 01545 580707/580604
(T)

DIRECTORY OF MARKETS & CENTRES

London

Alfie's Antique Market,
13-25 Church Street, NW8.
Tel: 0171-723 6066
Tues-Sat 10-6pm

Angel Arcade, 116-118
Islington High Street,
Camden Passage, N1.
Wed & Sat

Antiquarius Antique
Market, 131/141 King's
Road, Chelsea, SW3.
Tel: 0171-351 5353
Mon-Sat 10-6pm

Antiques & Collectors
Corner, North Piazza,
Covent Garden, WC2.
Tel: 0171-240 7405
9-5pm every day

Bermondsey Antiques
Market, Corner of Long
Lane & Bermondsey
Street, SE1.
Tel: 0171-351 5353
Friday 5am-2pm

Bermondsey Antiques
Warehouse, 173
Bermondsey Street, SE1.
Tel: 0171-407 2040/4250
9.30-5.30pm, Thurs 9.30-
8pm, Fri 7-5.30pm.

Bond Street Antiques
Centre, 124 New Bond
Street, W1.
Tel: 0171-351 5353
Mon-Fri 10-5.45pm,
Sat 10-4pm

Camden Antiques Market,
Corner of Camden High
Street & Buck Street,
Camden Town, NW1.
Thurs 7-4pm

Camden Passage Antique
Centre, 12 Camden
Passage, Islington, N1.
Tel: 0171-359 0190
Stalls Wed 8-3pm (Thurs
books 9-4pm), Sat 9-5pm

Chelsea Antiques Market,
245-253 King's Road, SW3.
Tel: 0171-352
5689/9695/1424
10-6pm

Chenil Galleries,
181-183 King's Road, SW3.
Tel: 0171-351 5353
Mon-Sat 10-6pm

Corner Portobello Antiques
Supermarket, 282, 284,
288, 290 Westbourne
Grove, W11.
Tel: 0171-727 2027
Fri 12-4pm, Sat 7-6pm

Cutler Street Antiques
Market, Goulston Street,
Nr Aldgate End, E1.
Tel: 0171-351 5353
Sun 7-2pm

Crystal Palace Collectors
Market, Jasper Road,
Westow Hill,
Crystal Palace, SE19.
Tel: 0181-761 3735
Wed 9-4pm, Fri 9-5pm, Sat
9-4pm, Sun 11-4pm

Dixons Antique Centre,
471 Upper Richmond Road
West, East Sheen, SW14.
Tel: 0181-878 6788
10-5.30pm, Sun 1.30-
5.30pm, Closed Wed.

Franklin's Camberwell
Antiques Market,
161 Camberwell Road, SE5.
Tel: 0171-703 8089
10-6pm, Sun 1-6pm

Georgian Village Antiques
Market, 100 Wood Street,
Walthamstow, E17.
Tel: 0181-520 6638
10-5pm, Closed Thurs.

Georgian Village,
Islington Green, N1.
Tel: 0171-226 1571
Wed 10-4pm, Sat 7-5pm

Good Fairy Open Market,
100 Portobello Road, W11.
Tel: 0171-351 5950/221
8977. Sats only 5-5pm

Gray's Antique Market,
58 Davies Street, W1.
Tel: 0171-629 7034
Mon-Fri 10-6pm

Gray's Mews,
1-7 Davies Street, W1.
Tel: 0171-629 7034
Mon-Fri 10-6pm

Gray's Portobello,
138 Portobello Road,
W11.
Tel: 0171-221 3069
Sat 7-4pm

Greenwich Antiques
Market, Greenwich
High Road, SE10.
Sun 7.30-4.30/Sat June-Sept

Hampstead Antique
Emporium,
12 Heath Street,
Hampstead, NW3.
Tel: 0171-794 3297
10-6pm, closed Mon & Sun.

Jubilee Market,
Covent Garden, WC2.
Tel: 0171-836 2139
Open Mon

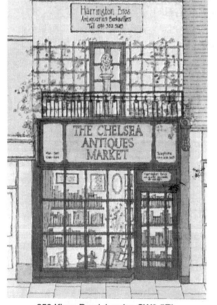

Kensington Church Street
Antiques Centre, 58-60
Kensington Church Street,
W8. 10-6pm

The London Silver Vaults,
Chancery House, 53-65
Chancery Lane, WC2.
Tel: 0171-242 3844
9-5.30pm, Sat 9-12.30pm

The Mall Antiques Arcade,
359 Upper Street,
Islington, N1.
Tel: 0171-354 2839
Tues, Thurs, Fri 10-5pm,
Wed 7.30-5pm, Sat 9-6pm

Northcote Road Antiques
Market, 155a Northcote
Road, Battersea, SW11.
Tel: 0171-228 6850
10-6pm, Sun 12-5pm

Old Crowther Market,
282 North End Road,
Fulham, SW6 1NH.
Tel: 0171-610 3610
Wed-Sun 10-6pm

Peckham Indoor Market,
Rye Lane Bargain Centre,
48 Rye Lane, Peckham,
SE15.
Tel: 0171-246 3639
Tues-Sat

Pierrepoint Arcade,
Camden Passage, N1.
Tel: 0171-359 0190
Wed & Sat

Portobello Road Market,
W11.
Sat 5.30-5pm

Rochefort Antique Gallery,
32/34 The Green,
Winchmore Hill, N21.
Tel: 0181-886 4779/363 0910

Roger's Antiques Gallery,
65 Portobello Road, W11.
Tel: 0171-351 5353
Sat 7-4pm

Steptoes Yard West
Market, 52a Goldhawk
Road, W12.
Tel: 0171-602 2699
Fri, Sat & Sun

Streatham Traders &
Shippers Market, United
Reform Church Hall,
Streatham High Street,
SW16.
Tel: 0171-764 3602
Tues 8-3pm

Wimbledon Market,
Car Park, Wimbledon
Greyhound Stadium,
Plough Lane, SW19.
Tel: 017268 17809. Sun.

Willesden Market,
Car Park, White Hart
Public House, Willesden,
NW10.
Tel: 0181-569 3889

World Famous Portobello
Market,
177 Portobello Road &
1-3 Elgin Crescent, W11.
Tel: 0171-221 4964
Sat 5-6pm

York Arcade,
80 Islington High Street, N1.
Tel: 0171-833 2640
Wed & Sat 8-5pm

Avon

Bartlett Street Antique
Centre,
5-10 Bartlett Street,
Bath.
Tel: 01225 466689
Mon-Sat 9.30-5pm,
Wed Market 8-5pm

Bath Antiques Market,
Guinea Lane,
off Lansdown Road,
Bath.
Wed 6.30-2.30pm

Bristol Antique Market,
St Nicholas Markets,
The Exchange,
Corn Street,
Bristol.
Tel: 0117 9224014
Fri 9-3pm

Clifton Antiques Market,
26/28 The Mall,
Clifton,
Bristol.
Tel: 0117 9741627
10-6pm, Closed Mon

Great Western Antique
Centre, Bartlett Street,
Bath.
Tel: 01225 424243
Mon-Sat 10-5pm,
Wed 8.30-5pm

Bedfordshire

Dunstable Antique Centre,
38a West Street,
Dunstable.
Tel: 01582 696953

Woburn Abbey Antiques
Centre,
Woburn.
Tel: 01525 290350
11-5pm Nov to Easter,
10-5.30pm Easter to Oct

Berkshire

Hungerford Arcade,
High Street,
Hungerford.
Tel: 01488 683701
9.30-5.30pm, Sun 10-6pm

Reading Emporium,
1a Merchant Place
(off Friar Street),
Reading.
Tel: 01734 590290
10-5pm

Twyford Antiques Centre,
1 High Street, Twyford.
Tel: 01734 342161
Mon-Sat 9.30-5.30pm,
Sun 10.30-5pm,
Closed Wed

Buckinghamshire

Amersham Antique
Collectors Centre,
20-22 Whieldon Street,
Old Amersham.
Tel: 01494 431282
Mon-Sat 10-6pm

Antiques at Wendover,
The Old Post Office,
25 High Street, Wendover.
Tel: 01296 625335
Mon-Sat 10-5.30pm,
Sun 11-5.30pm

Bell Street Antiques
Centre, 20/22 Bell Street,
Princes Risborough.
Tel: 018444 3034
9.30-5.30pm, Sun 12-5pm

Market Square Antiques,
20 Market Place, Olney.
Tel: 01234 712172
Mon-Sat 10-5.30pm,
Sun 2-5.30pm

Olney Antiques Centre,
Rose Court, Olney.
Tel: 01234 712172
10-5.30pm, Sun 12-5.30pm

Tingewick Antiques Centre,
Main Street, Tingewick.
Tel: 01280 847922
10.30-5pm every day

Winslow Antique Centre,
15 Market Square, Winslow.
Tel: 01296 714540/714055
10-5pm

Cambridgeshire

Collectors Market,
Dales Brewery,
Gwydir Street (off Mill
Road), Cambridge.
9.30-5pm

Fitzwilliam Antiques
Centre, Fitzwilliam Street,
Peterborough.
Tel: 01733 65415

Willingham Antiques &
Collectors Market,
25-29 Green Street,
Willingham.
Tel: 01954 60283
10-5pm, Closed Thurs

Cheshire

Davenham Antique
Centre, 461 London Road,
Davenham, Nr. Northwick.
Tel: 01606 44350
Mon-Sat 10-5pm,
Closed Wed

Nantwich Antique Centre,
The Old Police Station,
Welsh Row, Nantwich.
Tel: 01270 624035
10-5.30pm, Closed Wed

Melody's Antique
Galleries,
30-32 City Road, Chester.
Tel: 01244 328968
Mon-Sat 10-5.30pm

Stancie Cutler Antique
& Collectors Fairs,
Civic Hall, Nantwich.
Tel: 01270 624288

Cornwall

New Generation Antique
Market, 61/62 Chapel
Street, Penzance.
Tel: 01736 63267
10-5pm

Waterfront Antique
Complex, 1st Floor,
4 Quay Street, Falmouth.
Tel: 01326 311491
9-5pm

Cumbria

Carlisle Antique & Craft
Centre, Cecil Hall,
Cecil Street, Carlisle.
Tel: 01228 21970
Mon-Sat 9-5pm

Cockermouth Antiques
Market, Courthouse,
Main Street,
Cockermouth.
Tel: 01900 824346
10-5pm

Derbyshire

Derby Antique Centre,
11 Friargate, Derby.
Tel: 01332 385002
Mon-Sat 10-5.30pm

Derby Antiques Market,
52-56 Curzon Street,
Derby.
Tel: 01332 41861
Mon-Sat 9-5pm, closed Wed.

Glossop Antique Centre,
Brookfield, Glossop.
Tel: 01457 863904
Thurs-Sun 10-5pm

Devon

The Antique Centre
On the Quay, Exeter.
Tel: 01392 214180
10-5pm

The Antique Centre,
Abingdon House,
136 High Street,
Honiton.
Tel: 01404 42108
Mon-Sat 10-5pm

Barbican Antiques Centre,
82-84 Vauxhall Street,
Barbican, Plymouth.
Tel: 01752 266927
9.30-5pm

Dartmoor Antiques
Centre, Off West Street,
Ashburton.
Tel: 01364 52182
Tues 9-4pm

Shambles, 22 North Street,
Ashburton.
Tel: 01364 653848
Mon-Fri 10-5pm,
Sat 10-1pm

Dorset

The Antique Centre,
837-839 Christchurch
Road, East Boscombe,
Bournemouth.
Tel: 01202 421052
Mon-Sat 9.30-5.30pm

Barnes House Antiques
Centre, West Row,
Wimborne Minster.
Tel: 01202 886275
10-5pm

Bridport Antique Centre,
5 West Allington, Bridport.
Tel: 01308 25885
9-5pm

Gold Hill Antiques &
Collectables,
3 Gold Hill Parade,
Gold Hill, Shaftesbury.
Tel: 01747 54050

Sherborne Antique Centre,
Mattar Arcade,
17 Newlands, Sherborne.
Tel: 01935 813464
9-5pm

R. A. Swift & Son,
St Andrews Hall,
4c Wolverton Road
(off Christchurch Road),
Bournemouth.
Tel: 01202 394470
Mon-Fri 9-5.30pm

Wimborne Antique Centre,
Newborough Road,
Wimborne.
Tel: 01202 841251
Thurs 10-4pm, Fri 8.30-
5pm, Sat 10-5pm, Sun
9.30-5pm

Essex

Abridge Antique Centre,
Market Place, Abridge.
Tel: 01992 813113
10-5pm, Thurs 10-1pm

Battlesbridge Antiques
Centre, The Green,
Chelmsford Road,
Battles-bridge, Nr
Wickford.
Tel: 01268 764197

Essex Antiques Centre,
Priory Street,
Colchester.
Tel: 01206 871150
10-5.30pm

Grays Galleries Antiques
& Collectors Centre,
23 Lodge Lane, Grays.
Tel: 01375 374883
10-5.30pm

Kelvedon Antiques Centre,
139 High Street, Kelvedon.
Tel: 01376 570896
Mon-Sat 10-5pm

Maldon Antiques &
Collectors Market,
United Reformed Church
Hall, Market Hill, Maldon.
Tel: 01872 22826
1st Sat in month

Trinity Antiques Centre,
7 Trinity Street,
Colchester.
Tel: 01206 577775
9.30-5pm

Townsford Mill Antiques
Centre,
The Causeway, Halstead.
Tel: 01787 474451
10-5pm, inc Sun

Gloucestershire

Antique Centre,
London House,
High Street,
Moreton-in-Marsh.
Tel: 01608 51084
10-5pm

Antique Emporium,
The Old Chapel, Long
Street, Tetbury.
Tel: 01666 505281
Mon-Sat 10-5pm,
Sun 1-5pm

Charlton Kings Antique
Centre,
199 London Road,
Charlton Kings,
Cheltenham.
Tel: 01242 510672
9.30-5.30pm

Cheltenham Antique
Market, 54 Suffolk Road,
Cheltenham.
Tel: 01242 529812
9.30-5.30pm

Cirencester Antiques
Centre, 9 Silver Street,
Cirencester.

Cirencester Antiques
Market, Market Place,
Cirencester.
Tel: 0171-262 5003. Fri

Gloucester Antiques
Centre, Severn Road,
Gloucester.
Tel: 01452 529716
9.30-5pm, Sun 1-5pm

Cotswold Antiques Centre,
The Square,
Stow-on-the-Wold.
Tel: 01451 31585
10-5.30pm

Painswick Antique Centre,
New Street, Painswick.
Tel: 01452 812431
10-5pm, Sat 9.30-5.30pm,
Sun 11-5.30pm

Silver Street Antiques
& Things, 9 Silver Street,
Cirencester, GL7 2BS.
Tel: 01285 641600
10-5.30pm, Fri 9-5.30pm

Tewkesbury Antique
Centre, Tolsey Hall,
Tolsey Lane, Tewkesbury.
Tel: 01684 294091
9-5pm

Windsor House Antiques
Centre, High Street,
Moreton-in-Marsh.
Tel: 01608 50993
10-5.30pm, Sun 12-5.30pm

Hampshire

Creightons Antique Centre,
23-25 Bell Street, Romsey.
Tel: 01794 522758
9-6pm

Folly Antiques Centre,
College Street, Petersfield.
Tel: 01730 64816
10-5pm, Thurs 10-1pm

Kingsley Barn Antique
Centre, Church Lane,
Eversley, Nr Wokingham.
Tel: 01734 328518
10.30-5pm, closed Mon

Lymington Antiques
Centre, 76 High Street,
Lymington.
Tel: 01590 670934
10-5pm, Sat 9-5pm

Squirrel Collectors Centre,
9 New Street, Basingstoke.
Tel: 01256 464885
10-5.30pm

Hereford & Worcester

The Galleries Antiques
Centre, Pickwicks,
503 Evesham Road,
Crabbs Cross, Redditch.
Tel: 01527 550568
9.30-5pm, inc Sun

Hereford Antique Centre,
128 Widemarsh Street,
Hereford.
Tel: 01432 266242
9-5pm, Sun 1-5pm

Leominster Antiques
Market, 14 Broad Street,
Leominster.
Tel: 01568 2189
10-5pm

Worcester Antiques
Centre, Reindeer Court,
Mealcheapen Street,
Worcester.
Tel: 01905 610680/1
10-5pm

Hertfordshire

Antique & Collectors
Market, Market Place,
Hemel Hempstead.
Tel: 0171-624 3214
Wed 9-2pm

Bushey Antiques Centre,
39 High Street,
Bushey.
Tel: 0181-950 5040

By George Antiques
Centre, 23 George Street,
St Albans.
Tel: 01727 53032
10-5pm

The Herts & Essex
Antique Centre,
The Maltings, Station
Road, Sawbridgeworth.
Tel: 01279 722044
Tues-Fri 10-5pm, Sat &
Sun 10-30-6pm, closed Mon

St Albans Antique Market,
Town Hall, Chequer
Street, St Albans.
Tel: 01727 44957
Mon 9.30-4pm

Humberside

New Pocklington Antiques
Centre, 26 George Street,
Pocklington, Nr York.
Tel: 01759 303032
Mon-Sat 10-5pm

Kent

The Antiques Centre,
120 London Road,
Sevenoaks. TN13 1BA
Tel: 01732 452104
9.30-5.30pm, Sat 10-5.30pm

Beckenham Antique
Market, Old Council Hall,
Bromley Road,
Beckenham.
Tel: 0181-777 6300
Wed 9.30-2pm

Bromley Antique Market,
Widmore Road,
Bromley.
Thurs 7.30-3pm

Burgate Antiques Centre,
10 Burgate, Canterbury.
CT1 2HG
Tel: 01227 456500
Mon-Sat 10-5pm

Castle Antiques Centre,
1 London Road,
Westerham. TN16 1BB
Tel: 01959 562492
Mon-Sat 10-5pm

Cranbrook Antiques
Centre, 15 High Street,
Cranbrook.
Tel: 01580 712173.
10-5pm

Folkestone Market,
Rotunda Amusement Park,
Marine Parade, Folkestone.
Tel: 01850 311391
Sun

Hythe Antique Centre,
5 High Street, Hythe.
Tel: 01303 269043/269643
10-4pm, Sat 10-5pm
Closed Wed & Sun.

Malthouse Arcade,
High Street, Hythe.
Tel: 01303 260103
Fri & Sat 10-6pm

Noah's Ark Antiques
Centre, 5 King Street,
Sandwich. CT13 9BT
Tel: 01304 611144
10-5pm, closed Wed & Sun

Paraphernalia Antiques
& Collectors Centre,
171 Widmore Road,
Bromley. BR1 3AX
Tel: 0181-318 2991
10-5.30pm, Sun 10-2pm

Rochester Antiques & Flea
Market, Corporation
Street, Rochester.
Tel: 0171 262 5003
Sat 8-1pm

Sandgate Antiques Centre,
61-63 High Street,
Sandgate. CT20 3AH
Tel: 01303 48987
10-6pm, Sun 11-6pm

Tenterden Antiques
Centre,
66-66a High Street,
Tenterden.TN30 6AU
Tel: 01580 765885
10-5pm, inc Sun

Thanet Antiques Trade
Centre,
45 Albert Street,
Ramsgate. CT11 9EX
Tel: 01843 597336
9-5pm

Tudor Cottage Antiques
Centre,
22-23 Shipbourne Road,
Tonbridge. TN10 3DN
Tel: 01732 351719
10-5.30pm

Tunbridge Wells Antique
Centre,
Union Square,
The Pantiles,
Tunbridge Wells.
Tel: 01892 533708
Mon-Sat 9.30-5pm

Weald Antiques Gallery,
106 High Street,
Tenterden.
Tel: 01580 762939
10-5pm, Sat. 10-5.30pm

Lancashire

Blackpool Antiques
Centre, 105-107 Hornby
Road, Blackpool.
Tel: 01253 752514
9-5pm, closed Sat

Bolton Antiques Centre,
Central Street, Bolton.
Tel: 01204 362694
9.30-5pm, inc Sun

Bygone Times, Times
House, Grove Mill,
The Green,
Eccleston.
Tel: 01257 453780
8-6pm, inc Sun

Darwen Antique Centre,
Provident Hall,
The Green, Darwen.
Tel: 01254 760565
9.30-5pm, Sun 11-5pm,
closed Tues

GB Antiques Centre,
Lancaster Leisure Park,
Wyresdale Road,
Lancaster.
Tel: 01524 844734
10-5pm, inc Sun

Last Drop Antique
& Collectors Fair,
Last Drop Hotel,
Bromley Cross,
Bolton.
Sun 11-4pm

Levenshulme Antiques
Hypermarket,
Levenshulme Town Hall,
965 Stockport Road,
Levenshulme,
Manchester.
Tel: 0161 224 2410
10-5pm

Memory Lane Antique
Centre,
Gilnow Lane,
off Deane Road,
Bolton.
Tel: 01204 380383
9-5pm, inc Sun

Preston Antique Centre,
The Mill,
New Hall Lane,
Preston.
Tel: 01772 794498
Mon-Fri 8.30-5.30pm,
Sat 10-4pm, Sun 9-4pm

Royal Exchange Shopping
Centre, Antiques Gallery,
St Anne's Square,
Exchange Street,
Manchester.
Tel: 0161 834 3731/834 1427
Mon-Sat 9.30-5.30pm

Walter Aspinall Antiques,
Pendle Antique Centre,
Union Mill, Watt Street,
Sabden, Nr Blackburn.
Tel: 01282 76311
9-5pm, weekends 11-4pm

Leicestershire

The Antiques Complex,
St Nicholas Place,
Leicester.
Tel: 0116 2533343
9.30-5.30pm

Boulevard Antique
& Shopping Centre,
The Old Dairy,
Western Boulevard,
Leicester.
Tel: 0116 2541201
10-6pm, Sun 2-5pm

Oxford Street Antiques
Centre Ltd.,
16-26 Oxford Street,
Leicester.
Tel: 0116 2553006
Mon-Fri 10-5.30pm, Sun
2-5pm

Lincolnshire

Boston Antiques Centre,
12 West Street, Boston.
Tel: 01205 361510
9-5pm, closed Thurs

Eastgate Antiques Centre,
6 Eastgate, Lincoln.
Tel: 01522 544404
9.30-5pm

Hemswell Antique Centre,
Caenby Corner Estate,
Hemswell Cliff,
Nr Gainsborough.
Tel: 01427 668389
10-5pm, inc Sun

The Lincolnshire Antiques
Centre, 26 Bridge Street,
Horncastle.
Tel: 01507 527794
9-5pm

Portobellow Row Antiques
Centre, 93-95 High Street,
Boston.
Tel: 01205 369456
10-4pm

Talisman Antiques,
51 North Street,
Horncastle.
Tel: 01507 526893
10-5pm, closed Mon.

Stamford Antiques Centre,
The Exchange Hall,
Broad Street, Stamford.
Tel: 01780 62605
10-5pm

Talisman Antiques,
Regent House,
12 South Market, Alford.
Tel: 01507 463441
10.30-4.30pm, closed Thurs.

Merseyside

Hoylake Antique Centre,
128-130 Market Street,
Hoylake.
Tel: 0151-632 4231
9.15-5.30pm

Middlesex

Hampton Village Antiques
Centre, 76 Station Road,
Hampton.
Tel: 0181-979 5871
10-5.30pm

Hatch End Antiques &
Collectables, 294 Uxbridge
Road, Hatch End.
Tel: 0181 421 3056
Mon-Sat 10-5.30pm

The Jay's Antique Centre,
25/29 High Street, Harefield.
Tel: 01895 824738
10-6pm, Wed 10-1pm

Norfolk

Angel Antique Centre,
Pansthorn Farmhouse,
Redgrave Road,
South Lopham, Nr Diss.
Tel: 0137 988 317
9.30-6pm, inc Sun

Antique & Collectors
Centre, St Michael at Plea,
Bank Plain, Norwich.
Tel: 01603 619129
9.30-5.00pm

Cloisters Antiques Fair,
St Andrew's & Blackfriars
Hall, St Andrew's Plain,
Norwich.
Tel: 01603 628477
Wed 9.30-3.30pm

Coltishall Antiques Centre,
High Street, Coltishall.
Tel: 01603 738306
10-5pm

Fakenham Antique Centre,
Old Congregational Chapel,
14 Norwich Road, Fakenham.
Tel: 01328 862941
10-5pm, Thurs 9.5pm

Gostling's Antique Centre,
13 Market Hill, Diss.
Tel: 01379 650360
10-5pm, Thurs 10-7pm

Norwich Antiques &
Collectors Centre, Quayside,
Fye Bridge, Norwich.
Tel: 01603 612582
10-5pm

The Old Granary Antique
& Collectors Centre,
King Staithe Lane,
off Queens Street,
King's Lynn.
Tel: 01553 775509 10-5pm

Wells Antique Centre,
The Old Mill, Maryland.
Tel: 01328 711433
10-5pm, inc Sun

Wymondham Antique
Centre, No 1 Town Green,
Wymondham.
Tel: 01953 604817
10-5pm

Northamptonshire

Antiques & Bric-a-Brac
Market, Market Square,
Town Centre,
Wellingborough.
Tel: 01905 611321
Tues 9-4pm

Finedon Antiques Centre,
Church Street, Finedon,
Nr Wellingborough.
Tel: 01933 681260
9.30-5.30pm, Sun 2-5

The Village Antique
Market, 62 High Street,
Weedon.
Tel: 01327 42015
9.30-5.30pm,
Sun 10.30-5.30pm

Northumberland

Colmans of Hexham,
15 St Mary's Chare, Hexham.
Tel: 01434 603811/2
9-5pm

Nottinghamshire

Castle Gate Antiques Centre,
55 Castle Gate, Newark.
Tel: 01636 700076
9-5.30pm

Newark Antiques Centre,
Regent House,
Lombard Street, Newark.
Tel: 01636 605504
9.30-5pm, Sun 11-4

Newark Antique
Warehouse, Kelham Road,
Newark.
Tel: 01636 74869
8.30-5.30pm, Sat 10-4pm

Nottingham Antique
Centre, British Rail Goods
Yard, London Road,
Nottingham.
Tel: 0115 9504504/505548
9-5pm, closed Sat

Top Hat Antiques Centre,
66-72 Derby Road,
Nottingham.
Tel: 0115 9419143
9.30-5pm

Oxfordshire

Antique & Collectors
Market, Town Hall, Thame.
Tel: 01844 28205
8.30-3.30pm, 2nd Tues of
month

Cotswold Gateway Antique
Centre, Cheltenham Road,
Burford Roundabout,
Burford.
Tel: 0199 382 3678
10-5.30pm, Sun 2-5.30pm

Chipping Norton Antique
Centre, Ivy House, Middle
Row, Chipping Norton.
Tel: 01608 644212
10-5pm, inc Sun

Deddington Antique
Centre, Laurel House,
Bull Ring, Market Square,
Deddington.
Tel: 01869 38968
Mon-Sat 10-5pm

Friday Street Antique
Centre, 2 & 4 Friday
Street, Henley-on-Thames.
Tel: 01491 574104
9.30-5.30pm, Sun 11-5pm

Goring Antique Centre,
16 High Street,
Goring-on-Thames.
Tel: 01491 873300.
10-5pm, Sat 11-5pm,
closed Wed pm

Henley Antique Centre,
Rotherfield Arcade,
2-4 Reading Road,
Henley-on-Thames.
Tel: 01491 411468

The Lamb Arcade, High
Street, Wallingford.
Tel: 01491 35166/35048
10-5pm, Sat 10-5.30pm
Wed 10-4pm

Oxford Antiques Centre,
The Jam Factory,
27 Park End Street,
Oxford.
Tel: 01865 251075
Mon-Sat 10-5pm and 1st
Sun every month

Oxford Antiques Market,
Gloucester Green, Oxford.
Tel: 01865 242216
Every Thurs

Span Antiques, 6 Market
Place, Woodstock.
Tel: 01993 811332
10-5pm, inc Sun, closed Wed.

Shropshire

Bridgnorth Antique
Centre,
Old Smithfield,
Whitburn Street,
Bridgnorth.
Tel: 01746 768055

Cleobury Mortimer
Antique Centre,
Childe Road,
Cleobury Mortimer,
Nr Kidderminster.
Tel: 01299 270513
10-5pm, inc Sun, not Thurs

Ironbridge Antique Centre,
Dale End, Ironbridge.
Tel: 01952 433784
10-5pm, Sun 2-5pm

Pepper Lane Antique Centre,
Pepper Lane, Ludlow.
Tel: 01584 876494
10-5pm

Shrewsbury Antique
Market, Frankwell Quay
Warehouse, Shrewsbury.
Tel: 01743 350916
9.30-5pm

Shrewsbury Antique Centre, 15 Princess House, The Square, Shrewsbury.
Tel: 01743 247704
9.30-5.30pm

St Leonard's Antiques, Corve Street, Ludlow.
Tel: 01584 875573
9-5pm

Stretton Antiques Market, 36 Sandford Avenue, Church Stretton.
Tel: 01694 723718
9.30-5.30pm,
Sun 10.30-4.30pm

Telford Antique Centre, High Street, Wellington, Telford.
Tel: 01952 256450
10-5pm, Sun 2-5pm

Welsh Bridge Antique Centre, 135 Frankwell, Shrewsbury.
Tel: 01743 248822
9.30-5.30pm,
Sun 12-5.00pm

Somerset

Bridgwater Antiques Market, Marycourt Shopping Mall, Bridgwater.
Tel: 01823 451433
Fri 9-5pm, Sat 10-5pm

County Antiques Centre, 21/23 West Street, Ilminster.
Tel: 01460 54151.
10-5pm

Dulverton Antique Centre, Lower Town Hall, Dulverton.
Tel: 01398 23522.
10-5pm

Guildhall Antique Market, The Guildhall, Chard.
Thurs 9-3pm

Oscar's Antique Market, 13-15 Market Square, Crewkerne.
Tel: 01460 72718
10-5.30pm

Taunton Silver Street Antiques Centre, 27/29 Silver Street, Taunton.
Tel: 0171-351 5353
Mon 9-4pm

Staffordshire

The Antique Centre, 128 High Street, Kinver.
Tel: 01384 877441
10-5.30pm

Antique Market, The Stones, Newcastle-under-Lyme.
Tel: 0171-624 4848
Tues 9-4pm

Barclay House Antiques, 14-16 Howard Place, Shelton, Stoke-on-Trent.
Tel: 01782 274747
9.30-6pm

Rugeley Antique Centre, 161-3 Main Road, Brereton, Nr Rugeley.
Tel: 018895 77166.
9-5pm

The Potteries Centre, Stoke-on-Trent Antique & Collectors Centre, Winton Square, Station Road, Stoke-on-Trent.
Tel: 01782 411249
9-6pm

Tudor of Lichfield Antique Centre, Lichfield House, Bore Street, Lichfield.
Tel: 01543 263951

Tutbury Mill Antiques, 6 Lower High Street, Tutbury, Nr Burton-on-Trent.
Tel: 01283 815999
9-5pm every day

Suffolk

The Barn, Risby, Bury St Edmunds.
Tel: 01284 811126
10-5pm, inc Sun

Clare Antique Warehouse, The Mill, Malting Lane, Clare, Nr. Sudbury.
Tel: 01787 278449
9.30-5.30pm

Debenham Antique Centre, The Forresters Hall, High Street, Debenham.
Tel: 01728 860777
10-5.30pm, Sun 2-5pm

Long Melford Antiques Centre, The Chapel Maltings, Long Melford.
Tel: 01787 79287
9.30-5.30pm

Old Town Hall Antiques Centre, High Street, Needham Market.
Tel: 01449 720773
10-5pm

Snape Antiques and Collectors' Centre, Snape Maltings, Snape.
Tel: 01728 888038
10-6pm, inc Sun

Waveney Antiques Centre, Peddars Lane, Beccles.
Tel: 01502 716147
10-5.30pm

Wrentham Antiques Centre, 7 High Street, Wrentham, Nr. Beccles.
Tel: 01502 75376
10-5.30pm, Sun 2-5.30pm

Surrey

Antiquarius Antique Centre, 56 West Street, Dorking.
Tel: 01306 743398
9.30-5.30pm

Antiques Arcade, 22 Richmond Hill, Richmond.
Tel: 0181-940 2035
10.30-5.30pm, closed Wed

Antiques & Interiors, 64 Station Road East, Oxted.
Tel: 01883 712806
9.30-5.30pm

The Antiques Arcade, 77 Bridge Road, East Molesey.
Tel: 0181-979 7954
10-5pm

The Antiques Centre, 22 Haydon Place, corner of Martyr Road, Guildford.
Tel: 01483 67817
10-4pm, closed Mon & Wed

Cambridge Parade Antiques, 229-231 Carshalton Road, Carshalton.
Tel: 0181-643 0014
10-5.30pm

Dorking Antiques Centre, 17/18 West Street, Dorking.
Tel: 01306 740915
10-5.30pm

Duke's Yard Antique Market, 1a Duke Street, Richmond.
Tel: 0181-332 1051
10-6pm, closed Mon

Farnham Antique Centre, 27 South Street, Farnham.
Tel: 01252 724475
9.30-5pm

Fern Cottage Antique Centre, 28/30 High Street, Thames Ditton.
Tel: 0181-398 2281
10-5.30pm

Maltings Monthly Market, Bridge Square, Farnham.
Tel: 01252 726234
First Sat in month

The Old Smithy Antique Centre, 7 High Street, Merstham.
Tel: 01737 642306.
10-5pm

Reigate Antiques Arcade, 57 High Street, Reigate.
Tel: 01737 222654
10-5.30pm

Surrey Antiques Centre, 10 Windsor Street, Chertsey.
Tel: 01932 563313
10-5pm

Sutton Market, West Street, Sutton.
Tel: 0181-661 1245
Tues & Sat

Victoria & Edward Antiques Centre, 61 West Street, Dorking.
Tel: 01306 889645
9.30-5.30pm

Wood's Wharf Antiques Bazaar, 56 High Street, Haslemere.
Tel: 01428 642125
Mon-Sat 9.30-5pm

Sussex East

Antique Market, Leaf Hall, Seaside, Eastbourne.
Tel: 01323 27530
Tues & Sat 9-5pm

Bexhill Antiques Centre, Quakers Mill, Old Town, Bexhill.
Tel: 01424 210182/221940
10-5.30pm

Brighton Antiques Gallery, 41 Meeting House Lane, Brighton.
Tel: 01273 26693/21059
10-5.30pm

Brighton Market, Jubilee Shopping Hall, 44-47 Gardner Street, Brighton.
Tel: 01273 600574.
9-5pm

Chateaubriand Antiques Centre, High Street, Burwash.
Tel: 01435 882535
10-5pm, Sun 2-5pm

Cliffe Antiques Centre, 47 Cliffe High Street, Lewes.
Tel: 01273 473266
9.30-5pm

Cliffe Gallery Antique Centre, 39 Cliffe High Street, Lewes.
Tel: 01273 471877
9.30-5pm

The Collectors Market, The Enterprise Centre, Station Parade, Eastbourne.
Tel: 01323 32690

The Courtyard Antiques Market, 13, 15 & 17 High Street, Seaford.
Tel: 01323 892091
8.30-5.30pm

Foundry Lane Antiques Centre, 15 Cliffe High Street, Lewes.
Tel: 01273 475361
10-5pm, closed Mon

George St. Antiques Centre,
47 George Street,
Old Town, Hastings.
Tel: 01424 429339
9-5pm Sun 11-4pm

The Hastings Antique
Centre, 59-61 Norman
Road, Hastings.
Tel: 01424 428561
10-5.30pm

Kollect-O-Mania,
25 Trafalgar Street,
Brighton.
Tel: 01273 694229
10-5pm

Lewes Antique Centre,
20 Cliffe High Street,
Lewes.
Tel: 01273 476148
9.30-5pm

Mint Arcade,
71 The Mint, Rye.
Tel: 01797 225952
10-5pm

Newhaven Flea Market,
28 South Way,
Newhaven.
Tel: 01273 517207/516065
Open every day

The Old Town Hall,
Antique Centre,
52 Ocklynge Road,
Eastbourne.
Tel: 01323 416016
9.30-5pm, Sun 10.30-5pm

Pharoahs Antiques Centre,
28 South Street, Eastbourne.
Tel: 01323 38655.
10-5pm

Prinnys Antique Gallery,
3 Meeting House Lane,
Brighton.
Tel: 01273 204554
9.30-5pm

Seaford's Barn Collectors
Market & Studio Book
Shop, The Barn,
Church Lane, Seaford.
Tel: 01323 890010
Tues, Thurs & Sat
10-4.30pm

Sussex West

Antiques & Collectors
Market, Old Orchard
Building, Old House,
Adversane, Billingshurst.
Tel: 01403 783594

Copthorne Group Antiques,
Copthorne Bank, Crawley.
Tel: 01342 712802
Mon-Sat 10-5.30pm

Eagle House Antiques
Market, Market Square,
Midhurst.
Tel: 01730 812718

Mamies Antiques Centre,
5 River Road, Arundel.
Tel: 01903 882012
Thurs-Sun, 9-5pm

Midhurst Antiques
Market,
Knockhundred Row,
Midhurst.
Tel: 01730 814231
9.30-5pm

Shirley, Mostyns Antique
Centre,
64 Brighton Road,
Lancing.
Tel: 01903 752961
Mon-Fri 10-5pm

Petworth Antique Market,
East Street,
Petworth.
Tel: 01798 42073
10-5.30pm

Tarrant Street Antique
Centre, Nineveh House,
Tarrant Street,
Arundel.
Tel: 01903 884307
9.30-5pm, Sun 11-5pm

Treasure House Antiques
& Collectors Market,
31b High Street,
Arundel.
Tel: 01903 883101
9-5pm

Upstairs Downstairs
Antique Centre,
29 Tarrant Street,
Arundel.
Tel: 01903 883749
10.30-5pm, inc Sun

Tyne & Wear

Antique Centre Newcastle,
8 St Mary Place East,
Newcastle-upon-Tyne.
Tel: 0191-232 9832
Tues-Sat 10-5pm

Blaydon Antique Centre,
Bridge House,
Bridge Street,
Blaydon,
Nr Newcastle-upon-Tyne.
Tel: 0191-414 3535
10-5pm

Vine Lane Antique
Market,
17 Vine Lane,
Newcastle-upon-Tyne.
Tel: 0191-261 2963/
232 9832
10-5.30pm

Warwickshire

The Antiques Centre, High
Street, Bidford-on-Avon.
Tel: 01789 773680
10-5pm, Sun 2-5.30pm,
closed Mon

Antiques Etc., 22 Railway
Terrace, Rugby.
10-5pm, closed Tues & Wed

Dunchurch Antique
Centre, 16/16a Daventry
Road, Dunchurch, Nr Rugby.
Tel: 01788 817147
10-5pm, inc Sun

Leamington Pine & Antiques Centre, 20 Regent Street, Leamington Spa. Tel: 01926 429679. 9-6pm

Meer Street Antiques Arcade, 10a/11 Meer Street, Stratford-upon-Avon. Tel: 01789 297249

Meer Street Antiques Centre, Meer Street, Stratford upon Avon. Tel: 0189 297249

Old Curiosity Shop, 30 Henley Street, Stratford-upon-Avon. Tel: 01789 292485

Smith Street Antiques Centre, 7 Smith Street, Warwick. Tel: 0926 497864 10-5.30pm

Spa Antiques Market, 4 Windsor Street, Leamington Spa. Tel: 01926 22927 9.30-5.30pm

Stratford Antiques Centre, 60 Ely Street, Stratford-upon-Avon. Tel: 01789 204180 10-5.30pm

The Old Cornmarket Antiques Centre, 70 Market Place, Warwick. Tel: 01926 419119

Vintage Antique Market, 36 Market Place, Warwick. Tel: 01926 491527. 10-5pm

Warwick Antique Centre, 20-22 High Street, Warwick. Tel: 01926 495704 Mon-Sat

West Midlands

Birmingham Antique Centre, 141 Bromsgrove Street, Birmingham. Tel: 0121-692 1414/622 2145 Thurs from 9am

The City of Birmingham Antique Market, St Martins Market, Edgbaston Street, Birmingham. Tel: 0121-267 4636 Mon 6.30-2pm

Stancie Cutler Antique & Collectors Fair, Town Hall, Sutton Coldfield. Tel: 01270 624288 Wed monthly, 11-8pm

Wiltshire

Antique & Collectors Market, 37 Catherine Street, Salisbury. Tel: 01722 326033 9-5pm

The Avon Bridge Antiques & Collectors Market, United Reform Church Hall, Fisherton Street, Salisbury. Tues 9-4pm

London House Antique Centre, High Street, Marlborough. Tel: 01672 52331 Mon-Sat 9.30-5.30pm

The Marlborough Parade Antiques Centre, The Parade, Marlborough. Tel: 01672 515331 10-5pm, inc Sun

Micawber's, 53 Fisherton Street, Salisbury. Tel: 01722 337822 9.30-5pm, closed Wed

Yorkshire

The Ginnel, Harrogate Antique Centre, off Parliament Street, Harrogate. Tel: 01423 508857 9.30-5.30pm

Grove Collectors Centre, Grove Road, Harrogate. Tel: 01423 561680 10-4.30pm

Halifax Antiques Centre, Queen's Road/Gibbet Street, Halifax, HX1 4LR. Tel: 01422 366657 Tues-Sat, 10-5pm

Malton Antique Market, 2 Old Maltongate, Malton. Tel: 01653 692732 9.30-5, closed Thurs

Micklegate Antiques Market, 73 Micklegate, York. Tel: 01904 644438 Wed & Sat 10-5.30pm

Montpelier Mews Antique Market, Montpelier Street, Harrogate. Tel: 01423 530484 9.30-5.30pm

Treasure House Antiques Centre, 4-10 Swan Street, Bawtry, Nr Doncaster. Tel: 01302 710621 10-5pm, inc Sun

West Park Antiques Pavilion, 20 West Park, Harrogate. Tel: 01423 61758 10-5pm, closed Mon

York Antique Centre, 2 Lendal, York. Tel: 01904 641445 Mon-Sat 9.30-5.30pm

Scotland

Bath Street Antique Galleries, 203 Bath Street, Glasgow. Tel: 0141-248 4220 10-5pm, Sat 10-1pm

Corner House Antiques, 217 St Vincent Street, Glasgow. Tel: 0141-248 2560 10-5pm

King's Court Antiques Centre & Market, King Street, Glasgow. Tel: 0141-423 7216 Tues-Sun

The Victorian Village, 53 & 57 West Regent Street, Glasgow. Tel: 0141-332 0808 10-5pm, Sat 10-1pm

Wales

Cardiff Antique Centre, 69-71 St Mary Street, Cardiff.

Carew Market, Carew Airfield, on A477, Port Talbot. Tel: 01639 886822. Sun

Jacobs Antique Centre, West Canal Wharf, Cardiff. Tel: 01222 390939 Thurs & Sat 9.30-5pm

Offa's Dyke Antiques Centre, 4 High Street, Knighton, Powys. Tel: 01547 528634/528940 Mon-Sat 10-5pm

Pembroke Antique Centre, The Hall, Hamilton Terrace, Pembroke. Tel: 01646 687017 10-5pm

Port Talbot Market, Jubilee Shopping Hall, 64-66 Station Road, Port Talbot, Glamorgan. Tel: 01639 883184 Mon-Sat

Swansea Antique Centre, 21 Oxford Street, Swansea. Tel: 01792 466854 10-5pm

Wellfield Antiques Centre, Wellfield Court, Bangor, Gwynedd. Tel: 01248 361360 Thurs-Sat 10-5pm

DIRECTORY OF COLLECTORS' CLUBS

This directory is in no way complete. If you wish to be included in next year's directory or if you have a change of address or telephone number, please inform us by October 31st 1995. Entries will be repeated in subsequent editions unless we are requested otherwise.

Antique Collectors' Club, 5 Church Street, Woodbridge, Suffolk. IP12 1DS

Arms and Armour Society,
Field House, Upper Dicker, Hailsham, East Sussex BN27 3PY. Tel: 01323 844278

Association of Comic Enthusiasts,
17 Hill Street, Colne, Lancs. BB8 0DH.

Badge Collectors' Circle,
3 Ellis Close, Bramblefields, Quorn, Nr Loughborough, Leics. LE12 8SH.
Tel: 01509 412094

Beswick Collectors' Circle,
Corner Cottage, Hedgerley Lane, Gerrards Cross, Bucks. SL9 7NS.

British Art Medal Society,
Dept. of Coins and Medals, The British Museum, London. WC1B 3DG.
Tel: 0171 323 8170, extn. 8227

British Association of Sound Collections,
National Sound Archive, 29 Exhibition Road, London. SW7 2AS.
Tel: 0171 589 6603

British Button Society,
33 Haglane Copse, Pennington, Lymington, Hants. SO41 8DR. Tel: 01590 674044

British Matchbox, Label and Booklet Society,
122 High Street, Melbourn, Royston, Herts. SG8 6AL.

British Model Soldier Society,
22 Lynwood Road, Ealing, London W5 1JJ.

British Numismatic Society,
The Royal Mint, Llantrisant, Pontyclun, Mid Glamorgan. CF7 8YT.

British Teddy Bear Association, PO Box 290, Brighton, BN2 1DR

British Telecom Phonecard Collectors' Club, Camelford House, 87 Albert Embankment, London SE1 7TS.

Buttonhook Society,
2 Romney Place, Maidstone, Kent. ME15 6LE.

Cambridge Paperweight Circle,
34 Huxley Road, Welling, Kent. DA16 2EW.
Tel: 0181 303 4663

Clarice Cliff Collectors' Club,
Fantasque House, Tennis Drive, The Park, Nottingham NG7 1AE.

Comics Journal,
17 Hill Street, Colne, Lancs. BB8 0DH.
Tel: 01282 865468

Commemorative Collectors' Society,
25 Farndale Close, Long Eaton, Nottingham. NG10 3PA.
Tel: 0115 9727666

Corgi Collector Club,
PO Box 323, Swansea. SA1 1BJ.
Tel: 01792 476902

Costume Society,
c/o The State Apartments, Kensington Palace, London. W8 4PX.
Tel: 0171 937 9561

The Crested Circle,
42 Douglas Road, Tolworth, Surbiton, Surrey. KT6 7SA.

Cricket Memorabilia Society,
29 Highclere Road, Higher Crumpsall, Manchester. M8 6WS.
Tel: 0161 740 3714

Disneyana Club, 31 Rowan Ray, Exwick, Exeter. EX4 2DT.

Doll Club of Great Britain,
Unity Cottage, Pishill Bank, Henley on Thames, Oxon. RG9 6HJ.

Embroiderers' Guild,
Apartment 41, Hampton Court Palace, East Molesey, Surrey. KT8 9AU.
Tel: 0181 943 1229

English Playing Card Society,
11 Pierrepont Street, Bath, Avon. BA1 1LA.
Tel: 01225 465218

Ephemera Society,
12 Fitzroy Square, London. W1P 5HQ.

Fan Circle International,
79a Alcoldale Road, Westbury on Trym, Bristol, Avon. BS9 3JW.

Flag Institute,
10 Vicarage Road, Chester. CH2 3HZ.
Tel: 01244 351335

Friends of Blue,
10 Sea View Road, Herne Bay, Kent . CT6 6JQ.

Goss Collectors' Club,
4 Khasiaberry, Walnut Tree, Milton Keynes, Bucks. MK7 7DP.

Goss & Crested China Club,
62 Murray Road, Horndean, Waterlooville, Hants. PO8 9JL.

Great Britain Postcard Club, 34 Harper House, St James Crescent, London SW9 7LW

Hat Pin Society of Great Britain,
132 Hindes Road, Harrow, Middlesex. HA1 1RR.

Historical Model Railway Society,
59 Woodberry Way, London. E4 7DY.

Hornby Railway Collectors' Association,
2 Ravensmore Road, Sherwood, Nottingham. NG5 2AH.

International Bank Note Society,
43 Templars Crescent, London N3 3QR.

International Bond and Share Society,
6/7 Castle Gates, Shrewsbury, Salop. SY1 2AE.
**International Collectors' of Time
Association,** 173 Coleherne Court, Redcliffe
Gardens, London SW5 0DX
**International Correspondence of
Corkscrew Addicts,**
Ambrose House, 29 Old Church Green,
Kirk Hammerton, York. YO5 8DL.
Tel: 01423 330745
International Dolls' House News,
PO Box 79, Southampton. SO9 7EZ.
Tel: 01703 771995
King George VI Collectors' Society,
24 Stourwood Road, Southbourne,
Bournemouth, BH6 3QP.
The Lace Guild,
The Hollies, 53 Audnam, Stourbridge,
West Midlands. DY8 4AE.
Magic Lantern Society,
Prospect, High Street, Nutley, East Sussex
TN22 3NH.
**Matchbox International Collectors'
Association,**
The Toy Museum, 13a Lower Bridge Street,
Chester. CH1 1RS.
Tel: 01244 345297
Mauchline Ware Collectors' Club,
Unit 37, Romsey Industrial Estate, Greatbridge
Road, Romsey, Hampshire. SO51 0HR.
Model Railway Club,
Keen House, 4 Calshot Street, London. N1 9DA.
Mug Collectors' Association,
Whitecroft, Chandler Road, Stoke Holy Cross,
Norwich. NR14 8RG.
Musical Box Society of Great Britain,
PO Box 299, Waterbeach, Cambridgeshire.
CB4 4PJ.
National Horse Brass Society,
12 Severndale, Droitwich Spa, Worcs. WR9 8PD.
New Baxter Society,
c/o Museum of Reading, Blagrave Street,
Reading, Berks. RG1 1QH.
Old Bottle Club of Great Britain,
2 Strafford Avenue, Elsecar, Nr Barnsley,
South Yorkshire. S74 18AA.
Tel: 01226 745156
**Ophthalmic Antiques International
Collectors' Club,**
3 Moor Park Road, Northwood, Middx.
HA6 2DL.
Orders and Medals Research Society,
123 Turnpike Link, Croydon, Surrey.
CRO 5NU.
Oriental Ceramic Society,
31b Torrington Square, London WC1E 7JL.
Tel: 0171 636 7985
Passenger Ship Enthusiast Association,
PO Box 358 Coulsdon, Surrey. CR5 1AW.

Pewter Society,
Hunters Lodge, Paddock Close, St Mary's Platt,
Sevenoaks, Kent. TN15 8NN. Tel: 01732 883314
**Photographic Collectors' Club of Great
Britain,**
5 Station Industrial Estate, Low Prudhoe,
Northumberland, NE42 6NP.
Postcard Club of Great Britain,
34 Harper House, St James's Crescent, London
SW9 7LW.
Tel: 0171 733 0720
Pot Lid Circle,
c/o Keith Mortimer. Tel: 01753 886751
**Royal Doulton International Collectors'
Society,** Minton House, London Road,
Stoke-on-Trent, Staffs. ST4 7QD
Scientific Instrument Society,
PO Box 15, Pershore, Worcs. WR10 2RD.
Tel: 01705 812104
Shelley Group,
12 Lilleshall Road, Clayton, Newcastle-under-
Lyme, Staffs. ST5 3BX.
Silver Spoon Club,
Glenleigh Park, Sticker, St Austell, Cornwall.
PL26 7JB.
Tel: 01726 652269
Susie Cooper Collectors' Group,
PO Box 48, Beeston, Nottingham. NG9 2RN.
Sylvac Collectors Circle,
174 Portsmouth Road, Horndean, Hants.
PO8 9HP.
Tel: 01705 591725
Thimble Society of London,
Grays Antique Market, 58 Davies Street,
London. W1Y 1LB.
Tel: 0171 493 0560.
Tool and Trades History Society,
60 Swanley Lane, Swanley, Kent. BR8 7JG.
Tel: 01322 662271
Torquay Pottery Collectors' Society,
Torre Abbey, Torquay, Devon.
Train Collectors' Society,
29 Lammas Way, Ampthill, Bedfordshire,
MK45 2TR.
Victorian Military Society,
3 Franks Road, Guildford, Surrey. GU2 6NT.
Tel: 01483 60931
Wade Collectors Club,
14 Windsor Road, Selston, Nottingham.
NG16 6JJ.
Tel: 01773 860933/01374 209963
**Wireless & CEM National Wireless
Museum,**
52 West Hill Road, Ryde, Isle of Wight.
PO33 1LN.
Tel: 01983 567665
Writing Equipment Society,
4 Greystones Grange Crescent, Sheffield. S11 7JL.
Tel: 0114 2667140

INDEX TO ADVERTISERS

INDEX

MYSTERY OBJECTS?
Do You Know What These Items Are?

An ivory and silver tongue
scraper, 3½in (9cm) long.
£75–100 *PC*

A wife's cuckolding stool
manacle, 18thC, 5½in
(14cm) long.
£35–65 *WAB*

The Arnold Foster Mother,
an earthenware feeder,
11in (28cm) high.
£50–60 *JUN*

*These feeders were used for
rearing calves and lambs.*